The Serpent of Genesis

The Temple of Satan

The Serpent of Genesis

First Septenary
Book I

The Temple of Satan

Stanislas de Guaita

OUROBOROS

The Serpent of Genesis: The Temple of Satan
© and translation 2020 by Daniel Bernardo

All rights reserved under International and
Pan-American Copyright Conventions.

ISBN: 978-1-989586-30-3

OUROBOROS
https://ouroboros.publiebook.com

EVE AND THE SNAKE
(Original drawing by Mr. Wirth)

Esoteric plan of this work
Table of divisions and correspondences

	Chap. #	Tarot Arcanes	Analogic relations	Chapter Title
Book I — The Temple of Satan (First Septenary)	I	The Magician	The Unity. The Principle, the Object	The Devil
	II	The Priestess	The Binary. The Faculties, the Subject	The Sorcerer
	III	The Empress	The Ternary. The Relation, the Word	Works of Witchcraft
	IV	The Emperor	The Quaternary. The cubic base, the Power	Human Justice
	V	The Pope	The Quinary. The Will, its Instruments	The Sorcerer's Arsenal
	VI	The Lover	The Senary. Opposition, Reciprocity, Middle-course outcome	Modern Avatars of the Sorcerer
	VII	The Chariot	The Septenary. Triumph, Consummation, Fulfilment, Wealth, Superfluous	Flowers from the Abyss
Book II — The Key to Black Magic (Second Septenary)	I	Justice	Equilibrium, Balance, Harmony	Balance and its Agent
	II	The Hermit	Isolation, Power in the Astral	Mysteries of Solitude
	III	The Wheel of Fortune	Causality, Collective life, Future	The Wheel of Becoming
	IV	Strength	Energy, Means of deployment	Strength of Will
	V	The Hanged Man	Voluntary sacrifice, Interferences in projects	Magic Slavery
	VI	Death	Disintegration, Breakdown	Death and its Mysteries
	VII	Temperance	Mutations, Changes, Combinations, Exchanges	Magic of Transmutations
Book III — The Problem of Evil (Third Septenary)	I	The Devil	Fatal currents of instinct	Nahash, the Tempter of Eden
	II	The Tower	Collapse, Fall, Despair	The Fall of Adam (Involution)
	III	The Star	Ideality, Redemption, Hope	Redemption (Evolution)
	IV	The Moon	Trap, Construction (Hereb)	Travel Pitfalls
	V	The Sun	Splendour, Wealth, Expansion (Ihôah)	The Burning of Heraklès
	VI	The Judgement	Resurrection, Restitution, Return	The Resurrection from the Dead
	VII	The Fool	Subversion, Disorder, Dissolution, the Suicide of Evil defeated by its own weapons	Madness of Love
	Epilogue	The World	Universal syncretism, Thesis	Satan-Pantheus fades into God

The Serpent of Genesis

Table of Contents

Esoteric plan of this work..   vi

Summary.   1

Introduction   3

Catalogue.   13

The Temple of Satan

Chapter I
The Devil.   33

Chapter II
The Sorcerer   67

   The Sabbath   81

Chapter III
Works of Witchcraft   93

Chapter IV
Human Justice   123

   Trial and Revenge of The Templars   142

Chapter V
The Sorcerer's Arsenal..   169

   Inventory of the sorcerer's arsenal...   170

Chapter VI
Modern Avatars of the Sorcerer 211

Chapter VII
Flowers from the Abyss 271

Index 283

Summary

After some general insights into the state of mind and character of today's civilization, an *Introduction* explains the purpose and divisions of this work.

The **Serpent of Genesis** consists of three books (*The Temple of Satan, The Key to Black Magic* and *The Problem of Evil*) of seven chapters each: twenty-one chapters in total.

A twenty-second chapter forms the Epilogue, –and each of these subdivisions corresponds, as far as the general subject lends itself to it, to one of the twenty-two arcanes of the Tarot of the Gypsies.

The twenty-two subdivisions of the *Serpent of Genesis* do not require a regular commentary of the twenty-two keys of the Tarot.

Our work, dealing with a relatively limited subject, cannot lend itself to such developments (synthetic, mathematical, necessarily universal). We will content ourselves with exposing this object to light (the twenty-two arcanes); it will assimilate this light to the extent of its own receptivity; like a mirror, it will reflect for us only the rays that had met its surface.

Thus, the first Septenary –the *Temple of Satan*– refers to the first seven Tarot cards only in a very indirect and diverted way. However, the initiates will consider these analogical derivations less distant than one would be tempted to believe at first sight.

In *The Key to Black Magic* –the second Septenary– we come very close to the literal and immediate meaning of the Tarot cards 8 to 14; we even touch them almost constantly. The cause of this concordance is to be seen in the almost identical nature of the objects. Doesn't this book deal with the sacred mysteries of nature, whose hieroglyphs are presented to us in parallel with the Tarot? So we will have the opportunity, throughout the course of this second part, to describe and even comment on the Tarot cards numerically corresponding to the seven chapters that make it up.

The *Problem of Evil* –the third Septenary– diverts us a little from this central path, rejecting us towards derived and indirect interpretations. But, although sometimes indirect, the correspondences with the twenty-two keys of the *Book of Thoth* remain irreproachable to the end.

In short, our work is built entirely on the magical proportions of the Tarot. From one wing to the other, it has as its base and support, sometimes the constructions, sometimes the substructures of this vast monument of esoteric synthesis. May occultists judge our humble work solidly supported by the unshakeable edifice.

Introduction

I

As we write these lines, the intellectual world is in disarray. The triumph of the worst epidemic –agnosticism– is heralded by three alarming symptoms: the delirium of disrespect, the monomania of considering everything relative and the fever of individualism.

If only the modern doctors, pious in collecting the teachings of the past, as a son fulfils his father's last wishes, would respectfully question the will of the primitive sages.

If only the scientists, without neglecting the patient study of the accomplished facts, nor suspending the great analytical investigation, would see to the progressive sorting out of so many scattered elements, with a view to constructing a universal synthesis, in which the physical, moral, intellectual and divine sciences are arranged in four hierarchies.

If only the thinkers, finally, less anxious to appear original than sincere and truthful, were less quick to challenge any traditional authority than to inquire faithfully into the eternally absolute principles, whether or not they had been formulated by someone else.

If such were theologians, scholars and philosophers, then the nineteenth century would indeed be the century of the light and Paris the sun city.

But it is not. – Apart from the meticulous investigators of positivism, which tirelessly and inconclusively heap scrupulous remarks on the Ossas of minor observations, and on the Pelions[1] of scrupulous remarks; apart from the devout but blind

---

[1] Ossa and Pelion are two mountains in Greece. In Greek mythology, the mountain Pelion was held to be the home of the centaurs, and the giants were said to have piled Mounts Olympus and Ossa on its summit in their attempt to reach the heavens and destroy the gods.

partisans of the letter that kills the dragons of the holy cave, whose only merit is to preserve intact the symbolic treasure of the dogma, forever closed for them; what can we say of those who are still concerned about the big picture?

Since their ambition is limited to stamping their name on any system whatsoever –but which seems to be their own– they challenge the doctrine of their predecessors and push the emulation between colleagues to the point of the most petty denigration. No one wants to be the last to denounce their neighbour as seeing things from an inaccurate, erroneous and misleading point of view… As if the role of synthesis was not to embrace all relative points of view, in the same absolute contemplation of the true! This is High Science, and Spinoza defined it magnificently, saying that it views objects in a character of eternity.

Nevertheless, however desperate the holy cause of the integral Truth may seem at this hour, the attentive observer may perceive, besides the symptoms of decomposition and death, other no less certain signs of restoration and rebirth.

All these things are providential. From the slag in the crucible comes the noble metal, and the new world, in its laborious work of rebuilding, will use the minute debris of the old world, dissociated, disorganised to the point, to provide ready-made materials for the architects of the future.

Thus, the Future feeds on the Past; thus our Heavenly Mother[2] makes incorruptible life germinate and flourish on the dung of death, fertile ground that the universal roadway of ephemeral existences, accumulates day by day.

In distant centuries, when civilisations more colossal, but above all more noble and stronger than ours flourished –for they rested on the unity of Synthesis and not on the fragmentation of Analysis, on the healthy and holy Hierarchy and not on morbid and dissolving Anarchy–; in the distant centuries, Science and Faith were identified in the one and indivisible splendour of Total Knowledge; Priesthood and Teaching fraternised, opening two distinct paths to the same ideal; and venerable Religious Universities gathered young students in the study and worship of the True. Finally, the pontiff and the scholar were one master, the Hierophant,[3] in charge of initiating gradually worthy men into the four hierarchies of the sacred sciences, and to officiate with them in public ceremonies; thus, carried on the threefold wings of study, contemplation and prayer, the neophyte rose in degrees from the knowledge of what it is to the ineffable mysteries of the One who is eternally.

This is how scientific and religious teaching appears to us in the entire arbitral empire founded by Rama;[4] this is how, after Irshou[5] and the schism of the Yonijas,

---

2   The Sophia of the Gnostics, then of Bohemia and St. Martin; Nature, spouse of the pure Spirit; in a word, Providence or the universal consciousness of the life-principle.
3   The Hierophant was at the same time what we would call Metropolitan Bishop and University Rector; hierarchically grouped around him, the simple professor-priests took the name of Magi.
4   Rama or Ram, is a major deity of Hinduism.
5   A little before the Kali Yuga, the sacred books of the Brahmins say, nearly thirty-five centuries after Rama (i.e. around 3250 BC), the universal empire of Rama received, at its very centre, its first germ of dissolution. Emperor Ougra had just died, and his son Tarak'hya had succeeded him, but his younger son, Irshou, Regent of the Provinces, was extremely ambi-

INTRODUCTION

we still greet it in the regions that survived, such as Egypt and the Etruscan confederations, keeping intact the traditional treasure of ancient orthodoxy.

L'Histoire philosophique du Genre humain (Philosophical History of the Human Race),[6] by Fabre d'Olivet, leaves no doubt as to the certainty of these historical facts; but they are above all luminous evidence, for those who have meditated without bias on the more recent and less summary work of the Marquis de Saint-Yves d'Alveydre: *La Mission des Juifs* (Mission of the Jews).[7]

Wounded in its conceited self-importance, our civilisation of yesterday can put jeers on the lips of its sceptical defenders; contrast Voltaire's sneer with the voice inspired by the epopt,[8] which abruptly tears the veil of heroic times.[9] Nothing ultimately prevails over positively established facts, and when the Holy Truth utters its dazzling verb, it envelops in its thunderous rolls, the sour voice of the hisses. The hissers are free to prolong their squeaky protests afterwards... The fact remains –without question– , the thunder has spoken.

Yes, your titanic debris, Oh mysterious monuments of the old ages, testify to formidable and sacred civilizations, where Science and Faith (in their three times holy principle), lent each other mutual support: Religion consecrated the teachings of Gnosis; Gnosis verified the dogmas of Religion!... And the simple ones, through the frosted crystal of the exoteric fables, received the radiation of the Truth-Light, with a degree of attenuation proportional to the weakness of their eyes.

Saint-Yves d'Alveydre

---

tious and, unable to reach the sovereign power through legal and legitimate channels, he provoked a schism.
6 Paris, J. Brière, 1822, 2 vol. in-8°.
7 Paris, Calmann-Lévy, 1884, 1 vol. tall in-8°.
8 A seer; one initiated into the secrets of any mystical system.
9 Heroic times... a name as unfortunate as those of prehistoric or fabulous times; but to make us better understood, we must adopt the terminology consecrated by usage.

All the antinomies reconciled; all the knowledge classified; all the contingent realities leading to absolute truth, like finite rivers in the infinity of the sea; it was a strong synthesis, harmonious and hierarchical!... Such as, in the human body, the venous and arterial circulation; thus, through the organism of this colossus, two streams of intelligible order crossed each other, ascending and descending: one, originating from the multiplicity of positive observations, converged towards the unity of the transcendental and absolute Truth; the other, emanating from this sublime unity, branched out in radiant channels, infinitely, to go and spread its sap of light over the innumerable multitude of facts primitively observed.

A Science: that of Being; a Religion: that of God, merged into a scientific cult or sacred gnosis, by which the adepts rose to the total knowledge of divine Truth.

Educated in such a school, the men of that blessed era were giants; we are pygmies.

Their unanimous admiration saluted the great works of intelligence and justice; the best among us, titillated with unhealthy enthusiasm, prostrate themselves before the bloody idols of the arbitrary and brutal Force.

Our distant ancestors shouted: "Homeland!" with their eyes on the sky full of stars; drunk with blood and hatred, we cry: "Homeland!" as we stumble over the mounds of recent mass graves, and it is to the same refrain that we dream of future and more deadly hecatombs.

Are we not quite credulous in our presumption when we proclaim the contemporary advent of Science and Light? Like the crude centurion of Rome, who called the Greeks barbarians, we do not have enough disdain for the heroes of ancient civilisations. Apostles of scepticism, we shout down their naive faith; their serene enthusiasm makes us smile, jaded and with no energy left but for evil!

What if the dead were to return? At the sight of our rotten society, Rama or Zoroaster might well mock us in turn, if they didn't feel the urge to cry over us and our presumptuous decadence.

Is it the multitude of isolated, empirical, analytical knowledge; is it the progress of industry, luxury and comfort that a civilisation is measured by? – These things, no doubt, are of secondary importance in the edifice of a social state; but the real value of a society is measured by its intellectual and moral development, by the balance of its organic functions, and above all by the perfection of its unitary system.

The unquestionable progress of the positive sciences, the importance and variety of their applications, the gigantic development of industry, the apparent prosperity of the great nations, which always ends up swallowing up the small ones, the general increase (significant of selfishness) in material well-being, the very active diffusion of a beneficial but primary education; do not all these manifestations of progress, in the modern sense of the word, give us an illusion about the value and universality of our European social state?

But if we look only at the surface, from the point of view of social issues alone, does this state seem so wonderfully enviable?

Come on, let's go inside ourselves and appeal to our conscience to judge fairly!

The present state? – Let us see its fruits.

INTRODUCTION

The flagrant hostility between Science and Religion; the great struggle of the authoritarians and liberals, fiercer and more irreconcilable than ever; blind positivism disputing the sterile Eclecticism with the highest intelligences, when they do not sink into the shameless individualism of the sceptics; militarism invading everything, the city building the barracks and the barracks oppressing the city; Socialism allying itself too often with Nihilism, to triumph by dynamite or on the scaffold; Political Economy exhausting its ingenious verve to disguise, under euphemistic terms, the imminence of national bankruptcies, the harbingers of the worst debacles; all licences, in a word, under the name of Freedom; all misery, under the name of Equality, and, under the name of Fraternity, all selfishness! Are these the signs of a truly prosperous civilization?

The answer is doubtful, for those who have compared the present era, not to the Caesarian centuries of Assoûr and the Empire of Rome (tiny wrecks of a social state in full dissolution), but to the three thousand five hundred years of the peace of Aries, when the universal empire of Rama lavished the world with its glorious light, so bright and gentle, that the memory of the Golden Age has remained in human consciousness, as a comfort for the present and a hope for the future!

What material, intellectual and moral cataclysms were necessary to bring down this august edifice, this holy cathedral of the eternal androgynous harmony, the social Adam-Eve...? But standing, despite the dissolving action of the centuries –defying Saturn and his scythe, Neptune and his trident, braving Mars and his sword– the ruins of this grandiose past have remained: obelisks and pylons are still there, riddled with hieroglyphics...

A latent soul inhabits these skeletons of the past; a powerful verb will make the depths of these necropolises, sixty centuries old, vibrate for a few days, and apparent death will once again deliver the secrets of life to the null and void world!

While waiting for the posthumous Word to be exhaled from all these bones of holy antiquity, rare thinkers have deciphered the hieratic inscriptions of the ruined temples, the pantacles[10] of the decried manuscripts; they are in a position to preach the new Gospel with the appropriate prudence.

Long enough, from the top of his cross, the sorrowful Christ made the world resound with the most dreadful cry that ever came from the lips of a man, from the lips of a God who for a moment was failing, even to the point of doubting himself: *Eli, Eli, lamma sabachtani!*

The coming is close to the glorious Christ: he has come to suffer, to be crowned in blood and to assert himself in death... He will return to conquer, reign in peace and triumph in life.

Jesus Christ is the ideal sun of humanity; the law of eternal life is to be found in his Gospel, where his spirit is complete. But he himself (let us not forget) warned us of a veil that must be torn if we want Minerva to reveal herself to us in her chaste and marvellous nakedness: *The letter kills –he said–, only the Spirit gives life...*

---

10 In occultism, a pantacle is any geometric figure tending to express a universal structure, and within which are inscribed letters, words or symbolic signs.

It is to the oblivion of this divine precept that modern teachers owe it to themselves to hear the Gospel of Christ no better than they understood the Books of Moses, the Prophecies of Ezekiel, Daniel and Isaiah, the Apocalypse of Saint John. They take the sacred texts at face value, attributing to incomparable geniuses, such as Moses, Zoroaster or John, the cloths of nonsense that are the Pentateuch, or the Avesta, or the Apocalypse, provided that, attaching themselves to the literal narrative,[11] the interpreter forgets to extract from it the latent science, and if he neglects to awaken that Sleeping Beauty, which, in the Enchanted Forest –inextricable jumble of allegorical tales and symbols that are absurd in themselves– is still waiting for *Prince Charming, who must bring him back to life with a kiss.*

II

We have marked the abyss that separates our social state from that which the genius of Rama made prevail, for thirty-five centuries, over two-thirds of the then known world: for evidence abounds, and we cannot insist too much on this, the Golden Age is not a myth and the Reign of God on earth is a reality in the past.

Measuring our contemporary civilization against the pattern of the ancient one, we have specified, by contrast, the limits –so limited, alas– of its intelligence and morality. And despite the relatively enormous development of the conquests in which our positive science prides itself, we are able to affirm that the comparison would not be more to our advantage in this field than in the other two.

So far we have not spoken much about the fatal **Serpent**, and the few preceding pages may have seemed to the reader a singular aperitif: they are so only in appearance.

The esoteric interpretation –strictly unknown– of a text of Moses could not be presented without first insisting on the common ignorance where the Doctors are, of the hidden spirit of the Holy Books; on the other hand, before indicating to what extent religious exegesis is routine and superficial, it was important to put under the light, which has the effect of repelling the agnostic character of modern civilisation, the real cause of this routine and casualness.

But it is time to mark the stages we are about to take.

This Genesis, which the Doctors understand in a truly materialistic and anthropomorphic spirit, this Genesis "where scientific truth is hidden, frightening in its height and depth",[12] will provide the text of a study which will fill three successive books; for we will develop the two occult meanings of this text, after having exposed its demotic and vulgar meaning:

והנחש היה ערום מכל הית השדה עשר עשה יהוה אלהים :

(Sépher Bereschit, III, 1.)

---

11 Which is nothing less than a narrative.
12 *Mission des Juifs* (Mission of the Jews), page 66.

INTRODUCTION

Such is the sentence in Mosaic Hebrew; the accredited translation gives only the literal meaning and the material aspect: – *"However, the serpent was more crafty than any of the creatures of the earth that the Lord God had made"*.[13] Fabre d'Olivet, allowing the limpid spirit to filter through the cloudy thickness of the letter, translates: *"Now the original attraction* (greed, selfishness) *was the driving passion of all elementary life* (the inner spring) *of Nature, the work of Ihôah, the Being of beings"*.[14]

Be that as it may, in these two seemingly contradictory versions, let us implore the reader to be patient; the intimate meaning of the Mosaic text will become clearer in the course of later developments. For the moment it is sufficient to sketch out the scene of the first sin, at least as it appears to the most serious theologians, confident in the Vulgate's accounts.

The world has just come out of chaos at the call of the creative Word, and the first man, fashioned in the likeness of God himself, shares with the bride (whom, by a mysterious doubling, the Lord has brought forth from his side) the delights of an unparalleled garden, destined to be their immortal homeland.

Everything that the Earth, in the blossoming of a virginal sap, has been able to make gush from its womb under the caresses of the Sun, decorates the earthly paradise, these are only prodigies of green splendour and flowery majesty.

And the loving and naive couple –as king and queen of creation– walks through the wonders hatched for them alone.

Only a single tree is forbidden to their curiosity, and four rivers, taking their source in its roots, flow crosswise in the distance, dividing Eden into as many peninsulas, rivals of grace and fecundity. And the Lord said to Man: *But from the tree of the knowledge of good and evil, you shall not eat.*

But it is already certain that the magnet of the forbidden thing attracted the first woman; forgetting the mysteries of her new-born love, Eve could no longer move away from the tree, and dreaming, fascinated, murmured: "Since this fruit gives death, why shouldn't I taste it?..." The Bible (it must be said) presents another version, it attributes the temptation that gripped Eve to the Watching Serpent, coiled up on the trunk of the tree. But, for the sake of Adam's great-grandsons, Moses must have been mistaken on this point.

Let's move on. Our duty is to remain faithful to the Mosaic narrative, or rather to the version of the authorized translators of Genesis.

So the serpent, addressing the woman said: *By no means will you die a death. For God knows that, on whatever day you will eat from it, your eyes will be opened; and you will be like gods...*

And, less indecisive, the mischievous one reaches out his hand towards the golden apple. It is done, she succumbs to temptation... Eve, a precocious woman, cannot stop there: she needs her husband's complicity. She has bitten into the fruit, she makes Adam bite it, who shivers, drawn into crime, at the idea of the One who can call them at any moment...

---

13 See *any* Bible.
14 Caïn, Paris, 1823, in-8, page 27, and *Langue hébraïque restituée* (Hebrew language restored), Paris, 1815-1816, 2 vols. in-4. Volume II, page 95.

Already the voice of the Lord is raised and the couple flee in panic, ashamed, for the first time, of the nakedness of their flesh.

Covered in an improvised garment of fig leaves, Adam and his kind instigator appear before their judge in wrath.

– Adam, where are you?

– *I heard your voice in Paradise, and I was afraid, because I was naked, and so I hid myself.*

– *Then who told you that you were naked, if you have not eaten of the tree from which I instructed you that you should not eat?*

– *The woman, whom you gave to me as a companion, gave to me from the tree, and I ate.*

– *Why, woman, did you do this?*

And the poor weeping Eve said: *The serpent deceived me...*

– *Because you have done this –said the Lord–, you are cursed among all living things, even the wild beasts of the earth. Upon your breast shall you travel, and the ground shall you eat, all the days of your life. I will put enmities between you and the woman, between your offspring and her offspring. She will crush your head, and you will lie in wait for her heel.*

– *As for you –said the Lord to the man–, because you have listened to the voice of your wife, and have eaten of the tree, from which I instructed you that you should not eat, cursed is the land that you work. In hardship shall you eat from it, all the days of your life. Thorns and thistles shall it produce for you, and you shall eat the plants of the earth. By the sweat of your face shall you eat bread, until you return to the earth from which you were taken. For dust you are, and unto dust you shall return.*

Then the Lord, having clothed the guilty couple with coarse skins for clothing, drove the first human couple from the enchanted dwelling place of Eden. And on the threshold he put a Cherubim with a sword of flame, to forbid him entry for ever.

So there you have it, in substance, more or less, the mosaic fable of the original sin. I mean, in its most material and veiled version, as constantly rendered by translators, naive, or pretending to be so.

Let us ask ourselves, at this hour, what can this mystical and formidable Serpent be, whose perfidy knew how to lose Eve, then Adam... And according to the various meanings of this allegory, we will establish the divisions of our work.

III

What is this Serpent?

In the vulgar, apparent sense, it is easy to guess: it is the Spirit of Evil disguised as a reptile; it is the eternal Adversary, in Hebrew: שטן *Satan*.[15]

---

[15] This is not what can be called the positive meaning of the Symbol, but on the contrary an unfortunate attempt at superlative inter-prelation.
The positive meaning is the fact of drunkenness of some kind, which, invading man, makes him roll over to evil. – The Temple of Satan will give us the opportunity of analysing this drunkenness in its worst manifestations, in all the fury of its implementation: thus this First Septenary will serve as a commentary together on the positive meaning of the emblem and on the erroneous superlative meaning which the vulgar layman attributes to it.

In the first esoteric sense, it is the Astral Light, that implacable fluid which governs instincts; that universal dispenser of elementary life, fatal agent of birth and death; curtain of the invisible, behind which the various hierarchies of Powers hide, to which it serves both as a veil and a vehicle. This hyper-physical being –unconscious, therefore irresponsible– dominates the sorcerer as a master, meanwhile it obeys the magician as a valet. – To be or not to be… one must at all costs become master of it, if one does not want to become the plaything of the great currents that move within it, following invariable laws.

In the higher esoteric sense, the Serpent symbolises primordial egoism, that mysterious attraction of the Self towards the Self, which is the very principle of divisibility: that force which, by calling upon all beings to isolate themselves from the original Unity, to make themselves the centre and to take pleasure in their Ego, has caused Adam's fall from grace.

– The passage quoted from Genesis leads us to the problem of Evil: we must see in it the legend of the Human Fall, both collective and individual, which is followed, as a necessary complement, by the great epic of Redemption.

Hence the three parts in our work:[16]

1. – The Temple of Satan. – Our first book will therefore be devoted to an examination of the special works characteristic of Satan: Black Magic and its hideous practices, charms and evil spells. We will enumerate the infernal resources of witchcraft. We will challenge the prince of eternal darkness in his lair, and on the Sabbath, the monstrous goat with the breasts of a woman, whom the followers of these disgusting agape had to "kiss brutally under the tail, as a sign of great reverence and honour".

2. – The Key to Black Magic. – In this second book of the Serpent of Genesis, we will give the hidden meaning of the myth of Satan. – The study of the Astral Light, as the supreme agent of the tenebrous works of Goety,[17] will allow us to take up again the rites and phenomena that we will have described, and to analyse them in their real causes and effects, following the long secret doctrines of the Kabbalah and Occult Hermetism.

3. – The Problem of Evil. – Finally, the third part will be the philosophical synthesis of our Book; we will approach the great enigma of Evil, and we will raise, as far as our consciousness and our initiation allows us, the fearsome and beneficial veil that conceals from the eyes of the *profanum vulgus* the Great Arcanum of Magic. We will even push, further than any adept thought necessary, to that ultimate limit, so formidable to cross, where the emblematic Cherubim, with the sword of flame in its fist, threatens the daring contemplators of the most blinding of suns with blindness.

---

16 See the table entitled: *Esoteric Plan of this work*, at the beginning of this book (page vi). – It seems useless to repeat here what we have explained at the beginning of this book, concerning the number, sequence and distribution of the XXII chapters in three Septenaries and an Epilogue.
17 Invocation of evil spirits; black magic; sorcery, in a bad sense.

What is Evil? – Did God create it? – What is the origin of Evil, if it does not have a positive principle? – What, in the true sense, is the Edenic Fall? – What was the great Adam before the fall? What happens to him afterwards? – In what way does the Mystery of Creation identify with those of the Fall and the Incarnation? – In what way is the Mystery of Redemption complementary to these? – What is the Redeemer? The sorrowful Christ? The glorious Christ? – How are the five Hebrew letters (יהשוה) of the name of Jesus analyzed kabbalistically? – What is the esoteric resolution of the Social Question? – How does the inaccessible Unity reveal itself through the Ternary in the intelligible world and does it manifest itself through the Quaternary in the sensible world? – Where does Evolution lead to? – What is Nirvana?

By answering all these questions and a few others straightforwardly, we will show how a philosopher initiated into the mysteries of the Kabbalah can interpret Christian dogmas.

This is our sole intention, and to conclude this foreword to a book which claims not to disturb the peace of any conscience, we are very much to be excused for transcribing without comment what we wrote in 1886, at the bottom of a page where we were led to speak of the works of Christ: – *"To this divine mission, we think it prudent not to touch here; where Faith begins, perhaps it would be appropriate for Science always to stop, in order to avoid sad misunderstandings... And whenever, in the course of this brief study, we have to touch upon religious beliefs, let us declare once and for all that we are in no way competent in matters of Faith, we consider men and facts from the sole point of view of human intelligence and without ever claiming to dogmatise.*[18]

Stanislas de Guaita

---

18 *Essays of Sciences Maudites, I, Au Seuil du Mystère* (Essays of the Cursed Sciences I, On the Threshold of Mystery), by Stanislas de Guaita (Paris; Carré, 1886, 1 vol. large in-8), pp. 13-14. Second edition of the same, tripled text with figures; Paris, Carré, 1890, in-8, page 38.
Fifth edition of the same, corrected, with two beautiful magical figures after Henry Khunrath, a completely revised appendix and a preface by Maurice Barrès. Paris, Hector and Henri Durville, 1915, in-8.

Catalogue
of the main works in which the reader is sent back to *The Temple of Satan*

ANONYMS AND COLLECTIVES

ADVENT OF ELIJAH (*Avènement d'Élie*). – In France, 1734, 2 vols. in-12 (rare).

ALMANACHS OF THE DEVIL (*Almanachs du Diable*), containing very strange predictions for the years 1737 and 1738. – Aux Enfers. In-24 (very rare).

BAPTISTE FILES (*Dossiers Baptiste*). – (See details)

BRITISH LIBRARY (periodical).

CHYMICA VANNUS (Reconditorium ac reclusorium Opulentiæ Sapientiæque Numinis Mundi Magni; cui deditur in titulum)... Obtenta quidem et erecta auspice mortale cœpto, sed inventa proauthoribus immortalibus adeptis, etc... – Amstelodami, apud Jansonium, anno 1666, in-4, fig. (rare and singular work, published by the Rose + Croix).

FRIENDS OF SCIENCE (*Amis des Sciences*). – Scientific journal, edited by M. Victor Meunier.

INITIATION. – Independent philosophical journal of higher education. Hypnotism, theosophy, freemasonry, occult sciences. – Paris, Carré, large in-18, fig. (Estimated periodical, monthly, years 1888-1891.)

LEVITIKON or exposition of the fundamental principles of the doctrine of the early Christian Catholics, followed by their Gospels, an extract from the Golden Table and the Ceremonial Ritual for Religious Service, etc., preceded by a Statute on the

Government of the Church and the Levitical Hierarchy. – Paris, at the book-store of the Chrétiens Primitives, 1831, in-8 (now rare).

LOTUS (The). – Journal of Higher Theosophical Studies. Paris, Carré, in-8, monthly, 1887-1888.

MANUAL OF THE KNIGHTS (*Manuel Des Chevaliers*) of the order of the temple. – In Paris, at the home of Knight A. Guyot, printer of the Temple Militia. 707-1825, small in-12, massive (rare).

MYSTICAL CORRESPONDENCE OF J. CAZOTTE (*Correspondance Mystique de J. Cazotte*) with Laporte and Pouteau, Intendant and Secretary of the Civil List, during the years 1790, 1791, 1792..., preceded by a note on the life and works of this famous man, followed by his interrogation and judgement. – Paris, Lerouge et Cie, an VI, in-12, portrait.

NEW TESTAMENT. – (V, preferably the Sylvestre edition of Saèy.)

NOTICE TO CRIMINALISTS (*Avènement aux criminalistes*) on the abuses that creep into the Trials of Witchcraft, dedicated to the magistrates of Germany, a book very necessary at this time here, etc..., by Fr. M. S. I., Roman theologian, printed in Latin for the second time in Frankfurt, in the year 1632, and translated to French by F. B. de Velledor M. A. D. – In Lyon... by Claude Prost, à la Vérité, 1660, in-8 (very rare).

RED DRAGON, The (*Dragon Rouge, Le*), or the art of commanding the Heavenly, Aerial, Terrestrial and Infernal Spirits, with the true secret of making the dead talk, of winning every time we put in the lotteries, of discovering hidden treasures, etc., S. L., 1522, small in-12, figures. – (Printed at the beginning of the 19th century on the very rare edition of 1521).

RITUAL OF TOUL. – (Idem).

ROMAN RITUAL. – (Any edition.)

SALICAL LAWS (*Lois Saliques*) (Collection of 400 articles of which only Latin texts exist). – Often printed in collections of jurisprudence.

SECRET SOCIETIES, The (*Sociétés Secrètes, Des*) in Germany and other countries, Sect of the Enlightened, the Secret Tribunal, the Kotzebuë assassination, etc., and the Secret Tribunal. – Paris, Gide fils, 1819. in-8.

SEXT[1] DIALECTICAL AND POTENTIAL ESSENCE, The (*Sexte Essence Dialectique et Potentielle*), taken from a new way of convolution, according to the precepts of, the Holy Magic and invocation of the Demons. Paris, 1595, in-8 (not found).

TALMUD, The (*Talmud, Le*). – Collection sacerdotal of the rabbis, of which the most complete edition is that of Venice, 1520, in 12 vol. in-folio.

---

1 In the Roman Catholic and Greek churches, in religious houses, and as a devotional office in the Anglican Church, the office of the sixth hour, originally and properly said at midday.

A

ADAM (Paul). – *Being* (Être) (novel). – Paris, 1888, in-12.

AGRIPPA (Henri-Corneille). – *The Occult Philosophy* (La Philosophie occulte), divided into three books and translated from Latin. – In The Hague, at Chr. Alberts, 1727, 2 vol. in-8, fig. (Very rare, especially the large paper copies.)

ALBERT (The Solid Treasure of the Little One). – Or marvellous secrets of natural and kabbalistic magic… enriched with marvellous figures and how to make them. – In Lyon, among the heirs of Beringos frères, 6516, in-18.

ALBERT THE GREAT (Albert le Grand) (The admirable secrets of). – Containing several treatises on the conception of women, the virtues of herbs, precious stones and animals; augmented by a strange summary of physiognomy, etc., divided into four books. – In Lyon, among the heirs of Beringos Friars, 1799, in-12, fig.

AMMIEN MARCELLIN. – History of the Roman Emperors (*Histoire des Empereurs*), translated by Savalette. – Paris, 1848, large in-8.

ANDRÉ (Abbot J.-F.). – *The case of Rosette Tamisier* (Affaire Rosette Tamisier), preceded by a notice on Pierre-Michel Vintras and his sect. – Carpentras, impr. Devillario, Sept. 1851, in-12, fig.

AVTVN (R. P. Jacques, Capuchin). – *Scholarly incredulity and ignorant credulity about Magicians and Sorcerers* (L'incrédulité savante et la crédulité ignorante au sujet des Magiciens et des Sorcier), with the answer to a book entitled: Apology, for all the great figures who were falsely suspected of Magic. – In Lyon, at Jean Certe's house, 1674, in-4, massive.

B

BAISSAC (Jules). – *The Devil, the Person of the Devil and the Devil's Staff* (Le Diable, la personne du Diable et le Personnel du Diable). – Paris, Dreyfous, n. d., thick in-8. – *The Great Days of Sorcery* (Les grands jours de la Sorcellerie). – Paris, Rlincksieck, 1890, gr. in-8.

BAUDELAIRE (Charles). – *The Flowers of Evil* (Les Fleurs du Mal), poetry. – Paris, Poulet-Malassis, in-18.

BEAUNIS (Professor H.). – *Induced somnambulism* (Le somnambulisme provoqué). – Paris, J.-B. Baillière, 1887, in-18.

BEKKER (Balthazar). – *The enchanted world* (Le monde enchanté), where one examines common feelings, touching the spirits, their nature, their power. Translated from the Dutch. – Amsterdam, 4 vol. in-12, portrait and fig.

BERBIGUIER (Alexis-Vincent-Charles, from Thyme Newfoundland). – *The Goblins* (Les Farfadets), or all demons are not from the other world, adorned with 8 superb lithographed drawings. – Paris, the author, 1821, 3 vols. in-8.

BINSFELDII (Petri). – *Tractatus de confessionibus maleficorum and Sagarum*. Augustæ Treuiroruin, 1589, in-8.

BODIN. – *The Demonomy of Wizards* (De la Démonomanie des sorciers), to Monseigneur Chrestofle de Thon... revised, corrected and increased by a large part (with the Réfutation des opinions de Jean Vuier). – Paris, Jacques du Puys, 1587, in-4 (Rare).

BOGUET (Henry, dolanois, great judge in the land of Saint Oyan de Ioux, known as Saint-Claude, in the county of Burgundy). – *Discourse of the sorcerers (Discours des sorciers), with six opinions in fact of Sorcery, and an instruction for the judge in similar matters* (Discours des sorciers, avec six avis en fait de Sorcellerie, et une instruction pour le juge en semblable matière); being what the author has highlighted above on the same subject, only a sample of what is treated in this book (30th edition). – In Lyon, with Pierre Rigaud, 1610, in-8. (Only complete edition, extremely sought-after and rare).

BURGOA (R.-P.). – Geographical description of the province of Santo Domingo.

C

CADET OF GASSICOURT. – *The Tomb of Jacques Molay* (Le Tombeau de Jacques Molay), or secret and abridged history of ancient and modern initiates, Templars, Freemasons, Enlightened, and research on their influence on the French Revolution; followed by the key to the lodges (2nd edition, only correct). – Paris, by Desenne, year V of the French Era, in-12, fig.

CALMET (Dom Augustin, Abbot of Senones). – *Treatise on the apparitions of the Spirits* (Traité sur les apparitions des Esprits), on vampires or Revenants from Hungary, Moravia, etc... New edition (only complete). – Paris, Dehure, 1751, 2 vols. in-12.

CAYET (Palma). *Prodigious and lamentable story of Jeun Fauste* (Histoire prodigieuse et lamentable de Jeun Fauste), a great magician, with his will and his dreadful life. – In Cologne, at the heirs of Pierre Marteau, 1712, in-12, very strange frontispiece (rare).

CHABAS (F.). – *Studies on historical antiquity* (Études sur l'antiquité historique), based on Egyptian sources and monuments of prehistoric origin,, 2nd edition, revised and enlarged. – Paris, Maison-neuve, 1873, large in-8.

CHRISTIAN (P.). – *History of Magic* (Histoire de la Magie), the supernatural world and fate, through time and peoples. – Paris, Furne, Jouve et Cie, n. d., large in-8, engravings.

CLAVEL (F.-F.-B.). – *Picturesque history of Freemasonry* (Histoire pittoresque de la Franc-maçonnerie) and secret societies, ancient and modern, illustrated with 25 beautiful steel engravings (2nd edition). – Paris, Pagnerre, 1845, large in-8. (Very rare, most of the edition having been destroyed).

CATALOGUE

COLLIN DE PLANCY (D.-A.-S.). – *Infernal dictionary* (Dictionnaire infernal), or research and anecdotes about demons, spirits, ghosts, spectres, revenants, werewolves, possessed, sorcerers, Sabbath, wizards, salamanders, sylphs, gnomes, visions, dreams, wonders, charms, evil spells, wonderful secrets, talismans, etc.., In a word, about everything related to apparitions, magic, the trade of hell, divinations, secret sciences, superstitions, mysterious and supernatural things, etc. – Paris, 1826, 4 vol. in-8, with Atlas (this is the most complete edition). – Since then, the author has gone from extreme scepticism to extreme credulity; he has given a definitive edition, approved by the ecclesiastical authorities, of his completely revised Dictionary. – Paris, Plon, 1863, large in-8, fig.

COURT DE GEBELIN. – *Primitive world*, The (Monde primitif), analysed and compared with the modern world, considered in its allegorical genius and in the allegories to which this genius led. – Paris, 1777, 9 vol. in-4.

CROLLIUS. – *The Royal Chemistry* (La Royale Chimie), translated into French by I. Marcel, de Boulène. Followed by the Treatise of Signatures; or true and lively anatomy of the great and small world. – In Rouen, by Charles Osmont, 1634, small in-8 (very rare).

D

DAUGY (or Daugis). – *A treatise on magic* (Traité sur la magie), spells, possessions, obsessions and evil spells, where truth and reality are demonstrated with a safe and easy method to discern them and regulations against soothsayers, sorcerers, wizards, etc. By M. D..., small in-8. – Paris, 1732.

DAVID. *The Psalms* (see any Bible).

DELLON. – *Relation of the Inquisition of Goa* (Relation de l'inquisition de Goa). – Paris. Horthemels, 1688, in-12, fig.

DELRIO (R. P. Martin, Jesuit). – *Controversies and magical research* (Les Controverses et recherches magiques), translated by André Duchesne. – Paris, 1611, in-4° (rare).

DENYS (Ferdinand). – *Historical, Analytical and Critical Table of the Occult Sciences* (Tableau historique, analytique et critique des Sciences occultes), etc. – Paris, Mairet and Fournier, 1842, 1 vol. in-32.

DESMARETS (R. P.). – *History of* (Histoire de) *Magdeleine Bavent*, a nun of the Monastery of Saint-Louis de Louviers, with the general and testamentary confession, in which she declares the abominations, impiety and sacrileges that she practised and saw practised, both in the said Monastery and on the Sabbath, and the people she noticed there. With the ruling, etc... – In Paris, by Jacques le Gentil, 1652, in-4. (This original edition cannot be found, but the work has often been reprinted).

DU POTET (the baron). – *The Unveiled Magic or Principles of Occult Science* (La Magie dévoilée ou principes de la Science Occulte). – Saint-Germain, Eugène Heutte, 1875, large in-4, fig. (This work was not put on the market. Baron Du Potet reserved it for his insiders, to whom he gave it for 100 francs a copy and on a written oath not to transmit it to anyone, and not to reveal the secrets contained therein. Since the Baron's death, the Magic Revealed has been found quite often in catalogues, at more affordable prices).

E

ÉLIPHAS LEVI (Father Alphonse-Louis Constant). – *Transcendental Magic Its Doctrine and Ritual* (Dogme et rituel de la Haute Magie) (2nd edition, very enlarged, with 24 figures). Paris, Germer-Baillière, 1861, 2 vols. in-8. – *History of Magic* (Histoire de la Magie), with a clear and precise exposition of its procedures, rites and mysteries. – Ibid, 1860, 1 vol. in-8, fig. *The Key to the Great Mysteries* (La Clef des Grands Mystère), following Enoch, Abraham, Hermes Trismegistus and Solomon. – Ibid, 1861, 1 vol. in-8, fig. – *The Science of Spirits* (La science des Esprits). – Ibid, 1865, 1 vol. in-8.

ERDAN (Alexander). – La France mystique, a picture of the religious eccentricities of the time. – Paris, Coulon-Pineau, 1855, 2 vol. in-8, fig.

F

FABART (Felix). – *Philosophical and political history of the Occult* (Histoire philosophique et politique de l'Occulte); magic, witchcraft, spiritualism, with a preface by Camille Flammarion. – Paris, Marpon, n. d., in-12.

FABRE D'OLIVET. – *The Golden Verses of Pythagoras* (Les Vers dorés de Pythagore), explained and translated for the first time into French eumolpique[2] verse, preceded by a discourse on the *Essence and Form of Poetry* (Essence et la forme de la Poésie). – Paris, Treuttel and Wurtz, 1813, in-8. – *The Restored Hebrew Language* (La Langue hébraïque restituée) and the true meaning of Hebrew words re-established and proven by their radical analysis. This work brings together 1° an introductory essay on the origin of speech, the study of the languages which can lead to it and the aim which the author has set himself – 2° a Hebrew grammar, based on new principles and made useful for the study of languages in general – 3° a series of Hebrew roots, considered in new ways and intended to facilitate the understanding of language and etymological science; – 4° a preliminary discourse; – 5° a translation into French of the first ten chapters of the *Sepher*,[3] containing the Cosmogony of Moses, etc.; – 6° the first ten chapters of the Sepher, containing the Cosmogony of Moses. – In Paris, at the author's home, Barrois and Eberhart, booksellers, 1815-1816, 2 vol. large in-4. – *Philosophical history of mankind* (Histoire philosophique du genre humain), or man considered in his religious and political relations, in the social

---

[2] Name given by Fabre d'Olivet to rhymeless Alexandrian verses, where he alternately put masculine and feminine endings.

[3] Sepher or Sefer Yetzirah, the Book of Formation, or Book of Creation, is the title of the earliest extant book on Jewish mysticism, although some early commentators treated it as a treatise on mathematical and linguistic theory as opposed to the Kabbalah.

state, in all periods and among the different peoples of the earth. – (2nd edition of *The social state of Man* [l'État social de l'Homme]). – Paris, Brière, 1824, 2 vol. in-8.
– *Cain*, a dramatic mystery in three acts, by Lord Byron, translated into French and refuted in a series of philosophical and critical remarks; preceded by a letter to Lord Byron on the motives and purpose of this work. – Paris, Servier, 1823, in-8.

FLAUBERT (Gustave). – *The temptation of Saint Anthony* (La tentation de saint Antoine). – Paris, Lemerre, 1884, in-12.

FONTAINE (Jacques). – *Of the marks of the Sorcerers* (Des marques des Sorciers) and of the real possession that the Devil takes over the bodies of men; on the subject of the trial of the abominable and detestable sorcerer Louys Gaufridy, etc… dedicated to the Queen Regent – Lyon, Claude Larjot, 1611, in-8 (very rare).

G

GAFFAREL (J.). – *Unheard of curiosities on the talismanic sculpture of the Persians, horoscope of the patriarchs and reading of the stars* (Curiosités inouïes sur la sculpture talismanique des Persans, horoscope des patriarches et lecture des étoiles) (with 2 planispheres). – Rouen, 1632, in-8 (rare).

GARINET (Jules). – *History of magic in France from the beginning of the monarchy to the present day* (Histoire de la magie en France depuis le commencement de la monarchie jusqu'à nos jours). – Paris, 1818, in-8, frontispiece.

GIBIER (Doctor Paul). – *Analysis of things* (Analyse des choses), essay on future science, its influence on religions, philosophies, arts, etc. – Paris, Dentu, 1890, in-12.

GIRARD (Sur). – Proceedings in the Girard case, and in particular: *Factum for Marie Catherine Cadière* against J.-B. Girard, Jesuit. The Hague, with Henri Scheurleer, 1731, in-8. – *Instructive memorandum* for Father Girard, v. Catherine Cadière. Ibid, 1731, in-8. – *Continuation of* Catherine Cadière's proceedings against Father Girard, with response to the Jesuit's instructive memorandum. Ibid. in-8. – *Response* (other) *to the instructive memorandum*. Ibid. in-8.

GORRES. – *Divine, natural and diabolical mysticism* (La Mystique divine, naturale and diabolical), translated from German by Charles Sainte-Foi. – Paris, Vve Poussielgue, 1854-1855, 5 vol. in-8.

GOSSET. – *Cabalistic revelation of a universal medicine* (Révélation cabalistique d'une médecine universelle), followed by a dissertation on sepulchral lamps. – 1735, small in-8.

GOUGENOT DES MOUSSEAUX (the knight). – *The High Phenomena of Magic, preceded by ancient spiritism* (Les Hauts phénomènes de la Magie, précédés du spiritisme antique). – Paris, Plon, 1854, in-8.

GRANDIER. – *Treatise on the Celibacy of Priests* (Traité du Célibat des prêtres), published by M. Luzarche, based on a copy from the Jamet collection. – Paris, 1866, 1 vol. in-12 (doubtful text).

GRILLANDI. – *Tractatus de sortilegiis, ana cum J.-F. Ponzinibii tractatu de lamiis et excellentia juris utriusque.* – Francof. 1592, in-8.

GUAITA (Stanislas de). – *Essays of cursed sciences* (Essais de sciences maudites); at the Threshold of Mystery, new edition corrected, enlarged and recast, with two beautiful magical figures after Khunrath, and a completely new appendix. – Paris, Georges Carré, 1890, in-8, fig. – *Rosa Mystica,* poems, with a prose preface – Paris, Lemerre, 1885, in-12.

H

HEDELIN (F. lawyer in Parliament). – *Raw satyrs, monsters and demons* (Des satyres brutes monstres et démons), of their nature and worship, against the opinion of those who considered satyrs to be a species of men distinct and separate from the adamic ones. Dedicated to Mgr. le Mareschal de S. Geran. – In Paris, to Nicolas Buon, 1627, in-8 (very strange and extremely rare).

HELMONT (J.-B. van). – *The works, dealing with the principles of medicine and physics* (Les œuvres, traitant des principes de médecine et de physique), for the assured cure of diseases, translation by M. Jean le Comte. – In Lyon,. by Antoine Huguetan, 1671, in-4. (The treatise of *Magnetica vulnerum curatione* can only be found in the Latin edition of 1682, in-4).

HOMER. – *The odyssey* (L'odyssée) (translation by E. Bareste, 1842, or any other).

HONORIUS. – *Grimoire of Pope Honorius, with a collection of the rarest secrets* (Grimoire du pape Honorius, avec un recueil des plus rares secrets). Rome, 1670, in-16, fig. (extremely rare).

I – J

IAMBLICI. – *De Mysteriis Égyptiorum.* – 1602, in-12.

JABLONSKI. – *Pantheon Égyptiorum,* sive de diis eorum conurientarius, cum prolegomenis de religione et theologia Égyptiorum. – Francofurti, 1750-1752, 3 vols. in-8.

JACOLLIOT (Louis). – *The Sons of God* (Les Fils de Dieu). – Paris, Lacroix,. 1873, in-8. – *Spiritism in the world, initiation and occult sciences in India and among all the peoples of antiquity* (Le spiritisme dans le monde l'initiation et les sciences occultes dans l'Inde et chez tous les peuples de l'antiquité). – Paris, Lacroix, 1879, in-8.

JHOUNEY (Alber). – *Black lilies* (Les lys noirs), poems. Paris, Carré, 1888, large in-8.

JOACHIMI (Abbatis). – *Vaticinia siue prophetiæ, simul et Anselmi Episcopi Marsicani, cum imaginibus ære incisis,* etc... Venetiis, apud Hieronymum Porrum, 1589, in-4. – Engraved frontispiece and 34 figures in intaglio (extremely rare).

JOSEPH (Flavius). – *Jewish Antiquities* (Les antiquités judaïques) (in XX books), translation by Fr. Joachim Gillet. – Paris, 1756, 4 vol. in-4.

K

KELEPH BEN NATHAN (Dutoit-Mambrinj). – *The Divine Philosophy, applied to the natural, magical, astral, supernatural, celestial and divine lights* (La Philosophie divine, appliquée aux lumières naturelle, magique, astrale, surnaturelle, céleste et divine), or to the immutable truths that God has revealed about himself and his works, in the triple analogical mirror of the Universe, Man and written Revelation. – S. I., 1793, 3 vol. in-8.

KHUNRATH (Henrici). – *Amphitheatrum sapientiæ æternæ*, solius veræ, Christiano-Kabalisticum, divino-magicum, nec non physico-chymicum, tertriunum, catholicon instructore Henrico Khunrath, lipsensi, theosophiæ amatore fideli et medicinæ utriusque doctore... e millibus vix vni. – Hanuiae, excudebat Guilielmus Antonius, 1609, 1 vol. in folio, allegorical frontispiece, portrait and ten magic figures. (Very rare. Read a detailed description in our *Mystery Threshold* [Seuil du mystère]).

L

LA HARPE (J.-F. de). – *Complete works* (Œuvres complète). – Paris, 1821, 16 vol. in-8.

LAMARRE (de). – *Treaty of the Police* (Traité de la Police). – 4 vol. in-folio, 1710-1738.

LANCRE (Pierre de), adviser to the King at the Parliament of Bordeaux. – *Scheme of the inconstancy of evil angels and demons* (Tableau de l'inconstance des mauvais anges et démons), where he is amply treated of Sorcerers and witchcraft. A very useful and necessary book, not only for judges, but for all those who live under Christian laws. With a discourse containing the procedure carried out by the inquisitors of Spain and Navarre, in the town of Logroño in Castile, etc. – Paris, at the home of Nicolas Buon, 1612, in-4. With a Sabbath board (very rare and much sought-after).

LE LOYER (Pierre, King's Counsellor at the presidential seat in Angers). – *Discourse and history of the ghosts, visions and apparitions of spirits, angels, demons and urns visible to men* (Discours et histoire des spectres, visions et apparitions des esprits, anges, démons et urnes se visibles aux hommes). Divided into eight books, which, through the marvellous and prodigious visions and apparitions over the centuries, drawn and collected from the most famous authors, both sacred and profane, show the certainty of the spectres and visions of spirits; the causes of the various kinds of apparition of spirits, their effects, their differences and the means to recognise the good and the bad, and to drive out demons. Also treated are ecstasies and rapture; the essence, nature and origin of souls, and their state after the death of their bodies; plus wizards and sorcerers, and their communication with evil spirits; a collection of remedies to preserve oneself from diabolical illusions and deceptions. – In Paris, by Nicolas Buon, 1605, 2 vols. in-4 (the only complete edition of a rare and very strange book. Recommended to occultists).

LEBRUN (Father Pierre, priest of the Oratory). – *Critical history of superstitious practices* (Histoire critique des pratiques superstitieuses), which have seduced peoples and embarrassed scholars. With the method and principles to discern the natural effects from those that are not. – In Amsterdam, by J.-F. Bernard, 1733, 3 vol. in-8, figures.

LEGUE (Dr. Gabriel). – *Urbain Grandier and the possessed of Loudun* (Urbain Grandier et les possées de Loudun), unpublished documents by M. Charles Barbier. – Paris, art bookshop, 1880, in-4, fig.

LENGLET DUFRESNOY (the Abbot). – *Historical and dogmatic treatise on the apparitions, visions and particular Revelations* (Traité historique et dogmatique sur les apparitions, les visions et les Révélations particulières), with observations on the dissertations of the R. P. dom Calmet, Abbot of Sénones, on the apparitions and returnees. – Avignon, and is in Paris, at the home of J.-N. Leloup, 1751, 2 vol. in-12. – *Collection of old and new essays on apparitions, visions and dreams* (Recueil de dissertations anciennes et nouvelles sur les apparitions, les visions et les songes), with a historical preface. – Ibid, 1751, 4 vols. in-12.

LENORMANT (François). – *The occult sciences in Asia I. Magic among the Chaldeans and the Accadian origins* (Les sciences occultes en Asie I. La Magie chez les Chaldéens et les origines accadienne). – Paris, Maisonneuve, 1874, in-8. – The occult sciences in Asia: II. *Divination and the science of omens among the Chaldeans* (La divination et la science des Présages chez les Chaldéens). – Paris, Maison-neuve, 1875, in-8.

LEO III. – *Enchiridion* (of the pope), sent as a gift to Emperor Charlemagne. – In Rome, at the home of Father Angelo of Rimini, 1847, in-12, fig.

LIEBEAULT (the D.A.-A.). – *Induced sleep and similar states* (Le sommeil provoqué et les états analogues). – Paris, Dom, 1889, in-18.

LONGINI (Cæsaris). – *Trinum Magicum*, sive secretorum magicorum opus, etc... accessere nonnulla Secreta secretorum et mirabilia mundi, et Tractatus de proprii cuius que nati dæmonis inquisitione. Francofurti, sumptibus Conradi Eifridi, 1629, small in-12.

LUCAS (Louis, author of the *New chemistry* [Chimie nouvelle]). – *The alchemical novel or the two kisses* (Le Roman alchimique ou les deux baisers). – Paris, Michel Lévy, 1857, in-18 (very rare).

LUCHET (the Marquis de). – *Essay on the sect of the enlightened* (Essai sur la secte des illuminés). – Paris, 1789, in-8.

LUCIEN – *Complete works* (Œuvres complètes), translation Belin de Ballu. – 1788, 6 vol. in-8.

M

MARSOLLIER. – *History of the Inquisition and its origin* (Histoire de l'inquisition et son origine) – In Cologne, at Pierre Marteau's (À la Sphère), 1693, pet. in-8 (strange and sought-after).

MARTIN (Henri). – *History of France* (Histoire de France). Paris, Furne, 1860, 17 vol. in-8.

MEYNARDAIE (M. de la, priest). – *Examination and critical discussion of the History of the Devils of Loudun* (Examen et discussion critique de l'Histoire des Diables de Loudun), the possession of the Ursuline Sisters and the condemnation of Urbain Grandier. – In Liège, at Everard Kintz, 1749, in-12 (rare).

MICHAELIS (Le P.). – *An admirable story of the possession and conversion of a penitent* (Histoire admirable de la possession et conversion d'une pénitente) seduced by a magician, making her a witch and princess of sorcerers in the land of Provence, led to the Sainte-Baume, to be exorcised there in the year MDCX in November, under the authority of R. P. Sébastien Michablis, prior of the Royal Convent of Sainte Magdeleine in Saint Maximin, and of the said place of the Sainte-Baume. Committed by him to the Exorcisms and the collection of the acts the R. P. F. François Domptius, Doctor of Theology at the University of Louvain, all faithfully collected and very well verified. – Includes the (*Pneumatologie or Discourse of the Spirits* (Pneumatologie, ou Discours des Esprit) of the aforementioned Fr. Second edition. – In Paris, by Ch. Chastellain, 1613, 2 vols. in-8 (very rare and very strange).

MICHELET. – *History of France* (Histoire de France), illustrated by Vierge. Paris, S. D., 19 vol. in-8.

MIGNARD. – *Continuation of the monograph of the casket of the Duke of Blacas or Evidence of Manichaeism in the Order of the Temple* (Suite de la monographie du coffret du duc de Blacas ou Preuves du manichéisme dans l'Ordre du Temple). – Paris, 1853, large in-4, fig.

MIRVILLE (Mis Eudes de). – *Pneumatology. Spirits and their fluidic manifestations* (Pneumatologie. Des Esprits et de leurs manifestations fluidiques). Dissertation addressed to the Academy (with the Question of the Spirits, or defence of this dissertation). – Paris, Vrayet de Surcy, 1854, 2 vol. large in-8. – *Pneumatology. Spirits and their various manifestations* (Pneumatologie. Des Esprits et de leurs manifestations diverses). Second dissertation, *Historical manifestations* (Manifestations historiques). – Paris, ibid, 1863, 4 vol. large in-8.

MOSES. – *The Pentateuch* (Le Pentateuque), a new translation with the Hebrew facing it, accompanied by vowels and tonic accents, with philological and literary notes, by S. Cahen. – Paris, Barrois, Treuttel and Wurtz, 1831-1834, 5 vols. in-8 (rare).

N

NAVDE (Gabriel). – *Apology for all the great men who have been accused of Magic* (Apologie pour tous les grands hommes qui ont été accusés de Magie). – Paris, chez Augustin Besongne, 1669, small in-12 (estimated edition).

NYDAULD (J. de). – *On Lycanthropy, Transformation and Ecstasy of Sorcerers, with the refutation of Bodin's arguments* (De la Lycanthropie, transformation et extase des Sorciers, avec la réfutation des arguments de Bodin). – Paris, 1615, in-8 (very rare).

O

OLAI MAGNI. – *Historia de gentibus septentrionalibus*. – Rome, 1555, in-folio.

ORIGENI. – *Philosophumena* (treatise on heresies in ten books, also attributed to St. Ippolitus. The best edition is the one published by M. Miller, Oxford, 1851, in-8).

P

PAPUS (Gérard Encausse). – Absolute key to the occult sciences. The Tarot of the Gypsies, the oldest book in the world (Clef absolue des sciences occultes. Le Tarot des Bohémiens, le plus ancien livre du monde). For the exclusive use of initiates. – Paris, Carré, 1889, large in-8, fig.

PARACELSI (Aureoli Philippi Theoph. ab Hohenheim). – *Opera Omnia medico-chemico-chirurgica*, tribus voluminibus comprehensa. – Genevæ, sumptibus J. Antonii et Samuelis de Tournes, 1658, 3 vol. in-folio (very rare). – *Pro gnosticatio eximii doctoris Theophrasti Paracelsi*, ad illustissimum ac potentissimum principem Ferdinandum Romanorum Regem semper Augustum, atque archiducum Austriæ conscripta. – Anno 1536 (s. I.), 1 vol. in-4, with 32 figures in intaglio (untraceable and priceless).

PAUSANIAS. – *Historical journey to Greece* (Voyage historique en Grèce) (translation Clavier). – Paris, 1814-1821, 6 vol. in-8.

PÉLADAN (Josephine). – *Istar*, with a frontispiece by F. Rops. – Paris, Edinger, 1888, 2 vol. in-8.

PEUCER (Gaspar, very doctoral philosopher, mathematician and doctor of our time). – *Soothsayers or commentary on the main types of divinations* (Les devins ou commentaire des principales sortes de divinations). Distinguished in 15 books, in which Satan's tricks and impostures are discovered, solidly refuted, and separated from the Holy Prophecies and from natural predictions... Newly translated in French by S. G. S. (Simon Goulard, Senlisien) with the necessary tables and clues for the relief of the readers. – In Antwerp, by Heudrik Connix, 1584, in-4 (or large in-8).

PICO DELLA MIRANDOLA. – *Conclusiones philosophicæ, cabalisticæ and theologicæ*. – Rome, 1486, in-folio (rare).

PISTORII (Ioannis, Nidani, etc.). – *Artis cabalisticæ, hoc est reconditæ theologiæ et philosophiæ Scriptorum toinus I* (the only one published), in quo, præter Pauli Ricii theologicos et philosophicos libros, sunt latini pene omnes et hebræi nonnulli præstantissimi scriptores, qui artem commentarus suis illustarunt. – Basileæ, per Sebastianum Henricpetri, 1587, in-folio (very rare and highly esteemed).

PLATO. – *Complete works* (Œuvres complètes) (translation Victor Cousin). – Paris, 1822-1840, 13 vol. in-8.

PORPHYRE. – *A treatise on the abstinence from animal flesh, with the Life of Plotinus* (Traité touchant l'abstinence de la chair des animaux, avec la Vie de Plotin) by this philosopher and a dissertation on genius by M. Burigny. – Paris, De Bure, 1747, iii-12.

PRIERIAS (Sylvester). – *De Strigio magorum dæmonumque randis, libri III.* – Rome, 1521, in-4.

R

REGNARD (Dr Paul). – *Sorcery, magnetism, morphinism, delirium of grandeur* (Sorcellerie, Magnétisme, morphinisme, délire des grandeurs), illustrated work with 120 engravings. – Paris, Plon et Nourrit, 1887, gr. in-8.

REMIGII (Nicolaï). – *Demonolatriæ libri III.* – Lugduni 1595, in-4 (rare).

REUVENS. – *Letters to Mr. Letronne* (Lettres to M. Letronne). – In-4° with an atlas in-fol. of 6 plates. Leiden, 1830.

ROGER (Abraham, who made his residence for several years on the coast (of Choroniendel) and searched exactly for all that was most strange). – *The open door to the knowledge of the hidden paganism* (La porte ouverte pour parvenir à la connaissance du paganisme caché), or the true representation of the life, morals, religion and divine service of the Bramines, who lived on the Choromandel and the neighbouring countries. With remarks of the names and most important things. Enriched with several intaglio figures. Translated into French by Mr. Thomas la Grüe, master of arts and doctor of medicine. – In Amsterdam, by Jean Schipper, 1670, 1 vol. in-4 (strange and rare).

ROSENROTH (Knorr ab). – *Kabbala Denudata, seu Doctrina Hebræeorum transcendentalis et metaphysica atque theologica.* Sulzbaci, 1677. – Francofurti, 1684, 2 vol. in three massive volumes in-4 (extremely rare and much sought-after).

ROSSET (François de). – *The tragic stories of our time* (Les histoires tragiques de notre temps), in which are contained the fatal and lamentable deaths of several people, arrived by their ambitions, deranged loves, spells, robberies, rapes and by other various and memorable accidents. In Paris, printed by François Huby, 1614, small in-8 (very rare).

S

SAINT-AUBIN. – *History of the Devils of Londun* (Histoire des Diables de Londun), or of the possession of the Ursuline Sisters and the condemnation and torture of Urbain Grandier, parish priest of the same town. Cruel effects of the revenge of Cardinal de Richelieu. – In Amsterdam, Wolfgang, 1693, small in-12.

SAINT JEAN. – *Apocalypse.* It will be good to refer to the work of Adolphe Bertet (disciple of Eliphas Lévi), Doctor of Civil Law and Canon Law, lawyer at the Court of Appeal of Chambéry: *Apocalypse of Blessed John, apostle, nicknamed the theologian, unveiled* (Apocalypse du bienheureux Jean, apôtre, surnommé le théologien, dévoilée), containing the agreement of faith and reason, through the explanation of the mysteries of the kingdom of God, made available to everyone. – Paris, Arnauld de Vresse, 1861, 1 vol. in-8 (In addition to a very correct text and a good translation of the Apocalypse, one will find, in this little-known work, excellent esoteric commentaries on the 22 chapters of Saint John).

SAINT-MARTIN (Louis-Claude, Marquis de, the unknown philosopher). – *Unpublished correspondence with Kirschberger, Baron de Liebisdorf* (Correspondance inédite avec Kirschberger, baron de Liebisdorf), member of the sovereign council of the Republic of Bern (1792-1797). Work edited by Messrs Schauër and Chuquet. – Paris, Dentu, 1862, 1 vol. gr. in-8, portrait (out of print and now rare). – *The Crocodile or the War of Good and Evil* (Le Crocodile ou la guerre du bien et du mal), arrived during the reign of Louis XV; epico-magical poem in 102 songs. Posthumous work by a lover of hidden things. – In Paris, from the printing house of the Cercle social, year VII of the French Republic, 1 vol. in-8 (uncommon).

SAINT-YVES D'ALVEYDRE (Alexandre de). – *Mission of the Jews* (Mission des Juifs). – Paris, Calmann-Lévy, 1884, large in-8, portrait. – *Mission of the French* (La France vraie). – Paris, Calmann-Lévy, 1887, 2 vols. in-12.

SOULARY (Josephine). – *Complete works* (Œuvres complètes). – Paris, Lemerre, 3 vol. small in-12.

SPRENGER (Jacques). – *Malleus maleficarum of Lamiis and Strygibus and Sagis, aliisque Magis and Dæmoniacis mulieribus,* eorumque arte, potestate and pœna Tractatus tam veteruni quani recentiorum auctorum. – Francof. 1598, 4 vols. in-4.

SWINDEN (Doctor of Theology and parish priest of Cuxton). – *Research on the nature of the fire of Hell and the place where it is located* (Recherches sur la nature du feu de l'Enfer et du lieu où il est situé). Translated from the English by M. Bion, Minister of the Anglican Church. – In Amsterdam, by the Wetsteims and Smith, 1728, in-8, fig.

T

TAILLEPIED (F. Noël, Reader in theology). – *Psychology or treatise on the appearance of Spirits* (Psychologie ou traité de l'apparition des Esprits), that is to say, separated souls, ghosts, prodigies and marvellous accidents, which sometimes precede the death of great characters, or signify changes in the public thing. – In Paris, by Guillaume Bichon, 1588, small in-12 (very rare work; excellent edition, unknown to Messrs Brunet and Graësse, who gave the Rouen edition, published twelve years later, 1600, for the editions princeps).

TERTULLIANI (T. Septimi Florenti). – *Opera omnia.* – Venetiis, 1746, in-folio.

THIERS (John the Baptist, Dr. in theology, and parish priest of Vibraie). – *Treatise on superstitions regarding the sacraments* (Traité des superstitions qui regardent les sacrements), according to Sacred Scripture, the decrees of the Councils and the sentiments of the Holy Fathers and Theologians, 4th edition. – In Avignon, by Louis Chambeau, 1777, 4 vols. in-12.

TRITHEME (Abbot John). – *Polygraphy and universal cabalistic writing* (Polygraphie et universelle écriture cabalistique), translated by Gabriel de Collanges, native of Tours in Auvergne. – In Paris, by Jacques Keruer, 1655, 1 vol. in-4, fig. (very rare).
– *Steganographia vindicata, reserata et illustrata... ubi clarissime explicantur conjurationes spirituum...*, etc. Autore Wolfgango Ernesto Heidel. – Norimbergæ, apud Job. Fridericuin Rudigerum, 1721, in-4.

V – W

VALLEMONT (the Abbot of). – *Occult physics, or treatise on the divinatory wand* (La physique occulte, ou traité de la baguette divinatoire). – La Hague, at Adrien Moëtjens, 1762, 2 vol. small in-8, frontispiece and figures.

VINTRAS (Pierre-Michel-Eugène). – *The sword on Rome and his accomplices* (Le glaive sur Rome et sur ses complices). Coming and teachings of Elijah on the glorious advent of Jesus Christ. – London, at Dulau's, 1855, in-8.

VILLARS (the Abbot of Montfaucon de). – *The Count of Gabalis or Interviews on the Secret Sciences, new edition, augmented by the assistant geniuses and the irreconcilable gnome* (Le comte de Gabalis ou entretiens sur les sciences secrètes, nouvelle édition, augmentée des génies assistants et du gnome irréconciliable) (these last two works, attributed to the Abbot of Villars, are by Father Androl). – In London, at the Vaillant brothers' home, 1742, 2 vols. in-12.

WIER (Jean, doctor to the Duke of Cleves). – *Stories, arguments and speeches about the illusions and impostures of the devils, the infamous magicians, witches and poisoners; the bewitched and demonic and the healing of them; and of the punishment that magicians, poisoners and witches deserve* (Histoires, disputes et discours des illusions et impostures des diables, des magiciens infâmes, sorcières et empoisonneurs ; des ensorcelés et Démoniaques et de la guérison d'iceux item de lu punition que méritent les magiciens, les empoisonneurs et les sorcières), all of which are included in six books: with two dialogues on the power of witches and the punishment they deserve, by *Thomas Erastus*, professor of medicine in Heidelberg. – Geneva, 1579, in-8 (rare, reprinted in 2 vols. in-8, Delahaye and Lecrosnier, publisher, 1885).

WIRTH (Oswald). *The XXII Keys of the Kabbalistic Tarot, restored in their hieroglyphic purity* (Les XXII clefs du Tarot Kabbalistique, restitués en leur pureté hiéroglyphique). – Paris, 1889, in-18 format, Poirel, editor.

Z

ZIMPEL. – *The Millennium* (Le Millénaire), an extract from two works by Doctor ZIMPEL: the 11th hour of the Antichrist... and the popular explanation of the Apocalypse. 7th edition. – Frankfurt am Main, 1866, in-8 (most strange printed cover).

The Temple of Satan

The Temple of Satan (first book of the Serpent of Genesis) will be dedicated to the description of the special and characteristic works of Satan (vulgar meaning of the Mosaic emblem the Serpent).

There can be no question of explanatory commentaries, let alone esoteric teaching. Black Magic has nothing in common with High Doctrine.

We will limit to exposing and classifying the facts, real or legendary, pell-mell, without concern for providing a scientific explanation. However, when the occasion arises, care will be taken to qualify the exhibition, so as to make the authentic or illusory character of the alleged phenomena.

The exposition of the Doctrine will be given in the second Septenary (*The Key to Black Magic*); and in the third (*The Problem of Evil*) the metaphysical synthesis of the work will take on an appearance of firmness.

Beware, friend reader, of making a superficial or premature judgement, for such a judgement would be foolhardy.

THE GOAT OF THE GOETY
(after Eliphas Lévi)

Chapter I
The Devil
א

The Magician = the Unit = the Principle = the Object... *The Devil*

In the vulgar sense –familiar to all those who are not among the followers of Divine Science– the Serpent of Genesis symbolises the Devil, the Spirit of Evil personified in Satan. – Satan? the Devil? the Evil One?... Come on, you're joking! Who has ever seen this ghost made of smoke? Where does it show itself except in the fog of troubled and unhealthy imaginations, or in the dark kaleidoscope of weak and timid souls?... Has it ever taken a form accessible to our senses, in whose exclusive testimony we profess to believe? – No, it has not. No more than God, his tyrannical antagonist, no more than God, his merciless executioner, does Satan manifest his presence in the Universe... Would you like to teach us where the Devil lives?

To the materialists that speak this way, no one would dare to object with a rather simple reply: *He lives in you.*

Wherever the darkness of negation, which offends man's intelligence, abolishes the spiritual life in him and can obliterate that inner meaning which gives the intuition of the divine and the assent of the eternal, Satan is there in his metaphysical form: *Error.*

Wherever perversity corrodes poor souls to the point of dissolving the intimate bonds of solidarity that bind them together; wherever scepticism depraves consciences to the point of confusing the notions of right and wrong, in truth, Satan is there in his psychic form: *Selfishness.*

Everywhere, finally, where the free will of man, inducing Nature (the mirror of the divine) to the most dreadful lie, the strength to deny the glory of its heavenly type, substituting the arbitrary discordance of individual evil wills for the wise harmony of general laws, in truth, Satan is there in the sensible form: *Ugliness.*

Error, blindness of spirits! Selfishness, bad breath of souls! Ugliness, deformity of bodies... It is always the infamous silhouette of Satan, reflected in the three worlds of thought, feeling and sensory things.

But we shall probe at leisure, in our book III, the nature of this equivocal being; only the demotic meaning of the emblem should concern us here.

Let us admire the prudence of the teachings of the Church, which has always refused to define Satan and his empire, leaving it to its doctors to propose solutions, under the guarantee of their own fallible authority.

Various texts of the Holy Scriptures mention the existence of the Devil; this is a certain fact, but the interpretation of these dubious texts remains free: *In dubiis libertas*.[1] Allow theologians to argue for and against; no decision taken in Rome *ex cathedra* definitively fixes doctrine to the mould of an article of faith.[2]

As for the common feelings about the Devil, here it is: An angel fallen from his first splendour, a creature thrown into the abyss for claiming to be equal to the Creator and to rival his power, Satan occupies, with his legions of accomplices, the cursed abode of outer darkness, where tears and gnashing of teeth are to be found.

There, according to popular legend, the agents of eternal evil are twisted in the convulsions of eternal agony. Mixed up with his rebellious brothers, Satan rages for eternity. The only consolation allowed to his misfortune is in the growing multitude of damned souls, whom, as an insinuating and protean tempter, he endeavours to seduce from day to day in the earthly trial; just as in Eden, once under the figure of the serpent, he knew how to lose Eve, by the magical attraction of the forbidden fruit.

For it has to be said that as pure spirits –or, if one prefers, impure spirits– the Devil and his servants enjoy, in the imagination of the people and even in the belief of the masters of exegesis, the precious gift of *ubiquity*. While they suffer the penalty of their crime in *inferioribus terræ*,[3] they also roam the world of the living; constantly on the look-out for some weary and wavering soul on the road to salvation, they are ready to take advantage of the slightest failure to enlist souls in the army of Evil and to increase the infernal cohorts.

Thus, it is in the sheepfold and under the very leadership of the good shepherd, that the recruitment of the voracious wolf takes place, and the sheep succumb one after the other.

This, however, is the misinterpretation of the beautiful and profound words of Jesus: *Many are called, but few are chosen!*

---

[1] In doubt freedom.
[2] I beg Catholics to note this fact carefully. In vain will they object to the opinion formally expressed by some popes; this opinion has value and authority only in proportion to the science and particular inspiration of the pontiff, speaking in this case as a doctor and not as the infallible head of the Church; see the definition of infallibility: *the pope only is infallible when he ascends to the pulpit of St. Peter to promulgate a dogma* urbi et orbi. He only defines and imposes on the faith of the faithful a belief that was traditional in the Church.
Such is Catholic doctrine on this point, let us not forget that.
[3] Beneath in the earth.

It is astonishing that agnostic theologians, the perpetrators of such gloomy ineptitude, should remain pitifully indignant if some friend of the inflexible logic, pushing them to the wall, should, at close range, throw them into this captivating dilemma: God, you say, is *almighty, omni-prescient*, infinitely *merciful* and *good*. On the other hand, you teach that the great majority of men are going to Hell... You have to be consistent, even in theology. So God wanted Evil and Hell... If God did not foresee it, his omniscience is at fault; if he foresaw it but could not prevent it, I deny his omnipotence; if he foresaw it but could not prevent it, I deny his infinite mercy.

It was not by pushing to their last consequences the pitiful premises of such theologians that a poet and thinker of Soulary's stature was led to proclaim this sublime and diabolical blasphemy:

ET VIDIT QUOD ESSET BONUM...[4]

The man said: I wanted to know everything, I know everything!
In my narrow domain I can no longer stand still;
I have lived all my time, traversed all my space;
I have life in horror and the earth in disgust!
The Earth has said: My breast is exhausted and icy,
And my milk becomes a poison for men;
The leprosy of sin which invades it everywhere...
Stretches to my bones... *I am tired of giving birth!*
Heaven has said: *Lightning rusts with a burning sword...*
And the angel in the holy court is bored – waiting
Let an elected official finally start the number!
Hell has said: *Satan is tired of being squeezed*
The damned who swarm to the mass grave are getting in the way!
THE VERB SAID: NOTHINGNESS! IT HAS TO START AGAIN!

Aren't these fourteen verses really dreadful, especially the last one? Such is –let's face it!– the logical conclusion to the problem posed in such recklessly naive terms by the sacristy philosophers.

And while logicians like Pierre Bayle sneer at the infernal dilemma I have mentioned; while rare poets who are still thinkers dare, like Soulary, prostitute the language of the gods to such magnificent debaucheries of the verb, the theologians flatter themselves that they are solving the formidable problem of Evil, exhausting their dialectic in sterile disputes over *effective* and *sufficient grace*; the English doctor Swinden maintains, in a big book,[5] that the damned writhe in the fiery substance of the sun, which is none other than Hell visible to the naked eye[6] Dom Calmet seri-

---

4 Joséphin Soulary, *Poésies complètes* (Lemerre, in-12, 3 vols.). Ephémères, page 119.
5 *Research on the nature of Hell's fire and its location*. Translated by Bion. Amsterdam, 1728, in-8, fig.
6 Thesis taken up by M. Péladan in Istar and defended in a lyrical piece of the greatest allure: the Legend of Incest. – I must point out that the unanimous traditions of Theosophy agree to teach, on the contrary, that the sun is, for our whirlwind, the heavenly star par excellence: the blessed dwelling place of glorified souls.

ously discusses the virginity of St. Joseph, and the most authoritative doctors decide that the Devil himself presides over the dance of hats and pedestals!

But never mind. – The legend of the angelic fall is too universally known, and I would say popular, for it to seem useful to retrace the scene here.

Suffice it to observe that Moses makes no mention of the angelic revolt. He does speak of a certain Nahash? נח (already known to our readers), which the vulgar versions render by snake or serpent; he also mentions the fruitful union of the Bene-ha-Elohim בני האלהים or Sons of the Gods, with the daughters of men; the mysterious hymen from which the great race of *Gibborim* גברים, or of the Nephilim נפלים, from which giants were made; but it does not seem that the theocrat of Israel adopted it, nothing even proves that he knew the dogma of the angelic fall.

Leviticus names well the spirits Aôbôth אובות, who inspired the sibyls, but without specifying anything more.

The first among the authors of the Old Testament, Job designates under the name of Shatan שטן a spirit of the eighth hierarchy of the Kabbalists (Bene-Elohim), charged by the Lord with a special mission of trial. Further on, an obscure and vague phrase from Isaiah is customarily interpreted as an allusion to the fallen angel. – That's all.[7]

Examination of the *Talmud* suggests that the Hebrew Kabbalists brought this dogma from Babylon, a notorious borrowing from the dualistic theology of Zoroaster.

Everyone can see in what remains of the Avestas (sacred books of the Parses, due to the genius of these sacred texts) the constant antagonism of *Ahura-mazda* or *Ormuzd* (the Living Wisdom), god of Good, – and of *Angra Mainyu* or *Ahriman* (the Evil One), god of Evil.

The latter, a sort of divine Attila, dragging in his wake the horde of his implacable and cursed *Daevas*, relentlessly assaults and harasses the heavenly Benefactor, surrounded and defended by the holy legion of his *Amahraspands*. This is how Ahriman[8] justifies a name that inspection of the roots makes it possible to translate into English: *the malicious one*.

Let us hasten to say that the true initiates of esoteric Mazdeism saw in Ormuzd and Ahriman only princely principles, stemming from an ineffable cause

---

[7] One does find the word Shatan in *Numbers* (בפד בו ספר), twice, but it is a noun taken adverbially, in the sense of against (*adversus* of the Latins).
–Example: ויתצב סלאד יהוה בדרך לשטן לו (Numbers, XXII, 22). It can be translated as: *"And the messenger of Iod-heveh stood in the way, to be an obstacle (in Shatan) to him."*
Given this meaning of the Hebrew word שטן, it is curious to see how closely the word devil tightens its intimate meaning. Devil (in Greek διαβολος) comes from δια βάλλω, *throw across*; can the idea of obstacle be better translated?

[8] This is a strange thing and one that helps to explain how the rabbis, after Israel's captivity in Babylon, were so eager to see in the impersonal *Nahash* (the Tempter of Genesis) a distinct and personal being, a kind of god of Evil.
By a strange coincidence, the qualifier that Moses adds to the noun *Nahash* is precisely the word צדום, *Haroum* or *Harym*, whose *Ahriman* or *Harym-an*, the Mazdean name of the Adversary (ערומון, in Hebrew characters) differs only by the addition of the augmentative disinence ן, so there is not only resemblance, but identity.

–*Time without Limits*– which itself seems to be seen as the manifestation of a more unfathomably occult Unity (see *Vendidad Sadé*, 36th hâ). Moreover, as we pointed out in *The Threshold of Mystery*,[9] the androgynous couple *Mithras-Mithra* constituted, in the eyes of the followers, a principle of balance between Ormuzd and Ahriman. But the vulgar man did not understand it that way and the false intelligence of such a system generated incalculable evils.

Manes, later grafting the Mazdean dogma of the two principles onto Christianity as a young man, poisoned, so to speak, the sources of mystical life; his abominable heresy, though repeatedly struck with just anathemas, multiplied over time in changing forms like the dream of a crime; the doctrine of the best doctors was infested with it. It is clear that I am speaking of those who fought most fiercely against the progress of Manichaeism.

A real plague of the plague of human thought, this heresy! The contagion has spread everywhere. Without Manes and his all too often unconscious followers, *Nahash harym* would be healthily considered by all as an impersonal force of nature as a cosmic agent, in a word, not as the bogeyman of theology; and the odious spectre and jester of the Devil would not dishonour Christian Dogmatics at this hour, if one had known how to purge it of the last Manichean vestige.

A few verses from the *Apocalypse* (the misunderstood book of all those who do not possess the great keys of the Kabbalah) will find their place here. For if it is customary to attribute an agnostic and literal meaning to the fable of the angelic fall, it is not wrong to note that the vicious interpretation of these verses has had a lot to do with it.

"…And behold, a great red dragon, having seven heads and ten horns, and on his heads were seven diadems.

And his tail drew down a third part of the stars of heaven…

And there was a great battle in heaven. Michael and his Angels were battling with the dragon, and the dragon was fighting, and so were his angels.

But they did not prevail, and a place for them was no longer found in heaven. And he was thrown out, that great dragon, that ancient serpent, who is called the devil and Satan…" (*Apocalipsis*, ch. XII, v. 3 to 9, *passim*)

On the other hand, in the revelations of St. Hildegard, written supposedly under the dictation of the Word,[10] we read these words concerning Lucifer: "Then all the stars of his army, bathed until then in the streams of his light, completely extinguished today, seem like black coals burnt by fire. An irresistible wind is rushing them northward, away from the throne, and into such abysses that it will never again be given to anyone to see any of them".[11]

---

9   *Le Seuil du Mystère* (The Threshold of Mystery), 2nd edition.
10 The Son of God; God as manifested to man: same as Logos.
11 *Scivias*: an illustrated work by Hildegard von Bingen, completed in 1151 or 1152, describing 26 religious visions she experienced.

These lines of the saint are obviously a commentary on the verses transcribed earlier.

The Marquis Eudes de Mirville, the author of this wonderful comparison, invokes this fact, which struck him: that modern astronomy estimates that about a *third* of the intersidereal gap in the portion of the sky is accessible to its instruments. The result of these various comparisons was a stroke of genius for the Marquis, which left him somewhat stunned. How, in fact, in these lost stars, can one not see a *third* of the Tsebaoth that the red dragon swept off its tail during its fall into the abyss?[12] To deny the evidence, one must be in bad faith...

In any case, we shall leave M. de Mirville there, dizzy from such a sudden and luminous flash of light. – It would be better to resume our investigations into the essence of dyarchic doctrine.

The antagonism of the two principles constitutes a dogma that predates Zoroaster himself and dates back to the first cosmogonic cycles of India. "What gave birth to this dogma –says Fabre d'Olivet, in his admirable commentary on *Cain*– was an ancient tradition of the Hindus, in which it was learned that, from the very beginning of the world, the geniuses of the north and south of the earth had been divided over the drink of immortality, of which they also claimed exclusive possession. This division led to long and disastrous battles, the result of which was the complete rout of the geniuses of the south, called Assour, and their enslavement by those of the north called Devas. This tradition, which can be found in the Scandinavian Edda, almost in the same terms, was known to the Egyptians, Greeks and Romans as the War of the Gods against the Giants" (*Cain*, page 169).

It's quite prickly, as we can see the victors made themselves gods and inflicted the diabolical uniform on the poor defeated. I think I hear this from sceptics who are even more naive than irreverent... Perhaps, modelling things a little too much from above on those below,[13] do they imagine in very good faith that if the riot in heaven had succeeded, instead of failing, Jehovah, at this hour, slandered with horns and claws, would have been reduced to the unfortunate and subordinate role of a whisperer of bad advice! – Evil then would be *the Good*; cowardice would be called forgetting insults; baseness, modesty; charity would be considered a shameful weakness; chastity would be called infamy... As for vices, the reverse is true: pride would become greatness of soul; avarice would become wisdom; arrogance and anger would be the mark of a generous soul; intemperance and lust would be a guarantee of good physical and moral health; cunning and lies, and finally, proof of skill, finesse and spirit.

Is it possible that thinking beings could misuse such sophisms? It is to be pitied those who, trusting in the paradoxical deductions of a misunderstood or degen-

---

12 The hidden meaning of the angelic fall is really linked to the existence of the immense army of stars, but in a completely different relationship, which we will indicate in Book III: *The Problem of Evil*.

13 Too much, you say? And the axiom of Hermes: *quæ superius sicut et quæ inferius?*... And the analogical method, the foundation and criterion of Occultism? What do you do with it? – I leave it to Louis Lucas to answer, according to this method, by a comparison: man is the image of God, and yet God is not a vertebrate animal.

erate Mazdeism, persist in not wanting to realise that in the struggle mysteriously represented under this profound symbol, the Good has triumphed because it is order, norm, harmony, in a word because it is *the Good*; and that the necessary cause, infallibly assessed in advance, which, making Evil accidental and transitory, devotes it to future annihilation, is that it is disorder, arbitrariness, anarchy, and that it is called *Evil*.

We may find it strange that this insistence on cursing the doctrine of the two principles is the unequivocal source, in our opinion, of all degrading follies, the starting point of all the bloody excesses to which the Middle Ages wallowed (to confine ourselves to a single, albeit pitiful example); for, finally, all nations had their expressive myth of the evil spirit. Whether it is called Typhon, as in Egypt, or even Tchutgour, as among the Moguls, isn't the Devil always the Devil?

This is the way many honest people think, at least, which I regret to contradict. It is a principle that we are dealing with now, and we must be careful about it. And, although imperceptible nuances of form alone distinguish on the surface these different specimens of evil deities, I say that Ahriman (considered –wrongly, moreover– as the absolute principle of Evil, co-eternal with Ormuzd, the absolute Principle of Good), I say that Ahriman differs as profoundly from Typhon (or any other emblem of fortuitous and relative evil), as Error differs from Truth and Darkness from Light.

One cannot deny the *existence* of Evil (for its *essence*, it is something else.) Its manifestation in the Universe is certainly unmistakable, as are those of cold in winter and darkness at night. – But the light comes, and the shadow will vanish; the heat comes, and the cold will pass away, because shadow and cold are only endowed with a private existence; they lack their own essence, being negations. This is what happens to Evil, which is transitory, accidental, contingent.

To give an essence to Evil is to deny the essence to Good; to support the principle of Evil is to contest the principle of Good; to affirm the existence of the Devil as the absolute of Evil is to deny God. Finally, to support the coexistence of two contradictory absolutes is to utter blasphemy in religion and simple absurdity in philosophy.

What revolts the conscience, what outrages reason, is not so much the symbolic personification of harmful influences, in idols that are often odious and grotesque; it is the deification of Evil, disguised as an absolute principle under a mythological figure, and as such opposed to the principle of Good, similarly divinised.

But the Evil One is not only there where man has claimed to have drawn up his representative image, thus offering it in a notorious way to the common worship. No doubt, curious to unravel the figure of the Devil in all its pagan forms, we should take a quick look at these idols, more or less naive figurations of the forces reputed to be evil; on all sides, they can be seen fading away in the mist, these ghosts of sinister omen, if, descending in spirit the river of times gone by, we allow ourselves to drift among the confused vestiges of ancient civilisations and barbarities. – Let us take a careful look at both banks; apart from those deities that the nations proclaimed evil and thought they were honouring with a religious terror, others will appear to us as diabolical, others that these peoples had not yet marked with any stigma of disapproval. But the worship that was rendered to them soiled them with indelible abomination...

Has the esoteric depth of the famous text of the *Psalms* been fully understood: "Omnes dii gentium dæmonia"[14] (Psalms xcv, 5). It is up to human free will to deprave the most august concepts, and, by an obvious mystical law, every religious symbol, honoured with infamous rites, has by the same token been transformed into an idol in which Satan is incarnated.

Avatars of Satan, those vampires of the ancient Celtic, Thor and Teutad (or Teutatès), whose thirst, through the mouths of their thousand druidesses, howls, insatiable, from the depths of the night without dawn, to hasten the harvest of human blood.

Avatars of Satan, this bronze *Moloch* with a calf's head, the idol of the Ammonites, with arms wide open to embrace the victims, whose reddened metal entrails are about to devour the flesh! – And this *Belphegor* of Palestine, the bearded idol whose gaping mouth erected a colossal phallus in the shape of a tongue: less bloodthirsty divinity, but even more abominable, exclusively greedy, Philo tells us, of faecal and polluted offerings.

Avatars of Satan, this *Adramelech* of Sepharvaim (the magnificent king) and this *Melicertes* of Tenedos (the king of the earth); up to their nostrils rose, like cinnamon, the smell of roasted flesh on the burning altar where the young mothers offered their first-born child as a sacrifice.

And the prince of flies, the god *Beelzebub* of Syria, whose statue attracted all the mosquitoes of the country, because they took care to keep it dripping with blood!

And did not the god of *Mendes*, the pantheistic form of the Egyptian synthesis, incarnate Satan, when the fanaticism of the people immolated the modesty of virgins and the flower of young brides to the lasciviousness of the goat fed in the enclosure of his temple?[15]

Let's cross the Mediterranean. – Mention should be made of the very similar homage paid by the most serious matrons to the sacred shamelessness of the Priapus imported from Lampsaque in Italy, idols made of wood, always impassive, under their cinnabar layer, on the threshold of gardens and crossroads? – Is it necessary to recall the infamy of certain Etruscan deities and the impure rites celebrated on the feasts of the *Good Goddess?*... Shall I repeat all those scandals whose frequency decried the degenerate *Mysteries*, and which outdated devotional garments have long been the abomination of sanctuaries?...

Satan-Pantheus, formidable and multiform, specified himself under a thousand faces, to defile all the altars.

Towards the time of the Messiah, the word of the Psalms received its complete fulfilment: as many gods, as many demons: *Omnes Dii gentium dæmonia.*

---

14 For all the gods of the Gentiles are demons.
15 See Jablonski: "...Nempe Thumi in templo Mendetis, mulieres hirco huic se submittebant (*Pant. Egypt.*, book II, ch. VII)".
The analogy is close with the Baphomet of the Templars, also a symbol of the Pantheistic Synthesis, whose cult (if the trial documents are to be believed) was no less abominable than that of the god of Mendes.

THE DEVIL 41

And so all the stars of the mystical firmament became pale in the dawn of the divine sun rising in Bethlehem!

However, all these idols were only mythological representations of the Supreme Powers; ancient symbols of perfect science and poetry, sometimes full of greatness, which are undoubtedly worthy of our veneration... But the foul or bloodthirsty practices of these cults consumed their dishonour. The rite defiled the myth, the tabernacles collapsed in shame, and the invigorating spirit flew away from the rubble of the dead letter.

It would certainly be a tedious task to go further in counting the number of cursed forms in which Satan, the usurper of divine tributes, was complicit.

There is not a country in either world where the divine vices have not, under thousands of names, multiplied their sacrilegious altars. It is not without astonishment that we can see the hyenas and jackals of the Spanish emigration in the XVI century, suffocating in their cradle the young and peaceful civilisations of Mexico and Peru, finding at least this excuse for their cowardly and perfidious ferocity, that Heaven was wrathful at the spectacle of human blood shed on altars of idolatry. – What could be more similar to the dolmen of the druid priests than the pointed stone on which American priests immolated countless victims each year in front of the consecrated statue of the god-snake, *Vitzliputzli*?

Even now, in the middle of the nineteenth century, in the heart of this Hindustan that England so rudely kneaded in the Western mould between its leopard claws, can we not hear the Devil claiming aloud his tribute of carnage in the form of the god *Shiva* and the goddess *Kali*, the king of suicide and the queen of assassination?

Wishing to spare the public the detail of the dreadful tortures in which the devotion of the Solitary and the Fakirs, prompt to all mutilations in the colour of meritorious austerities, is indulged, we shall at least mention the fierce joy of Shiva's fanatics, devoting themselves enthusiastically to achieve the most hideous dead; the sacred chariot of the god, the heavy chariot with the four rolling millstones will lacerate their flesh and crush their bones; they know it, and it is with cries of triumph, with the gleam of a free sacrifice in their eyes that they lie down by, dozens on the path of the crushing idol.

What can we say about this monstrous Kali –the man-eater– for whose worship priests are not enough? An immense secret society envelops the whole of India with its networks; its followers are called the Thugs, intrepid purveyors of the mystic ogress, and their entire existence is devoted to her cult. They go abroad when necessary (they are Hindus!) to strike victims who have been marked in advance and who, having been warned in time to take the liner, thought they were escaping their imminent bad fate.[16] Christian, in his *History of Magic*,[17] reports the last words of a Thug chief, the famous Dourga,[18] which the English police had managed to seize. They are typical and well worth transcribing:

---

16 Since the English have for some time been succeeding in preventing the frequency of such massacres, it would be a mistake to suggest that the black band has been dissolved.
17 *Histoire de la Magie,* Paris, Furne et Cie, s. I, 1 thick vol. in-8, with engravings.
18 Dourga is one of the mystical names of the Goddess, mother of Kali (Bhavani, wife of Shiva).

"Our brothers –the thug told his judges–, had learned that the foreigner of whom you speak had to leave with an escort of fifty men. We simply formed a troop three times that number, to go and wait for him in the jungles, where an image of the goddess Kali stood. As we are forbidden by our priests to engage in combat, because our sacrifices are only pleasing to Kali as long as our victims are surprised by death, we welcomed the travellers, offering them to walk together, in order to protect each other from any danger. They accepted without mistrust; after three days of company, we were friends..., each stranger walked between two Thugs. The night was not quite dark; in the light of the starry twilight I gave the signal to my brothers. At that moment the two Thugs that were guarding each victim acted; one tied a noose around his neck, while the other grabbed him by the legs and knocked him down. This movement was performed in each group with lightning speed. We dragged the corpses into the bed of a nearby river and then scattered."

The Indian was under no illusion about the fate that English justice had in store for him; this can be seen from the few words he uttered, by way of peroration: *"Only one man has escaped us; but the goddess Kali has her eyes open on him; his destiny will be fulfilled sooner or later!* As for me, I was once a pearl at the bottom of the ocean; today I am a captive... The poor pearl is chained: they will drill a hole to hang it from a wire and it will float miserably between heaven and earth. This is how the great Kali wanted it, *to punish me for not having offered her the number of corpses that belonged to her.* Oh black goddess, your promises are never in vain, you whose favourite name is *Kouiz-Kali* (the man-eater), you who drink unceasingly the blood of demons and mortals".[19]

As he predicted himself, the Thug was hanged...

It seems that we can leave it at that; these gloomy examples are sufficient authorization for us to call all these hideous idols unscrupulously Satan's Avatars.

From the sad reality, let's move on to the traditional legends of the old world. No matter how unhappy they may be, we move away for a while from the scenes of actual barbarity where our pen has necessarily lingered.

Here the abundance and diversity of documents forces us to make a choice. The grimoires of the rabbis are of such an excessive richness that deep lessons can be drawn from them, under the bark of these fables, sometimes coarse and always of dubious taste!

One would have much to say about the *Cacopneumatics*[20] of the Talmudists and the followers of the Kabbalah. Those who stick to the letter of their parables attribute to these doctors teachings as absurd as they are picturesque, on the role of the Tempter and the nature of original sin. We reveal elsewhere the esoteric significance of these fables.

It is written in the Zohar Hadasch (Yitro section, page 29) that the Tempter (Sammael סמאל) plotted, together with his wife Lilith לילית, the seduction of the first

---

19 *Histoire de la Magie* (History of Magic).
20 *Neumatic*: In theology, relating to the spirit or pneuma, as distinguished from both soul and body; spiritual.

human couple. The companion of the Evil One had no difficulty in corrupting the virtue of Adam, which she defiled with her kiss; the beautiful archangel Sammael did the same to dishonour Eve, and such was the cause of human death.

The *Talmud* does not express itself in any less formal terms; I quote: "At the time when the Serpent *mingled with Eve*, he threw in her a defilement, the infection of which was transmitted to all her descendants..." (Shabbath, fol. 146, recto). (Shabbath, fol. 146, recto). Often expressions become so crude that one hesitates to translate them.

On other pages, the male demon takes the name of *Leviathan* לויחן and the she-devil takes the name of *Heva* חוא.

This Heva would have played the role of wife to Adam for a long time in Eden, before the Lord had drawn the true Eve from her side (originally *Aisha*, אשה, then *Heva* or *Chavah* חוה). Out of the love of Adam and Heva-serpent, legions of larvae, succubae and semi-conscious (elemental) spirits would have been born.

Moreover, the rabbis turn *Leviathan* into a kind of infernal androgynous, whose male incarnation (Sammael) is for them the *insinuating serpent* and whose female incarnation (Lilith) is the *tortuous snake* (see Sepher *Ammudé-Schib-a*, fol. 51, col. 3 and 4). These two monsters will be annihilated at the end of time, as we can read in the Sepher *Emmeck-Ameleh* – "In times to come, the Most High (blessed be he!) will kill the unholy Sammael, for it is written (Is. XVII, 1): In that time Jehovah will visit with his terrible sword Leviathan, the serpent who is Sammael, and Leviathan, the crooked snake who is Lilith" (fol. 130, col. 1, ch. XI).

Lilith is not, according to the rabbis, the only wife of Sammael; they name three others: *Aggarath* אגרח, *Nahemah* געמה and *Mochlath* רעלס. But of these four devils, Lilith alone will share the terrible punishment of her husband, for having helped him alone to seduce Adam and Eve.

Aggarath and *Mochlath* play only a rather self-effacing role; the same is not true of the other two sisters.

Let us pray to Eliphas Lévi to complete these few details and we will be done with this demonology of the rabbis:

"According to the Kabalists there are two queens of the stryges[21] in Sheol—one is Lilith, the mother of abortions, and the other is Nehamah, fatal and murderous in her beauty. When a man is false to the spouse set apart for him by heaven, when he is abandoned to the disorders of a sterile passion, God withdraws his legitimate bride and delivers him to the embraces of Nehamah, who assumes at need all charms of maidenhood and of love; she turns the hearts of fathers, and at her instigation they abandon all the duties owing to their children; she brings married men to widowhood ; while those who are consecrated to God she coerces into sacrilegious marriage. When she assumes the role of a wife she is, however, unmasked easily, for on her marriage-day she appears in a state of baldness, that hair which is the veil of modesty for womanhood being forbidden her on this occasion. Later on she assumes airs of despair and disgust with existence; she preaches suicide, deserts him who cohabits with her, having first sealed him

---

21 Nocturnal and evil spirit that can be the metamorphosis of a living or dead human being.

between the eyes with an infernal star. The Kabalists say further that Nehamah may become a mother but she never rears her children, as she gives them to her fatal sister to devour."²²

Nothing is more common among all peoples than these legends of love, very often fertile, confusing gods and mortals in a jumble; at all times the Sons of Heaven –whether reproved or not– seemed to be eager to seduce the daughters of the Earth. We need only look to Genesis for examples; who hasn't read in Suetonius this peculiar tradition, brought back from the Θεολογουμενα of Mendesian Asclepius, about the birth of Octavian?

Atys (mother of the future emperor), having gone to a solemn sacrifice in honour of Apollo at night, had her litter put down in the temple where the other matrons were already asleep, then fell asleep herself; suddenly a snake slithered up to her and came out of bed a few moments later. When Atys wakes up, she has to undergo the usual purification, for she has conceived; but the image of a snake has spontaneously imprinted itself on her body, as if it had been painted on it, known as Suetone –*velut depicli draconis*– a stigma which later did not want to disappear, to such an extent that she is forced to renounce the public baths forever… Ten months later Augustus was born, and everyone hastened to proclaim him the son of Apollo.²³

The adventure of Pauline and the Roman knight Mundus will seem no less strange. The historian who vouches for it is not one whose testimony can be decently challenged.²⁴ Moreover, it is no longer a myth or a legend, but a true and most significant history; does it not mark the extent to which the opinion of a possible marriage with the Immortals was widespread in Rome under Tiberius? What is more, one can infer from it the frequency of such adventures, since no one even thought to be surprised that an Invisible wanted to unite in love with Saturnin's wife.

Here are the facts. – Mundus, a young debauchee, fell madly in love with the honest matron; but his assiduity earned him nothing but insults. In desperation and on the advice of Ide, one of his freed women, Mundus corrupts the priests of Anubis, who will soon resort to a sacrilegious fraud, in order to deliver to him the overconfident Pauline. They summon her; they declare that she is loved by a god and that Anubis burns to possess such a beautiful and virtuous young woman, but that his free consent is required. Although very flattered, Pauline is a wife; she hesitates to commit herself without her husband's permission. Her husband, Senator Saturnin, who is himself greatly honoured by Anubis' choice, becomes a pimp out of devotion. Not only did he allow and advise his wife to spend the night in the temple, he also

---

22 Eliphas Lévi, *Histoire de la Magie* (History of Magic).
See also Rosenroth's *Kabbalistic Dictionary* and the treatise *De revolutionibus animarum* (1st and 3rd volumes of the *Kabbala denudata*, 1684, 3 vols. in-4).
23 "In Asclepiadis libris lego, Atyam, quum ad solemne Apollinis sacrum media nocte venisset, posita in templo lectica, dum cæteræ matronæ dormir, obdormisse; draconem repente irrepsisse ad eam, pauloque post egressum illam expergefactam quasi a concubitu mariti purificasse se, et statim in corpore ejus extitisse maculam, velut depicti draconis, nec potuisse unquam eximi; adeo ut mox publicis balneis perpetuo abstinuerit; Augustum natum mense decimo, et ob hæc Apollinis fihium existimatum." (Suet., *Duodecim Cæsares: Octavionus*, XCIV).
24 Flavius-Joseph, *Antiquities of the Jews*, book II, chap. IV.

ordered her to spend the night in the temple. It is there, under the auspices of the God who did not mind disturbing a sacrifice whose glory remains his, that Mundus makes his pleasure of the chaste Pauline and dishonours the proud virtue that has so disdained him… But the success of such a stratagem intoxicates the happy lover to the point of encouraging him to betray the mystery of iniquity himself; he makes a cynical request to his mistress for one night; why should she now be with him from now on, sharing a happiness she has already known? The reckless Mundus has deceived himself, counting on the silence of his victim; the indignation lends this new Lucretia the audacity to proclaim her dishonour. She cries out for vengeance to the Emperor Tiberius, who confines himself to banishing the main culprit, whose senseless love seems to mitigate the attack; but the temple of Isis is demolished by order, and the statues of the goddess and Anubis are thrown into the Tiber. As for the perfidious instigators of this adulterous sacrilege, Ide, the freed slave, and the complicit priests, both die on the cross.

It would be an interminable and unfortunate task in every respect to suppress all the stories, whether historical or legendary, in which –to speak the language of Aristotle– Eudaemon and Cacodemon[25] played their small part. Since we are once again reduced to making a choice, let us skip the first centuries of the Christian era; the twilight of a savage civilisation gives way to the growing darkness of an even more terrible barbarity. A sinister scarecrow and jester stands in our way, it is the ghost of the devil in the Middle Ages… Nevertheless, before confronting the noisy flock of the possessed and the raging pack of demonologists, it is not without interest to show by what artifices, always and everywhere the ape of God, Satan opposes, in the imagination of peoples, the diabolical ascetic to the divine ascetic and the Antichrist to the Redeemer.

Deplorably grafted onto the dogmatic tree of Catholicism, the Manichean doctrine of a Demon rival of God[26] was to have as its first consequence to evoke an evil Word in front of the divine Word; an infernal Messiah in front of the heavenly Messiah.

The *Apocalypse* speaks at length of two monstrous beasts, one generated from the waves of the Ocean, the other from the bowels of the Earth, and then of a false prophet, a sort of fatal and grandiose magician, who is the man of the Beast and to whom tremendous power is given for lies and evil. He deceives men and subjugates the nations… Saint John, in chapter XIX, describes in these terms the final defeat of the messengers of hell:

{19:19} And I saw the beast and the kings of the earth and their armies, having been gathered together to do battle against him who was sitting upon the horse, and against his army.

{19:20} And the beast was apprehended, and with him the false prophetess, who in his presence caused the signs, by which she seduced those who accepted

---

25 A cacodemon (or cacodaemon) is an evil spirit or (in the modern sense of the word) a demon. The opposite of a cacodemon is an agathodaemon or eudaemon, a good spirit or angel.
26 I say rival of God, not equal to God, nor coeternal with him.

the character of the beast and who worshiped his image. These two were cast alive into the pool of fire burning with sulphur.

{19:21} And the others were slain by the sword that proceeds from the mouth of him who was sitting upon the horse. And all the birds were sated with their flesh.[27]

Perhaps one day, interpreting the Johannite tradition, we will be allowed to lift the triple veil that conceals such formidable mysteries from secular eyes. Be that as it may, to carry out such a task would require the latitudes of a special setting. The *Apocalypse*, built on the metric standard of Dorian synthesis, with its twenty-two chapters, combined with infinite art on the occult numerations of the cyclic ternary, septenary and duodenum, is a book of Kabbalah as profound as the *Bereschit* and *Siphra of Zenihouthas*; in this appropriate athanor, the Spirit blows in great currents: so many words, so many mysteries.

Here such comments would be irrelevant; it suffices to point to the Apocalypse as the original cradle of the famous myth of the Antichrist.

A learned pontiff of the first centuries,[28] paraphrasing this beautiful definition of the beloved apostle: *the Antichrist is the one who divides Christ*, St. Gregory the Great, delivers the intimate meaning of the symbol; there are, he says, two loves, two spirits that divide men into two classes, synthesising these classes into two distinct bodies; there are two worlds, two societies, or, to speak with St. Augustine, two cities. One of these cities, one of these worlds, one of these bodies, will be called Christ; the other will be called the Antichrist; but an essential dissimilarity distinguishes them; the *head* of the heavenly *body* has already appeared, it is Jesus Christ; its members, forming and growing little by little, constitute its church. The body of the Antichrist, on the other hand, is a complete fabrication;[29] but the head will not appear until the end of time.

An anonymous mystic of the last century compares the Antichrist *to a dragon which would be born by first showing its tail, later would produce its body and whose head would be born last.*[30]

The comparison is not only a happy one, as we shall see later, it fits perfectly with the esotericism of the myth. But most modern theologians are only satisfied with a literal and entirely anthropomorphic interpretation.

Does this mean, then, that at the end of time, according to the thesis that is so precious to them, a man in flesh and blood, endowed with irresistible power and infernal malice, should appear? Many Fathers believed it; the ambiguity of certain texts even led many to believe that the Antichrist would appear twice; in this version, Elijah and Enoch reincarnated would be opposed to him at his first coming,

---

27 Compare this quotation from *Apocalypse* with the one already made above. In the first text we usually see the fall of the rebellious Angel; in the other, the final defeat of the Antichrist. One of the scenes opens the cycle of time in the depths of the past, the other closes this cycle, at the end of an unfathomable future.
28 End of the 6th and beginning of the 7th (540-604).
29 In this sense, even in the time of the Messiah, St. John announced that the Antichrist was already in the world: *Et nunc jam est in mundo*.
30 *L'Avènement d'Élie* (The Advent of Elijah), s. 1., 1734, tome II, page 135.

but since he had won, these two men of God would die at his hand. – At his second appearance, Christ would come in person to fight him and bring him to naught.

Isn't it really curious how these traditions about the Antichrist are an exact copy, but in reverse, of those about the Redeemer? It is like an image reflected upside down on the surface of a filthy pond. We are told of the two comings of the Messiah of darkness and the two comings of the Messiah of light, with the difference that, according to the law of inversion already mentioned, the *glorious Antichrist* (if we can say without blasphemy) comes first, and the torment of the *painful Antichrist* must mark precisely the definitive triumph of the glorious Christ at the end of time.

I don't know if the author of *The Advent of Elijah* measured with a conscious eye the secret depth of his comparison mentioned above – the insiders know that the occult meaning of the word *head* (in Hebrew *Ræsch* רא) is compared to the *virtual power of unification*, to the superlative *Principle of living unity*. They will have no difficulty in understanding that the mystical body of Christ (or his Church) is alone in possessing a homogeneity of essence and a reality of archetype; therefore his head (his virtual essence or principle) is represented as pre-existing to the development of his body and this head is Jesus Christ. – As for the Antichrist, his mystical body, all of false contribution and aggregation, is painted *without a head*, that is to say, without its own essence and radical principle. This head, in fact, which appears late in the consumption of the ages, being only the resultant and the product of the body, is a contingent and not absolute synthesis, totalised and not radical, consequent and not anterior to the elements grouped in it.

Because –either the Devil or the Devil's Messiah, or Satan or his Antichrist– the eternal symbol of discordance, schism and negation, cannot in any way become a principle of unity. It is only *an abstract type of an accidental and transitory state, or, in another light, a relative synthesis of evil beings, seen as evil, and not as beings.*

The Antichrist, some very enlightened doctors predict, will be conceived from Belzebuth in the bosom of a sacrilegious nun. Always the same parallel of opposition with Jesus Christ, conceived of the Holy Spirit in the womb of an immaculate virgin?

The false Messiah will only have a fluid or spectral body and will speak in all tongues. Boguet adds that he will continually be at war and persecute the righteous, and that he will perform the most amazing wonders and mark his followers with a sign on their foreheads and hands.

Our friend Jhouney, in his beautiful esoteric poem by *Sorath*, thus apostrophe the Antichrist:

Thou shalt raise the cross in thy bold hands,
Thou shalt even work miracles through the cross.[31]

Let us underline in passing these two verses of a truly occult scope. The poet of the *Black Lilies* knew how to strike the rock to bring forth its living spring; but this is not the usual case of the mystics who spoke of the Christ of Darkness –and we cannot compile all their often ridiculous and contradictory prophecies. The curi-

---

31 *Les Lys noir* (The Black Lilies). Carré, 1888, in-8, page 3.

ous will consult with interest the works of *Abdeel, Raban-Maur* and *Malvenda,* the masterpieces of the genre.

Never, of course, has some dangerous heresy or some daring philosophical innovator appeared on the world stage to lead people into error, or into too abrupt a current of truth (considered premature, risky, inopportune), without the anthropomorphists of orthodoxy shouting at the Antichrist.

Simon the Magician, Apollonius of Thyana, Marcion, Manes, Valentine, Anus, Luther, Zwingle and Calvin[32] were among the gratification of this peremptory imputation. – On the basis of the beautiful definition of St. John –*spiritus solvit Christum*– it can be said that all these opinions, no doubt too feverishly intransigent, contain a part of truth, and the reader will see us subscribe to it, to a certain extent, in Chapter II.

But not even Mohammed, the illustrious civiliser of Africa, the Moses of Ishmael –a missionary from on high, almost a son of God– was given this insulting honour.

The same suspicion was also levelled at a number of political figures, such as Julian the Wise (known as the Apostate), Frederick the Great, Robespierre, Napoleon I and even Napoleon III. An incredible number of pamphlets have been published in support of these last two theses.[33]

Men of letters, philosophers and scholars were no better protected from suspicion: Voltaire, Rousseau, Diderot, d'Alembert and d'Holbach were especially denounced in the XVIII century, and I would be very surprised if some brave clergyman had not, in ours, believed to have deciphered on the foreheads of Darwin and the honest Littré this stigma of reprobation.

It has always been the ambitious mania of the most orthodox theosophists to read the fulfilment of ancient predictions in the mirror of contemporary facts…

In short, the Antichrist was sought and found everywhere, even and above all where he was not; but who dared to see him where he obviously was: under the biretta of the inquisitors, the hood of the exorcists and the doctoral cap of the demonographers?…

All three are dreadful in the perpetration of their respective labours: odious, gloomy labours…

---

32 The heresiarchs and their proponents soon retaliated by pointing to the pope as the true Antichrist, and the political Catholicism of Vatican Caesars as the beast of the Apocalypse. Edifying exchange of reciprocal amenities.

33 I have a curious one, entitled *Millénaire* (Millennium) (Frankfurt am Main, 1866, in-8). This pamphlet is the work of a certain Dr. Zimpel, whose mental faculties seem to be in disarray. On the pink cover there is a double engraving, showing the Beast of the Apocalypse with its seven heads, one of which is that of Napoleon I. The engraving is a double engraving of the Beast of the Apocalypse. – The upper print shows the Beast walking slowly from right to left; the heads and tail are low; a young deity (probably the image of Liberty and Civilisation) sits on his back; his right hand, armed with a sceptre, weighs on the seven heads; his left hand holds a cup from which parchment scrolls are released. – The lower print shows a young woman lying on the ground; the Beast has turned around and is now running from left to right. A half-bodied man has suddenly pushed, like a protrusion, over the animal's neck: it is Napoleon III, very similar; he clenches his left fist in anger and, armed with a spear, he strikes the overthrown goddess in the flank with his right.

THE DEVIL

The role of the exorcist is limited to tormenting the poor sick, but it is less with the intention of curing them than with the vague hope of hearing them, during a fit of frenzy, incriminate some poor man for having cast a spell on them.

The task of the inquisitor is more atrocious, it consists in undertaking the body, soul and spirit of the accused, by means of a series of tortures that are artfully graduated and diversified, by the perfidy of honeyed promises and the artifice of insidious interrogations, until the fatal moment when, with his heart failing, a cleverly extorted confession finally springs from his lips.

But the work of the demonographer[34] is the most barbaric and the most execrably efficient! Is it not he, first of all, who, by the contagion of insanity that he spouts out under the guarantee of his doctoral seriousness, creates wizards and witches in abundance? Is it not also he who, by pointing out the victims to the ferocious industriousness of the judge, devotes them to the fatality of a supposedly redeeming death? – For it is his bastard and pedantic jurisprudence (all tangled up in casuistry and stinking of false theology) that taxes the sorcerer as a criminal so damnable, alas! that the mere atonement at the stake is supposed to be sufficient to bend the wrath of Heaven in favour of such a guilty party and thus charitably save him from eternal flames!

Let us look at the legal authorities of the seventeenth century on this point.

First of all Pierre de Lancre, the elegant and worldly *adviser to the king in the Parliament of Bordeaux*; a few lines of his pen will tell us what the crime of the sorcerer is and what punishment he deserves.

– "To dance indecently, to feast naughtily, to mate diabolically, to sodomise horribly, to blaspheme scandalously, to take insidious revenge, to chase after all horrible, dirty and brutally denatured desires, to hold toads, vipers, lizards and all kinds of poison preciously; to love a stinking goat ardently, to caress it lovingly, to hug and mate with it horribly and impudently. Are these not disordered features of a lightness not equal to that of the other, and of a vile inconstancy, *which cannot be atoned for by any other fire than that which divine Justice has housed in hell?*"[35]

Let us consult Boguet, *this great judge of Saint-Claude in the county of Burgundy*, who had a woman burnt because the cross of her rosary had been chipped, he claimed to see there a certain sign of pact with the devil. Let's ask him if it is appropriate to pardon repentant sorcerers.

"As for me, I will always be of the opinion that on the slightest foundation they should be made to die, when there is no other reason than that which I have touched many times, namely that they never change their lives".[36]

---

34 A writer on demons and demonology; a demonologist.
35 *Inconstance des démons* (Inconstancy of the demons), Paris, Buon, 1612. Thus Lancre does not even admit, in his preface, that burning at the stake is sufficient atonement. – So why burn? What right do we have to usurp the role of Providence, to anticipate the hour marked by it?... But elsewhere this magistrate contradicts himself; he agrees with the common opinion concerning the redemptive virtue of the pyre. He too will therefore burn for the tenderness of his soul...
36 *Discours des Sorciers* (Discourse of the Sorcerers). Lyon, 1610, in-8, page 405.

These two examples may suffice to give us the demonologists' note. Let us add that this language is still moderate, close to that of Bodin, Sprenger and Michaëlis; I am not talking about Remigius, a criminal judge in Lorraine, all the more ferocious because he was afraid of those he condemned. He himself boasts of having, in the space of a few months, burned more than eight hundred women, accused of witchcraft; as for the men, he doesn't count them.

The article of possessions is no less sinister and hardly worthy of attention. It seems wise to confine our pen to a sketch of one of those hystero-demonopathic scenes[37] embellished with exorcisms –oil on the fire– To narrate them all, we would need a volume, since they multiplied, always identical, from the Middle Ages onwards and especially around the seventeenth century, when their next consequence was a famous series of bonfires, blazing in different parts of Europe and France.

URBAN GRANDIER

CORNELIUS AGRIPPAS

As these infernal tragicomedy manners are almost always accompanied by capital trials on witchcraft charges, Chapter IV will soon offer the public other stories of the same kind. Then all these scenes, as we have said, seem slavishly modelled on each other...

To what extent could the free will of the actors or even the calculations of the interested organizers (of profit or fame) have been consciously exercised on an already known theatrical canvas? – This is what I want to leave to others to clarify.

---

37 To speak the language of Dr. Calmeil.

If I choose, among so many cases, the perhaps too banal one of the Ursulines de Loudun,[38] The fact that no one appears so complete in this genre is that possession is complicated by a formal accusation of witchcraft, by a trial and a torment; we shall see in it the contribution of the reigning superstition, of reason of State and of particular grudges, conspiring to lose a man who remains himself an enigma, a man from whom, on more than one side, powerful interests were certainly to be disposed of.

The parish priest of Saint-Pierre de Loudun and one of the brilliant socialites, an eloquent and outspoken theologian, who had become even more popular through the fame of his good fortune than through the resonance of his words; it seems beyond dispute that Urbain Grandier was passionate, if not precisely for magic, at least for singular research on various points of theology and science, to the study of which the Church has always shown a certain repugnance to see the faithful devote themselves.

It is worth recalling that among the papers of all kinds seized at Grandier's –and without taking into account the alleged pact,[39] obviously apocryphal, the work of his enemies and perhaps of his judges– a manuscript *against the celibacy of priests* was burnt, a daring work if ever there was one (M. Luzarche had previously published an edition (1866), based on a copy from the Jamet collection, the authenticity of which, unfortunately, seems highly dubious); finally, two pieces of at least equivocal verse were found, the obscurities of which were considered *dirty and shameless*.

On the other hand, various libels,[40] more than insulting to the character of Cardinal de Richelieu, had appeared a few years earlier. It is known that the almighty minister, with his acrimonious and resentful nature, resented the fact that a superior man manifested brilliantly, apart from the beam of light he had grouped around his own. Little inclined by temperament or by politics to forget the insults and to disdain the quibbles which certain parties did not spare him, he had put his police on tenterhooks to discover the author of these virulent pamphlets; but as all his enquiries had been in vain, his resentment had to be satisfied with the decision of Parliament, which had not been ashamed to condemn the printer to the gallows, in the absence of the pamphleteer.

---

38 I classify this complex case in the article *Possessions*, and consequently in Chapter I, entitled *The Devil* (this same chapter). – On the other hand, I refer the equally complex and similar cases of Gauffridy, Picard and Girard to Chapter IV: *Human justice*. Where does this apparent anomaly come from? It is quite simple; for me, these last three are low-level sorcerers, and I believe in the innocence of Urbain Grandier.

39 What seems monstrous is not so much the fact of a pact signed by Grandier; we shall see that sorcerers were in the habit of writing them; it is the presentation to the judges and the display at the trial, as evidence, of the double so-called written and signed copy of the Princes of Darkness. It is written in incredible terms, with the words in one corner: "The original is in hell (*Extractom ex inferis*)". – A letter from the devil Asmodeus to the exorcists is also kept in the National Library! The death sentence was pronounced on the examination of these mirific pieces.

40 The one that made a racket is entitled: *La cordonnière de Loudun* (The shoemaker of Loudun).

Poor revenge! It is true that in Loudun the public voice, or rather the rumour of a whole clan in the town, denounced Urbain Grandier; faced with these clues Richelieu was only waiting for a pretext to doom the presumed libellist...

The opportunity was not long in coming. It offered itself, superbly, in 1633.

The devil had just settled at the Ursulines of Loudun. This convent, which had long been rather unfamiliar, offered a spectacle as scandalous as it was extraordinary: most of the nuns, including Jeanne de Belciel, the superior, were convulsing, possessed by the evil spirit. The surprising wonders that characterise the state of fanaticism, burst forth in all its occult strangeness.

It is known that the Rituals distinguish four decisive signs by which one can recognise that a possession is real and not feigned: 1° hearing and speaking unknown languages; – 2° revealing future or distant things; – 3° manifesting forces above human nature; – 4° rising into the air and remaining suspended in it without any support. All these phenomena were manifested, mixed with trickery, in certain number of nuns; not a single sign was missing from the check list. In the very terms of the definition given by the theology and under the guarantee of the criteria proposed by the Rituals, possession was no longer questionable. Screams, contortions, obscene poses and remarks, erotic fury unleashed without any constraint, no debauchery that was foreign to the oddball. It was a pandemonium in which all cynicisms were at play, since they were blamed on the Evil One... Exorcisms were attempted on a daily basis, but to no avail.

The prodigies were, moreover, accentuated in intervals, so positive and of such striking authenticity, that their sight determined the sudden conversion of a famous non-believer, adviser to the Parliament of Brittany, who ran from the depths of his province to make fun of exorcisms; the nuns, calling by name Sir Kériolet, overwhelmed him from the outset by such revelations, that he stopped, petrified on the threshold. Then, penetrating his innermost thoughts, they threw in his face some of his past actions, the last vestiges of which he believed to be buried in the depths of his heart. The old atheist came in the hope of laughing a lot and felt moved to tears. Loudun was his road to Damascus, he confessed and promised to make amends. In short, the devil converted him to God, and so well, that after a hard penance, this gentleman, who professed to believe in nothing, spent the rest of his days in the practices of the most exalted asceticism.

Incidit in Scyllam, cupiens vitare Charybdim.

However, the possessed, so clear-sighted with Sieur de Kériolet, persisted in denouncing, in the person of the priest of Saint-Pierre, the magician guilty of having cast a spell on them...

In the meantime, Laubardemont, the Cardinal's handyman, was staying in Loudun, to supervise the demolition of the castle, too suitable to serve as a refuge for Protestants in times of trouble... He took care to inform Richelieu of all these abnormal events, and even ran away to Paris to decide his master to punish severely; then he soon left, armed with discretionary powers and an imperative warrant for the arrest and trial of Urbain Grandier. The trial proceeded slowly; Laubardemont had requested the assistance of a few judges from neighbouring bailiwicks, carefully

THE DEVIL

selected to help him in his task; the sentence he would pronounce was decreed in advance, sovereign and without appeal.

The unfortunate parish priest of Saint-Pierre was lost in advance. – First of all, he had declared himself very foolishly, with his usual frankness, to be on the side of those who opposed the dismantling of the castle with all their might. He had long been suspected of having an intelligent relationship with the political leaders of the Huguenot party, and in the course of very serious disputes with his bishop, he had also invoked directly the king's justice, as if the cardinal-minister had not been all in the state. The latter had felt all the more offended that the king, who –perhaps flattered that he had been approached– had thought he should grant the request.

Almost at the same time, the Cardinal de Sourdis, Archbishop of Bordeaux, acquitting Urbain, issued a decree of definitive rehabilitation in his favour. The parish priest of Saint-Pierre, somewhat vain and boastful by nature, had not been able to keep secret his intention to humiliate his enemies. Simultaneously victorious before the civil and religious authorities, he had allowed himself an insolent return to Loudun, in an attitude of ancient triumph, with a laurel branch in his hand.

But that is not all yet, for it seems that poor Grandier really enjoyed piling up one reckless act upon another. A much admired preacher, a much sought-after confessor of the ladies,[41] he had alienated himself from the Ursulines, refusing to accept the direction of the convent which had been offered to him with a haughty air. As I have already said, it was a peculiar convent; its morals and way of life were not very edifying. The Ursulines, by dint of their hostility against the disdainful priest, ended up evoking him in the astral and seeing him. He was, according to the sisters, a formidable magician; he appeared at night, although the doors and windows were closed, and already most of them shamelessly accused themselves of having nothing more to refuse him. Thus the hallucination, combined with resentment, induced them to charge the poor Urbain with an accusation of witchcraft, so dreadful in the seventeenth century.

Inextricable situation! Only Laubardemont could have saved the parish priest of Saint-Pierre; but this chief, in a feline mood and at first wily, was not a man to let his prey escape.

In vain Grandier, considering the procedure to be arbitrary, appealed to the Parliament; a judgement of the Council of State declared his appeal null and void. In vain did honest and courageous citizens address petitions and protests to Louis XIII, initialled with the most honourable and respected names of the town. In vain they denounced the sickly fanaticism of the Ursulines, the scandal of the exorcisms and the partiality of the magistrates in charge of the investigation: Laubardemont

---

41 Urbain Grandier had a mistress who loved him tenderly. It was for this young girl, named Magdeleine de Brou, that he had written his treatise against the celibacy of priests. – Magdeleine was circumvented; no promises or threats were spared to obtain some revelations from her. But this courageous girl drew from her love the necessary constancy to emerge victorious from all these traps. She would have let herself be torn apart rather than say a word that could have compromised the priest of Saint-Pierre. They had to give up trying to get anything out of her.

silenced Grandier's party and terrorised the whole town by issuing a series of ordinances, the like of which had never been seen before.

The accused, in his cell, saw himself facing the last vexations: he had no bed. We read in a letter to his mother that he asks for one, for *if the body does not rest* (he said), *the spirit succumbs*; he prays that a Bible and a Saint-Thomas may be sent to him *for his consolation*.

It was not until April 14, 1634 that Grandier was confronted for the first time with the nuns who had been mercilessly accusing him for so many months, while by means of incessant exorcisms, sometimes public, sometimes behind closed doors, sometimes together and sometimes individually, care was taken to exasperate and stiffen their evil and fierce obstinacy, by repeating the same exercises of fantastic slander and devout imprecations every day.

The exorcists Barré and Mignon had long been the main regulators of these little daily scandals, then it was the turn of the Capuchins Lactance and Tranquille.

Various pacts and charms, composed of curdled blood, nail clippings, ashes and other unknown materials, were placed before the eyes of the parish priest of Saint Pierre. Finally, to make matters worse, he was forced to take the stole and the bottle brush to exorcise the possessed nuns himself. Jeanne de Belciel and her companions took advantage of this to splash him with the most coarse insults, and as he was about to question them in Greek, in order to catch the Devil at fault, the Evil One replied through the mouth of the Superior: *Ah! How fine you are! You know very well that it is one of the conditions of the pact made between you and us not to answer in Greek.* All these so-called revelations from beyond the world were reputed to be gospel words, despite the strangest intermittencies in the lucid state of the subjects, for it was accepted that *the Devil cannot resist the authority of the Church*.

An amusing detail, a vaudeville trait in this gloomy drama: Laubardemont made a profession of admitting, with his eyes closed, on the faith of the exorcists, the infallible truthfulness of the devils who were compelled according to the rites. However, it happened that one of them declared clearly, by the mouth of a duly exorcised nun, that the lord of Laubardemont was a *cuckold*. – The latter, without mistrust, and who was not in the habit of rereading the minutes, signed gravely at the bottom of the page, adding with his hand: *What I attest to be true*. This burlesque, but perfectly authentic piece, in which the magistrate vouches for the husband's disgrace, appeared in the case file (see ms., n° 7618 of the *Fonds Français*).

Let us cut short all these details. Suffice it to say that the exorcists were so successful in their laughter that Laubardemont had to rant and rave about an order more incredible than the previous ones, threatening serious prosecution[42] to anyone who would interfere in blaming or ridiculing the nuns and good fathers… Thus every precaution was taken, so that both could be odious or ridiculous in peace.

But then an incident occurred, which no one had foreseen: a wind of repentance suddenly blew over the oddball; the Superior of the Ursulines and two other nuns were seen to throw themselves, in a lucid moment, at the knees of the accused,

---

42 Ten thousand pounds of fine and other larger sums and corporal punishment, if the case goes ahead… (The very text of the Ordinance).

then at the feet of the commissioners, confessing that they had damned themselves to lying and proclaiming Grandier's innocence out loud! – They were silenced; the remorse which had dictated their approach was made to pass by a new trick of the impure Spirit, anxious to snatch a magician from the pyre which was already demanding him.

The poor priest was condemned to death; he was burned alive on the day of the ruling (August 18, 1634).

He had not been spared the humiliations, outrages and successive refinements of ordinary and extraordinary torture, in order to extract a confession from him… It was all in vain: he died, sublime in gentleness and resignation, but unshakeable.

At the stake itself, it is said that Lactance held him up to kiss a metal crucifix reddened by the fire. The unforeseen pain of the burning would, it was thought, make him throw his head back; so the people, too eager to believe him innocent, could no longer doubt that he died in impenitence, with his lips drawn back sharply, simulating a refusal.

At the end of this infamous trap, Grandier was the victim of an even more infamous perfidy. He had been promised to be strangled as soon as the wood caught fire, but the exorcists had tied knots in the rope, and despite the executioner's best efforts,[43] Grandier fell alive into the heart of the blaze. He could still be heard crying out in the flames: "My God! My God! Forgive my enemies!"

At that very moment, a flight of pigeons swirled over the martyr's head. The halberdiers exhausted themselves in vain reels to make them flee. After Grandier was dead, the flock of birds, flying fast, got lost in the clouds. It is easy to see how the poor man's slanderers were able to take advantage of this unexpected incident; they shouted that a band of demons was rushing to receive the magician's soul. Others, on the other hand, were convinced that these doves had come to bear witness to the perfect innocence of such a victim!

What appeared –as brochures and memoirs for and against Grandier were published– is hardly believable; these battles of opinion have long fascinated people's minds. I give here a few stanzas which form the Epilogue of an excellent book published in Holland by Mr. Aubin (Saint-Aubin, following others), and which enjoyed a surprising popularity in France at the time: *l'Histoire des Diables de Loudun* (The History of the Devils of Loudun) (Amsterdam, 1693, small, in-12).[44] These verses, of an unusual hardness and sharpness, seem to have been written yesterday:

> Hell has revealed that through horrible plots
> I made a pact with Hell to corrupt women.
> No one complains about this last offence.
> And the unjust Judgment that puts me to the torment,

---

[43] The executioner was forced to step back, just as he was making his efforts; for, without waiting for the signal, Father Lactance had set the fire with his own hands, and the flame was rising.

[44] The success of this work, due, as we know, to a Protestant pen, enraged the partisans of possession and exorcisms. One of them offered a wonderfully inept refutation under the title: *Examen critique des Diables de Loudun* (Critical examination of the Devils of Loudun), by the Abbé de la Meynardaie. Liège, 1749, in-12.

The Demon who accuses me is author and accomplice,
And received as a witness to the crime he faked.

The Englishman, to get his revenge, burnt the Maid.
Such fury made me burn like her.
The same crime was falsely imputed to us.
Paris canonizes her, and London hates her.
In Loudun some believe me to be a manifest enchanter,
Others absolve me, and a third party suspends his judgement.

I was, like Hercules, foolish for women.
I died like him consumed in the flames.
But his death made him a god.
From mine, injustices have been veiled so well,
That we do not know whether the fires are bad or good,
Blackened me for Hell, or purged me for Heaven.

In vain, the torments has shined my constancy,
It's a magical effect. I die without repentance.
My speeches are not in the style of the Sermons.
Kissing the Crucifix, I spit on his cheek.
Looking up to Heaven, I pout at the Saints.
When I call upon my God, I call upon the Demons.

Others, less warned, say, in spite of envy,
That one can praise my death without approving my life;
That being good and resigned is a sign of hope and faith;
That to forgive, to suffer, without complaint, without murmuring,
It is perfect charity, and may the soul be purified,
No matter how badly we lived, dying like me.

Heaven seemed to avenge the memory of the poor priest, beating all his executioners. Laubardemont was the first one, struck down by family affections, fall into disgrace with the Cardinal; the Fathers Lactance and Tranquille died almost immediately in a frenzy that was blamed on the Devil. Father Surin, another exorcist, went mad. As for the surgeon Mannoury, who was so cruel to the poor accused, the spectre of his victim never left him, harassing him relentlessly to the grave.

Urbain Grandier had predecessors; he was not the last to be put to death on the denunciation of oddballs, all claiming to be more or less dishonoured by a man who in his life had never had the opportunity to see or speak to them. This is how tradition intended it: the possessed always prided themselves on being fawning sycophants.

Possession (or, as Dr. Calmeil calls it, Hystero-demonopathy) is undoubtedly one of the most mysterious diseases, which is proliferating in astonishing manifestations, and which the Faculty of Medicine would be somewhat embarrassed to report, according to the currently accepted laws of its doctrinal professors; but what

THE DEVIL

can be inferred from this? – That certain mysteries remain impenetrable, even when official science intervenes to clarify them.

Exorcists do not hear with their ears, and this is the style in which they are accustomed to vaticinate:

> *The Devil is the author of all phenomena that cannot be explained by the known laws of Nature. – Duly exorcised, the Devil is compelled to tell the truth; his testimony must be believed in the face of justice.*

These two formulas, artfully combined, have resulted in the final condemnation of many innocent people. Fortunately, if the Devil still wants to testify in court, justice no longer cares about the Devil's testimony. Nobody complains today about this small change…

I am mistaken, my friend and reader; you must admit it.

A whole contemporary school, of which I want to say a word, seems to regret the era of daily exorcisms and witchcraft trials. – But before you get to know the Marquis Eudes de Mirville and his friend, the Chevalier Gougenot des Mousseaux, be patient and let me introduce to you a modern hierophant, who was, around 1820, even more curious to see the pyres rekindle.[45] He is the author of fourteen hundred pages in-8 on the Goblins,[46] a work decorated with figures and a portrait at the bottom of which the author gives, with the best grace, his names, titles and qualities: "Alexis-Vincent-Charles Berbiguier de Terre-Neuve-du-Thym, native of Carpentras, living in Avignon, temporarily domiciled in Paris…." Here we are informed.

He is a truly possessed, who sees everywhere only demons (whom he calls *Goblins*) and sorcerers (whom he calls *physicists*). He complains bitterly about an *infernal-diabolic* society (*sic*), whose main accomplices –doctors, students, lawyers, pharmacists…– he unmasks in the face of heaven. The incessant persecutions that these wretched people inflict on him poison his existence; he thinks he is taking revenge by denouncing their names.

A simple madman, one might say. Why prolong this chapter (already too massive), mentioning such a being? – The famous Abbot of Villars could answer: "God has given me the grace to recognise that madmen are in the world only to give lessons in wisdom".[47]

---

45 Indeed, his sweetest hope was to bring, through his revelations, the sovereigns to revive the old decrees against the followers of magic. He constantly intersperses with such threats the invectives he ranted against his persecutors: "What fruit will you reap from your infamous methods? The certainty that one day they will be locked up in the dungeons of the Holy Inquisition, so wisely instituted to punish spirits, sorcerers, magicians and even all those who would doubt for a moment the power of the supreme God".
"*I hope one day to read the names of all those who seek to persecute me, on the bloody lists of this dreadful Tribunal!*" (Volume I, page 143).
He goes so far as to make this charitable vow: "Great God… let there grow on the earth enough wood to be able to build pyres big enough and spacious enough to contain and pulverise the whole race of leprechauns everywhere" (vol. III, p. 197).
46 *Les Farfadets* (The Goblins), or all demons are not from the other world…. Paris, published by the author, 1821, 3 vols. in-8.
47 *Le comte de Gabalis ou entretiens sur les sciences secrètes* (The Count of Gabalis or interviews on the secret sciences). London, 1742, 2 vols. in-12 (Volume I, New Interviews, page 2).

And Berbiguier is not a madman like the others; his madness is peculiar in that it is based on the perception –absolutely indirect and distorted, I agree– of a very real world which sensible people do not suspect, and which my book will only make known to them, moreover, if they resign themselves to becoming madmen themselves; I mean beings susceptible to notions and perceptions to which most of their fellow men remain closed.

Berbiguier is certainly the victim of a swarm of *larvae*; but he attributes these vexations to sorcerers transformed into monsters of all kinds and sizes. From this point of view the examination of his engravings is most peculiar; those whose eyes are not made for the astral can at least study in this mirror the protective nature of the larvae, capable of assuming, with inconceivable flexibility, the most paradoxical and varied forms; it is enough for the poor *possessed*, whether their horrible presence, to have the apprehension or obsession of some hideous figure, and the larvae *mould* themselves in that fashion immediately. It is a hallucination that takes shape; it is a thought that becomes objective and is informed by the ambient plastic substance, as I explain in detail in *The Key to Black Magic*.

"When you hear –says our man–, the sound of big birds flapping their wings, they are only goblins; it is the same when you hear monsters of a prodigious size or of a dreadful shape walking, but which you do not see either; when, in the most enclosed flats, you hear a dreadful wind, which frightens people who think they are safe... Then you must arm yourself with great courage, arm yourself with a weapon of some kind, sharp or pointed, if you can, move constantly from right to left, as if you were spying, and you may hear the blood of the person or persons whom you have had the good fortune to wound" (Berbiguier, volume III, pages 83-84).

The variety of forms in which the larvae multiply is perfectly described in these lines; but what is most astonishing is that this unlettered maniac.[48] They had the precise intuition of the real weapons capable of dissolving these fake and fleeting beings; steel points, sharp blades – and also (*Les Farfadets* (The Goblins), volume II, page 27-63) special fumigations!... Moreover, let us not insist: further on we will find Berbiguier and his entire arsenal of offensive and defensive weapons (ch. V).

I quote him here only as a modern demonologist, and as such I wish to provide a further sample of his style.

All those who believe in the Devil and Hell are characteristic in this respect. The quirkiness of language does not give way to the quirkiness of ideas; the form is worthy of the content.

Listen to this diatribe against cats: "May this chapter ... disgust the ladies of Paris with the love they bear for these leprechauns; I never feel greater pain than when I see a pretty mouth on the muzzle of a beast of the tiger breed. My pain is no

---

48 All the erudition (what erudition!) is indeed compiled; as for the style, Mr. Pascal Brunet, lawyer, and Mr. François-Vincent Raspail had to, while carefully respecting its precious flavour, make the spelling and grammatical errors that enamelled it disappear from the manuscript.

less great when I hear a pretty woman calling her husband my cat; it seems to me that by telling him my cat, she is inviting him to be received as a leprechaun!"

"*I will never be the cat of the virtuous woman I have to marry.* One of the clauses of my marriage contract will forbid the woman who will associate her destiny with mine to give me other titles than those which flatter honest people. I would much rather be told my friend than be called by names that love and nature reject!" (Volume II, pages 307-308).

The scourge of the goblins (as he calls himself) thinks he brings to the world the revelation of a new science, and at the same time the means of reducing Hell to impotence: "I do not always agree with the scientists; often *when I compare them to myself, they are nothing but fools in my eyes*" (Volume I, p. 324). With such an opinion of himself, Berbiguier does not despair of taking his place among the Fathers of the Church: "I am at the height of joy when my thoughts are shared by an apostle of the Christian faith; that is why I make it my duty not to miss a sermon... My book will be full of material that the preachers will be able to consult when, in the silence of the cabinet, they compose their speeches. They have provided me with material for my essays; *I flatter myself to return it to them with improvements...* What a new enjoyment for me when I go to the sermon and hear myself quoted by the preacher, as St. John, St. Mark, St. Matthew or St. Paul is quoted...." (Volume III, pages 63-64, passim).

Joseph Prudhomme visionary: here is Berbiguier. The guests of Hell appear to him in an obviously traditional, classical and commonplace form.

But seventy years have passed since the publication of *The Goblins*. Let us be modern; after *Satan rococo*, we are going to see *Satan fin-de-siècle*.

At a time when this prince of darkness is being denied his empire by the most determined spiritualists –for the very people for whom ghost appearances are a simple and familiar thing, laughing at the mere mention of the Evil One!– Conrart's prudence seems to have won over even the most devilish paragons of diabolism. Prompted to relegate the litigious facts of witchcraft to the history of bygone ages, these doctors willingly admit that times have changed, and that the Devil shows some reluctance to perform *in person*, in front of an irreverent public, quite capable of laughing in his face, if he showed it.

This invincible repugnance should not be believed. Eliphas Lévi tells us[49] of the adventure of a Paris worker whom the demon Astaroth visited, in the figure of a gigantic ox-headed swine. It was around the beginning of the Second Empire.

But, respectful of correct dress and the customs that are de rigueur today, Satan sometimes shows himself to be less indecently archaic; he even sacrifices to decorum, to the point of curbing his well-known taste for legendary travesties.

We could not close this chapter more agreeably than by reporting the true adventure that was certified to the Chevalier Gougenot des Mousseaux, by a bishop of his friends. It is with the express permission of the penitent and to the shame of

---

49 *La Clef des grands Mystères* (The Key to the Great Mysteries). Paris, Baillière, 1861, in-8 (pages 167-176).

the apostles of scepticism, that the prelate invites M. des Mousseaux to publish the confession of a poor girl, seduced and outrageously disappointed by a devil in black habit.

The story we are going to transcribe (with a slight abbreviation) takes up pages 376-384 of the book entitled: *Les Hauts phénomènes de la Magie* (The High Phenomena of Magic) (Paris, large in-8, 1864). The name of the Chevalier des Mousseaux, author of this and several other similar works,[50] made some noise thirty years ago and the religious authority gave the most solemn sanction to the theories ardently defended by him and his master the Marquis de Mirville.[51]

There was quite a outcry, in the ultra-Montane camp, in favour of doctrines that were at least outdated, whose pyres had been burnt at the stake from the XII to the XVII century above all, the very logical conclusion and the legal translation.

I would be mercilessly accused of exaggeration in such a serious matter if I did not put before the eyes of the reader some of the laudatory appreciations of all those entitled: Mgr. Donnet, Cardinal Archbishop of Bordeaux; Mgr. Césaire, Cardinal Archbishop of Besançon; the T.R.P. Ventura de Raulica, General of the Theatins, Consultor of the Congregation of Rites, Examiner of Bishops, etc.; the R.P. Voisin, etc... – These approvals, all formal, some of them enthusiastic, can be read at the beginning of the book from which I extract the following story. As they are very extensive, I will only quote a few of them:

FROM CARDINAL DONNET: "Already, Sir, in your book of *Magic in the XIX century*, you examined modern magic in its principle; you showed its demoniacal characteristics... Today, in your work of the *Mediators*, you go further; you go to the heart of your subject, and in the triple light of history, religion and philosophy, you delve into the depths of the foundations of Magic."

"Continue, Sir, to fight against error and *to put your zeal and knowledge at the service of Catholic truth... Continue to defend the truth, to disillusion the peoples*, and the beautiful words of Scripture will be applied to you: *Qui erudiunt multos, quasi stellæ in perpetuas æternitates* (of July 26, 1863.)".

FROM THE ARCHBISHOP OF BESANÇON: " ...I can assure you that *your works are not only very orthodox*, but also very endearing and very complete..." (October 9, 1863).

FROM THE GENERAL OF THÉATINS: "...*You have treated your subject with mastery*; your vast knowledge, your immense erudition, brings out the *indisputable reality of the facts*. Your ruthless logic demonstrates *the supernatural character and the demonic nature*."

"*Perfectly orthodox*, you have managed to avoid the mistakes of Gœrres..."

---

50 Other works by M. des Mousseaux, published by Plon (large in-8): *Mœurs et Pratiques des Démons* (Habits and Practices of the Demons) (2nd edition), 1865; – *Médiateurs et moyens de la Magie* (Mediators and means of Magic), 1863; – *Magie au XIXe siècle* (Magic in the XIXth century), 1864.

51 *Les Esprits et leurs manifestations diverses* (Spirits and their various manifestations), by the Marquis de Mirville (Paris, 1854-1863, 6 vol. gr. in-8).

"An old proverb of your nation says: *noblesse oblige*, and no one better than you, Sir, puts this axiom into practice. With your latest work, *you have just won letters of nobility in the Church*, which impose new obligations on you."

"*Don't stop on such a beautiful path. God will bless your efforts, and the veneration and gratitude of truly Catholic souls will one day honour your memory and your tomb*" (1863).

FROM R.P. VOISIN: "*...Everywhere you are at the height of your subject... Everywhere you present yourself as a sagacious philosopher of perfect orthodoxy... I congratulate you on your beautiful and good book, a useful work not only for seculars, but also for many clergymen, and not only for simple people, but also for scholars. Continue your role as a Christian champion and Orthodox apologist*" (November 3, 1864).

After these quotations, which were useful, as we will agree later, I come to the confession of the penitent. As above, I transcribe with a faithful pencil, but by pruning out what is neither essential nor typical:

"On a summer's evening –it was July 17, 1844– our young daughter and sixteen other girlfriends were all together in the same house, only two men were in the midst of that commotion. We promised each other a happy and noisy life: *If you want –said one of the gentlemen–, I will send for ONE who knows about pleasures (sic)*. – Yes, yes, we should do that! What will he do? We look at each other. The doors are closed, well closed, the windows closed; the speaker opens a book which he calls the *Great Albert* and mutters a few words... We wait, we are about to laugh. But all of a sudden, oh surprise! Then, as a ghost would appear, *a very handsome gentleman appears (sic)*... – *Yes, yes, I promise to amuse you carefully*, says the newcomer to this merry brood of fools, the one who has just become visible from the invisible: We have to agree, however; I'm going to put an easy condition on it, aren't I?

Opening a book and presenting each of them with a sheet of white paper, the stranger dictates these words to which he asks them to subscribe: *I renounce my name* (five of them were called Marie), *I renounce faith, heaven and hell; I give myself to you for ever*. And all of them are successively asked to sign this form with their blood...

A series of strange, risqué, voluptuous, dishevelled, vile dances that end in scenes of debauchery, opens this period of promised happiness. The night passes, and we see, at a given moment, the *impudent and handsome gentleman vanish, like a shadow would vanish*. A week and months go by.

But who was this cynical and prodigious character, entering and leaving through closed doors, appearing like a ray of sunshine, disappearing as a ghost would disappear? *Who was this dreadful bon vivant, suddenly out of nothing, whom everyone had seen so closely and felt so strongly?*... He was what was needed for the mad women he was trying to capture. He had that day the figure of a young man, a face of some thirty years old, an elegantly cut outfit and no more and no less claws than a coquettish woman. We can say this with full knowledge of the facts, for he quickly became at ease, *and soon nothing remained hidden from him, neither his feet nor his hands; let us repeat that each of our young and unwise licentious women owed it to the plenary grace of contact to know what he was...* The testimony of their meaning was, alas, only too complete.

But let us limit ourselves to the features that refer to one girl; she was alone and occupied in her room on July 17, 1845, that is to say, on the anniversary of this apparition.... Suddenly the same being, *suddenly appeared before her eyes*, appeared to her and made her shudder with surprise. *Do you remember the 17th of July?* he said to her as he approached her... *Would you hesitate? Sign quickly, or I'll kill you!* – And every year, from now on, thus surprised, I had to renew the lease of my person... Once this was done, we became good friends again; everything had to happen again in marriage, and it was like that every time he appeared. I saw him, I touched him, I spoke to him, and the time of his visits was, at least, a good three hours. *Eleven years in a row he came...* His visits usually began with a conversation of almost a quarter of an hour, and then he would take hold of me...

How do you do it –I asked him–, *appearing and disappearing with closed doors and windows? – I have permissions. – But for a body it is inconceivable; if you are a devil and therefore a spirit, how can you be like a man for us? – I take a dead body and with it I do what I want (sic)!*

– You will never die –he said– as long as you are faithful to me; you will be eternal; I mean that at death I will have the power to bring you back to life.

What did he mean by these words?

What is certain is that, *by a marvel of God's grace*, life came into my soul as a result of remorse... Today the pact is broken, thank God! It was not without difficulty. I belong to God; *it was about time*. Remorse no longer tears my soul apart, but my repentance is deep...

– Are you sure that all your answers to these questions are real and not illusions? – Yes, perfectly certain; as certain as I can be of anything in the world... *The certainty of my former friends* –she added– *is unshakeable and the same as mine.*

Having completed this writing M. des Mousseaux warns us, *on the basis of the notes and on the answers which, for the past three years, have been successively transmitted to me by Mgr. X... and following the conversations I had with him on this point, I submit it to him; he finds it exact and good for publication as I am publishing it here*".[52]

The Chevalier Gougenot des Mousseaux is too pungent a historian of satanic morals for us not to give in to the temptation to let him speak for a few moments longer.

New avatar of the Evil One. – The author describes to us what fantasies of dubious taste the Devil indulges in, when curiosity gathers, around a fashionable medium, elegant and (this time at least) more prudish daughters of Eve:

---

52 *Hauts phénomènes de la Magie* (The High Phenomena of Magic), pages 376-384, *passim*.

"From time to time, a mysterious and indiscreet breath would engage under the women's skirts, inflate them and balloon them. Several ladies, belonging to the most distinguished society and perfectly foreign in their relations with one another, assured me that they had experienced this unpleasant effect in the most sensitive manner, which, more than once, made them retreat precipitously. Until then, nothing but innocent enough; but one day, between two ladies of my most intimate acquaintance, the younger of whom, Madame the Countess of ***, at a respectable age of maturity, a third was sitting, a friend of both. Suddenly, isolated as she was from the medium and his companions, she uttered a cry of distress, stepped back and raised her hand to the lower part of her bust. She is beside herself...

Another day, a lady of fairly ample stoutness was sitting a few steps away from the medium, and a rib from her petticoat, on which the full weight of her bust was borne, was as violently extracted from her backdrop as a tooth would be from its socket. At the same moment, a scream escaped from the mouths of the other women, who *all at the same time* felt the same part of their bodies being touched. Half respect for the truth, half respect for themselves, this part was called the *knees* by these ladies. I do not speak at random, but I would be lapidated if I said any more"[53]

Decidedly, Lucifer is a bad taste joker, or rather a fellow in very bad company. But, believe me, the fault lies with certain mediums who tolerate such deplorable company in a familiar way. If brothers and husbands believed me, being unable to reach the mischievous inconveniences of the Invisible, they would –by proxy– pull the ears of mediums guilty of enlisting in their troupe such unfortunate actors and producing in their places scenes of such indecency.

Not all of them have such compromising guests; this is fortunate enough for the profession, for since such supernatural caresses are not usually to the taste of these ladies, and even less to the taste of their husbands and wives, mediums would risk taking the Devil's blame, and Spiritism would risk taking the blame for the mediums' wrongs; in short, however recreational they may be, the deserted sessions would be a warning to them, a little late in life, to raise better their otherworldly brats!...

The knight's style is no less endearing than the anecdotes he vouches for; so we shall end by throwing down on paper the few flowers of rhetoric with which he has sprinkled the Epilogue of his account:

"The same and identical *version, coming from the mouth of the second witness, reached my ear with the help of a slight ricochet from a friend*, which I had simply set in motion, *so that I could raise my documents above the regions of doubt*" (page 350).

It's delicious, isn't it? Here's something better; a vehement wrath hugs the knight by the throat; he thinks of Christians bad enough as Catholics to doubt the wonders he reports and the universal consensus of demonographers:

---

[53] *Hauts phénomènes de la Magie* (The High Phenomena of Magic), pages 349-350.

THE SORCERER IN THE GRIP OF THE FOUR ELEMENTAL FORCES
(original drawing by Mr. Wirth)

"*Shame, however* –he exclaims– *in the vineyard of the father of the family, to those Protestants of the second vintage,* who dare to prefer their weak and vacillating lights to the *unfailing* lights of the Church, *their poor and wiped out reason only surrendering to the religious authority* when the latter, *pressing the point of condemnation on their throats,* shouts at them: Believe or go to hell! Surrender or die!

Textual. – Ah, I'm not making this up. It's in full text, page 133.

It was part of my plan to bring out the language of the doctors of demonology.

After the Vincent Berbiguier style, I gave my audience a taste of the Gougenot des Mousseaux style...

THE DEVIL

What a sad face you make, everywhere and always, old Satan! When you are not obnoxious, you are grotesque.

The mire of foolishness in which you wallow splashes your opponents, and the intense ridicule you give off reflects on all those who believe in you, either to curse you or to adore you!

Your science is a mockery: *Sorcery* (that magic in reverse, which ignorant and envious people have all too often confused involuntarily or on purpose with the *Holy Kabbalah*), sorcery mixes at any moment, in its impure goblet, turpitude with fanaticism, crime with folly!

Darkness is no more; only light exists... You have only one excuse, Oh Prince of Darkness, and that is that you do not exist!... At least you are not one conscious being, an abstract negation of the Absolute Being, you have no psychic and voluntary reality other than that which each of the perverts in whom you incarnate lend you. – And in these very incarnations, you can be recognised everywhere by your essential characters which are Non-Being, Misery, Impotence, Stupidity and Envy... In your domains, Oh Satan, we enter with our heads held high.

To manifest the inanity of the infernal darkness is to enhance the radiance of divine splendour; to unmask the foul and sacrilegious practices of the necromancer is to glorify the august works of the Magi.

Here we are again, reader, on the *threshold of mystery*, but of the mystery of opprobrium and error, of night and iniquity.

Let us not stand in front of the portico, unworthy of our attention; but, in order to penetrate into the heart of this temple, which is only a hovel and a den, let us arm ourselves, as if with a talisman, with the naive and contemptuous motto with which Henry Khunrath sealed his *Amphitheatre of Eternal Wisdom:*

PHY DIABOLO, TERQVE QVATERQVE ISTI PHY:
ATQVE ITERVM PUY IN ÆTERNVM!

CHAPTER II

The Sorcerer
ב

The Papess = the Binary Faculties = the Subject... *The Sorcerer*

Throughout history, superstitious and wicked men are sought magical science, inquisitive about mysteries in order to profane them, jealous of Science in order to abuse it, ambitious of power in order to reign in disorder and through crime.

Magic appeared to these perverts as a triple instrument of tyranny, pleasure and intimidation; and this unholy dream of a despotism without restraint or control, based on the monopoly of knowledge forbidden to the vulgar, seduced, deceived and lost them. For this science is of divine right; he who covets his treasures in the hope of unpunished prevarication, wanders into the underground that leads to the secret vault; he sinks into the depths if he thinks he is going up, and the distant light he takes for the lamp of the threshold is only the anticipated reflection of the pyre of atonement.

However, Nature, respectful of free will, has endowed man with means of action, in iniquity as in virtue; the occult agent obeys every will, holy or perverse, and if the egoist is unfit to conquer the True, at least he can do Evil.

In what circumstances is the qualification of sorcerer applicable to him? The question seems a delicate one. Indeed, superior beings who make science serve dark works are not strictly speaking sorcerers, although they perform cursed rites.

Neither tumblers are necessarily sorcerers, although many tumblers are sorcerers, or if one prefers, many sorcerers are tumblers.

Let us explain. – There is a fairly common agreement that sorcerers are daring charlatans. I am careful not to say that they are always wrong. History is there to attest to their moral degradation; it shows them to be steeped in the dregs of crime, and such men can only be hypocrites. In this case, by dint of mystifying others, have they not ended up mystifying themselves? I would like to think so.

But we want to generalise this hypothesis. If there are sorcerers who are more or less charlatans, it is certain that none of them is an absolute sceptic. Their intellectual and moral decay –inciting them to believe what is absurd to the exclusion of the things that reason admits– provides us with the key to this anomaly.

Are we talking about the classic sorcerer? About the dark follower of black magic? This one believes in his own power. He is not wrong, for it is real; but he does not suspect the mediating cause any more than he discerns the mediating agent.

Are we talking about *mediums* and other contemporary sorcerers? – They are subject to intermittencies; the Force which they claim to direct and which leads them, unleashes them at will and chains them to the fatality of its own movement; so that they find themselves reduced to the role of jugglers, as soon as it is lacking.

This is how we have been able to catch a *medium* of unquestionable power in the act of committing the grossest deceptions, a medium who the day before had succeeded –under conditions of scientific control and even overwhelming evidence– in achieving manifestations that were a hundred times more surprising. But yesterday the *mediator* was assisting the medium; today it is missing, and since pride or greed dominates the poor experimenter, he prefers to cheat (should he be caught in the act!) rather than confess to being in fact a humble slave of the occult powers of which he boasted of being the high and powerful lord.

Let this example, taken from the sorcerers of the day –absurd gallants of Occultism and tenors of the Mystery,[1] tightrope walkers with an invisible rope, puppets in black robes whose strings are hidden–, let this example not distract us from the legendary, foul and dreaded pariah sorcerer of the Middle Ages and the Renaissance; fanatical and narrow-minded, fearful like all suspects, daring like all hunted cowards.

Between the modern magicians, those who are forced to hold public meetings, and the spell-breakers of yesteryear, there are connections and differences. Both are puppets, equally unaware of an Agent whom they claim to enslave, both have unshakeable faith in spiritual essences; but if the medium, convinced of the existence of the *disembodied*, persists in denying Satan, the sorcerer, on the other hand, believes with all the strength of his being in the power of the Prince of Darkness and in the terrible reality of his favours.

What am I saying? Viewed in its normal setting (the ambient life of the XV and XVII centuries), we see it as a *pact* in all its forms.

This pact with the Spirit is by no means an object of mystification or intimidation for onlookers; it is a contract drawn up by the sorcerer with meticulous care and unequalled conviction, at the risk of his own life; the discovery of this single piece is enough to cause his death at the stake, following the most dreadful torments.

We will have to return to the pacts concerning the witchcraft trials; let us not anticipate. Reserving for Book II –as far as it is possible for us– everything that resembles a scientific explanation, we shall take another brief look at the character

---

1   I am referring here only to certain dubious and charlatan mediums; but it must be admitted that conscientious mediums are the exception. Among the latter, we must also take into account the unconscious fraud frequently observed among them, as M. Donald Mac-Nab shows us in his remarkable work on the phenomena of spiritism.

of the vulgar sorcerer, that wandering Jew of occult crime,[2] often pursued from den to den and fugitive from exile to exile; slipping like a shadow in solitary places, mumbling incomprehensible words, their eyes always moving, misled, staring everywhere with stupid looks of resentment or charged with dread...

But they are not always threatened. Sometimes they are protected by the great, tradition also shows them with their heads held high, strutting around in the odious and grotesque apparatus of his pretentious nullity; it is even in these latter characters that it will be easier for us to recognise and denounce them in all their disguises. For they are protean, changing according to the times and environments; but the *satanic claw* remains indelibly on their forehead.

Being Satan –as we have already said– the prototype of nothingness and hateful vanity, it follows that the seal of his domination, the imprint of his presence; his *moral signature*, in a word; necessarily offer all the distinctive marks of non-being, misery and envy.

This triple criterion is infallible. The reader himself will be able to convince himself of this in chapter VI, devoted entirely to the description of the sorcerer in his modern avatar (so different in form from its past form), this chapter will not surprise anyone; and placed face to face with the familiar people of Beelzebub, in black smocks or black habit, no one, thanks to the above description, will doubt not hesitate to recognise them.

It is a fact that in all climates as in all ages, evil manifests itself in a variety of ways: aberration of the spirit, perversion of the soul, defilement of the body, these are the same follies, the same passions, the same vices and, as Eliphas Lévi says somewhere, "the Spirit of darkness is hardly inventive".

Black magicians can be found throughout the history of peoples and it would be impossible to say which period or country was spared this kind of plague.

Ask the annals of antiquity; there is not a writer who does not bear witness to their existence and the terror that gripped people as they approached. The Fathers of the Church proclaim that the first centuries of the Christian era were plagued by them.

According to the chronicles of the Middle Ages, they swarmed across the face of Europe, with the appalling fertility of the accursed races.

They are the larvae of this long twilight... Like the dragonflies in our ponds, born from the vapour of water under the influence of a ray of sunshine; they seem to be born from the thickening of darkness on the vapour of spilt blood.

But they are not mere ghosts, alas! For the great dawn of the Renaissance does not dispel them. They are only too formidable a reality. Far from diminishing, their number is increasing day by day; the ferocious zeal of the magistrate is matched

---

2 It would be a badge of naivety to believe that Perversity, Guile and Power are incompatible with Ignorance and Stupidity.
Ignorant and foolish shepherds are often fearsome persons who bring bad luck, in whom instinct is supplanted by abortive intelligence. They have at their disposal coarse fluids, accumulated at high tension, and the gullible terror of the masses submits to the ascendancy of beings infinitely superior to themselves, but subjugated by fear and superstition.

only by the perverse cunning of the criminal, and witchcraft trials, which are always capital, leave no judge, prosecutor or executioner unemployed.

This leads us to the middle of the XVIII century!...

At this very hour, when torture is abolished and when necromancers are hardly in danger of coming into conflict with the law, except for some harmless prosecution for swindling or vagrancy, it would be a serious mistake to support the disappearance of their fatal posterity.

Being hybrid, almost uniformly malicious and foolish, the sorcerer only by exception shows a intelligence already half-darkened in fanaticism. Ingenious by instinct at the most incredible travesties, he has changed his appearance, morals and language. Under the peasant's coat, under the doctor's frock coat, elsewhere again we find it, almost as widespread and I would add perhaps more dangerous in its new modalities... alas! Also under the priest's robe. It is a matter of statistics; in all times, moreover, it has always been so. Just as doctors provide the opium and its equivalents with the most serious contingent, so too, and for similar reasons, Satan's army has always been recruited preferably from the priesthood. This connection is not only piquant, but easy to check on both sides.

I repeat: never have sorcerers been bolder and more evil than in those days, when they are denied.

There is perhaps some courage to break the visor of the prejudices most *honourably received*; but I will support with examples what I'm exposing, I will demonstrate with facts; finally, I will explain by bringing to light a singular and little-known doctrine, the mediator of free reason and popular institutions, the conciliator of the most distrustful science and the most august traditions.

The sorcerer –I said–, can be found in all times, in all latitudes.

To go back to the most remote civilization –so vaguely blurred in the mists of the past, that all the documents gathered on it by researchers would fit on half a page– we know however that the Atlanteans, whose cataclysm without example in history engulfed the continent more than nine thousand years before our era,[3] had their soothsayers and their sorcerers.

India has always known sorcerers; but originally they concealed their malice and disguised their nameless practices, which were not tolerated by the wise successors of the great theocrat Rama. They only began to appear on the peninsula at a time when the social state, deafly worked by the fermentation of the impending schism, was tending imperceptibly to decline.

For the modern Hindus have descended to the last rungs of superstitious beliefs; the enchanter is at the same time, in them, oracle, magnetizer, exorcist, acrobat and beggar. They are above all the Fakirs and even some low-level priests (*Pourohitas*), then the ascetics and the monks who are seekers: all of them compete with mummies and manifestate surprising phenomena, with the help of *mentrams*,[4] and invocations to the *Pitris*.[5] One can read in Louis Jacolliot's interesting works

---

3 See Plato (Dialogue of *Timaeus*).
4 Conjurations.
5 Disembodied spirits, souls of the ancestors.

–*Le Spiritisme dans l'Inde* (Spiritism in India), specially in the *Fils de Dieu* (Sons of God)– details as complete as they are unexpected about these kinds of people. They are universally admired and venerated in the countryside. The Brahmin *pandits*[6] and the initiates of the High Doctrine: *Dwidjas*[7] and true *Yogis*,[8] *Chelas* and *Shabérons*;[9] they are almost alone on the peninsula, quite free from this moral leprosy; if we leave the priestly caste, hardly a few *Rajahs* and the elite of the *Kshatriya*[10] are exceptions.[11]

Among the ancient Hebrews, Black Magic was limited to the evocation of the spectres of negative light, Aohoth, אובות, so severely proscribed by Moses. The refinements of witchcraft were not introduced into Israel until relatively late.

But the Finns and the Accadians are less novices in criminal operations, and François Lenormant points out a thousand characteristic details about the necromancy of Accad. One can see, in the many monuments he comments on, the theurgist clearly distinguished from the sorcerer, who is withered with the name of the *wicked man*. Evil spells are called the *work*; incantations, the *word*; philtres, the *mortal thing*.[12]

We will only mention for the record the existence of the magicians of Evil in other parts of the East. It is not that they are rare or that their influence is nil; but apart from Ceylon, where Shivaism degenerated into witchcraft (which is the case of all dead cults) is waging a hard war against Buddhism as a religion, oriental sorcerers lack characteristics; they all seem to be fashioned on the same pattern.

There is, moreover, a misunderstanding that cannot be cleared up with too precise a pen, a confusion customary to all historians of oriental mores and which travel narrators –missionaries or official explorers– seem to be taking on the task of perpetuating. On this delicate point, they heap up compelling darkness at will. Whether it is a matter of contemporary accounts or documents on the most remote

---

6 Scholars.
7 Twice Born.
8 United in God.
9 *Shabérons*: Buddhist monks of the Tibetan monasteries; – *Chelas*: disciples of Occult Science. There are quite a few of them in India itself.
10 *Rajahs*: Hindu princes – *Kshatriya*: nobles of the warrior caste.
11 Let us recommend in this connection a very old and little known book, whose documents, gathered day by day in India, were grouped together and brought to light by a 17th century traveller, a Protestant missionary, *Abraham Rogerius*, "who made his residence for ten years on the Choromandel coast, and in the neighbouring countries": *La porte ouverte pour parvenir à la connaissance du Paganisme caché* (The open door to the knowledge of Hidden Paganism), translated into French by Th. La Grüe (Amsterdam, Jean Schipper, 1670, 1 vol. in-4, frontispiece and very curious engravings). The reader will find precious documents, memories perhaps a little mingled with mirages, but endowed with the rare and penetrating flavour that is characteristic of virgin impressions, absolutely sincere and naive. One feels this book written from the daily investigations of a new observer, ignorant of oriental philosophies, like all those of his time, but scrupulous in recounting things seen, without pretensions with a beautiful spirit, and what is perhaps even better, without school bias. This treatise covers well the superstitions of India and the evil spells that are practised there.
12 There was hardly any difference between philtre and poison.
See *La Magie chez les Chaldéens* (Magic among the Chaldeans) (1874), *La Divination chez les Chaldéens* (Divination among the Chaldeans) (1875). 2 vol. in-8, Maisonneuve, editor.

period, historians and narrators are happy to speak of magic; but they use the same noun and use the same epithet to describe the initiated theurgist of the sanctuaries and the lowly necromancer whose art, prostituted with dark and criminal works, is not averse to the most vulgar methods of concealment.

Now, Black Magic has the first characteristics of being furtive and anti-sacerdotal, and the most suspicious rites cannot justify the name witchcraft, when they are celebrated in broad daylight, by priests of any religion, before the assembled faithful.

However, extenuating circumstances can be found in the misunderstanding of ethnographers. – These writers hardly go back beyond the so-called historical times, when the multiple debris of the ancient religious synthesis was becoming increasingly fragmented, and the misunderstood Polytheism of its sectarians and even its priests was, in their eyes, robbing the Catholic tabernacle of Unity. There is no doubt that public worship at that time –especially around the altars consecrated to gods of an analytical and particular order– consisted of a thousand ceremonies whose character can rightly appear dark. Human sacrifices, to take a significant example, were almost universally consecrated and legitimised by a priestly symbolism, already materialised for a long time, and which depraved or venal priests always took it upon themselves to keep up with their passions and lusts –in a word, with their interests, great or small.

The theocratic confederation of Aries had long since ceased to exist, dislocated by schism, heresy and political dissension; only a few fragmentary regions of this vast religious empire remained faithful to the integral teaching as well as to traditional worship. – They were still opposed, petrified in their immutable orthodoxy, to the rising tide of iniquity and corruption, rising in ever more threatening waves around them. But everywhere else, recent autocracies, discordant enough to have appropriated for themselves each of the new laws, customs and rites, agreed at least to introduce into their public customs, and to assume religious sanction, the abominable principle of human blood shed by man, in favour of the divinity.

Real but obscurely revealing a profound decadence in esotericism (in vain monopolised by schismatic sanctuaries), this impure and sacrilegious rite manifested the Great Arcanum now misunderstood in one of its most sublime corollaries: the ineffable identity of the Great Adam and the Divine Word, or, if you like, the Hominal Synthesis in God, of whom Universal Man.[13] is the first exteriorization, the first development of a purely intelligible order.

So, if we enter the full Cycle of Assumption, in that cursed epoch of which the Bull of the Zodiac becomes once again the antisocial emblem after having been, so many centuries before, the astronomical hieroglyph of the *Bharat Cycle*,[14] we find the human sacrifice sacerdotally enthroned in all climates.

From India, where Kali and Shiva still claim their bloody tribute today, to the various Phoenician states, where the entrails of the monstrous Rutrem and the

---

13 We envisage here, of course, *Universal Man* as being none other than the *Human Reign*, conceived in its principle of transcendent universality...
14 The *Bharat Cycle* will start 107 centuries from ours, according to the revelations of the infallible Brahmanic chronology.

gigantic Moloch swallowed batches of human victims on a fixed date; to the Celts, where the druids of Thor and Teutad accumulated heroes' hecatombs on the mystical dolmen; – and among the Greco-Latin peoples, from Hellas immolating Iphigenia and paying an annual royalty to the Cretan bestiality, the flower of the ephebes and the virgins of Athens; to Caesarian Rome, making the Gallic prisoners fall under the sacred knife, these are but streams of human blood on the altars of the nations.

Israel did not shirk this custom of iniquity, and, as the author of the *Science des Esprits* (Science of Spirits) maliciously points:[15] "the God of the Jews thirsted for the blood of kings, and Joshua offered him hecatombs of defeated monarchs. Jephthah sacrificed his daughter and Samuel cut King Agag into pieces on the sacred stone of Galgal. Moloch differed from Jehovah only by lack of orthodoxy, and the God of Jephthah had mysteries similar to those of Belus". – We will add, without having the bad taste to insist too much, that the autos-da-fé of the Holy Roman Inquisition were not without some resemblance to the idol of the Carthaginians, whose reddened bronze entrails were always hungry for flesh and thirsty for blood.

But, to return to the ancient cults, let us beware of detailing here *priestly* practices that are essentially not suspected of witchcraft. In the preceding chapter (the Devil), the outline of these dark divinities was noted; for if the man who, with the consent of the mislaid people, sacrifices his fellow man on the altar of an idol is a priest and not a sorcerer, on the other hand, these idols, in whose honour all this blood was religiously shed, are true incarnations of the vague and terrible spectre that is commonly known as Satan.

It would be wrong, moreover, to believe that in those centuries when daytime religions had rites so close to necromancy, necromancers were more unemployed. Between the sanctuary with its golden candelabra and the vaulted cellar with its black candles, antagonism was constant; hierophants and sorcerers always were hostile in the mutual accomplishment of often fraternal works.

In Greece, the goetic magic ran an enchanted drug shop. One potion inspires love, another brings death; so much so that a mysterious relationship closely links these two fierce divinities, both sovereign mediators between the Relative and the Absolute, the finite and the infinite – between man and God! A thousand superstitions, of Asian and Phrygian origin, have acclimatised under the beautiful sky of Hellas. The Ophiogenes of Hellespont seem to have inherited some infernal Orpheus and learned at his school the art of charming the most repugnant and feared beasts: toads and vipers, asps and *tards*.

Poetry itself is contagious: Erato becomes a witch. Doesn't *charm* come from *Carmen*; – *Incanter*, from *Cantus*? The incantation of the women of Thessaly, skilled at mixing perfidious juices and poisonous words in honour of the triple Hecate, has become legendary:

> Noxious vegetable with a majestic port,
> Your seeds germinated on a cursed night,
> Under the eye of a tawny, hostile and monstrous star.

---

15 By Eliphas Lévi, 1 vol. in-8, Paris, 1865.

Your very names, suspicious to the Wise One who meditates,
Were banished from the Word, in those ancient times.
Where to know your virtues was forbidden.

From the Sagas of Colchis and the Egyptians
Deterred, under the horror of the bloody Moon,
Your root, dear only to magicians,

Who, combining the bitter sap of a plant
With dead lymph extracted from white bones,
Under the modulated incantation in a slow voice,

Distilled, around midnight, these overpowering philtres,
How the chastity of the virgins of Greece
Falling down, exposing the treasure of their flanks...[16]

Everyone knows the legends of Ionia: what marvellous metamorphoses were accomplished by the voice of the magicians, and how their poems –to borrow the language of M. Rollinat– *ghostly* the whole of Nature. Mystical lamps were lit at the corners of the triangles, in the burial places; then legions of pale spectres came out of the tombs, dressed in borrowed bodies to spread terror. The Vampires (nowadays *Broucolaques*)[17] would lurk in the alcoves, to suck the blood and the strength of the humans – *sanguinem and robur*... Finally, it would be a mistake to think that the *Werewolf* was invented in the Middle Ages. *Lycanthropy* was then as common and perhaps more feared than in the 15th century AD.

Necromancy, like its sisters *Lycanthropy* and *Erratic Vampire*, is linked to the cult of the bloody Hecate. An ancient Hellenic tradition states that spectra, in order to appear, borrow a fluid envelope –or phosphorescent body– from the very substance of the lunar rays. In this respect, let us quote an entire text of evocative conjuration, brought back from Origen (*Philosophumena*, page 72), and which can be translated as follows:

"Come, Oh triple Bombo, Goddess infernal, and earthly, and celestial; Goddess of paths and crossroads! Enemy, night-bearer of light, yet one who brings light to us, friend and companion of the Night... Wandering among the shadows and graves, you enjoy the long barks of the dogs and the steam of the spilled blood. You desire blood and bring terror to mortals... Oh Gorgo! Mormo! Multiform moon, favour with a favourable ray a sacrifice offered in your honour!"

As for the sacrifice itself, ask Theocritus about the saga ceremonies that were customary: the Sabbath itself, the foul Sabbath of the Middle Ages, does not reach this level of horror.

In Rome Horace is the echo of Theocritus, and from Greece to Italy the rites vary little; the Latin painter also arouses disgust by the intensity of his paintings. But for the nausea to be extinguished in a burst of laughter, one must read Lucian: with

---

16 *Rosa Mystica*, by Stanislas de Guaita. Paris, Lemerre, 1885, in-12, page 101.
17 *Broucolaque* is a greek word (*vrykolaka*) for vampire.

what straps he pinned this hideous scoundrel, ingenious in tripping the horrible into the rut of ridicule! – Lucien, the *Faux Prophète* (False Prophet).

It was above all on the decline of the great Republic, when the bloody competitions of the dictatorship heralded the next establishment of the Caesars, that sorcerers of all kinds gained a foothold in Rome and the provinces. The clashes of arms of the Civil War sounded the death knell of freedom, the hour of the licence had come. A whole spontaneous generation of the larvae of false occultism hatched. Spellcasters, fortune-tellers, Phrygians trading clandestinely in philtres, charms and amulets; false astrologers, so-called Chaldeans, who were considered to be versed in the depths of all secret and forbidden knowledge; the dregs of the people had invaded the great city in fermentation. In the absence of science and morality, these charlatans, who were not lacking in audacity, competed fiercely with omens, flames and other aruspices; the people were inclined to mummies, already disenchanted with the religion of their ancestors, and the world's police victors welcomed with favour the most degrading superstitions of the defeated barbarians.

However, soothsayers and astrologers were favoured; some citizens were seen to acquire at a high price and to consult in the greatest mystery some collections of enigmas, which they insisted on looking at as authentic and priceless copies of those famous scrolls that the Sibyl of Cumae had burnt, according to the legend, in the presence of Tarquin and his disdainful attitude.

Magic became poisonous in Rome with Locust, as in Colchis and Thessaly with Medea. The death of Britannicus, scrupulously recounted by Tacitus down to the last detail, attests to the knowledge and use, during the reign of Nero, of toxic substances whose formula we no longer possess. The fact that the young prince was struck by lightning as soon as the cup touched his lips, made most ancient authors think of *Prussic Acid*, the only one[18] of the poisons known at that time, whose action on the organism was fast enough to explain the very precise description of the death given by the contemporaries.

But this hypothesis itself seems to us to be unfounded. – We remember that the emperor, by a truly exquisite perfidy, and one that was quite capable of deflecting suspicion, wanted a slave to be the first to taste the drink he intended for his victim. But Britannicus cried out, the drink seemed so hot to him and, without mistrust, poured cold water into it. And the cold water alone was poisoned... Thus death slipped –stealthily, so to speak– into the cup of the imperial host.

Hydrocyanic (or prussic) acid is as volatile as ether. Mixed with a liquid almost in boiling point, it would immediately have been released in torrents of acrid vapours; and not only would Britannicus have staggered, suffocated, without having been able to raise the cup to the level of his lips; but the asphyxia would have further struck down the cup-bearer himself, and perhaps the immediate neighbours of the prince. In any case, a subtle and penetrating odour of bitter almonds, invading the whole room, would have revealed at once, by inconveniencing the guests, the nature

---

18 All the substances likely to have produced such a rapid death, –*Nicotine, Conicine, Amyl Nitrogen*– are also volatile, the last two especially, and all three endowed with an odour as strong as it is revealing.

of the liquid poured. Let us refer to the accounts of Tacitus and Suetonius; nothing of the kind took place.

What can we conclude from this? Does this mean that Locusto possessed a secret of toxic substances unknown to science today?... Or was the drink she prepared *more* or *less* a poison, in the modern acceptance of the term?...

The theurgic school of the Neo-Platonists, founded in Alexandria, belongs in one way or another to the history of High Magic. It nevertheless comes near certain practices that are more than suspect, and it is without injustice that it has often been accused, despite its science, of tendencies tainted by an obvious superstition.

This same complaint applies even more equitably to the various schools of Gnosis, even the less eccentric ones; born from the very cradle of Christianity, these sects, under the pretext of a protest of the *spirit* against the *dead letter*, created the *Antichrist*[19] in the Church, by determining the schism: This crucial point of view, once set aside, it is hardly to be denied that several of these dissident communities almost immediately indulged in the darkest practices of Goetia.

Simon the Magician (the man with the bag of tricks, but also, like most of those we will mention, Simon, the terrible manipulator of astral forces), continues in the apotheosis of Helen, his concubine (incarnation of Selene or the Moon), the rehabilitation of the dullness and debauchery.

The black Montanus turns his eunuch body into a veritable tripod, where, hysterical sibyls, Maximilian and Priscilla, his Doves, stammering words without a sequel, twist themselves into the prey of all the frenzies of an unattainable love.

Marcion (perhaps the guiltiest, certainly the most learned) founds the sect of the Ophites. Not content with laying an evil hand, a knowingly sacrilegious hand, on one of the inviolable Kabbalistic veils, he also materialises the most formidable and occult manifestation of ceremonial magic, to the point of synthesising –in this case, it's confusing– the secret notions of *Agathodemon* and *Cacodemon* in the therefore equivocal form of a snake; finally (abominable parody!) makes the sacred ὀφίς, the physical instrument of the most detestable mysteries!...

Elsewhere, the deacon Marcos, ordaining prophetesses and priestesses of Christ the young girls deflowered and consecrated by him, takes them to the altar naked and throbbing with the breath of his mouth: for with an impure breath he has been able to kindle in them the flames –often twin, alas– of magnetic *vaticinium* and of absolute debauchery.

---

19 *Spiritus qui solvit Christum*... we already know this profound definition of the Antichrist: it is the spirit of sectarianism, intolerance, division...
It is understood that we are not talking here about the orthodox Gnostics: Saint Irenaeus, Saint Denis the Areopagite, Saint Clement of Alexandria, Synesius, etc.
As for certain dissident Gnostics, such as Marcion and Valentin, we blame them as sectarians, putting themselves outside the unity; but we cannot ignore the Science of these esotericists, which still radiates, although mixed with errors, under the unfortunately *eclectic* and consequently bastard veil of their symbolism. – The same can be said of Manes himself: while we fight with all our strength against his doctrine (which is, in short, erroneous in the bad sense in which it must inevitably have been understood), we willingly salute in him a beautiful, errant genius.

All of them have prostituted Holy Magic to Evil, some with a power of conscious perversity, truly infernal... And these are so many examples taken at random, and which will suffice to make us glimpse the abysses of shame and madness, where the exaltation of a mysticism almost always ascetic at the beginning, makes ardent and generous natures roll, born for the fight of life. One wanted to deny the Flesh, or better to spiritualise it by masturbating it under the compression of the Spirit; but it is the Spirit who descends from his ecstasy to come and pollute the Flesh!

Ah, what revelations we shall have to make in Chapter VI on a large number of similar facts, the authenticity of which cannot be doubted! We shall offer the reader a shower of contemporary turpitudes, born of a mysticism mad with pride and delirium; for where pride sows in foolishness, it is always Satan who reaps in shame.

It is then that Pascal's famous words will come back to mind: "Man is neither angel nor beast, and whoever wants to be an angel, becomes a beast."

We have said it elsewhere,[20] all the heresies of the first centuries are imprinted with a varnish of the blackest taste; all the heretics are sorcerers. Here is the profound reason, as protestors of the Spirit against the Letter formulated by the Teaching Church, they want to become the magi of primitive dogma, revealed in its esotericism, well or badly understood by them. But they forget that by provoking a schism, they have acted as anarchists, and that their work is thus vitiated in principle and sterilised in its germ.

When one sets out to cure a sick person, one must not first amputate, under the pretext of protecting him from contagion, the only limb which the disease has not yet reached; for the sick body, even deprived of a limb, can heal, heal and live; while the healthy limb separated from the body decomposes and dies. – In the same way, if one aspires to reform the Church, one must first of all remain in the Church; She is the living entity and the very principle of Unity.

This is what the early *Protestants* could not understand. Their ambition was to become the pontiffs of a renewed cult, the wrong lot of swelling the number of cursed sects[21] fell to them alone.

While the struggles of Arianism bloodied Europe, Manichaeism –a Christian re-edition of the antagonistic dogma of the Persians, as disfigured by the less clear vision of the second Zoroaster– affirmed (as we have explained in the previous chapter) the equality of origin and power of the two principles: Good and Evil, the Divine Word and the Evil Word, Christ and the Antichrist.[22]

To disregard the relative and transitory nature of Evil was to raise to the Divine Evil Principle a temple and an altar of darkness – a true rallying point for all devil worshippers. It meant recruiting in advance and into the future ages all false mystics and sorcerers.

We would not end up pursuing this deceptive and fleeting heresy in all its forms; the essence of its mysteries will reveal itself when we study the rites and

---

20 *Au Seuil du Mystère* (On the Threshold of Mystery), 2nd ed., p. 44.
21 Without examining the work and doctrine of these sects, we can say that they are marked a priori with at least one of the characters in which one recognises sorcerers: they all bear the anti-sacerdotal stamp.
22 For more details see chapter I.

ceremonies of the Sabbath. We do not hesitate to maintain this allegation, however insulting and paradoxical it may seem. Albigensians, Cathars, Waldensians, shakers of the Cévennes and sorcerers from the country of Labourt are all Manichean sects barely disguised; and the trial of the Manichean Templars[23] will shed new light on the infernal and dualistic nature of this monstrous heresy.

Nor can we track down the elusive personality of the sorcerer in these disguises, through the history of the Middle Ages and modern times. Even if it were traced *currente calcmo*, such a monograph would be duplicative: by pointing out, in chapter IV, some of the most famous trials, whose invariable outcome leaves so many bloodstains on all the pages of our Christian annals, we will be able to distinguish the true sorcerer from the false one.

The appellation of *false sorcerer*, which might surprise the reader, is justified in itself, when one considers that all great men, provided they did not resign themselves to the donkey cap of *doctor scholasticus* before the public, were fatally accused of evil and heresy! At the same time, they risked imprisonment, torture, burning at the stake...

Any recalcitrant superiority was stamped with the fatal label, not only in the eyes of the clerics and their envious mediocrity, but also in the court of secular opinion.

To all lords, all honour: Albert le Grand, Trithème, Agrippa are worthy of being cited in the front line. – They were magi; how could they not have been turned into sorcerers...? Saint Thomas Aquinas himself, the Angel of the School! cannot escape the suspicion of witchcraft, nor can his contemporary, the monk Raymond Lulle de Palma, *the very enlightened doctor.*

In a mood of universal mistrust, the monomaniacs of demonology did not even spare the papal throne. It is likely that Popes Sylvester II and Gregory VII were still regarded in the XVII century as followers of Beelzebub, since the scholar Gabriel Naude pleads their innocence in the excellent and courageous book he published in 1625: *Apologie pour tous les grands hommes qui ont été accusés de magie* (Apology for all the great men accused of magic).[24] He is also bitterly taken up of his scepticism by the Capuchin *Jacques d'Autun* (or his real name, Mr. Chevannes), the author of an inept in-4°, of more than a thousand pages, entitled: *l'incrédulité savante et la crédulité ignorante au sujet des magiciens et dessorciers* (Learned disbelief and ignorant credulity of magicians and sorcerers).[25]

Nothing is more buffoonish than the accusations made against all geniuses by the stubborn maniacs of the supernatural – accusations of which the honest Naudé is indignant. We shall cite two examples.

On *Cornelius Agrippa*: Delrio reports that "being in Louvain, as the devil had strangled one of his boarders, he ordered him to enter his body and make him walk seven or eight laps in front of the public square before leaving it, so that he would not be punished and suspected of his death when all the people would have judged

---

23 Chapter IV: *Human Justice.*
24 Paris, 1625, in-8.
25 Lyon, 1674, in-4.

THE SORCERER 79

it sudden and natural". Similarly, Paul Ioue say in his Éloges (Praises), that he died very poor and abandoned by everyone in the city of Lyon, and that touched by repentance, he gave leave to a great black dog who had followed him all the time of his life, taking off his collar full of magical images and figures, and telling him in anger: *Abi perdita bestia, quæ me totum perdidisti*; whereupon the said dog rushed into the Saône, and was not seen or met since."[26]

On *Saint Thomas Aquinas*: Naudé is saddened to hear that the bad grimoire *Essentiis Essentiarum* is attributed to this Father of the Church. There it is said that after the flood Abel withdrew from a stone a treatise of hermetic astrology, having broken the stone; and "from it he learned the art of making images under certain planets and constellations. As he was inconvenienced in his studies by the great noise of the horses that passed by his window every day to go and drink, he made the image of a horse, according to the rules of the said book, and after putting it in the street 2 or 3 feet into the ground, the grooms were afterwards forced to look for another way, as they were not able anymore to make any horse pass through that place."[27]

These legends show clearly that the passion –a real moral epidemic– to see magicians everywhere was rampant.

Many more were told about Agrippa; we will not burden these pages with such a jumble. Let us listen instead to Naudé; after recalling a number of particularities in praise of the man who was then known as the *arch-sorcerer*, in particular "that he was chosen by the Cardinal of the Holy Cross to assist him at the Council..., that the Pope wrote him a letter urging him to continue to do well, as he had begun to do; that the Cardinal of Lorraine wanted to be godfather to one of his sons in France". ... etc... and finally that he was a singular friend of four cardinals, five Euesques[28] and all the doctrinal men of his time; that Paule Joue called him *portentosum ingenium*, that Jacques Gohory put him *inter clarissima sui sæculi lamina*; that Lud Vvigius called him *Venerandum Dominum Agrippam, litterarumque omnium miraculum et amorem bonorum*, etc...";[29] Gabriel Naudé, who is not lacking in logic,"would willingly ask Delrio... why the Pope's judgment, the authority of so many Cardinals and Euesques, the favour of two Emperors and so many Kings, are not such good and legitimate evidence to prove his innocence..."[30]

---

26 Naudé, *Apologie pour les grands hommes* (Apology for the great men) (Paris edition, Besonge, 1669, small in-12, page 305). Having only this edition of Paris, 1669 before my eyes, I always indicate its pagination. – "The black dog of Agrippa, whom he called Monsieur, when Agrippa died in the hospital of Grenoble, threw himself into the river in front of everyone and has never been seen since" (*Réfutation des opinions de Jean Vvier* (Rebuttal of Jean Vvier's opinions), supplement to *La Démonomanie des Sorciers* (The Demonomy of Sorcerers), Paris, 1587, in-4, page 241). Thus Jove and Bodin agree on the prodigy of the suicide of this poor dog; but they cannot agree on the city where Agrippa died: one says it was Lyon, the other Grenoble... This is very characteristic.
27 Ibid, page 350.
28 Euesque was a clerical dignitary.
29 Naudé, *Apologie...* p. 294.
30 Ibid., p. 296.

All these quotations have no other purpose than make the reader understand, by which accusations some tried to tarnish, and by which arguments others tried to defend the memory of a scholar such as Henry Corneille Agrippa And these things were being debated at the end of the seventeenth century!

One last trait, very suitable for revealing the state of mind at that time: "Nicolas Remigius, a criminal judge in Lorraine, who had eight hundred women burned alive, saw magic everywhere, it was his fixed idea, his madness. He wanted to preach a crusade against sorcerers, with whom he saw Europe filled. Desperate not to be taken at his word when he claimed that almost everyone was guilty of magic, he ended up denouncing himself and was burned on his own confession".[31]

Such facts can be taken as typical; their eloquence is repugnant to any commentary. If we are to believe Ferdinand Denis,[32] an intelligent compiler of all the ancient chroniclers, there were, in Paris during the reign of Charles IX, more than thirty thousand sorcerers.

In order to be impartial (and even if we give much credence to the exaggeration of our contemporaries, motivated by the common mania for seeing legates of hell everywhere), we have to agree on one thing, wizards were in *abundance* at the time, and one can imagine the panic of the people; it is not to the point of blindness on the part of the magistrates that we do not realise it by deploring it. For –we cannot repeat it too often– witchcraft is not an empty word; evil spells, bewitchments, spells have always had and still have a formidable reality… There is no doubt that the accusation of black magic has been abused, and we have just produced some astonishing examples; but is this really a plausible reason to affirm that witchcraft is *never* but a dream. Are *all* the bewitchers miserable jugglers without power? Are the *bewitched always* poor victims of their sick imagination?

To the blind man who would support such a thesis, modern science –yes, the very science of universities– would come to inflict daily denials. Without invoking here the undeniable reality of occult phenomena which doctors of spiritualism would be appalled by (they claim to be not surprised by anything!), I beg the incredulous public to simply refer to the experiences of Doctors Liébeault, Bernheim, Beaunis, Charcot, Luys and other university teachers.

Whoever, having read the scientifically recorded facts of these masters of hypnotism, and having reflected a little on the essence of these phenomena, still denies the possibility of a spell, in my opinion, lacks common sense or good faith… This is what I hope to prove in due course; but here such a discussion would be an appetizer.

I return to my subject and find myself in the presence of the sorcerer, as our fathers knew him from the XII to the XVIII century. This is the average, truly classical type. I was looking forward to him.

---

31 Eliphas Lévi, *Rituel de la Haute Magie* (published in English as Transcendental Magic Its Doctrine and Ritual).
32 *Tableau historique et philosophique des Sciences occultes* (Historical and Philosophical Table of the Occult Sciences). Paris, 1842, in-32, page 159.

THE SORCERER

Michelet, in his astonishing monograph,[33] considered than sorcerers, from beginning to end, lost compared to witches: "For one sorcerer –he says-, there are ten thousand witches".[34] The statistics of judicial convictions would say something else. Here, as everywhere, Michelet brutalises the facts a little to force them into his thesis, which is always preconceived, and very eloquently pleaded, by the way. Be that as it may, the bias, which is evident on every page, is very detrimental to the verisimilitude and sometimes even the interest of his depiction of the time – and if he has, in short, done an admirable work, it is because all his stories, even the illusory ones, are transfigured by the breath of wild poetry that was within him.

Witches or sorcerers, what does it matter, anyway? The question is asked in these terms: what is a *sorcerer*, either male or female?

Let us judge the tree by its fruits.

It would no doubt be easy to transcribe the long and confused descriptions of Bodin, or of any other demonographer, but we believe that the best way to make the sorcerer known is to stage him, in the exercise of his sad duties, on the ground of the *legendary Sabbath*.

By offering the reader a Sabbath image, we are going to allow his imagination to bring these madmen back to life in the fantastic setting where their madness was practised. For it is important to note that all the incredible stories that we are going to summarise in a way have come out of the mouths of the defendants prosecuted for the crime of witchcraft; they are taken at face value by their often spontaneous confessions and not always extorted by the questions. What is more, the accused knew in advance, that such confessions condemned them to an inescapable death, condemned them without possible remission to the atrocious torment of the pyre.[35]

Not all woods, says Pythagoras, are suitable for carving a Mercury; nor are all places suitable for reviving these weekly assemblies[36] of sorcerers and evil spirits, which have been called Sabbaths.

There are sites where the mother-nature seems to smile at her children and, through the mute language of things, speaks to them of hope and happiness. There are also arid and ravaged places, which only inspire disenchantment, terror and madness in the heart of man...

The Sabbath

Daisy hunting enthusiasts often encounter darker green circular bands on the grassy hills, where the thicker vegetation is also half the height. These bands are often hemicyclic, sometimes spreading out in a perfect circumference, and differ in diameter and width; they appear to be compass-shaped and in autumn they are filled with a tiara of brightly coloured sponges and other cryptogams.

---

33 *La Sorcière* (The Witch). Paris, Hetzel, 1862, in-12.
34 That witches were more numerous than sorcerers is a bit of an exaggeration, that's for sure. Surely the proportion is inaccurate.
35 Sometimes they convinced the executioner to strangle them before throwing them into the flames.
36 Biweekly, according to some authors.

An old tradition tells us that the fairies danced their ronde under the moonlight...

And, as the Fairies –innocent and mad deities of Nature– never go without the wand of metamorphosis in their hands and the smile of benevolence on their lips, their exuberant joy spreads around them in marvellous gifts, and under their light steps the grass grows in abundance, and the night lights up with the phosphorescent glow of their silvery flight... They are Life itself, embodied in the splendour of the feminine forms; they are Love which fertilizes everything with a ray of its sweet eyes!

But haven't you seen, near the unpleasant ruins haunted by evil spirits, around abandoned cemeteries or on the cliffs, bitter trails where grass never grows, as if some impure breath had sterilized the clod as it passed by? – Move forward: an icy breath has run through your hair... Take a walk along these sinister-looking brushwoods; an infallible instinct guides you with shivers... To your left, leave the *wizard's pond*, a puddle of water rotting in a hollow, hidden by a willowy mist with bleached foliage. The naive traditions of the people forbid you to approach it; these swamps, shaded by pale shrubs, very low, are as many sighing holes of hell! – Oh fairies! Good fairies! You don't live there, where are you?

Have you not felt it? – A ghost has taken your hand; it is he who guides you and you obey his embrace in silence... You go up the steep slope where the red bushes seem like spectres crouching in the vapours of the twilight.

A fold in the ground is still to be crossed; here you are on the ridge; the path leads to a solitary moorland; the very rare grass is yellow in places...

In front of you stands a wild building... Come closer again, it is a dolmen, you see the gigantic stone, where the sacred knife of the druids was used for the prescribed sacrifice, in honour of Thor and Teutad.

Night has fallen completely.

But now a sinister and bloody light strikes the ancient altar of the Celtic Moloch. It looks like blood and perhaps it is! The moon has risen red on the horizon of the woods in the distance; the scene is illuminated by a strange day; the air is heavy, foul and rotten...

> But, like a wandering breath of cooled inferno,
> In the valley that takes on a strange figure,
> A lukewarm, dumb and ominous wind
> Eating on the rare grass and the rosy bush...[37]

Now that the enormous moon, which rises slowly, is illuminating the moor, indicating the objects which were at first indistinct..., is it a path, tell me, this circular strip which goes around the dolmen?

It is not a path. The grass is mowed there and, as if ravaged by a corrosive vapour, it's right on the ground. *It is the exact opposite of the fairy circle.*

Fertility and life have disappeared.

---

37 Maurice Rollinat, *Les Névroses. L'alée des Peupliers* (Neuroses. The avenue of the Poplars).

THE SORCERER

A few minutes more and death will vomit out all the spectres of his empire[38] they are indecisive larvae which oscillate and condense with difficulty; flying toads, crocodiles whose eyes blaze and suddenly alternate; dragons with the mouths of hippopotamus, with the wings of enormous bats, cats with soft and uncertain legs, like octopus tentacles... Here come down naked women, screaming and wild and dishevelled, caracoling on a broom that runs and rears up in turns...

We are on the Sabbath!

. . . .

An incanter witch crouching at the foot of the dolmen; a handful of sticks has caught fire in her right hand; she dips two fingers of her left hand in a sandstone jug between her knees. – Aye Saraye! She shouts, Aye Saraye[39]... A glimmer of light shines from the bottom of the pitcher, and behold, a small animal escapes from it, light, ready, and the size of a squirrel: it is *Master Leonard*.

The witch stood up as a sign of respect. Leonard, in a second, has grown two metres, and at that moment he is a monstrous goat with crooked horns. The fluorescent wave that his whole body seems to exhale like a pale atmosphere is lost in spirals and stinks strangely.

A thousand will-o'-the-wisps flutter here and there across the moor.

Suddenly one seems to rush, crackle and suddenly settles between the devil's horns.

For Master Leonard it is the Devil!...

They rush from the four corners of the horizon, from the four cardinal points of the air one can see sorcerers, witches and demons melting in a jumble. The sky is scratched in the flight of the spirits, and under the fiery eye of Hecate the gloomy air vaguely darkens; vaguely the earth fades away from the moving shadows that intertwine.

– Har! Har! Sabbath!... Shout the arrivals, hurriedly gathered in groups around the Master, who, in turn, with graceful eagerness, offer each one his behind to kiss. But instead of the gaunt buttocks of a goat, it is a young face of marvellous beauty – and every affiliate receives on the mouth the caress of two fresh and lively lips.

---

38 Our information is drawn from a large number of authors. To quote our authorities at every detail would be tedious, unbearable..., at every line, one would need references.

The bettter sources are BOGUET, *Discours exécrable des Sorciers* (Sorcerers' execrable speeches). Lyon, 1610, in-8. – Nicolas REMIGIUS, *Demonolatria*. Lugduni, 1595, in-4. – BODIN, *Démonomanie*. Paris, 1580, in-4. – LE LOYER, *Histoire des spectres* (History of spectres). Paris, 1605, in-4. – Jacques d'AUTUN, *La Crédulité savante* (Scholarly Gullibility). Lyon, 1674, in-4. – DEL RIO (translated by DU CHESNE), *Controverses magiques* (Magic Controversies). Paris, 1611, small in-8. – BINSFELDIUS, *De confessionibus maleficorum*, August. Trev..., 1591, in-8. – TAILLEPIED, *Apparition des Esprits* (Appearance of the Spirits). Paris, 1588, small in-12. – DOM CALMET, *Esprits et Vampires* (Spirits and Vampires). Paris, 1751, 2 vols. in-12. – GARINET, *Histoire de la Magie((History of Magic). Paris, 1818, in-8*. – MICHELET, *La Sorcière** (The Witch). Paris, 1862, in-12. – Paul ADAM, *Être* (Being). Paris, 1888, in-12.

39 By corruption of the Hebrew אהיהאשראהיה (Æhieh asher Æhien: the Being is the Being).

Fires of heather and cypresses are lit up all over the moor: they are ardent and blazing, colourful. Slow melodies, which seem to come from an invisible harmonica, sparkle their pearly notes, with a liquid timbre and an ineffable purity...

And it is with the screams of the familiar that a strange contrast is created.

Now, after the homage of his faithful, Master Leonard resumes a bored look; disdainfully, he goes to the high golden pulpit where the druidic altar serves as a pedestal, from there he dominates the whole assembly.

The Master of Ceremonies is standing in front of him, his staff in his hand. It is then that the names are called and the marks or stigmata are checked.

But behold, a black sheep with glowing eyes runs like a hurricane from the northern parts. He bleats to reassure the one he is carrying: superb girl[40] naked, straddling her soft fleece. She torments herself hard and cries... She is the expected victim, she is the *Queen of the Sabbath*.

People hurry around her with all the signs of respectful impatience. She gets down from her mount and while she is being cheered, she veils her shame in the disorder of her long hair.

The Master of Ceremonies solemnly raises his golden wand; the Devil rises and greets the young girl; he finally comes down from his pulpit and the Black Mass is about to begin.

Humble goat-foot have dug a hole in the ground to the left, Leonard goes there with great pomp and circumstance to urinate first. The principal members of the congregation imitate him. This is the lustral water for sprinkling – and which is used to baptise the newcomer. Then the witches, dipping two fingers of their left hand into it, devoutly sign themselves backwards.

Here comes the procession again. The virgin whom the Goat is to initiate is brought back to the altar of Teutad, where she receives all the sacraments of hell in succession.

Having done this, she is coated with an ointment containing cantharides and stramoine, and the ticklish drunkenness invades her poor, spasms-unaware body by degrees, and there she is now, distraught in her modesty by the automatism of desire.

In the *Introit*, Satan prescribes that the children, too young to take part in the great mystery –in the great sacrilege of the universal communion of love– should be kept away. They go down to the devil's ponds, white wafers in hand, to pasture the troop of countless toads, all baptised and dressed in green velvet or scarlet silk, with a bell on their collar.

Between them and the Great Assembly, the *elves of the Air* weave a thick cloud, and Leonard proceeds to the *Rite* of the Newcomer.

---

40 "All those we have seen called Queens were sweet and of some beauty more singular than the others" (Pierre de Lancre, *Inconstance des démons* (Inconstancy of the demons). Paris, Buon, 1612, in-4, page 223).

THE SORCERER 85

Turned upside down on the altar, frightened and gasping for breath, she receives the bitter kiss of the god. It is a dreadful tear, the burning of a red iron stake, and then immediately the anguish of an abundant, icy flood.[41]

Let us abbreviate. – All the demonologists dwell on too many details,[42] that we have not been take care to reproduce.

A frantic ronde, snaking around the couple with shouts of fierce joy, mixes, confuses the sexes and the ranks, back to back. The chain is only broken for the adulterous, incestuous and sodomitic frolics, scattered across the moor in the moonlight... Incest is above all in honour, for the Sabbath becomes through it the eternal nursery of Satan: "There was no perfect sorcerer and sorcerer's witch, who was not begotten of father and daughter or of mother and son".[43]

However, on the very body of the new priestess –a pulsating altar– the *Snapping Goat*[44] officiates, he offers wheat to the Spirit of the Earth who makes the harvest grow; he gives rise to little birds that carry, through the night sky, the wishes of the assistants to the demon of Liberty.

Then a symbolic cake is kneaded, baked and consecrated on the priestess' bloody loins. It is the *Confarreatio*, the host of impure love, the offering of universal evil, the infernal communion that is distributed to the whole assembly...

The time has come for a fraternal feast, and the prepubescent pastors bring back from the pasture the battalion of toads entrusted to their vigilant care.

The old furies, for whom love is but a twice-sterile reminiscence, have prepared various carrion and cooked with enchanted herbs the children who died before baptism.

The mead circulates in the bowls, people enjoy themselves, they get drunk all over. Hermaphroditic monsters and imps in various disguises decorate the tables where the peasants fraternize with the Lord and the Prelate, where the proudest ladies elbow their way through the rough and tumble. What would the chatelaines that still despise de villains would do?... Nobles and commoners, all mixed up together, hasn't the great blind Lust mixed their blood and spit?...

A big grey cloud has devoured the moon. The braziers glow red, lighting up the moor alone.

Then a dreadful voice, without a distinct tone, a hoarse and mournful voice is heard twice: Avenge yourself, or you will die! Immediately, raising his bushy tail, whose presumptuous shamelessness he veiled,[45] Leonard drops blackish seeds under him, in a rosary, and then some very stinking powders. Large pieces of cloth have been spread out, according to the rite, to receive these variously precious droppings;

---

41 *Igneam esse diaboli mentulam, frigidum vero semen ejus, Sabbathi meretrices unâ voce confitur.*
42 We shall quote only one, in Latin: "*Aliquid turpissimum (quod tamen scribam), astruunt: videlicet dæmonem incubum uti membro genitali bifurcato, ut simul utroque vase abutatur*". This quotation from Sylvester Prierias says enough: on reading this nameless turpitude, taken at random from among a thousand, one can easily imagine what the others can be.
43 Bodin, *Démonomanie de Sorciers* (Demonomy of Sorcerers), book IV, ch. V.
44 I'm not inventing anything: Lancre, *Inconstance*, preface, towards the end.
45 *Immane scrotum, torvamque mentulam.*

they are poisons, elixirs and philtres: they are for love, for madness, for death and also for mysterious healings... Some are intended to make fields sterile, others to infect the air for the production of epidemics. It is made for general distribution.

Finally, her hairs scattered, all emboldened and feverish, the Queen of the Sabbath rises up, and with a bright voice, threatening Heaven with her fist: *Thunderbolt of God*, the triumphant victim cries out, *Thunderbolt of God, strike, if you dare!...* Then she throws herself on one of the toads, which she tears with rage between her teeth: *Ah, Philip, if I had you!...*

The horizon pales, however, at the first light of dawn. Suddenly, the Goat has metamorphosed into a monstrous rooster, all black, with a crest of dazzling flames – and a formidable crow can be heard.

The assembly disperses in a hurry and everything has disappeared...

One should not believe that one could condense in this short description all the insanities, all the turpitudes especially, of which abound in the writings of Bodin, Lancre, Delrio, Boguet, Sprenger, Michaëlis and other demonologists.

Without mentioning the interminable chapter of lewd frolics –restricted by us to the space of a few still refined lines– we have said nothing of the dance of the toads, nor of the complaints that these interesting little beasts made against the witch who was too careless of their dear health, nor of the confession to the devil of the sins that were omitted to be committed, nor of the periodic harvests of human flesh under the gallows, nor of the interminable other details, of equally exquisite taste.

Our great ambition was to reconstruct the tragicomedy as a whole, it goes without saying that in our efforts to group the main scenes logically, we were unable to reconcile the opinions of all the authors. Far from agreeing on the order of the ceremony, each of them artfully interchanged the various phases of the ceremony. The substance remains invariable in all of them, but for certain details of form it would be difficult to reach a perfect agreement.

In the course of Book II, we are looking for the real in this fabric of legendary phantasmagorias – where each person will see, at his or her own discretion, either the most fearsome drama or the most burlesque pantomime, depending on his or her point of view.

To complete this picture, let us report in a few lines what popular traditions say about Evocation, the Covenant and transport on the Sabbath.

Eliphas Lévi, in his *Transcendental Magic Its Doctrine and Ritual*, conscientiously lists the bizarre, odious and ridiculous ceremonies required in Goetia to ward off the Devil.[46] We refer researchers, curious about such specifications, to them. But absolute rules are made to be violated, imperative prescriptions are promulgated to be eluded, and in fact never or hardly ever did a sorcerer deploy this device to compel Satanas to appear.

The annals of witchcraft are full of tales of evocation, having succeeded perfectly, without all this luxury of staging. We even see the Devil appearing without

---

46 See in our chapter V, the article on *Evocation*.

any intention of being called, and exclaiming in a voice of thunder: *Why did you call me?*[47] Most often, the hero of the adventure is a poor schoolboy, who –out of curiosity– looked through the eyes of a grimoire that chance had placed there... What craftsmen of misfortune are chance and curiosity! The Devil, who is a clever being, and, what's more, a bad sleeper, has big eyes and a loud voice; he doesn't want to be disturbed for nothing; he threatens, he storms. In short, he demands that we bind ourselves to him by a freely consented contract.

The reckless poor man is trembling with fear and does not know how to get out of such a bad situation. But Satanas, suddenly softened, becomes paternal and itemises to him the most seductive proposals. It is not so rare and envied that he promises him, on condition, however... Oh! Almost nothing! He only wants two lines of commitment, signed by this hand that is still trembling.

A *Pact*, here we go! In four years, ten years, or thirty years, the pupil will be acquired by the devil body and soul – in return for which the devil, during this period, undertakes to serve him with all his resources and to defend him with all his art. The moneybag of the poor will be inexhaustibly full of doubloons and piastres; he will seduce the most prudish women with a single glance; he will transport itself wherever it pleases, with the speed of thought, and his wishes, whatever they may be, will be granted, as soon as they are formulated in its heart. The offer is seductive; the unfortunate man cannot resist it. He signs the double contract with his blood, the Devil takes one; as for the other, oh wonder! Placed on the pinprick he has made in his arm, it enters the flesh, without enlarging the scratch, which is on the contrary healed by the blow.

Those who want to know the epilogue of these kinds of adventures (again according to legend) will read for their information the rare and curious work by Palma Cayet: *Histoire prodigieuse et lamentable de Jean Fauste, grand Magician, et sa vie épouvantable* (The prodigious and lamentable story of Jean Fauste, a great magician, and his dreadful life).[48]

This is the type of almost all the legends of evocation, the background does not vary, the form hardly varies.

This is what can be called a coincidence; on the other hand, the pact is voluntary and perfectly expressed.

For it must be said that theologians readily distinguish between the expressed or *formal* pact and the unexpressed or *tacit* (*ipso facto*) pact. By eating the apple, according to them, our mother Eve made a tacit pact with the Devil...

But enough of this scholastic's quibbling. It remains for us to say a word about the Sabbath. The mode differs according to the authors and according to the country; the elastic person of the Devil lends himself to all uses; his morals change, according to the beings he plots to seduce.

---

47 Between us, I believe that if the Devil appears when he is not called, he generally refuses to come when he is called.
In both cases, to get it to come, *it has to be predestined.*
48 Cologne, heirs of Pierre Marteau, 1712, small in-12, with an engraved frontispiece, which we reproduce in this same page.

At times the witch feels abducted, with the sound of midnight, by an unknown force, and carried away in the air, with the speed of the wind, to the place of the Sabbath. Sometimes Satan appears to her clearly, in the form of a goat or a sheep; he then takes her on his back or on his horns and takes her away, as above, through the chimney opening. – Elsewhere, he communicates to the broomsticks the virtue we know; in the hands of their owner, these modest utensils become, when the time comes, tireless, lively and faithful mounts.

DOCTOR FAUST IN HIS CIRCLE SURROUNDED BY DEMONS.

But an hour or two before the rapture (in whatever way the rapture takes place), whoever wishes to go to the Sabbath must grease his or her body, especially the thighs, stomach and groin, with a special ointment –the composition of which varies little– which Satanas and his companions take great care to keep constantly supplied for the faithful of the Synagogue (1).

THE SORCERER

The reader should not forget this particularity; this is the most important point to take note of... In the second book, we shall return, as befits the occasion, to the question of the magic ointments; we even promise to make revelations about them that are as curious as they are unexpected.

Sometimes the candidates for the infernal agape hastened the marvellous virtue of the ointment by the secret properties of an electuary which they absorbed in the form of a rather large pill. All these very interesting details want to be examined in all seriousness; here we are merely pointing out them.

Whereas the chapter VI of the *Temple of Satan* will edify the reader on the problem of the sorcerer in his most modern incarnations, let us leave it alone – and let us end with a strange adventure, which we have from the very mouth of the peasant from Lorraine to whom it came.

We will record it, as far as possible, in the very terms in which it was told to us. The one who speaks is a man of about thirty-five years of age.

– "It happened when I was a child, sir. I could have been five or six years old. It was in Cutting (a village in the annexed Lorraine) in the autumn of 1859. One evening, when the sky was like ink, we were chatting as a family near the fireplace in our kitchen, when a *music*[49] of a very funny character could be heard outside. It was like the song of fifteen or twenty people, all of whom, for the occasion, would have taken on a sharp and reedy voice.[50] The tune modulated on only two or three notes was not lacking in charm; its very monotony was impressive.[51]

I hurried outside and saw nothing. The voices seemed to come from a very great height; they became noticeably clearer, as if the choir had come closer to us.

I was very frightened and my mother's words were not to reassure me: *Take care, my son, this is the High Hunt* (this is how we call the air journey of witches and sorcerers on their way to the Sabbath).

I stiffened myself against fear and began to sing mockingly, imitating these monsters and to shout insults at them. Then the song suddenly died out. As I was preparing to go home, a human corpse bone, falling on my cap, almost knocked me out; but I could not bring myself to take it in my hand, so terrible was its stench.

I found my mother as terrified as I was; nameless carrion had fallen into the hearth, right down to her feet, through the hole in our chimney.

I won't be caught *mocking the High Hunt* any more!..."

We will take care to add to this anecdote a single commentary. We give it for what it is worth, believing at least that the narrator is a sincere and convinced man.

---

49 Melody.
50 High register of the human voice using the upper cavities of the vocal apparatus to make sounds resonate.
51 Here I translate the peasant's long circumlocutions to the best of my ability.

As we have said, the sorcerer is also sincere: most of the time unshakeable in his belief in the devil –his master– it is in the name of Hell that he vainly promises, threatens, curses and, although based on his faith in a lie, his power is not in vain.[52]

Faith turns mountains upside down, said Christ... Sad faith, you will think, the faith of these people! But sad or not, blind or enlightened, passive or active, it is always FAITH.

Whether it is a magician or a sorcerer, do not look elsewhere for the secret of the Occult Force.

– It is there.

---

[52] We are careful not to claim that the power of sorcerers extends to all the works that we have attributed to them, legend in hand. It will be seen later in this work that we may be less gullible than many unbelievers by profession.

EVOCATION OF THE DEVIL

(original drawing by Mr. Wirth)

CHAPTER III
Works of Witchcraft
ג

The Empress = the Ternary = the Connection = the Word... *Works of Witchcraft*

But the Magician is not in question; only the Sorcerer is. – The worker being known to us, it is time to come to its work. It will provide the subject of this chapter III.

We will deal with witchcraft, which can be defined as the putting into action, for evil purposes, the occult forces of nature.

Already earlier, sketching the silhouette of the Devil and the portrait of the sorcerer, we have more than touched on the theme of this discourse. This was necessary for the pleasure of our first pages. The painting of the Sabbath, in particular, has synthesised and concretised on the spot the ceremonial of a certain number of evil spells, performed in the traditional order of their grouping.

But after the synthesis, whose role is to drown the details in the harmonious fusion of an overall view, must come the analysis which, bringing these diverse objects one after the other to the foreground, restores the firmness and the line to their contours; to their surfaces, the variety of shades that nuance them... In short, we had to reserve for this hour the examination of the spells by the menu and the scrupulous specification of the usual rites of the black magician.

It is not a folly reading but that of a Ritual, and to sum up the ritual of the saddest of pontiffs is, in short, our present task. Let us hope that the benevolent attention of the audience will not grow too weary of the implacable monotony of such a nomenclature. At least let us try to break the didactic boredom, with the help of a few anecdotes.

Need I remind you that we repudiate any explanatory comment at the moment? *The Key to Black Magic*[1] will open up for us these mysteries, and we shall

---
1 Second Septenary of *The Serpent of Genesis*.

then distinguish what is real and terrible in the almost unlimited power which the unanimous consensus of the peoples has constantly lent to the sinister practitioners of Goetia; the raison of being of this power will be revealed to us at the same time as the mechanism of its effects.

It is only then that the judicious reader will consider himself in a position to give an opinion, and will be able to do so without presumption, by comparing the documents provided with his proper examination and the explanations offered with his sagacious evaluation.

Until then, it would seem that any opinion should be postponed.

The same cannot be said of the writer, whose first duty is to sacrifice the very logic of his plan for the sake of interest and, in all things, for the sake of clarity.

If, in this first septenary, in which the summary of commonly accepted opinions should alone find its place in relation to the alleged facts, the author sometimes allows his own feelings to be prejudged, or betrays his doctrinal preferences by chance, he certainly apologises for this as a *defect of form*. But the correction of the *dogmatic content* is the essential thing. At least he believes so, and the goal he has aimed at will undoubtedly be achieved if his conclusions, prematurely guessed or sensed at the wrong time, find their justification twice, in the eloquent plea of the facts themselves, and in the rational sequence of the hypotheses explaining these facts.

As we have seen, the Devil is the ape of God; the sorcerer is the ape of the priest. The analogy may well extended, for witchcraft has always been the depraved image of religions, as an inverted priesthood.

What, in fact, is a religion? – It is, on the one hand, a set of dogmas and expressive symbols of the great truths of the celestial Mysticism; on the other hand, a set of sacramental rites, which are the active translation and living adaptation of these symbols: all things destined, as it were, to serve as a link between the divinity and men, between heaven and earth.

The purpose of *Religion* is to *connect* (*religare*) fallen humanity with its heavenly type, the Eternal Word.

If we turn this definition upside down, it would be perfectly suited to witchcraft, a kind of religion reflected in the infernal mirror, which reverses and distorts its image. Imagine God upside down, and you will have the Devil; this is one of the well-known axioms of the Kabbalah: *Dæmon est Deus inversus*.[2]

Witchcraft has its negative dogmas, its symbols of error and its rites of abomination. It has its sacraments; one can even distinguish in them *matter* and *form*, like those administered by the Church.

The matter of the spell consists of a sensitive object, which serves as a symbolic basis for the false faith of the sorcerer, as an express translation to his evil intention, as well as to his fatal will it still serves as a support. – The form of the spell is the

---

2 One reads in the *Collection des Kabbalistes de Pistorius* (Kabbalistic Collection of Pistorius) (*Artis cabbalisticæ*... Tomus 1, *ex Pistonii Bibliotheca*, Basileæ, 1587, in-folio, page 792): "Eædem sunt litteræ nominis Cacodæmonis (which is princeps mundi huius) and nominis יהוה. And qui sciuerit ordinare transpositum, deducet unum ex alio."

expressive sign of the diabolical infusion, the occult manifestation of the intentional verb, which consecrates the matter for a prefixed purpose and strives it in the desired direction in advance.

All the theorists of Goetia, with Jamaica in mind, speak of *substances suitable for receiving the gods* (pneumatic impregnation) and of *signs* that have the virtue of *binding the gods* to these substances. Who would not immediately recognise the matter and form of the magic sacrament?[3]

Sacramental theory is identical in Religion, in Black Magic and in High Magic. Whether we examine the priest in the administration of baptism, the sorcerer in the practice of bewitchment or enchantment, or the magician in the making of a talisman or a pantacle, it will likewise be impossible for us to ignore the sacramental character of these three operations,[4] holy or sacrilegious, beneficial or harmful, whatever. Now, this character is twofold; it consists essentially –and this cannot be over-emphasised– in the combination of two complementary and mutually indispensable elements: the matter of the sacrament and its form; in other words, the *body* of the sacrament and its *soul*. The intention alone varies, – but either natural water for baptism, or a wax figure for bewitchment, or a metal washer for talismanic infusion, these various objects constitute the sacramental material. And, on the other hand, either celestial invocation, infernal imprecation, or magical consecration, the words spoken constitute the sacramental form.

Having said this, and without insisting further on this threefold comparison, let us leave the reader the easy task of deducing the numerous analogies similar to this one; let us finally enter into the exclusive domain of Black Magic, to stick henceforth as much as possible to the pure and simple description of its rites and mysteries.

We can divide the spell-makers into three main categories, according to the motive attributable to them. The first class would include the dupes of unhealthy curiosity or foolish pride: to impose them on other men by the ostentation of a supernatural power, what a dream!… The second class would embrace those who are devoured by blind hatred or jealousy, who are drunk with vengeance and do evil for evil's sake. Finally, the third class of black magicians would be those who have allowed themselves to be seduced by the prospect of imaginary lucre, by the suggestions of avarice or lust, and whose aim is to satisfy their greedy or brutal passions.

As for the sorcerer's own works, they can be more naturally divided into three main classes: his crimes against God, against himself and against his neighbours.

Less synthetic and less complete, though more detailed, is Bodin's distribution in Book IV of *Démonomanie* (Demonomany). – He counts fifteen detestable crimes, which, if we are to believe him, burden the conscience of almost all sorcerers: "It

---

[3] The famous Cornelius Agrippa, indirect and late heir of this school, more learned than irreproachable, is no less formal on this point; he returns to it very often in his *Occult Philosophy*. Read in particular chapter XI of Book One: How the occult virtues are infused into the species of things through ideas, through the soul of the world, etc… There we find this excellent formula, which gives the key to talismanic science: Things below receive as much strength and virtue from heaven as matter is willing to receive, *Occult Philosophy*. The Hague, 1727, 2 vol. in-8, figures, – page 32.

[4] I use the terms *sacrament* and *sacramental*, in their widest sense.

has been well verified –he says–, that sorcerers who have express dealings with the Devil are usually guilty of all or most of these wickednesses".⁵ (1) Here is a shortened enumeration: 1° divine lese-majesty; – 2° blasphemy; – 3° homage to the Devil; – 4° abandonment to the Devil of children born or unborn; – 5° sacrifice to the Devil of the said children; – 6° their consecration to the Devil from the womb; – 7° oath of satanic propaganda; – 8° oath taken in the name of the Devil and in his honour; – 9° incest; – 10° homicide, in order to obtain the flesh and human organs required for the making of charms; – 11° anthropophagy, customary for Sabbath guests; – 12° the use of poisons and philtres; – 13° the sort that kills cattle; – 14° the sort that sterilises the earth, causes hail and destroys the harvest; – 15° finally, carnal copulation with demons and monsters vomited by hell.

It would be easy, from the retrospective point of view of the laws in force throughout the Middle Ages and of the jurisprudence that still prevailed at the time Bodin lived, to point out the gaps that make this classification incomplete and vicious: it is important to note, among other things, the omission of the crime of heresy, infallibly imputable to any sorcerer. This crime –in the same way as those of evocation and adoration of the Devil, discussed in the previous chapter– falls, depending on one's point of view, into the two categories of insult to God and serious offences against oneself.

In any case, we will have to deal above all with evil spells, or spells perpetrated with a view to harming one's neighbour.

Harming our neighbour is the great ambition of Satan's vassals.

But, before going into the details of the most common superstitious practices of these wretches, it seems appropriate to produce, by way of example, an obvious and well-established fact of an effective spell, which we borrow from the judicial chronicles of the seventeenth century.

It is fair to observe, to the honour of the Parliament of Paris, that the tradition was to show, in matters of witchcraft, a relative moderation. The jurisprudence of the Boguet and Remigius was not allowed there; but, in contrast to the provincial parliaments, where it was customary to light pyres for the simple offence of superstition,⁶ the magistrates of Paris usually only delivered to the flames sorcerers, after being were duly convinced that they had, by their manoeuvres, caused the death of a person, or at least material damage, such as the loss of livestock or the ruin of harvests.

The Bailiff of Pacy had sentenced several shepherds to the torments of rope and fire for the latter crimes, but in the absence of conclusive evidence (this was between 1687 and 1691), and Parliament felt it had to overturn the verdict of the court of first instance and replace the death penalty with that of the galleys. The guilt of the defendants, who were the authors of the damage suffered, was held to be a constant, but was the devastation caused by magical operations or simply by natural means? – The Court was reluctant to rule.

---

5   *Démonom.*, p. 221, a.
The least of these crimes deserves, according to Bodin, exquisite death.
6   The sovereign courts of Bordeaux and Rouen were distinguished above all else by their indescribable fanaticism...

The decisive evidence was not long in coming, and the evidence in the trial of Shepherd Hocque was so conclusive that the resonance of this series of cases tired all the echoes in Europe.

The facts are peculiar. I want to provide a brief summary of them.

The trial against Hocque had as its motive the strange contagion which was then decimating the cattle. The public voice denounced him as the author of this calamity.

Sentenced only to the galleys by the Haute-Justice of Pacy, on September 2, 1687, Hocque appealed against the bailiff's sentence. However, in the disputed witchcraft case, the Paris court only reviewed death sentences. This was not the case with his sentence, which was confirmed by a decision of Parliament on the following October 4. The first judge's leniency, this time in line with the case law of the appeals chamber, betrayed his doubts as to the efficient cause of the epidemic, as he had only pronounced the sentence on the poisoners of herds "by means of drugs and other natural means". In the meantime, notwithstanding the arrest of the shepherd, mortality was more intense among the livestock. Hence a thousand conjectures and the suspicion that they had been mistaken.

In order to clear up the matter –Hocque was still in prison in Paris– it was decided to give him a certain Béatrix as his chain companion, who was one of the variety of snitches that had been named after *sheep*.

Let us follow the course of events. The trick succeeded as well as one could wish. Beatrix made the shepherd drink and he, without any mistrust, explained the enigma. He confessed to having buried, in a stable he indicated, "a magical poisoning charge, called the nine conjure words". The epidemic will not stop, he said, until the spell is destroyed.

What does Beatrix do? He goes to tell everything to the Commandant de la Tournelle, a man of prudence and advice, who orders him to make the sorcerer drink again, in order to obtain from him the breaking of the spell. Hocque, in the fumes of the wine, consents to everything, without thinking that the immediate effect which must follow the lifting of the spell will be the of his author. For there is a fearsome law in Goetia –the so-called law of *shock in return*– that any magical poisoning current, diverted from the goal it was supposed to strike, returns to its point of emission with double violence; from then on, the bewitcher is lost without resources, if he does not have the skill to deflect the deadly influx on the head of a third person – substitute victim who would die in his place.

Quite drunk, the shepherd writes to his son Nicolas Hocque to have the charge lifted by a Burgundian sorcerer named Bras-de-fer; he relies on this colleague, limiting himself to prescribing that his own name not be pronounced. But when, barely sober, Hocque learns that his letter has gone, he becomes lucid again, and rages with indescribable fury against Beatrix: "You are going to be the cause of my death –he exclaims–, you will die! Because you entrapped me". And with the help of other convicts, always eager to punish a snitch, he sets about strangling Beatrix. No doubt the snitch would have died there, had it not been for the sudden intervention of the Commandant of the Tournelle, who shows himself already surrounded by people at arms, suppresses the sedition that is rumbling, and puts Béatrix in safety.

However, Bras-de-Fer, called to Pacy, manages "by means of execrable figures and impiety, to discover the spot in the stables where the poisoning charge lies, which he digs up and hastens to burn, in the presence of the farmer and the farm boys.". But, at the moment –says the authentic account– he testified that he was very sorry and that the Spirit had revealed to him that it was Hocque who had made the charge and that he had died six leagues from the said Pacy in the time he had lifted it (without knowing that he was in Paris in prison). *This turned out to be true, as much by the information given by the Commissary the Marié at the Château de la Tournelle, as by that given by the judge of Pacy on the spot, that on the same day and at the same time that Bras-de-fer had begun to lift the charge, Hocque, who was one of the strongest and most robust men, had died in an instant, in strange convulsions and tormenting himself like a possessed man,* without wanting to hear about God or confession; which made it clear that there was something supernatural about the shepherds' spells..."

The Court clerk's office has kept the authentic documents "of Bras-de-fer trial, as well as the trial of the children of the said Hocque, and those named Pierre Petit and Jean Berger, who were found to be accomplices..." The account continues in these terms: "The shepherds were found to have seized handwritten books containing various means of killing cattle, and to have attempted to kill men and women. *And those who were caught and interrogated admitted having made charges of poisoning the cattle, called among them* THE BEAUTIFUL SACRED GOD, *with parts of the Holy Host that they took at communion, animal excrement and a writing with blood of the same animals mixed with holy water and the words mentioned in the trial.*"

In 1691, two sorcerers from the same band, Pierre Biaule and Médard Lavaux, were again seized and hanged and burned on December 2, 1691, in execution of a sentence of the Bailiff of the Chatelain of Pacy, dated October 2 of the same year and confirmed this time by Parliament four days before the execution.

We know now what our fathers called a charm.

More than one may be surprised to see this hideous object decorated with such a charming name. The etymology justifies everything; *charm* (*charme* in French), which comes from *carmen*, therefore expresses a preparation made effective by the virtue of magic words, most often rhythmic in origin –*carmina*– sometimes sung; hence the word *Incantation*, which means the very act of this consequence, or rather of this verbal execution, chanted by the *Enchanter*.

We know that charms are all the more powerful, that mixed substances are stranger, more incompatible, more repulsive and, on all things, of such a nature as to confuse the mind by the contrasts of their mixture. *The Key to Black Magic* will make you understand why. It is for a motive very similar to this one that Pico della Mirandola teaches this axiom: "The most incomprehensible words, the most apparently absurd formulas of evocation, are magically the most effective".[7] It is therefore not surprising to read, in the grimoires and even in certain rituals of high theurgy,

---

7 One also reads in the *Oracles* attributed to Zoroaster (cap. de *Dæmonibus et sacrificiis*): "Nomina barbara nunquam mutaveris; sunt enim nomina apud singulos a Deo data, potentiam in Sacris ineffabilem habentia". (Trinum Magicum. Francofurti, 1629, small in-12, p. 345).

whole words and sentences that are rebellious to the wisdom of the most learned linguists. Long before Pico della Mirandola, the theosophist Jamblique, in his book *De Mysteriis* (cap. *de Nominibus divinis*), also resolved the objection raised by Porphyry, touching on the impenetrable meaning of such barbaric names, used in religious ceremonies, these names, he said, which are obscured by their antiquity, deserve all our veneration; ineffable and revealed from on high, they are closer to the language of the gods. – Without disputing these opinions, I note the manifest predilection of the followers of the Goetie for unintelligible words and unheard-of mixtures.

Whether the enchanter elaborates charms with a view to sowing death or letting go the bridle of deranged passions, he always takes care to incorporate holy, blessed or consecrated things, with the most repugnant and often the most obscene materials. This is a peculiar fact to remember; for, as an impure dyarchy, his delirious ambition constantly seems to be to achieve the most sacrilegious and, so to speak, the most intimate profanation, by giving the essentially disparate substances he kneads together a monstrous appearance of homogeneity.

Always this Manichean fury of opposing Heaven and Hell, to mix them up, confuse them, pervert them and thus outrage them one with the other.

Let us take a historical example from the confessions of Magdeleine Bavent, the most famous of the Sisters of Saint Elizabeth of Louviers, whose possession we mention in chapter IV. These confessions were published in the form of Memoirs or Autobiography, by R. P. Desmarets, priest of the Oratory and sub-penitentiary of Rouen, who was Magdeleine's repentant confessor. At the beginning of Chapter VI we read: "Barely fifteen days had passed before Picard (the director of the convent) made some pretext in the garden, where I was with some of the nuns. For this reason I had the discomfort of my periods. He followed us, and as we were stopped at a certain place, he took a Host from a book he was carrying, with which he collected a few lumps of the blood that had fallen into the ground. Then he wrapped it in it, and calling me to him towards the cemetery, took my finger to help him put it in a hole near a rosebush. The girls who were exorcised have said that it was a charm, to attract the nuns to lechery. I don't know what to say… but it was certainly that, for my particular one, I was very inclined to go to the same place where I was assaulted by dirty temptations and fell into impurity." (*Histoire de Magdeleine Bavent, ensemble l'arrêt* (History of Magdeleine Bavent, with the judgement)… etc…, by R. P. Desmarets. Paris, Jacques le Gentil, in-4).

However revolting these details may be, we have had to quote them in support of what we have to say.[8]

The suggestive *charms* of impure love take the characteristic name of Philtres (from the Greek φιλεῖν, to love), especially when they consist of elixirs, drinks that the sorcerer makes his victim drink, or powders, electuaries, which must be mixed with food.

---

8 At least the passage we have chosen can be transcribed; there are others, in the same guise, which we could not bring ourselves to put before the eyes of the public. This is unfortunate for our thesis, but we have respect for the reader. Let's just point out to him, as very interesting from the point of view we are dealing with, the last twelve chapters of this book, rated LK7, 4183, at the, Bibliothèque nationale.

As for murderous charms, it is not appropriate that some authors have given them the name of Philtres... We have seen them qualified more correctly, it seems, as magical poisoning charges.

Sorcery generally refers to any operation of dark magic. The *evil spell* (*maléfice* in French), already a less vague term, although still very elastic, designates any witchcraft rite performed with the aim of harming one's neighbour (mal *facere*). As for the operation perpetrated at a distance, and whose effect must be to make the maleficent languish and perish, or to beat him to death, it is *Bewitchment* itself. "Bewitchment –says Eliphas Lévi–, is a very energetic word in its Gallic simplicity (*envoûtemenet* in French), is the action of taking, so to speak, and *enveloping someone in a whish*, in a formulated will".[9]

In any case, the charmed object is none other than the sacramental matter and the Evil Spell and *Enchantment* is its form.

In Enchantment or Bewitchment (the same thing), the matter takes the name of *Volt* (from the Latin *vultus*, effigy) and the form is called *magical execration*.

The Volt of the classic bewitchment is the figure, modelled in wax, of the person whose loss is sought. The more perfect the resemblance, the more likely the spell is to succeed. If, in the composition of the Volt, the sorcerer can bring in, on the one hand, a few drops of holy chrism or fragments of a consecrated host; and on the other hand, nail clippings, a tooth,[10] or hair of his future victim. The sorcerer thinks that these are all assets in his game, and if him can steal from the victim some old effects, worn a lot, he considers himself happy to carve the fabric he will dress the figure with, as much as possible following the example of his living model.

Tradition dictates that this ridiculous doll should be given all the sacraments that the recipient of the spell may have received: Baptism, Eucharist, Confirmation, Priesthood and even Extreme Unction, if the case arises. The execution is then carried out by piercing this object with poisonous pins, with a great explosion of insults to excite hatred, or by flaying it at certain fateful hours, with shards of glass or poisonous thorns, all disgustingly dirty with corrupted blood.

A toad, to which the name of the one you wish to bewitch is given, also sometimes replaces the wax volt, but the impregnable ceremonies remain the same. Another recipe is to bind the living toad with the hair that one has obtained in advance; after spitting on this ugly bundle, one buries it under the threshold of one's enemy or in any other place that it frequents every day, out of necessity.[11] The toad's elemental

---

9 *Dogme de la haute Magie* (Transcendental Magic Its Doctrine and Ritual).
10 Hence the popular threatening expression, which has become a vague formula for hatred or simply resentment: *Let him beware, I have a tooth against him.*
11 An example of a rather similar spell:
One summer night in 1619, the gravedigger of the Saint-Sulpice cemetery, was awakened by the barks of his watchdog and saw three women busy with an evil spell. They went around the church walls, drawing circles on the ground with their sticks. Soon they went to dig a hole near a carpenter's grave to put their spell in.
The good man, having thought that they were burying the victim of some infanticide, consulted his wife, to find out what course of action to take in such a case. When he returned with his brother, whose help he had asked for, the three witches were on the run. Only one of them,

spirit now attaches itself to the victim and persecutes him to the grave, unless he know how to send him back to the bewitcher.

Eliphas Lévi, who reports this strange rite, observes that the victim can thwart the manoeuvre if he takes care to carry a live toad in a horn box. The same author adds about this repugnant amphibian:

> "The toad itself is not venomous, but it is a sponge for poisons, and is the mushroom of the animal kingdom. Take, then, a plump toad, says Porta, and place it with vipers and asps in a globular bottle. Let poisonous fungi, foxgloves and hemlock be their sole nourishment during a period of several days. Then enrage them by beating, burning and tormenting in every conceivable manner, till they die of rage and hunger; sprinkle their bodies with powdered spurge and ground glass; place them in a well-sealed retort; and extract all their moisture by fire. Let the glass cool; separate the ash of the dead bodies from the incombustible dust which will remain at the bottom of the retort. You will then have two poisons – one liquid, the other a powder. The first will be fully as efficacious as the terrible *Aqua Toffana*; the second, in a few days' time, will cause any person who may have a pinch of it mixed with his drink to grow wilted and old, and subsequently to die amidst horrible sufferings, or in a state of complete collapse. It must be admitted that this recipe has a magical physiognomy of the blackest and most revolting kind, and sickens one by its recollections of the abominable confections of Canidia and Medea".[12]

The rites of bewitchment multiply in a large number of more or less picturesque modes. Eliphas Lévi also mentions the one which consists in nailing in the shape of a cross all the vestiges imprinted on the ground by the one who is thus tried to torment. Strong-headed nails are used "consecrated for works of hatred with the stinking fumigations of Saturn and invocations to evil geniuses".[13]

We shall leave it at that, at least in the traditional forms in Europe and according to the indications mainly collected in the Grimoires that the Middle Ages bequeathed to us.

But how can we ignore the occult and devastating agent of the Voodoo followers, that elusive *nescio quid*, called by them *Mandigoës-Obi*; that unknown power which, in the form of a periodic epidemic, decimates the populations of Santo Domingo and other islands of the West Indies?

The Voodoo sect, if we are to believe Abbé Bertrand, is a brotherhood, or rather a cult brought back from Africa. What would confirm this assertion is, on

---

the wife of the dregs of the people, named Claire Martin, was seized and publicly castigated by the bailiff of Saint-Germain-des-Prés.
But the gravedigger and his brother were unable to discover any newborn child: "Having dug a little earlier with a bone of a dead man's rib, they found a sheep's heart full of nails, dropped in the shape of a half-cross and with bunches of pins attached to it; a horrible thing, which they did not want to touch with their hands, but raised it up and placed it on a fire shovel…"
The witch did not try to deny this spell; she was only treated so gently because of the spontaneity of her confession.
12 *Dogme de la haute Magie* (Transcendental Magic Its Doctrine and Ritual).
13 *Rituel de la haute Magie* (Transcendental Magic Its Doctrine and Ritual), p 242.

the one hand, the striking similarity of the terms *Obi, Oibiyah*, with the typhoonian *Obeah* mentioned in the *Papyrus Anatasi*, the *Ob* of the Hebrews and their spirits *Oboth*,[14] words of Egyptian and perhaps Ethiopic origin, and, on the other hand, the invariable concordance of the magical meanings of these terms, maintained over several scores of centuries, and several thousand leagues away.

The capital ceremony of the followers of Voodoo has a strange air of kinship with that of the Sabbath of the Sorcerers, as described in Chapter II. "The scene –says M. de Mirville–, takes place in the most impenetrable depths of the forest, on the toughest of mountains, on the edge of volcanoes or in the pestiferous marshes. The roll call of the faithful, the observation of the *presence of the Obi*, the bringing of the sistrum[15] and the boiler, the slaughter of a goat that must offer itself to its executioner and die without uttering a single cry, the orgiastic dance, the kneeling before snakes, the dreadful howling, acts of revolting infamy and too often, it is said, the *immolation of a child*. This is the whole programme of the mysterious festival during which all the names designated for revenge are written down.[16]

And the enemies of the sect perish in turn, struck by a mysterious evil, a consumption without appreciable cause!

A European living in Jamaica, M. Lond, tells that, on the denunciation of a poor dying woman by the fact of Voodoo, an exact search was carried out in the hut of an octogenarian black woman, a formidable magician, notoriously designated as such and convinced that she had *unleashed the Obi* on a considerable number of natives… They were new victims every day. A few cords and some small bones; then an earthenware vase full of clay pellets, kneaded, as far as we could make out, with hair and bits of linen; finally, the skull of a cat, the teeth and claws of the same animal, and variously coloured glass beads; this was all that could be seized from the suspect in this hut, which we took care to burn with all that it contained… Immediately, as if by magic, the epidemic ceased.[17] (See the *Bibliothèque Britannique* (British Library), t. IX, page 521).

The Voodoo god, whose power seems limitless, is none other than a sacred serpent for his faithful. Like all those dishonoured by this symbol of all mystical abomination, his cult is linked to the arcane of the Incubus, about which it is so often spoken of in our work.

Powerfully grouped around their high priest, omnipotent minister of occult vengeance, the followers of Voodoo constitute a formidable secret society, which is not without analogy with the Indian sect of the Thugs, already known to our readers.

---

14 *Ob, Oboth*, is the true pronunciation of the terms אוב and אובות, already mentioned, and which are written *Aôb* and *Aôbôth*.
15 A musical instrument much used in ancient Egypt and other Oriental countries.
16 *Des Esprits et de leurs manifestations diverses* (The Spirits and their various manifestations). Paris, 1864, 6 vol. large in-8; volume V, pp. 317-318.
17 These events took place in the latter part of the XVIII century. – The sect of Voodoo is far from being extinct today. Some authors even claim that, since the famous Santo Domingo Revolution, which was undoubtedly its work, this sort of barbaric Freemasonry has taken on a notable extension.

The serpent of Voodoo is, in short, the same tortuous power of destruction, which the Goetian of ancient Egypt evoked in these terms, to help them with their grudges: "Oh you who hate, because you have been driven out, I invoke you, almighty sovereign of the gods, destroyer and depopulator, you who shake up everything that is not defeated! I invoke you, Oh Typhon-Seth!... Behold, I perform the rites prescribed by magic, I summon thee by thy true name. Come to me in truth, for you cannot refuse me... And I too hate this house which is prosperous, this family which is happy: come against them, and overthrow them, for them has insulted me.[18]

Whatever the proper substance of this formidable Agent, whose serpent has always been one of the hieratic emblems, it is certain that she bends to the accomplishment of all mysterious works. And those moderns who think they are directing (under the name of electric fluid), and vaguely suspect (under that of magnetism) two very indirect modifications of its energy, have an inaccurate and distant idea in all respects of the powers that can be developed in oneself by the man who has been able to penetrate the essential nature of this Agent.

Acquiring such knowledge is given only to a rare elite, and those who do acquire it are far from possessing the privileges of the perfect magician. To achieve this, science is only an insufficient condition: one has to combine absolute dominion over the flesh, considerable training, unfailing audacity and the most unalterable composure. That is to say how few *initiates* have become true *adepts*. The author should not flatter himself to count himself among those St. Michaels of the Occult, for whom the dragon is an ever docile and unarmed slave. But such demigods did exist –as witnessed by Moses, Orpheus, Apollonius and so many others– and perhaps even exist today...

They are characterised by a distinctive feature, which makes them unerringly recognisable. They have always and everywhere made use of the magic sceptre for the general good, or at least for the collective good; nowhere and never for personal interest or petty ambition.

Let us close this parenthesis. The works dealt with in our book have nothing to do with these living miracles of science and will. We have pronounced their great names only to awaken providential echoes in the dark crypt where Satan receives the homage of his worthy pontiff: the black magician.

At first glance, he appears to be clothed with the same prerogatives as the Magician of Light. They are sometimes even confused. It is by an optical error, or, as our fathers would have said, it is by the effect of an infernal mirage, that the serpent's liegeman manages to give himself the air of a prince.

The sorcerer has nothing in the world at his disposal: on the contrary, it is the *impersonal* Spirit of Evil that disposes of his poor person and plays with him. – The sorcerer does not accomplish his magic by means of Hell; it is Hell that accomplishes it by means of the sorcerer, whom he drags into his whirlwind of fantastic madness, fatal perversion and universal disorder!

---

18 See the Papyrus Anastasi and Sallier, commented by the Egyptologist Reuvens, in his *Lettres à M. Letronne* (Letters to M. Letronne).

No valet is less free than the black magician, calamitous puppet of the Invisible, unconscious puppet of Evil, he abdicates all *true personality*;[19] he drowns his free will in the fatal ocean of which he will become a wave. But instead, he will be this wave, and the great Occult Power will now act within him, and then –through him– out of him.

This Power will manifest itself in all aspects of evil and disorder. It is through it that we have already seen the last of the slaves, clothed in apparent mastery, influence living beings from a distance, striking them with death, consumption or madness. But the region accessible to his evil spells is not limited to this, as the following will show.

First there are charms that attack the reproductive sense, either to exalt it or to abolish it.

No one is unaware of the despotic empire that has always exercised this unfortunate tyrant of the organism, which has been called the sixth sense, over most men. We know how variable are the whims of his appetite – sometimes stubbornly greedy for the saddest of dishes, or sickly contemptuous when, for him, the table is laid with magnificence.

Sorcerers have always exploited such a random predisposition, to make this fallacious tide of desire rise or fall at will is still a favourite game for certain village charmers, and I must say that they excel at it; it is marvellous to see them depress the venereal appetite to the point of dead calm, or exasperate it to the point of delirium.

I would not swear that the skilful use of stimulants and aphrodisiacs was completely unrelated to their spells; many certainly use these artificial means, which, coming rather from the physiological study of medicine, seem to have nothing to do with witchcraft. But, it must be admitted, these funny people most often demand from black magic practices a result that is neither less immediate nor less effective.

My readers already know the general composition of philtres. As a matter of curiosity, I indicate a few less atrocious, if not less ridiculous recipes to inflame a woman's love; the grimoires prescribe to make her smell an ointment of chypre and ambergris, ground up with the marrow extracted from the left foot of a wolf, or else to give her the left half of a frog skeleton, which one has obtained by placing the living frog on an anthill (the right half would incite hatred, as the left half excites love). According to other classics of witchcraft, the unfortunate woman must be made to take half a drachm of the following preparation: hare testicles and dove liver powdered in a mortar, with the crumbly scales of the blood that has been carefully drawn in April, on a Friday, and dried in the oven, in a small glazed pot. The whole thing is seasoned with sacrilegious ceremonies and magical words, devoid of any reasonable sense.[20]

---

[19] The Magician, on the contrary, abdicates all false personality. This will become clear in Book II.

[20] I quote the incredible recipe proposed by the *Great Albert*, as an antidote to these various philtres: "If a woman has given something to a man to make him love her, and he wants to be free, he shall take her shirt (the woman's) and piss through her head and through her right sleeve; he shall immediately be delivered from all evil spells." (Book II, page 147).

It is well thought that all these recipes of high taste are in themselves vain and without virtue; everything depends, Paracelsus tells us, on the interior and occult Magnesia, that is to say, on the more or less direct power of the charmer on the astral.

The most grotesque formulas are the most effective, the most ridiculous mixtures are the best in the hands of a true sorcerer; since the very contrasts of these incoherent mixtures constitute an adequate element for his disordered will, a base that can serve as a point of support for him.[21]

But let us beware of anticipating the theories of Book II. Our framework restricts us to the sketch of the main spells.

If the spell of love is called a *philtre*, the spell of impotence to love takes the picturesque and naive name of the *nœud de l'aiguillette*.[22]

It is here one of the most usual grievances of the people against sorcerers. What unfortunate people have been killed under this pretext is almost incalculable; it must be said that many times it was done a little lightly? What more frequent displeasure, in fact, at the first nights of love, than this paradoxical stagnation of the flesh, when the heart is nevertheless very interested? In these cases, for want of any other ill-intentioned enchanter, Dame Emotion seems a very sufficient magician to *nœud de l'aiguillette*. This is what our fathers did not want to agree to. If a disappointment of this kind lasted, they would cry out for the curse! They would then go through all the people they knew, or suspected of trading with the Devil, or simply judged capable of harbouring some old grudge against one of the spouses... And woe betide the poor person on whom the suspicions weighed! In the animal world he is less enduring than a lover disturbed in his happiness; it was enough of a confidence mumbled in the ear of the magistrate, that he immediately, with the aim of discovering the real culprit, ordered that all the suspects be subjected to ordinary and extraordinary questions.

Be that as it may, impotence spells have always been one of the most popular charms in every country and, despite its relative innocuousness, one the universally feared, and that attracted mercilessly punishing revenges: "The practice is more common today than ever, since even children are involved in *nœud de l'aiguillette*, which deserves an exemplary punishment...", wrote Boguet, during the reign of Henni IV.[23]

Pierre de Lancre, a contemporary of Boguet, tells us that the terror of this evil spell was so widespread at the beginning of the XVII century that most marriages were celebrated in great secrecy and as if by stealth.

---

21 "...Everything in the mind of a man who loves ardently is effective for love, and everything in the mind of a man who hates greatly is effective for harm and destruction. It is the same in all things to which the spirit is strongly attached, because everything it thinks and does, coming from characters, figures, words, speeches, gestures and the like, *helps the appetite of the soul* and acquires admirable virtues... (Corneille Agrippa, *Philos. occult.*, Volume I, p. 191-192).
22 A spell that was believed to have the power to prevent the consummation of the marriage. This is indeed an old impotence spell. The counter-spell was *dénouer l'aiguillette*.
23 *Discours exécrable des Sorciers*. (Despicable Speech of the Sorcerers). Lyon, Rigaud, 1610, in-8, page 212.

This calls for a word of explanation. It should be noted that the most common rite for this ligature was commonly performed in the Church during the wedding ceremony. The rite is very simple: after having tied a shoelace, one attends the celebration of the marriage. When the rings are exchanged, a first knot is tied with the lace; a second knot is made when the priest pronounces the words essential to the sacrament; and finally, when the spouses are under the sheet, a third knot is made and the impotence spell is done (*Bodin*).

Another procedure consists of interlacing the fingers of one's hands, twisted with the palm out; one begins with the little finger of the left hand and continues slowly until the two thumbs meet, then the charm is perfect. This rite must be performed in the church, at the moment when the husband presents the ring to his wife.

We do not flatter ourselves to detail all the methods of venereal ligature, which, according to Bodin,[24] are more than fifty. Moreover, Abbé J.-B. Thiers, in his great work on *Superstitions qui regardent les sacrements*,[25] treats the question in all its detail, and we refer the reader to pages 503-527 of his volume IV.

THE HAND
OF GLORY

The grimoires mention a large number of other ligatures, which we will dispense with listing them in the menu. Those who are curious will find details of them in chapter XL of Agrippa's first book.[26]

It is difficult for us, however, to pass over in silence this famous numbing spell, which is said to have been used by some thieves to rob a house, without running the chance of being disturbed. This spell is famous in the countryside, under the rather strange name, in truth, of *Hand of Glory*. I confess – says the apocryphal *Little Albert*–, that I have never felt the secret of the Hand of Glory; but I have been present three times at the final judgement of certain scoundrels who confessed under torture... that in the thefts they have committed .... the use of the Hand of Glory was to stupefy and render immobile those to whom it was presented, so that they could move more than if they were dead".[27] It is the hand of a hanged man that is dried in the bright sun, after having been soaked for fifteen days in a mixture of zimat (*sic*), saltpetre, salt and long pepper.

It is then dried in an oven heated with verbena and fern, and a candle is made from the fat of the hanged man, virgin wax and "Laponian sesame". When the thieves want to plunder some house at leisure, they light this candle and,

---

24 The *Grand Albert* gives a more impertinent and buffoonish recipe: "Let us take the penis of a newly killed wolf; let us go to the door of the one we wish to bind and call him by his own name. As soon as he has answered, they will tie the penis with a white thread lace, and the poor man will be powerless at once."
It must be admitted that one would hardly invent a more ridiculous recipe than this. – The recipes for *dénouer l'aiguillette* are of the same kind.
25 *Traité de Superstitions* (Treatise on Superstitions), Paris, 1741, 4 vols. in-12.
26 *La Philosophie occulte* (The Occult Philosophy), Volume I, page 101.
27 Page 117, in the bad modern edition of Paris, Renault, 1839, in-12.

WORKS OF WITCHCRAFT

using the hand of the hanged man as a candle-holder, they enter boldly into the place where they are dealing with; convinced that there were twenty people there, armed to the teeth, all of them will be struck at once with stupor and numbness, so that they will be able to plunder without fear, for not one of the witnesses of their crime will flinch, as long as the magic candle is not extinguished.

This, at least, is what the grimoires compilers, who sing the praises of this prestigious secret, maintain.

The *Glaneur indou-chinois* (Hindu-Chinese Gleaner), which was published in Malacca in the first half of the 19th century, is an example of charm, not without analogy with the glorious hand. Unfortunately, we have no details about the ceremonies used to accomplish it; only the result is known to us:

"Public curiosity –says the Gleaner–, has been aroused in recent days by the discovery of a gang of child thieves of both sexes

This discovery was made by the zeal of a silk weaver, who, while walking through the streets of Canton, recognised his master's child, who had been lost for a few days. *The child turned a stupid glance at him and refused to recognise him.* The weaver took him by force to his father's house.

He was still under the spell of stupidity, but it was not until the Buddha's priests had been called and the effective ceremonies performed on such occasions that the *charm disappeared* and the child, shedding tears, recognized his master and his father. The affair and the miracle were immediately communicated to the government, who found the child thieves. They were six men and three women, who had been doing that job for more than twenty years. They had abducted several thousand children during that time; only ten remained in the house, *all under the influence of the stupefying charm, which, like the one thrown on the weaver's child, disappeared through the prayers and ceremonies of the priests of Buddha*".[28]

This competence in exorcisms is common to the ministers of all the regular priesthoods; it is not unimportant to analyse it.

Earthly representatives of the Heavenly Humanity and proxies of large groups of earthly candidates for this humanity, the priests of all worships have the power to conjure up the collective forces of Evil, in the name of that collective Power of Good which is called the communion of the Chosen Ones. In this case, the immediate success of the Exorcism –for it is one– proves abundantly that the state of stupor into which these children were plunged was not the effect of some narcotic or any other artificial means, but the result of an occult action, whether one wishes to call it a stupefying charm like M. de Mirville who reports the anecdote,[29] or that one prefers to give it the less archaic, and more fashionable name today, of *suggestive phenomenon.*

Before beginning to describe another order of spells, we will again point out the so-called charm of *taciturnity,* so famous in the judicial splendours of Sorcery. *Anaesthetic charm* would be a more exact locution.[30]

---

28 The *Glaneur indou-chinois* (Hindu-Chinese Gleaner) of July 8, 1820.
29 *Des Esprits et de leurs manifestations diverses* (The Spirits and their various manifestations), t. I, page 262.
30 The sorcerer's taciturnity is, in fact, only a consequence of his anaesthetic state.

It was, in essence, a diagram most often drawn on an extremely thin strip of paper. The magicians prosecuted by the justice, having reduced this diagram to the most imperceptible volume, would hide it under their toenails or in a lock of their hair. As long as this palladium was not taken away from them, they faced the most abominable tortures without feeling the slightest discomfort, and without risking losing their way, by letting slip, unexpectedly, the decisive confession of their misdeeds.

Therefore, the first care of the torturer was to cut the patient's nails, to shave his hair (if necessary, his beard), and finally to remove all hair on all the surfaces of his body. Happy could the accused say to himself, that one deigned to stick to these humiliating preliminaries, without carrying out even more outrageous surveys.

There are countless examples of impassive attitudes due to the *spell of taciturnity* in front of the executioner. It is a diploma of stoicism, a patent of sovereign indifference to the cruellest treatments. Its effective virtue cannot be doubted; it is therefore of almost universal use, according to its authors.

In that way, at the height of the torture, one can well hear the sorcerers moaning or even shouting, but it is a fact that we do not see them shedding a tear, no matter how hard they try. What is more, the magistrate is so fully aware of his inability to manifest a phenomenon that is a normal, immediate and primary consequence of physical pain, that he draws a serious indication from it for the accused. This is the case, he believes, for ordering further searches. As soon as the diagram is uncovered and burned, the dry grunts turn into screams interspersed with confessions – and tears flow abundantly.

All authentic relationships agree on this. As for the conclusions to be drawn from this, we have faith in the wisdom of the reader, who is aware neither of the miracles of autosuggestion,[31] nor of the so frequent cases of hysterical anaesthesia.

The pernicious influence of the Sorcerer is not limited to the ruin of man and cattle. *Nuisance is his lot*, says the proverb, to justify this saying in every way is his ambition. The spells cast on the harvests did not once pass for the slightest evidence of his universal malevolence. His gaze alone was credited with the sinister privilege of sterilising the earth and harming all beings animated by the breath of life; hence the popular saying: *He has the evil eye.*

Moreover, this scoundrel, an expert in the worst trades, ran a shop selling powders for achieve inheritance, contagion charges and compensation elixirs. His goal? – To abolish all happy fertility; to abort crops and women; to sow death at home and in the stable. The worker of these precious tasks showed two faces like Janus; poisoner or sorcerer – the choice was yours: double competence!

The mould, collected at night from the skulls of the hanged men, soaked in his boxes or distilled in his retorts with the foam of toads and the drool of vipers. The vegetable kingdom provided its poisons, the animal kingdom its venoms, in a jumble; and pale, ragged, sordid, one could see the irreconcilable enemy of men and things consuming, with homicidal or sacrilegious words, the subversive union of

---

31 Let us hasten to add that there was something more to it.

these heterogeneous ingredients, astonished to feel themselves kneaded together, at the fancies of the sorcerer's madness.

We have indicated above the ridiculous origin of the elixirs that the Devil himself, if we are to believe the Legend, distributed to the faithful of the Black Mass. "A witch told in the year 1583 that she threw certain powder into the air, which her Master had given to her, from which were born those beasts that gnaw away at the fruits of the earth in a short time".[32] It goes without saying that she was burned.

It would be easy to multiply similar examples, but I prefer to tell a slightly different anecdote, reported by several demonographers.[33]

A farmer from the diocese of Trier watching his daughter (only eight years old), who is planting cabbages in the vegetable garden, sees that she is doing very well and congratulates her on her skill. – I'm good at a lot of other things –the child answers mysteriously. You see, the weather is serene, the sky without a cloud: well, tell me where in the garden you want me to make it rain? – The astonished father points to a small lawn in the enclosure; then he observes the little girl who has withdrawn to a secluded spot. With increasing astonishment, he sees her digging a hole in the ground with the help of a hazel stick; this fills the pit with a peculiar liquid, the origin of which I leave it to be guessed; the fact is that she doesn't look for it very far, having only to crouch down for this exercise... At last he sees her beating with her wand the surface of this artificial pond, mumbling words that don't reach him. Suddenly a shiver seizes the spectator, whose scepticism had not been shaken by these strange preparations, he thought he saw a faint cloud condensing above the square of grass; no doubt about it, because the sun, always as bright as ever in such a limpid azure, drapes its rays over this light fog, determining a perfect rainbow; – and now the meteor resolves itself into fine and abundant droplets... The rain is wonderfully contained within the agreed limits, not a single drop falls outside. The brave man, dismayed to have such a precocious witch in his family, wants to know who was her master in an obviously suspicious art. The child, pressed by her father questions, ends up confessing that her mother led her to the Sabbath; as for her knowledge, she keeps it as a secret with her *good friend*, the Lord with the forked foot. It is clear that these revelations are not to alleviate the father's terror, which is mixed with fierce scruples of conscience... In short, long perplexed, he resigned himself to taking sides and, being a good Christian, he handed over his own wife to the magistrate, washing his hands, like Pilate. "And she was burned alive", concludes the chronicle. Nothing could be simpler or more natural.

Hail, storms, drought or thunderstorm, as the case may be, were obtained by recipes quite similar to this one. This is at least what results from the concordance of confessions and free testimonies given in court by those accused of witchcraft.

Without entering into a discussion of the facts, we cannot fail to note in passing the air of kinship that links these spells to the phenomena obtained every day by the Hindu Fakirs, by the admission of even the most sceptical witnesses.[34]

---

32 Boguet, *Discours des Sorciers* (Discourse of the Sorcerers), page 243.
33 Among others, Delrio.
34 See *Le Spiritisme dans l'Inde* (Spiritism in India), by Jacolliot, pp. 228-361.

These bewitchers seem to act with relative omnipotence on an igneous fluid (AKASA) more subtle than lightning, so famous itself in the splendours of the supernatural.

If demonologists are to be believed, the Fire of Heaven is a vehicle dear to the evil spirits, who have become accustomed to using the whole of nature to contribute to our ruin. In this respect, witchcraft libels are full of conclusive anecdotes – and these legends from another age seem to have nothing to surprise us.

For it is well known how zealous our forefathers were in endowing a conscious self to all the impersonal or merely instinctive forces of nature; this was the naive Christians' ultimate protest against idolatry, abjured in its pagan form, but ingenious in its most orthodox travesties, and always alive, despite appearances.

The gods, precipitated from Olympus, had taken refuge in Hell; now mere demons, they had acquired the right of citizenship in the new faith, at the price of a double sacrifice of self-respect, the acceptance of a subordinate role and the opprobrium of a virtual torture, it is true, but exacerbated by a corrosive flow of anathemas and exorcisms without respite.

Surely, among all natural agents, lightning is superlatively mysterious and fateful in appearance. That, from then on, any lightning, more livid and blinding than any other lightning was, for the imaginations of the Middle Ages, a pretext for a sudden outbreak of imps, one more strike, there is nothing there that surprises us.

But what will we think of the serious and disturbing confessions that a very honourable contemporary scientist, who is certainly a naive only in name,[35] once confided to the *Ami des Sciences* (Friend of Science), the journal of Mr Victor Meunier? Here are the words of this physicist:

"I have a discovery that frightens me!.... There are two electric forces: one, raw and blind, is produced by the contact of metals and acids; *the other is intelligent and clairvoyant*. Electricity coming from the hands of Galvani, Nobili and Mateucci; the raw current followed Jacobi, Bonelli and Moncel, while the *intellectual current* followed Boisrobert, Thilorier and the Chevalier Duplanty... *The Thunder in a Ball, or globular electricity contains* A THOUGHT *that disobeys Newton and Mariotte, to do as it pleases.*

In the *Annals of the Academy* there are thousands of proofs of Lightning's intelligence... But I realise that I am getting carried away. I have hardly let go of the KEY that will show us the universal principle governing the two worlds: the material and the intellectual".[36]

What could be stranger than such confidence coming from a serious person, if it were not for the reticence of a man of such weight, a scientist renowned throughout Europe for the firmness of his mind, the extent of his knowledge and more than one discovery in the field of the natural sciences?

But no more comments; this is not the place to discuss the opinions of the physicist Jobard. In this first septenary, we will simply collate the facts.

---

35 Jobard, a French scientist, who died in Brussels in 1861. In French *jobard* means naive, gullible.
36 *L'Ami des Sciences* (Friend of Science), No. 2 March 1856, page 67.

WORKS OF WITCHCRAFT

We will quote two rather typical ones, on the high exploits of the Spirit Lightning. The first one has no other authenticity than the testimony of simple people, most inclined to retrospective hallucination. Told by a XVII century author, quoted by Abbot Lenglet-Dufresnoy. The anecdote is significantly pushed to the supernatural;[37] nevertheless, it is curious enough to find its place in a chapter dealing with devils and witchcraft.

THE GREAT FIRE, THUNDER AND LIGHTNING OF THE SKY *occurred on the Cathedral Church of Quimpercorentin, with the vision of a horrible and very dreadful Demon in the fire on the said Church.*[38]

"On Saturday, the first day of February 1620, a great misfortune and disaster occurred in the town of Quimpercorentin, when a beautiful and high Pyramid covered with lead, on the nave of the great Church and on the crossing of the said nave, was completely burnt by lightning and fire from Heaven, from the top to the said nave, without being able to bring any remedy. And to know the beginning and the end, it is that on the said day of the seven and a half hours tending to eight in the morning, there was a terrible thunderbolt and lightning among other things; and at that moment there was seen a horrible and dreadful Demon, in a great wave of hail seizing the said pyramid from above and below the cross, being the said Demon of green colour, having a long tail of the same colour. No fire or smoke appeared on the said pyramid until about one o'clock in the afternoon, when the smoke began to come out from the top of the pyramid and lasted for a quarter of an hour; and from the same place the fire began to appear little by little, increasing in size as it descended from the top to the bottom, so much so that it became so great and so dreadful that it was feared that the whole Church might be burned, and not only the whole Church, but also the whole city. All the treasures of the said church were pulled out, the neighbours of the church had their goods transported as far as they could for fear of fire. More than four hundred men worked to extinguish the fire, and they could do nothing about it. Processions went around the Church and other churches, each one in prayer. Finally, the fire kept growing, as it found more wood. Finally, for any resolution, the Holy Relics were placed on the nave of the said Church, near and in front of the fire. Gentlemen of the Chapter (in the absence of the Bishop) began to conjure up this evil Demon, whom everyone could see openly in the fire, sometimes green, sometimes yellow and blue; throwing the Agnus Dei into it and about one hundred and fifty barrels of water, forty or fifty carts of dung, and yet the fire continued. And as a last resolution, they had rye bread thrown from four floors, in which they put a consecrated Host, then they took holy water with milk from a woman nurse of good life, and all this was thrown into the fire, and immediately the Demon was forced to leave the fire, and before he went out, he made such a

---

37 The word supernatural is in our eyes highly inappropriate, and we will be careful to avoid it in metaphysical developments where it could create confusion. Everywhere else, we shall use it in the vulgar sense which usage has consecrated.
38 First published in Rennes, by Jean DURAND, 1620; then reprinted in Paris, by Abraham SAUGRIN.

great commotion, that it seemed as if we were all burnt, and that he was going to take the Church and everything with him: and whistling, he went out at half past six in the evening of the said day, without doing any harm (thank God) that the total ruin of the said pyramid, valued in at least twelve thousand crowns.

After this wicked being was out, the fire was overcome. And a short time later, the said rye bread was still in essence, without being damaged in any way, because the crust was a little black.

And at about half past eight or nine, after all the fire had been put out, the bell rang to gather the people together to give thanks to God.

Gentlemen of the Chapter with the choristers and musicians sang the *Te Deum* and a *Stabat mater* in the Chapel of the Trinity at nine o'clock in the evening.

Thanks be to God, no one died, although three or four were wounded.

It is not possible to see anything more horrible and dreadful than the said fire." – END.[39]

This narrative is doubly precious to us, in that it consecrates, by means of a singular example, popular belief in the demons of lightning, and above all in that it describes in detail the exorcisms and other religious ceremonies which our fathers of the last centuries were accustomed to in such cases. — Moreover, although examples of collective and spontaneous hallucinations are quite frequent and duly noted, we would tend to believe that the eyewitness, the narrator of this prodigy, had knowingly put on, on the day of the fire, some magnifying or, to say the least, enchanting glasses.

But here is a more modern fact affirmed by reliable witnesses, and which is not incredible, from any point of view that one examines it. We condense the somewhat diffuse account of M. Gougenot des Mousseaux.[40]

"MARIA OPTIMAM PARTEM ELEGIT, QVÆ NON AVFERETVR AB EA."

It was this beautiful and consoling word of Christ that a great Polish lord had engraved in gold letters on the tomb of his beloved daughter, who died at the age of eighteen from a languid illness. Half a day is not over when a storm rumbles in the sky; lightning bursts a pale flash of lightning, branching off into a viper's sting, destroying the metal inscription in two places... Four melted letters, volatilized by the shock of the fluid, leave the holy text mutilated – and with a formula of heavenly love and hope, make a sentence of eternal and supreme reprobation.

"MARIA... IMAM PARTEM ELEGIT, VÆ NON AVFERETVR AB EA". *Mary has chosen her place in the depths of the abyss; anathema on her! Her place will not be taken away from her.*[41]

---

39 See Lenglet-Dufresnoy: *Recueil de Dissertations anciennes et nouvelles sur les Apparitions, les Visions et les Songes* (Collection of Old and New Dissertations on Apparitions, Visions and Songes). – Paris-Avignon, Jean-Noël Leloup, 1754, 4 vol. in-12, volume II, pp. 110-114.
40 Gougenot des Mousseaux, *Mœurs et Pratiques des Démons* (Demonic Habits and Practices), 2nd edict, recast. Paris, Plon, 1865, in-8, pages 15-16.
41 This anecdote is reminiscent of the dazzling omen, the harbinger of Augustus' death.
   In the year 14 of Jesus Christ, lightning struck the inscription on the statue erected in the Champ de Mars in memory of the Conqueror of the Gauls, mutilating the first letter. From

So much for lightning. Let us add that, rightly or wrongly, our ancestors attributed plagues, contagions and food shortages to the influence of evil spirits, as well as unforeseen cataclysms such as cyclones, eruptions and earthquakes.

The Church's exorcisms are the best proof of this attribution, a belief commonly held and sanctioned by the clergy at least as far as the disturbances of the elements are concerned: "I adjure you, hail and wind, that you may resolve yourselves into rain, etc.," we read in the *Rituel de Toul* (Ritual of Toul), page 538. The *Rituals* are full of these formulas.

Now, who where these demons, who –according to the people– unleashed their malevolence through peaceful nature? – The followers of Black Magic!

This is how the Middle Ages, to the great joy of exorcists, rejected any abnormal phenomenon on the account of Hell and its malice, and motivated the vengeful anger of the monsters of Hell, by denouncing the perfidious instigation of the Sorcerer...

Our fathers wanted to find a reason for the miracles; today we deny a priori the possibility of a prodigy. They went too far, perhaps we are falling too far short. They were gullible to the point of often becoming visionaries; we are suspicious to the point of stubbornly closing our eyes to the splendours of the evidence.

The Magician has always been regarded as the confidant of spirits and ghosts from beyond the grave; if his science is royalty, the art of evocation is, without a doubt, the most beautiful jewel in his crown.

It is useless to return here to the evocation of the Devil and the pact which results from it; all the more so as in Chapter V we will touch it.

In Chapter VI, on the subject of spiritists and spiritualists, we shall deal with the evocation of the dead or of any beings who give themselves up as such.

In this chapter we wish only to ask the old Homer for the poetic testimony of the traditional rites of this operation, which is certainly the most daring, whether man is allowed, or rather forbidden, to undertake. Let us open the Odyssey to the first pages of his book IX. Ulysses will scrupulously describe the details of his attempt; let us rely on the competence of a guide who will lead us by the hand through the maze of dark Hades.

For the king of Ithaca it is a matter of consulting the spectre of the divine Tiresias, the magical ceremonies are about to begin.

Having dug a deep pit, Ulysses, in honour of the thin spirits, spreads there in turn honey and pure wine, clear water and flour. Then he passes from prayers to invocations, and, brandishing the sacred iron, he finally slits the throats of the victims on the pit, where the blood flows in black streams.

CÆSAR, the Fire of Heaven made ÆSAR, which was, among the Etruscans, the generic name of the Beings belonging to the race of Gods (אלהים of the Hebrews).

The Thrasyllic magus consulted, saw in the letter C struck down, *the symbol of the one hundred days that still separated Augustus from Apotheosis.* Consequently, he predicted that at the end of this period, he would be placed among the gods. And in fact, death, a hundred days away, struck Caesar Augustus!

Suddenly, from the depths of Erebus, the shadowy people rise up from the shadows; thirsty for the blood they spill, they hurry and scream around the pit, the Prince standing, with his sword in his hand, blocking their path. The repressed shadows are frightened and dissipate, their protective vapours unfurling in volutes. But new ghosts follow them, rushing from the depths of Erebus; Ulysses recognises several comrades-in-arms in the numbers, and these deceased friends beg him to let them drink the mysterious liquid which must lend their inconsistent substance a fleeting objectivity!…

Inflexible, the necromancer, following the occult rite, holds the tip of his sword firmly to the surface of the bloody drink, which the evoked spirit of Tiresias should touch –before anyone else–, with his lips. But now the Prince, hitherto impassive, feels his courage falter: an august and beloved shadow has risen from the abyss… he has recognised his mother!… Unfortunately, the sacred prescriptions do not tolerate any modifications; the law of Fate is not to be trifled with. And, while a sob breaks in his chest, he pushes away the ghost of Anticlea.

At last Tiresias appears, an old man with white hair and a golden sceptre in his hand: "Get back, son of Laertes", he cries out, "take your sword out of this pit and let me drink black blood. When I have drunk, I will reveal the future to you! The soothsayer stretches out his lip to the bloody purple and unravels the weft of Destiny…

The mother of Ulysses is still there, dark and mute; she doesn't recognise her child. The king, dismayed, asks Tiresias for the means to reveal himself to her. The soothsayer's answer is worth noting: "The one of the shadows, whom you will allow to lean over the pit and wet her lips with the blood of the victims, will suddenly recognise you. You will be able to learn from her what you wish to know. But any ghost that you draw away from the sword will flee into the deep night." Ulysses drew his sword from the pit; at last his mother came near, and as soon as she had drunk, she saw him and cried out: "Oh my son, how could you came down to Sheol of Darkness?" While she is talking to him, he rushes three times to kiss the dear dead woman, who three times faints in her arms, like a shadow without consistency, or like a dream that fades away, when one thinks one grasps it.

Such is, in short, Homer's story, a conscientious witness to the rites of his time, and revealing, under this fabulous appearance, more than one profound mystery. Moreover, these ceremonies belong to Black Magic, through the use of sword and blood. The mystical shedding of blood is abominable, as will be explained later (*Key to Black Magic*).

We have nothing to say here about Evocation through the stellar pantacle and the consecrated perfumes; these arcana are those of the High and Divine Magic, and the science of which they are a part will remain a dead letter for the Sorcerer forever.

His science, as a magician of darkness, is quite different. He evokes the spirits of disorder and unconscious perversity; he evokes sexual aberrations and the blind deployment of this subversive force of perdition, which, by compacting the invisible, gives the ghosts of his delirium a harmful objectivity; he evokes vampirism and degrading metamorphoses that gradually assimilate his astral form to the inferior types of animality; he evokes the nameless voluptuousness of the incubus trade.

These are the works of the black magician and truly worthy of him. Of these last two we have said nothing yet, and we want to say a word.

The Incubus and the Succubus are the two spectral forms of a convertible hermaphrodite, if I may say so, predominantly phalloid or cteismorph, depending on whether the brutal being whose appetite evokes it is a witch or a sorcerer.

Named éphialtes by the ancient Greeks, Incubus and Succubus were, in the popular imagination, the personification of the nightmare. Indeed, in painful dreams, the genital organ is often affected. Pleasure, which then takes on all the characteristics of anguish, has paroxysms that are more like suffocation than spasm. Often the two coincide; it is the fusion of all the opposites: suffering and pleasure, desire and disgust. It's the love grumble, Eros' game turned tragic, with a monster for a partner. For the lustful shadow, commonly indecisive, suddenly takes on horrible contours.

Sometimes this fallacious object offers itself in a less fierce aspect, or even with a friendly face. Its manners are more agreeable; the violence that it manifests is gentler; in short, it behaves politely.

In chapter one, we have transcribed in detail the confession of a poor girl, victim of a relatively presentable incubus, brutal and at times violent in intimacy, but not unkempt... In short, more than one young girl would be content with such a gallant, considering it quite possible, despite his extraction. – Le Loyer, adviser to the king at the presidential seat of Angers, offers us another example, which would be judged less tolerable, unless there were special tastes:

"In the land of Marree, there was a girl who found herself fat because of the Devil. She didn't give her parents cause to think about who might have knocked her up, because she abhorred weddings and did not want to be married. They pressed her... She confessed that it was the Devil who slept with her every night, in the shape of a handsome young man. The parents were not satisfied with the girl's answer, they spoke with her chambermaid, who at night brought them into the room with torches. It was then that they saw in the girl's bed a very horrible monster, not shaped like a man. The monster was not content to leave the bed, and a priest was brought in to exorcise it. Finally, the monster went out, but it was with such a din and shattering that he burnt the furniture that was in the room and when he went out he made a hole in the roof of the house. Three days later –said Hector Boëce–, the Witch gave birth to a monster, the ugliest ever born in Scotland, which the midwives suffocated".[42]

This is what Lancre would call "*an unjust disappointment!*"

After the incubus, the succubus!... Hear the story attested by the English Doctor Barnelt. It is about a young guy from Sommerset County, robust and healthy, that a quick consumption leaded in a few months to the threshold of the grave. Every night, visited by a spectre of lust, he succumbed to temptation, in spite of the wise resolutions taken and renewed every day. Finally, terrified by the prospect of imminent death (for evil always gets worse), the young man arms himself with cour-

---

42 *Histoire des Spectres* (History of Spectres), Paris, 1605, in-4, page 315.

age and goes to bed, determined to unmask the ghost. Around midnight, he feels the young succubus slip into bed. With the speed of lightning, he grabs the hair of the nocturnal visitor with his two hands and cries out for light. While some is being brought in, she manages to free herself in a supreme effort, leaving in her lover's hands two handfuls of *white hair*. She was a horrible witch from the neighbourhood, as old as Sarah when she was abducted by Abimelech.[43] And yet the young man asserts that the breath of this creature was a true child's breath, and the firmness of her flesh and her whole being at last announced a twenty-year-old girl, healthy and vigorous. By what illusion could this old hideous woman have given herself such an appearance? Mystery! In any case, here is the portrait drawn by Goerres, from whom I am borrowing this anecdote: "For fifty years, this old woman had passed for a witch. She was thin and dry, bent with age and walked only on crutches. Her voice was hollow, solemn, mysterious, but hypocritical at the same time. His eyes cast a penetrating light that inspired fear".[44]

The story told by Barnelt can serve as a transition between the proper facts of incubus and those of transformation by enchantment on the one hand, and vampiric erraticity on the other.

Who hasn't read some appalling tale of vampires decimating an entire country? The facts are so numerous, so concordant and so solemnly attested, that to deny the real existence of this kind of posthumous disease would be bad faith!

All the narratives are similar: a man with a troubled reputation, a man suspected of trading with Hell, comes to die. Often he has issued some strange prescriptions concerning the manner and place of his burial; after an ambiguous life, he seems to have been concerned to maintain a disturbing attitude until death... In any case, his last intentions are respected by his family, he will sleep his murderer's sleep underground; he has gone from being a sorcerer to being a vampire.[45]

Soon, in fact, many people in the country were dying, victims of a strange and supernatural evil. Well-respected witnesses claim to have seen every night a vagrant ghost assailing passers-by, sometimes in human form and sometimes in the form of a monstrous dog. The same ghost also enters houses and attacks those who are immobilised by sleep; it suffocates them by compressing their chests, several are found dead in their beds in the morning... Those who survive after receiving his harmful visit, drag themselves along painfully, thin, pale, exhausted. All vitality seems to have been taken away from them, in the monster's embrace, so pale are they, for his

---

[43] She was then ninety years old, according to the Vulgate's own account (Genesis, chap. xvii, verse 17). This presupposes that the king of Gerar who kidnapped her (Genesis, chap. XX) had either a very keen taste for pieces of sexual archaeology, or gallant habits whose very violence seems to be the last word of courtesy; or, on the other hand, it proves that perhaps it was neither gallantry nor mature womanhood, but ideographism and allegory.
The small approximation of dates, revealing this anomaly, makes the twentieth chapter a page that militates in favour of the spiritual sense, in spite of modern theologians who deny it in Genesis, as in the other books of our two Testaments.
[44] Goerres, *La Mystique divine, naturelle et diabolique* (The divine, natural and diabolical mysticism), translation Sainte-Foi, Paris, 1854, 5 vol. in-8; tome V. p.303.
[45] Vampirism would be a hereditary evil. Several authors cite families where this disease was regularly transmitted from father to son.

breath and blood was sucked from these unfortunate people. If the vampire's kiss is renewed, they die in the second or third assault…

There is a general consternation.

Then a rumour rises, which grows, accusing the dead. There are whispered accounts of similar events, traditional in some families. It is known that in such circumstances the burial of the bandit from beyond the grave must be violated. Notorious sacrilege, the only remedy for such a great evil.

Are individuals reluctant to take the initiative in such an act? Public pressure is so strong and tenacious that the authorities are forced to intervene. The corpse is exhumed, and the sun shines on the most chilling of shows: a cold, motionless dead body in perfect condition, but the lips are glassy and sometimes the eyes are wide open. The beard, the hair, the nails have grown in an extraordinary spray. The strength seems to have been concentrated in useful places, to preserve the vegetative vitality of the corpse. They follow the custom that has been handed down, nailing the hideous vampire to the ground, passing a stake through his heart. He then shakes his marble sleep and twists, with a last scream, in the convulsions of posthumous agony; streams of red and fluid blood gush out under the iron…, and, according to the energetic expression of Eliphas, the vampire has *woken up in death*. However, it is not all over yet, and in many cases the ghost continues its nocturnal ravages; the cursed corpse must be reduced to ashes so that everything can return to normal.

However unlikely these facts may be, they must be admitted, otherwise all the criteria of historical certainty will be invalidated. Where will the scepticism of scholars stop if they reject the most formal testimonies and invalidate the authentic reports drawn up on the spot by the judicial or municipal authorities?

Moreover, the faith of reasonable people in the existence of vampires must be corroborated to the point of evidence, by comparing these more or less ancient facts with modern facts, if not all the same, at least entirely similar and certified by witnesses who are just as difficult to challenge as the former.

I am referring to the burial of Fakirs in voluntary lethargy, several feet into the ground – and their resurrection, recorded by doctors, after months, sometimes a year of burial in the ground. Every precaution was taken; care was taken to operate with peremptory meticulousness, in order to achieve certainty, which is scientific, unquestionable and absolute. In order to prevent even the possibility of a temptation to commit fraud, cereals were sown and then harvested on the site of the mysterious burial place, where sentries in charge of watching over every moment were renewed night and day, without interruption. Eliphas, in his *Transcendental Magic Its Doctrine and Ritual* reports, with great luxury of detail, a rather conclusive example, vouched for by Doctor Mac Gregor, the English officer Obsborne and General Ventura.[46]

Doctor Gibier, a professor at the Museum, cites a very recent case, which is also reported in *Le Temps*, N° 31, October 1885. I borrow from his beautiful book, the *Analyse des choses* (Analysis of Things)[47] some excerpts relating to this experi-

---

46 The burial of the Fakir lasted ten months, from June 1838 to the end of April 1839.
47 Paris, Dentu, 1890, in-12.

ence, transmitted in great detail by Doctor Honigberger, and certified by Sir Claudius Wade, English minister in residence in Lahore.

After long preparations, Harides the Yoghi tried his luck, in front of Runjet-Sing, rajah of Lahore.

"The adept, surrounded by his disciples and accompanied by the rajah and his court, made his way seriously to the place of the trial. After a linen shroud was laid on the ground, he stood in the middle and turning his face to the East, he sat cross-legged in the pamadzan attitude of Brahma sitting on the Lotus. He appeared to meditate for a moment, then he fixed his gaze on the tip of his nose, after spilling his tongue in the back of his throat. Soon his eyes closed, his limbs stiffened; catalepsy... was manifested.

The followers of the hermit then hastened to colour his lips and close his ears and nostrils with wax-coated linen pads, probably to protect him from insects. They gathered the four corners of the shroud over his head and tied them together. The seal of the rajah was put on the knots and the body was enclosed in a wooden box measuring four by three feet, which was closed tightly and was also covered with the royal seal.

A walled vault, prepared three feet below ground to contain the body of the yogi, received the box, whose dimensions were exactly adapted to this tomb. The door was closed, sealed and filled completely with clay.

However, sentinels were ordered to keep watch day and night around the sepulchre, which was surrounded by thousands of Hindus who had come in pilgrimage to the burial of the saint.

At the end of ten weeks, the agreed term for the exhumation, an even greater number of spectators flocked to the site of the event. The rajah had the clay that had sealed the door removed and recognised that its seal, which closed it, was intact.

The door was opened, the box was taken out with its contents, and when it was found that the seal with which it had been sealed was also intact, it was opened.

Dr. Honigberger remarked that the shroud was covered with mould, which could be explained by the humidity in the vault. The body of the solitary man, hoisted out of the box by his disciples and still surrounded by his shroud, was pressed against the lid and then, without discovering it, hot water was poured over his head. Finally, the shroud that wrapped him was stripped from him, after having checked it and broken the seals.

Then Dr. Honigberger examined him carefully. He was in the same attitude as on the day of the burial, only the head rested on one shoulder. The skin was wrinkled; his limbs were stiff. The whole body was cold, except for the head which had been sprinkled with warm water. The pulse could not be felt in the radials, nor in the arms or temples. The auscultation of the heart indicated nothing but the silence of death...

The lifted eyelid showed only a glassy and deadened eye like that of a corpse.

The disciples and servants washed the body and rubbed the limbs. One of them applied a layer of warm wheat paste to the yogi's skull, which was renewed several times, while another disciple removed the ear and nose pads and opened his mouth with a knife. Harides, like a wax statue, gave no sign that he would come back to life.

After opening his mouth, a disciple took his tongue and brought it back to its normal position, where he held it, as it tended constantly to fall back on the larynx. He rubbed fat on her eyelids and a final application of warm paste was made on his head. At this moment, the ascetic's body was shaken by a twitch, his nostrils dilated, a deep breath was taken, his pulse beat slowly and his limbs warmed up. A little melted butter was put on the tongue, and after this painful scene, the outcome of which seemed doubtful, *the eyes suddenly regained their glow.*

The resurrection of the yogi was complete, and when he saw the rajah, he simply said to him:

–Do you believe me now?

It had taken half an hour to revive him, and after an equal amount of time, although still weak, but dressed in a rich robe of honour and decorated with a necklace of pearls and gold bracelets, he was enthroned at the royal table.

Some time later, the rajah probably challenged the yogi and he was again buried, this time six feet below the ground. The earth was beaten around his coffin, the vault was walled up, earth was poured over it and barley was sown on it. Again according to the same eyewitnesses, Haridès was left in this tomb for four months, after which time he was brought back to life as he had been the first time".[48]

To whatever power one attributes the lethargy of the fakirs and Hindu yogis, and so distant as to suppose it to be from the vampiric state, as we have already described above, one will agree nonetheless that these various examples, also attested and certified several centuries, as well as several thousand leagues apart, support and corroborate each other.

As for *Lycanthropy*, a close kinship obviously links it to vampirism. In both cases, the murderous spectre runs around the countryside in various animal forms; in both cases, it willingly attacks the beings it encounters; the essential difference consists precisely in the fact that the *werewolf*, while its astral form wanders outside, is a living sorcerer sleeping in its bed; and the vampire, on the contrary, is a dead sorcerer who vegetates in its grave.

The term *Lycanthropy* is a very unsuitable term, for the erratic transformations of the sorcerer must be confined to the general form of the wolf; the traditions of dark magic show us that the followers of the Sabbath vary the animal disguises in which they return, once the assembly is over: cat, dog, goat, sheep, and even snail, slug or toad; – the only embarrassment is that of choice. This allows the rabid *demonologists* to come across magicians and witches quite frequently on their way back from the Sabbath, for it would be bad luck not to see any of these various animals on their way.

Returning to the werewolf, let us say that in the real cases of pseudo-morphic bilocation, the instantaneousness of the repercussion phenomenon has been noted many times, which imprints on the inert and absent material body the trace of the

---

48 *Analyse des choses* (Analysis of Things), pages 171-175.

blows and the stigma of the wounds that are borne to the erratic ghost. – An example: "We read that in the diocese of Argentina three damsel witches attacked in the form of cats a villager[49] who was chopping wood, and defending himself, he hit and wounded them badly; for which he was soon afterwards taken prisoner, and there apologising, he made it clear that he had not wounded women, but three cats, who, as evil spirits, had assaulted him to kill him, from which it is discovered that it was a illusion of the devil".[50] The three witches were burnt, as is well known.

It would be appropriate to add here what happened in the year 1588, in a village about two leagues away from Apchon in the high mountains of Auvergne. "A nobleman, being on the vespers at the windows of his castle, saw a hunter of his acquaintance passing by, and asked him to see him when returning from the hunt. The hunter, continuing his way along a plain, was attacked by a large wolf, against which he shot with his arquebus, without wounding him; then he grabbed the wolf by the ears, but at last, being weary, he got rid of the wolf, and stepping back, he took a large hunter's knife which he was carrying, and struck the wolf with it, cutting off one of its legs, which he put back into his pouch after the wolf had fled. Then he went back to the castle of the gentleman, at whose sight he had fought the wolf. The gentleman asked him to tell him about his hunt, which the hunter wanted to do, and thinking of pulling the leg from his pouch, he pulled a hand, which had a golden ring on one of its fingers, which the gentleman recognised as his wife's; this made him suspect her, and having entered the kitchen, he found his wife warming herself, with her arm under her forearm. When he pulled his arm, recognised that her hand was cut off. The gentleman took her harshly and soon, after presented with her hand had, she confessed that she was the one in the shape of a wolf, who had attacked the hunter, and since them she been burned in Ryon".[51]

This wonderful story bears all the characteristics of the apocrypha, that the chatelaine was wounded by repercussion in the hand is not impossible, as we shall see in Book II; but the metamorphosis of the paw in hand, in the hunter's *pouch*, constitutes, in the very hypothesis of such a phenomenon, a notoriously false addition. This detail is, on the part of the judge of Saint-Claude, a stylistic arabesque. Moreover, he does not cite Riom's judgment and reports the adventure only by hearsay. – As it stands, it seemed worthy of being transcribed.

The werewolf was commonly believed to devour the victims of its aggression, preferably young children. Even today, are not terrified toddlers threatened with the werewolf when they are not obedient enough?

Pierre de Lancre has devoted an entire book of his *Tableau de l'inconstance* (Chart of Inconsistency) (pages 235-329, 95 pages in-4) to the werewolf. You should

---

[49] Bodin, reporting the same fact, is even more explicit: "... There were three witches near Strasbourg, who assaulted a ploughman in the form of three big cats and, defending himself, he wounded and chased away the cats, who found themselves in bed sick in the form of very injured women at that very moment…" (*Démonomanie*, page 108, B.).
[50] Valderama, *Histoire générale du monde* (General History of the World). Paris, 1619, in-8. Volume II, page 262.
[51] Boguet, *Discours des Sorciers* (Discourse of the Sorcerers), pp. 341-342.

read his account of the trial of 1603, and of the decision pronounced in red robes at the Bordeaux Parliament, against a thirteen-year-old werewolf guilty of having devoured a boy and a girl. As he went foolish to the court, he was treated leniently, he only was confined to a convent for the rest of his life. Lancre, who went to see him in this retreat, with the praiseworthy aim of supervising his conversion, was frightened by the persistence of his anthropophagous tastes: "He confessed to me, without any ceremony, that he still had an inclination to eat the flesh of small children, among whom the little girls were or would be his delight. I asked him if he would eat it if it were not prohibited, he told me frankly that he would, and better girls than children, because they are more tender And the religious told me, that when they first put him in the convent, they saw him eating in secret the guts or entrails of the fish they were preparing....."[52]

The accusation of anthropophagy has always been maintained in the imagination of the peoples as one of the worst grievances invoked against the servants of Hell. The Stryges, Lamies and Wizards were supposed to cut the throats of children taken from baptism on the Sabbath. Their tender and tasty flesh seemed particularly prized in the Synagogue. However, the following text leads us to believe that, in the absence of thrushes, the witches attacked the blackbirds: "That if the Stryge is convinced that she has eaten a man, she will pay two hundred coins". This is in the chapter LXVII of the *Salic Laws*.

But this isolated text would give rise to a misconception; the commensal of satanic orgies must confess to us his favourite tastes. Rarely leopard, rather hyena or jackal, carrion is his customary and favourite prey. See the trials of all the maniacs whose depositions before the judge have provided material for our description of the Sabbath.

The Sabbath! Pandemonium of turpids and scoundrels, embodied in all forms of ugliness: this is the official theatre of classical and legendary witchcraft.

What should we think of this gloomy comedy, set in an even gloomier setting? What reality should we recognise in it? Did it exist only in the manner of this marvellous forest of Brocéliande, still visible to certain mystics of Finistère (the friends of the enchanter Merlin and the fairy Viviane), but disappeared from the indifferent eyes, and which one would look for in vain on the map of Brittany... – Here is our answer.

First of all, it is certain that flesh and blood sorcerers have held, and still hold, assemblies where all the mysteries of ignominy are practised. We know of some, for our part, which regularly function in the heart of Paris and elsewhere. We bear witness and guarantee their existence; we are eyewitnesses and disgusted guarantors, we shall return to this subject in the sixth chapter.

But there is another Sabbath elsewhere, more formidable and more occult. The physical, material, apparent world is only the crude reverse side of a more subtle world, just as real, *if not more so*: the astral world. This is the domain where Sorcery unfolds all the delirium of its furious intoxication, all the luxury of its arrogant infamy, all the pomp of its criminal nothingness. It is here that it sketches out, in the

---

52 *Tableau de l'inconstance*, page 317.

power to be, the monstrous works which every day abort, in act, on the visible plane; for physical nature can only bring to term the disastrous effects of a discordant cause by violating itself, antipathetic to the harmonious laws of the universe. Thus, since the runts are hardly viable, the evil is less, though still perceptible.

Thus, on the level of material existence, spells and curses have, for sure, disastrous effects, but rarely come to full maturity... This is nevertheless a distressing frequency. Imagine a treacherous, tireless hand sowing poisonous seeds in profusion on the world of the living, but most of these seeds fall on infertile sand, rot in the rain or dry out in the sun, instead of germinating under these two combined influences. Few of them grow a slender, sickly stem and die with the flowering; still few of them bloom and bear fruit: bitter, sparse fruit! It doesn't take much more to poison the passer-by who picks them...

Have you understood the apologue, dear reader?

The sorcerer only manages to do harm unexpectedly and by exception, just as an escaped galley slave commits a crime before being caught, but he is always dragging his ball and the gendarmes are not far away!

The sorcerer has coveted the dictatorship, but he is a slave. Sometimes he revolts and shakes his chain; but the fortune of Spartacus is short-lived and the world has no more to fear from the domination of the black magicians than Rome had to fear from the triumph of the slaves.

Even though the Sorcerer succeeded in doing evil, his works of hatred did not benefit him; he was the first victim.

His great ambition, always disappointed, would be to strike others without receiving the repercussion. It is the universal law of solidarity that causes his misery and his condemnation.

He wallows and struggles in the despair of his final impotence, like the laggards of the Sabbath among the slimy slopes of the gallows orgy.

CHAPTER IV

Human Justice

ד

The Emperor = the Quaternary = the Cubic Base = the Power... Human Justice

מכשפה לא תחיה
ספר ואלה שמות
Maleficos non patieris vivere.[1]
(*Exodus*, XXII, 18)

This laconic verse of Moses, which prescribes *not permit practitioners of the black arts to live* (textual!) serves as an epigraph to the fanatical work of Councillor Pierre de Lancre, who, as all the jurisconsults who have dealt with the crime of magic, never failed to invoke it in support of their bloody thesis, as the divine precept. Therefore the most barbaric laws and ordinances, brought against the Sorcerer by the various legislators, would be nothing more than the legal adaptation and, in a way, the legal echo of this text, propagated from age to age.

---

1 In *Tableau de l'inconstance des mauvais anges et démons* (Scheme of the inconstancy of evil angels and demons...), on its title page. – Lancre mistranslate מכשפה by *Malevolent* (French *Maleficos*); it is a singular feminine meaning the Witch. (*Praestiqiatricem* is the exact term, given by B. Arias Montanus in his Hebraic Bible with an interlinear Latin translation.)
In the twentieth chapter of Leviticus, verse 27, we read: "A man or a woman, in whom there is an oracle-like or a divining spirit, shall be put to death. They shall stone them. So let their blood be upon them".
And in Deuteronomy, chapter XVIII, verse 10-12: "Do not let there be found among you one who would purify his son or daughter by leading them through fire, nor one who consults seers, nor one who observes dreams or omens. Do not let there be found among you one who practices the occult, nor one who uses spells, nor one who consults demonic spirits, nor a diviner, nor one who seeks the truth from the dead. For the Lord abominates all these things..."

123

The customs of stupid ferocity enthroned in the Middle Ages are far from disappearing with it, a resurgence of fanaticism signals the whole of the XVI century and the first half of the XVII.

Burning at the stake seemed –to the most moderate people– to be not only a very just atonement, but barely sufficient, for such heinous crime; since, according to Bodin (one of the authorities on the subject), the spell breaks down into fifteen detestable crimes,[2] the least of which, at his discretion, deserves an *exquisite and crying death*.[3]

Around this time, two voices rose up alone to protest against the excessive rigour that was customary: those of the doctor Jean Wier or Wierus and the Protestant pastor Balthazar Bekker.

Wierus, in his treatise of *Lamiis*,[4] and especially in his great work of the *Illusions et impostures du Diable* (Devil's Illusions and Deceptions),[5] maintains that the sorcerer is not a criminal to be burned, but a sick person to be cured. A proposition that is all the rarer and more unexpected, since Wier disputes neither the power of demons nor the reality of witchcraft. It was a universal outcry of indignation against this generous thinker, to plead the madness of wizards, was it not to declare oneself for them? Then he was the pupil and friend of Cornelius Agrippa, the author of the *Occult Philosophy*, another pretext to put him under suspicion. In short, it was insinuated that he was pleading *pro domo et patria*,[6] and that he himself was a servant of Hell.

Bodin immediately published, following his *Démonomanie*, the *Réfutation des opinions* (Rebuttal of opinions) of Jean Vvier,[7] which begins: "At the end of this work, and about to go to press, the Printer to whom I had given the task sent me a new book of *Lamiis* by Jean Vvier, doctor, in which he supports the sorcerers... Which gave me the opportunity to answer him, not out of hatred, but first of all for the honour of God, against whom he has armed himself. Secondly, in order to dispel the opinion of some judges, to whom this man boasts of having made them change their minds, boasting of having gained the point through his books that sorcerers should be now released, pure and plain,[8] I was astonished at this, for such an opinion must be that of a very ignorant or, indeed, very wicked man. Judging him by his books Jean Vvier, he is a monster, since he is not ignorant; although he is a doctor he teaches in his books a thousand damnable sorceries ... which I have not been able to read without horror"[9] – Further on, we must see with what superb style Bodin dresses him down, as a humble medicaster incapable of high theology, based on "a foundation of urines"!

---

2 See our Chapter III, pages 95-96.
3 *Démonomanie des Sorciers* (Demonomy of Sorcerers), pages 217-220.
4 Basileæ, 1577, in-4.
5 Geneva, 1579, in-8.
6 Master and country.
7 Paris, 1587, in-4.
8 The criminal justice of those times was thus subject to strange intermittences; but it was, on the contrary, around that time, and especially at the beginning of the seventeenth century, that perhaps the most sorcerers were burned.
9 Pages 238-239.

Poor Wierus was preaching in the desert! – Almost a century later, in his *Monde enchanté* (Enchanted World).[10] Balthazar Bekker, in the name of Jesus Christ and charity, took up and accentuated the thesis that Wierus had defended in the name of physiology and medicine; he was no more successful. He was accused of denying the existence of the Devil, and the affair caused a scandal… He was deposed from his ministerial duties by his Dutch colleagues at the synod, to the detriment of his fellow believers.

By denying the figure of the sorcerer, Bekker went too far, it would have been better to stick to Wierus' opinion. I agree in many cases that the goety's adepts are madmen, but first of all they are evil madmen. We know the terrible words of a president of the Assize Court: "If monomania is a disease, it must, when it leads to capital crimes, *be cured in the Grève*".[11]

Many will consider the remedy a little radical… I think, for my part, that human justice cannot and must not prosecute anyone under the charge of casting spells;[12] but the trial of the Marshal of Retz will shortly provide us with an example of the appalling crimes for which spells are sometimes used as a cover; such crimes, without doubt, it is the duty of human justice to seek them out and reach the perpetrators.

In order to judge fairly the cruel Middle Ages and the implacable courts that survived it for centuries, we must know how far the evil influence that those they hunted down under the name of sorcerers could have spread. To get an exact account of the practices familiar to necromancers, to discover the darkness of Black Magic; to distinguish between legend and history, between imagination and reality; to appreciate in a healthy way, both the wickedness and the stupidity of these exploiters of public credulity –who often fool themselves first–; the range of their weapons, the sometimes illusory and sometimes effective nature of their manoeuvres, is more difficult than one might think.

Discernment, penetration, and the special knowledge required make it a delicate task… And without justifying the torture, always atrocious and reprehensible, only a few scholars are able to understand and admit to themselves that most of the spell-breakers deserved, if not the pyre, at least the scaffold.

Moreover, it would be appropriate to allege, in the defence of the judges, the panic of the populations involved and the obscurantism of such a pitiful era. This twofold *mitigating circumstance* will influence the outcome of the impartial history, when all the evidence of the supreme trial is finally gathered and closed, and the counsels and prosecutors will in turn appear at the bar for posterity.

The torment of many innocent people is undoubtedly to be deplored and the wheel of the blind Fortune has crushed more than one! – The panic of the accused,

---

10 Dutch book translated into French (Amsterdam, 1694, 4 vols. in-12).
11 *Grève* was a public square in Paris, situated on the banks of the Seine, in front of the Town Hall, where executions were once carried out.
12 It is not that I contest in certain cases the responsibility of sorcerers, nor above all the criminal character of evil spells; but I challenge, in matters of pure magic, the competence of the magistrate.

the stupidity of the witnesses, the inadequacy of the criminal investigation, too often summary, and committed at the hands of incapable or biased persons; everything conspired to render illusory the securities that any fair legislator always takes care to multiply, around the helpless accused. How often the accused, prematurely treated as guilty, fell victim to the individual ferocity of a prosecutor, or to the collective negligence of magistrates convinced in advance of the crime.

Moreover, when it came to witchcraft, the customary procedure no longer imposed its salutary brake on the examining magistrates, and no longer guaranteed the accused the guarantee of his beneficial routine: it was a *crime of exception!* The powers of the magistrates became discretionary, and often their jurisdiction was declared sovereign in advance and without appeal. It was thus in 1609, when King Henry IV delegated MM. d'Espagnet, President of the Parliament of Bordeaux, and Lancre, councillor, "for the search for sorcerers in the country of Labourt and other neighbouring areas…". And this, in order to make and perfect the trial for them sovereignly, notwithstanding any opposition and appellations".[13] It was thus, in 1634, when King Louis XIII, impatient to alleviate the Cardinal's grudges, gave full powers to Sieur de Laubardemont to go, in Loudun, to strike down the indomitable parish priest of Saint-Pierre, Urbain Grandier.

On the other hand, such criminalists, devoted to demonology had been wise to formulate the Code of Fanaticism in their writings.[14] Unheard of! These incredible regulations were accepted by bailiffs, parliaments, ecclesiastical or mixed tribunals as having the force of law.

It was the victory of delirious prejudices over justice and common sense; it was the apotheosis of arbitrariness, trampling on the law.

Excited, rightly or wrongly, by the weakest clues, public reprobation pointed the finger at the suspects, – and they could say they were doomed, in advance, to be burned at the stake.

All this sad state of affairs seems to imputable to the prejudices of the times more than to men… Whatever the fate of these poor people, and how many ears of pure wheat may have fallen under the sickle, mixed with the chaff, let us not lightly anathematise these judges of the past, they believed it was their duty to cauterise with red-hot iron a leprosy which was growing prosperously everywhere; these terrible surgeons did not fail in their mission; – and the conclusion of this work will, I think, not be, no doubt, their justification, but certainly their honourable excuse.

---

13 Pierre de Lancre, *Inconstance*, etc… (Preface).
14 I am referring above all to Boguet's book (already quoted), whose editions multiplied in a way that was so prodigious for the time: *Discours exécrable des Sorciers, avec six avis en fait de Sorcellerie, et une instruction pour un juge en semblable matière* (Discourse of the Sorcerers, with six opinions on witchcraft and an instruction for a judge on similar matters), by Henry Boguet, Dolanois, Great Judge in the land of Saint-Oyan de Ioux, known as Saint-Claude in the county of Burgundy, being what the author has above brought to light on the same subject, only a sample of what is treated in this book (3rd edition). In Lyon, by Pierre Rigaud, 1610, strong vol. in-8.
This 1610 edition is the *only complete* edition of this long authoritative book.

The truth obliges us to recognise that witchcraft was proscribed at all times by the legislators of the nations and was everywhere punished with the utmost rigour. Let us note the main examples of this.

The *Vendidad-Sadé*[15] forbids, under the most severe penalties, the practice of incantations and charms. This sacred book attributes its invention to the *Yatus*,[16] the enemies of the Zoroaster. If we believe François Lenormant, the Accadian priests taught the art of conjuring bewitchment and making it fall back on the head of the witch guilty of having cast it, by a kind of shock in return: "May she die, and I live," such was the formula of the dismissal.[17]

The *Harris Papyrus*, a very old manuscript discovered in Thebes in 1855, provides the most valuable information on practical magic in Egypt. The translator of this important piece,[18] Mr. Chabas, has deciphered what remains of another manuscript of the same provenance, also traced in secret hieroglyphs; it concerns the trial and death sentence, under Ramses III, of a steward of flocks, perhaps a simple Egyptian shepherd... Among the spells noted against this *hai* (pervert), there is mention of a hand paralysed by the *man of Menh*,[19] as well as other "great abominations. The judgement, conceived in vague terms, reads: *Let him die himself, according to the order of Pharaoh, according to what is written in the lines of the divine language.*

We only need to recall the three formal texts of Moses transcribed at the beginning of this chapter.

No one has forgotten this characteristic feature of the *Book of Kings*: Saul in the pythoness of Endor.[20] Tormented by prophetic terrors, which his conscience, however hardened it was, could not suffocate in her, the king is led, in disguise, to a woman renowned among the people for the divinations she performed, in favour of the *Aôbôth* ghosts; he orders her to evoke the shadow of the prophet Samuel. The witch has some difficulty in obeying, objecting to the law of death renewed against the diviners by Saul himself. The latter reassures her and that decides her; but as soon as the apparition appears to the eyes of the pythoness, she cries out with a loud cry: – Ah, why have you deceived me, for you are Saul.... – Fear not –said the king–, but what have you seen? – I saw the earth open and a god rising from the depths... It is the figure of an old man, draped in a mantle. – Saul, recognising the holy prophet, prostrated himself to the ground; but, worthy of our attention, before predicting his defeat and death to the rejected king of Iod-heveh, Samuel bitterly reproached him for having disturbed his rest from beyond the grave, and especially for having forced him to pass through the dark door that every mortal must pass through only once.

If we pass through Greece, we find a law against enchanters: "It provides that all those who, by charms, words, ligature, waxen image, or other evil spell, enchant

---

15 *Vendidad-Sadé*, I, pp. 52-56.
16 A kind of spirit corresponding to the Greek daimon.
17 *La Magie chez les Chaldéens* (Magic among the Chaldeans), Paris, 1874, in-8, pp. 55-56.
18 Published by him in 1860.
19 Everything suggests that it was a spell by a wax figure.
20 Kings I (Samuel I), XXVIII, verses 7 to 21.

or charm someone, or who use them to kill men or livestock, shall be punished by death".[21]

Plato[22] reports this law. Demosthenes cites its application: Lemnia, witch, put to death on the denunciation of a servant girl. Pausanias[23] mentions a chamber of justice, specially established by the Republic of Athens, to repress the crime of witchcraft, and to put an end to all dangerous and disastrous superstitions in the worship of national gods.

In Rome, the *Law of the Twelve Tables*[24] also strikes with death any citizen guilty of having harmed, by charms or incantations, either persons, livestock or crops. This old legal text even stigmatises the sorcerer by declaring him abominable: *Sacer esto!* – It is known that the Romans did not abuse this imprecation, which was, as Lamarre observes very well, a mark of the highest indignation.

Pierre de Lancre[25] recalls the execution of 170 witches in Rome, under the Consulate of Claudius Marcellus and Valerus Flaccus they had cursed various people, greasing the doors with enchanted ointments.

Under Augustus, exactly all the books of magic that could be found in Rome were searched for: they were immediately burnt, numbering 2,000, by express order of the Emperor. Tiberius and Nero confirmed, with new edicts, the validity of the ancient laws. The latter even banished all philosophers from Italy on the pretext that they were secretly engaged in the art of divination; this did not prevent the prince, with such praiseworthy zeal, from evoking the spirit of his mother Agrippina.

The Christian princes repressed, of course, with the utmost severity, the practice of the cursed sciences, confusing under this name the highest Magic and the most abject Goetia, against which the Council of Ancyre threw its anathemas (314).

In 319 Constantine promulgated a law against the Aruspices; but two years later, another law partially retracted the first one... An increase in severity was seen under Constantius, who ordered (357) that all enchanters should have their heads chopped off.

After the polytheistic restoration attempt of Julian the Wise (known as the Apostate), Magic is generally confused with Paganism itself, in the edicts of the Christian emperors who succeeded him: Jovian, Valentinian, Valens, Hononus, Theodosius, Arcade and Leon.

As for the barbarians who settled in Gaul around this time, their princes were no less severe. Long before the conversion of Clovis to Christianity (496), the Salic law mentions and punishes the crime of spells. Chilpenic III issued an edict against the Sorcerers in 742, and in 772 Charlemagne founded the Holy Vehme to exterminate them in Germany.

Several kings of France provided, by successive ordinances, that such scum should be hunted down and decimated according to the rigour of the laws. We will close this already tedious and yet very incomplete list by mentioning the orders of

---

21 *Traité de la Police* (Treaty of the Police), by M. de Lamarre, volume I, title VII.
22 Plato, *De Legibus*, Book II.
23 Pausanias, *in Elia*..., book V.
24 *Leg. duodecim tabular*..., rt. 55, 68, 69, etc.
25 The *Inconstance*, etc..., page 138.

HUMAN JUSTICE

Charles VIII (1490), the Provost of Paris (1493), Charles IX to the States of Orléans (1560), Henri III to the States of Blois (1579); the royal letters of Louis XIII, dated 20 January 1628, and finally the already less barbaric edict of Louis XIV, dated July 1682, which the Parliament of Paris registered on August 31 of the same year.[26]

As for the bulls thundered by the popes against sorcerers, the decisions of councils, episcopal mandates and other documents emanating from religious authorities, my manager forbids me to touch them, even briefly. – To deal with the story of the competitions between the ecclesiastical and civil powers, the conflicts between the Tribunals of the two orders, and the creation of Mixed Courts, etc... May be the patience of the reader is running out (I imagine), after the dry and monotonous enumeration through which he had the courtesy to follow me earlier.

I will only say, in general terms, as regards France, that an act of parliament, decreed in 1281, at the request of the Bishop of Paris, reserved knowledge of the crimes with which we are concerned exclusively to the clergy;[27] but towards the fifteenth century, case law finally settled down and the judges seized the matter again.

I would again point out the unspeakable Bull of Innocent VIII (1484), which instructed magistrates not to tolerate that the sorcerer (often an idiot and very incapable of defending his life) were represented by a lawyer, or even by a voluntary defender. – In the vast majority of cases, the most ferocious and unscrupulous judges ignored this prohibition, but it is nevertheless typical and indicative of the priestly spirit in the Middle Ages.

Moreover, this defence was, and always will be, a defence of excessive prescriptions that are likely to revolt the public conscience; they were openly violated and, above all, everyone hastened to make them fall into disuse.

Are there any other examples of this? – The *Roman Ritual* reminds the sick that, by the decrees of the Lateran Council and by the writs of several popes, it is forbidden for any doctor, under the most serious penalties, to visit his clients more than three times, without having demanded proof that they have confessed and received absolution for their sins.[28] When was such a prohibition observed?.... I do not know that it was taken into account, even at the time of the most execrable fanaticism.

---

26 There are two related ordinances, both of which are reproduced *in extenso* towards the end of Daugy's work: *Traité sur la Magie, le Sortilège, les Possessions, Obsessions et Maléfices* (Treatise on Magic, Sorcery, Possessions, Obsessions and Curses)... In Paris, by Pierre Prault, 1732, in-12.

These are: 1° *An Edict of the King punishes the various crimes committed by the soothsayers, magicians, sorcerers, poisoners*, etc... (Soothsayers banished from the Kingdom, sacrileges and poisoners punished by death...).

2° A *Declaration of the King issued against the Bohemians and those who give them shelter*... (Gypsies to be sentenced to life imprisonment; Bohemians to be shaved and, in case of recidivism, castigated and banished).

27 For further details see Goerres (*La Mystique*, already cited, volume V, page 358).

28 Here is the exact text of the RITUAL: "An si opus fuerit, tam infirmo quam ejus familiaribus vel propinquis in memoriam revocet, quod Latranensis Concilii, ac plurium Summorum Pontificum decretis *cavetur sub gravibus pœnis, ne medici ultra tertiam vicem ægroios visit, nisi prius certo constet confessionis sacramento rite expiatos fuisse*". (Chapter Visitation and Cura Infirmorum).

Third example. What Rome is so bitterly reproached for having prescribed in barbaric centuries, the Government of Louis-Philippe was not ashamed to repeat in 1832, after the riot in the cloister of Saint-Merry. No, I am mistaken: he dared much worse. M. Gisquet, Prefect of Police, issued a circular, enjoining all doctors to denounce to the Councils of War the wounded to whom they had given their care! For the honour of the French medical profession, this unfortunate civil servant was disobeyed in every respect, not one denunciation was made. This circular had caused such nausea in the public opinion that King Louis-Philippe (either by contagion or modesty) thought he too had to testify that he had been heartened by it.

But let us return to the legal mores of the last few centuries with regard to witchcraft. The last centuries, we say, because, however atrocious the Middle Ages may have been, capital executions, seasoned with nameless cruelties, had never multiplied in history as they did under the last Valois and the first Bourbons.

The jurists, as we have said, had classified the facts we are dealing with as crimes of exception, but we shall see what they meant by this: these crimes are "more serious and more directly aimed at public damage and afflict the Republic in a marvellous and very special way, such as the crime of lese-majesty... heresy... witchcraft... treason... conspiracy... the counterfeiting of money... the robbery..., which crimes are commonly called excepted, because they are truly excepted from the common and ordinary provision of the law, so that in the prosecution and punishment of such crimes, one is not obliged to the common and ordinary proceedings that the law orders for others".[29]

Thus, in matters of Magic, the majority of jurisconsults agree that public rumour, pointing to an individual, legitimises his arrest and torture (Boguet).

That privileges on the basis of age, gender and rank must not be applied (Delrio).

That the son is allowed to testify against his father, the daughter against her mother.[30] (Bodin). A single witness is enough (Boquet).

That under no circumstances should one be spared torture "which is excellent with young girls, young children, and dainty or delicate women". (Bodin.)

It is necessary to shave the whole body of the accused, man or woman, in order to see if he does not hide a charm of taciturnity, "*etiam in partibus secretioribus, si feminæ, sint à feminis, si viri à viris*". (Delrio.)

"One can pass to condemnation of atrocious and secret crimes on the basis of clues, conjectures and presumptions". (Boguet.) – "Spell is indeed a more serious crime than poisoning". (Bodin.)

If there is evidence, or serious presumptions, or if the accused confesses in torment, very rarely is his head cut off; almost everywhere the punishment is a pyre. Sometimes he is buried alive. If he shows great repentance, he may be able to obtain "to be strangled and muzzled before being burned"; this was promised to poor

---

29 *Avis aux Criminalistes sur les abus qui se glissent dans les Procès de Sorcellerie* (Notice to the Criminalists on the abuses that creep into the Witchcraft Trials), etc., in Lyon, by Claude Prost, 1640, in-8, very rare (page 7).

30 In Bodin we find this abominable sentence: "And as for daughters, if they have accused their mothers before they were accused, they deserve forgiveness. A few whips will suffice if they are young and penitent" (Bodin, *Démonomanie*, page 293).

Grandier, but they didn't keep their word; the reader remembers that he was thrown alive into the flames.[31]

If the evidence is completely lacking, the sentence of banishment will be applied, "without ever acquitting any accused" (Boguet).

It was strongly recommended to place letter boxes in churches, where witches could be denounced by anonymous notes (Bodin).

In order to get the suspects to confess, they must be persuaded that, since their accomplices have denounced them, we know where they stand on their crimes. In this way, the judge will be able to see if the accused is confused (Bodin).

Everything we have just read is singularly odious, isn't it? Well, it's not much, and here anything goes!

It is permissible and "an excellent deception" (*sic*) to convince the sorcerer that *the confession will be very useful to him for the redemption of his life; by this we mean eternal life*, the one that must surely be the most precious to him and which he can always deserve by his repentance and sincerity before the judges, his constancy in torture! (*Jesuit Delrio*).

Also they promised the sorcerer that if he confessed, we would be feed with meat and drink wine for the rest of his life, and even they could promise to build him a house. This leaves you free to formulate a small *mental restriction, where the house means a wooden cage in which he will be burned alive, by the rest of his days means the days before he faces the final agony.* Such a ruse is lawful and a good ruse (the same *Delrio*).

Ditto: the sorcerer's lawyer will be allowed to talk freely and alone with his client; but a clerk, hidden in a corner of the room, will have to take notes, in order to condemn the poor devil, caught in the act of confessing (Delrio – Bodin).

But enough of these iniquitous regulations.

It would remain for us to detail the various tortures in use, in order to hasten the "confession" of the guilty party, but we give up on this task, at least on our own; we ask for mercy, our hearts fail us in the end! Brodequin, whip, estrapade, collar, rack, question[32] of water, fire, etc… etc… – We mention instead of describing with confidence that our readers will be grateful for this reserve.[33]

---

31 See our chapter I. – *Urbain Grandier et les Possédées de Loudun* (Urbain Grandier and the possessed of Loudun), by Dr Gabriel Legué (Paris, Baschet, 1880, in-4, fig.).

32 *The Question!*… Isn't there in this single word, taken to be synonymous with *preliminary torture*, the unexpected euphemism of a truly savage irony? *The Question… call for a free confession!…*

33 It is important, however, to give a quick indication of the most common forms of torture. Dr. Regnard summed up the essential details in a few precise and summary lines. We have been able to spare the sensibility of the audience by omitting these descriptions in the body of the speech; since we intended to transcribe in a note this curious excerpt from Dr. Regnard:

"The most ordinary torture in witchcraft trials was the question of the boots (*brodequin*). The leg of the accused was placed between two saws, or between two planks tightened with ropes, and between the leg and the planks wedges were driven in with a mallet. The tightened leg would finally burst, to the point, says an old author, that one could see the *marrow coming out of it*.

Other torture was the *estrapade*, the accused was hanged by the hands from a rope tied to the ceiling, and weights were attached to his feet. He would be left like this until he screamed in pain. Then the judge would order him to confess; if he refused, the executioner would beat him

If there is some overly conscientious person, who pushed the courage of the spirit to the point of wanting to go into everything in depth by the menu, or some pervert who revels in the details of these paintings from another age, we would send them back to the demonographers and historians of the Inquisition. It is there that they would find the perfect and methodical enumeration of all kinds of tortures.[34] We would point out to them, in particular, Book V of Delrio's, *Controverses magiques* (Magic Controversies),[35] which this good Father devoted almost exclusively to torture. Finally, we would point out to them the remarkable lessons of Professor Regnard, brought together in a beautiful volume under this title: *Sorcellerie, magnétisme, morphinisme, délire des grandeur* (Sorcery, Magnetism, Morphinism, Delirium of Greatness).[36] The author, who seems to us to be a delicate person, a researcher and a bibliophile, has reproduced a large number of very curious old woodcuts and copperplates, taken from the books, moreover quite rare and almost unknown, of Guaccius (1608), Gilbert de Vos (1025) and Abraham Palingh (1659). Several of these engravings represent various tortures.

Mr. Regnard had the happy idea of reviving some astonishing verses, long forgotten and which he will allow us to quote after him.[37] The author is that famous judge from Lorraine, Nicolas Remi (or Remigius), who claimed that, out of three people taken at random in the street, there were at least two sorcerers. We remember that he took revenge for the relative disbelief of his contemporaries by denouncing himself, and died happy, burnt alive on his spontaneous confession! The poem he wrote, in order to allow himself this last fantasy, and left as a singular testament to his monomania, had been lost. It seems curious enough to merit the honours of

---

violently with rods, and the jolts that the pain caused to his body would double his torment. If the confession did not come, the executioner raised the witch with a pulley up to the ceiling and let her suddenly fall back onto the pavement of the room. And it would start all over again until the confession.

If the *estrapade* was impotent, we had the rack. It was a triangular wooden beam with a sharp upper angle, on which the accused was placed on horseback. Then a series of weights were hung from her feet. (Thirteen-year-old Marie Carlier was put on the rack in 1647 and remained there for several hours, and it was necessary to add three more weights to make her confess. She was burned alive. Because of her young age, and to avoid the crows having pity of ther, the execution took place at dawn).

We still had the resource of the collar. They called it an iron circle, with nails inside. It was attached to a post, and the accused's neck was placed on it. The spikes were calculated to barely enter the flesh. But the legs of the defendant were roasted with burning embers, and the pain caused her to shake the iron spikes into her throat." (Dr Paul Regnard, *Sorcellerie, magnétisme, morphinisme, délire des grandeur* (Sorcery, magnetism, morphinism, delirium of grandeur). – Paris, Pion et Nourrit, 1887, grand in-8, P. 32-35).

34 At the time of going to press, we are aware of the recent book by M. Jules Baissac: *Les grands jours de la Sorcellerie* (The great days of Witchcraft) (Paris, 1890, large in-8, of more than 700 pages). Although far from subscribing to all the author's conclusions, we cannot ignore the high merit of this study and the immense amount of scholarship to which it bears witness. M. Baissac deals thoroughly with the question of torture and we can do no better than to refer the curious to it. See especially pages 149-167.

35 Translated and condensed by André du Chesne, 1611, p. in-8.

36 This is the work from which we have borrowed the note on the previous page.

37 We will only restore the spelling of the time.

reprinting, so commonly accorded to mediocre and insipid pieces. May a publisher-artist make this wish come true!

> ...In my presence one day this fact happened
> As to my questions, with an embarrassed look on my face
> The witch remained completely mute,
> I guessed a secret cause near her.
> She lowered her eyes and then raised them again.
> By her own gestures, help was calling for...
> I demanded the reason for such great fear;
> The Witch then, deposing the constraint:
> "Alas!" she cried out in great pain,
> "This is the abominable author of all my ills!
> "He stands on this wall, placed in this slot;
> "To cut off my voice, he sows terror.
> "His paws have the contour of the legs of a lobster;
> "He moves in the crack, in and out,
> "Same as the snail that meets a stone.
> "Ah, he's now retreating with his double horn!"
> From the society of wise moderators,
> Of all crimes committed inflexible avengers,
> Judges, don't be afraid to be strict.
> ....
> In your judge to punish the witch.
> On this fact, pronounce the agony of the burning pyre:
> All the centuries will praise these acts of justice!...

The rhyme is not rich and the style is old..., but this piece makes you want to know the rest.

It seems that we have compiled enough information to be granted dispensation from new nomenclatures.

It is not in a few lines that we can retrace the exploits of the demonologists, almost all of whom were judges and legislators. But there would be a beautiful, terrible and captivating book to be made! Each of them signed his work with a stamp of his own; – and this psychological stamp could easily be found when examining the various hecatombs they bloodied around the territory of their respective jurisdictions.

Nicolas Remigius is a mystic of ferocity; the nine hundred witches that he burned in Lorraine in a short space of time are not the only evidence of this; fourteen accused women committed suicide, in order to avoid going through his hands, and he boasts about it in the preface of his book, dedicated to the Cardinal of Lorraine (1596).

The Bishop of Geneva, a great lord of the most haughty, is no less expeditious, some fifteen chandeliers earlier: it was in three months that he burned his five hundred sorcerers.

Grillandus, inquisitor in Arezzo, (1520) confessed one thousand seven hundred and seventy victims; inflexible and solemn, without anger or pity,[38] he is a priest; and no other Doctor, except perhaps the Jesuit Delrio, is more systematic and casuistic.

Sprenger, on the other hand, is compassionate and good; it is out of charity that he grills his thousand or so litigants (1485); he wants to save them from hell, first of all; then, moved by the plagues and miseries of the people, commonly attributed to the followers of black magic, he wants to put an end to this state of affairs, exterminating every last magician.

Pierre de Lancre, adviser to the Parliament of Bordeaux, a man of benevolent nature and easy morals – in love with pretty witches when he didn't burn them. Pierre de Lancre confessed, with incredible flippancy, to having condemned six hundred of them, in the space of three months, in the land of Labourt (1609). According to some historians, it said that it was a thousand.

At the same time, the most ferociously stupid of them all, Henry Boguet, judge in Saint-Claude, had six hundred of them burned at the Burgundian pyres (around 1602).

The author of the *République* (Republic), eloquent lawyer, liberal writer and well ahead of his time, Jean Bodin sketched himself out with the stroke of a pen; he expressed the wish to see the hundreds of thousands of wizards who infested the world gathered together, so that Bodin himself could burn them in a single heap.

As for the *autos-da-fé* of the Roman Inquisition, we shall not insist on them in this chapter; good souls might find it ungodly to assimilate to the justice of men the execution of what they believe to be the justice of God. On the other hand, when we are asked for the benefit of this nominal category, other good souls might well find it ironic – and here we are adrift, from Charybdis to Scylla!

No one can please everyone and his father, says the fable. Will we at least be allowed to get out of this by using a medium-term solution? It will be to limit our pen to indicating the sources, where everyone will be free to go up or not. *L'Histoire de l'Inquisition et son origine* (The History of the Inquisition and its origin),[39] on the one hand, and on the other the *Relation de l'inquisition de Goa* (Relation of the Inquisition of Goa)[40] have always seemed to us to leave nothing to be desired in this respect. The great work by Llorrente, general secretary of the Inquisition, the *'Histoire de*

---

38 A characteristic of Grillandus, told by Michelet: A young man crossing the countryside at the first hour of dawn and following a brook hears himself called out in a very soft, but fearful and trembling voice. And he sees an object of pity there, the white figure of a woman almost naked, except for a pair of pants. Shameful, shivering, she was huddled in the brambles. He recognises a neighbour; she begs him to pull her out of there. "What were you doing there?" – I was looking for my donkey. He doesn't believe it, and then she breaks down in tears… The devil led her to the Sabbath; when he brought her back, he heard a bell and dropped her. She tried to be discreet… Unfortunately the fool could not hold his tongue. She was burnt. Grillandus speaks of her complacently, and says (the sensual butcher): "She was beautiful and quite fat, *pulchra et satis pinguis*." (*La Sorcière* (The Witch), page 445).
39 Cologne, à la Sphère, chez Pierre Marteau, 1693, small in-8.
40 Paris, 1688, in-12, figures.

l'Inquisition d'Espagne (History of the Spanish Inquisition)[41] is still fruitful; nothing could be written more judicious and balanced on such a burning issue.

One of the most important magic trials whose echoes have resounded throughout history is undoubtedly that of the Knights Templar. It would come, in order of date, at the top of the two or three others that we are going to report on, but we believe we have excellent reasons to put it aside. We will come to it last.

Leaving aside the archangelical figure of Joan of Arc and her dazzling epic, the conclusion of which seems as shameful for the King of England (who stubbornly wanted such baseness) as it is for the King of France (who did not risk his crown and his life to prevent it); it is time to remember that we have promised to sketch the profile of the famous Marshal of Brittany, whose legend has taken hold of him to make him Bluebeard.

This magnificent and deplorable Gilles de Laval, lord of Retz (or Raiz), who had the blood of the noble Montmorency family, was, around the first half of the XV century, one of the most intrepid warriors and above all one of the most opulent lords of the time. His jet beard had the cyanic reflections of a raven's wing, hence the nickname Bluebeard, and his oblique eye, flashes of contained ferocity and equivocal lust.

The insolence of his pomp was so out of proportion with his fortune, which was colossal for the time, that he devoured it in a few years, says Garinet.[42] "two hundred thousand gold crowns and more than thirty thousand pounds of annuities, which are worth at least three hundred thousand today".[43]

He indulged in the ostentations of devotional luxury, dressing his chaplains as prelates, all in gold. He set out every day in search of new altar boys, on the pretext of providing for the magnificent chapel of the Castle of Tiffauges, which his wife, Catherine de Thouars, had brought him as a dowry.

Threats were skilfully mixed with promises, in order to obtain from poor parents the abandonment of these young boys, whom the Marshal wanted to protect and launch into the world. Children were recruited in a more mysterious way. Michelet tells us that "an old woman, called *the Meffraie*, used to roam the countryside, the moors. She approached small children who were looking after animals or begging; she flattered and caressed them, but always holding her face half hidden by a black cheesecloth; she lured them to the castle of the Sire of Retz, and they were never seen again...". As their boldness grew, they came to those of the towns.[44]

However, the habits of the lord were becoming more and more strange. Gilles de Laval would not take another step without dragging after him two sinister guests, one, an apostate priest from the diocese of Saint-Malo, and the other, a Florentine adventurer by the name of Prélati. Since the arrival of these two men at the castle,

---

41 Paris, 1817, 4 vols. in-8.
42 *Histoire de la Magie en France depuis le commencement de la Monarchie jusqu'à nos jours* (History of Magic in France from the beginning of the Monarchy to the present day). Paris, Foulon et Cie, 1818 in-8, frontispiece.
43 The authors disagree: "His income was estimated at one million nowadays," says Christian in his *Histoire de la Magie* (History of Magic) (page 396).
44 Michelet, *Histoire de France* (History of France), tome VI, page 335.

not a day went by without one of the altar boys disappearing.[45] Was there any desire to learn what had become of him? The Lord of Retz did not joke about this. He had strictly forbidden any indiscreet questions and even curiosity, the expression of which he regarded as a personal insult.

Eventually terror spread to the surrounding area. For a long time contained, finally it rose like the waves of the sea; the public voice designated the Marshal as a murderer and a sorcerer.

One morning in the year 1440, the castle was taken over by the orders of John V, Duke of Brittany, and the Marshal was arrested in the midst of its pomp and power – and the attentive world was afraid of the revelations of the most scandalous trial in the annals of Christianity.

The Lord of Retz, ruined to the core and riddled with debt, would, in desperation, wallow in the abominations of the blackest goetic arts. The charlatans to whom he had confided had lulled him for a moment with fanciful dreams; one was to compose mountains of gold for him by means of alchemy; the other flattered himself by obtaining for him, with Satan's help, the possession of inexhaustible mines, where the solar rose blossoms on the tree of metallic sephiroths; and the access to marvellous caves, all studded with stones. But the so-called disciple of Hermes succeeded above all in dissipating the little gold that the usurers had still provided; as for the sovereign master of the Powers of Darkness, he had persuaded the Marshal that the devil would give his help only on terrible conditions: at the price of daily renewed sacrifices, of the most innocent and purest blood...

Since the children could not be found, the justice system had a search carried out. The underground passages of the various castles of Champtocé, Machcoul and Tiffauges vomited more than two hundred horribly mutilated corpses into the light of day. They were found even in the latrines of the Suze castle.

But that was not all. A mixed tribunal, in which the Bishop of Saint-Brieuc and Jean Blouyn, official of Nantes and inquisitor of France, appeared as clerics, was convened under the chairmanship of the Seneschal of Rennes, Pierre de l'Hospital; the trial immediately took a singular turn and gave striking confirmation to the most insulting suspicions.

Indeed, it had been clearly noticed that Gilles de Laval, always surrounded by his pages, was showing an indifference towards women which was from then on considered highly suspicious; in short, his scandalous austerity had been accused of infamy. But such words only were whispered; never had these whisper ever taken shape, because the marshal was such a great and powerful lord... Now the investigation established that all the shameful vices had met at Tiffauges, and that the one there knew how to marry the best of superstitious greed with the most ferocious of lusts. Pleasure, which always escaped him, could only be attained on the triple condition of practising, in sodomy mode, on prepubescent victims, throbbing with the last spasms of agony! Sentenced to the fire on October 25, 1440 as a murderer,

---

45 Like master like valet: the lord of Retz was well served. – A doctor from Poitou, named Corillon; Sillié, the Marshal's businessman; Ponton, one of his pages; and his chamberlain, Henriot, were his other accomplices.

sodomite, heretic and sorcerer, he went up to the stake in the Magdeleine meadow near Nantes, delighted to have obtained as a last favour to be surrounded to the point of his torture by that royal luxury which had been his life, and which was collapsing with him in death.

Eliphas Lévi, who recounts this lamentable trial at length,[46] provides, against his habit as a scrupulous storyteller, details whose authenticity seems questionable, but which marvellously make the story of the lord of Retz coincide with the legend of Bluebeard. Those who are curious should refer to them.

We do not need to retrace all the impertinence and obscenities that fill the numerous documents of that era; so many others have, since the end of the last century, looked at what was still typical of the archives of parliaments and bailiwicks!

We will only mention as a reminder the public exhibition of Master Guillaume Edeline, prior of Saint-Germain-en-Laye, who saved the spontaneity of his confessions, confessed that he had devoted himself to the devil, to obtain from the Great Seducer the means to satisfy all the requirements of his natural gallantry, *and especially to please a lady knight*. He described the Sabbath assembly, where, having been carried on horseback on a broom, he paid back his duties to the Devil, disguised, for this time, as a sheep *which he kissed brutally under the tail and in the bottom, as a sign of great reverence and homage*. With a mitre in his head, he was led to a square in Evreux, where the inquisitor urged him, in the interest of his soul and "for the edification of each one", to bear public witness to his repentance. This advice was not repeated; *at the time the said Master Guillaume Edeline began to groan and condemn himself for his misdeed, asking for mercy to God, the King and the justice* (Chroniques de Monstrelet). He was condemned to life imprisonment and a diet of dry bread soaked in water, like the thinnest schoolboy.

Such clemency was rare.

The demonologists therefore made a big fuss about the acquittal of a poor, three-quarters stupid girl, whom the Inquisition wanted to burn in Metz as a witch, and who owed her life to the energetic attitude of Corneille Agrippa. Advocate General and Syndic of the city (recounts Naudé), "he directly opposed the proceedings of Nicolas Sauini, for then inquisitor of the faith in the said city, who wanted to have a poor village woman punished as a witch, and had her released, and all informers and witnesses fined heavily."[47]

Get a witch acquitted! Conviction of witnesses as slanderers! What a scandal in the Christian world!

Demonologists therefore rely on this fact, among others, to make Agrippa "the greatest sorcerer who ever lived his age".[48]

On April 13, 1611, a man died in the flames in Aix en Provence, a man whom contemporaries do not designate under a less flattering title: He is the *Prince of the Synagogue and the greatest and most distinguished magician who ever was, head of*

---

46 *Histoire de la Magie* (Transcendental Magic Its Doctrine and Ritual), pages 281-290.
47 *Apolog.*, page 297.
48 Bodin, *Dém.*, p. 240.

all the sorcerers of Europe from Constantinople to Spain, Messire Loys Goffredy (or Gaufridy), *parish priest of the Church of the Accoulez, in Marseille.*

The decision of the Parliament states that after having made amends before the Church of Saint-Sauveur in Aix, "bareheaded and barefoot, the rope at the neck, holding a burning torch in his hands, and having asked for forgiveness from God, the King and Justice…, afterwards will be delivered to the executor… Taken and put in the rack at all the places and crossroads of this city of Aix, with burning pincers in all the places of his body, he will be burned alive and his ashes thrown to the wind…, and his body will be burned alive…, and his ashes thrown to the wind… And before being executed, will be put and applied to the question, in the most serious Gehenna that can excite himself, to have from his mouth the truth of his accomplices… etc…" (Judgement quoted by dom Calmet, in his *Traité des Apparitions* (Treaty of Apparitions),[49] text completed and corrected according to the version given by Jacques Fontaine, in his book *Marques des Sorciers* (Marks of the Sorcerers).[50]

A few days after this barbaric execution, the exorcists, whose relentlessness pursued the priest of Les Accoules to death, published a *Confession by Messire Louys Gaufridy*. Whether this piece was composed by Fathers Michaëlis and Domptius, or whether the confessions were really extorted from Gaufridy by the acuity of the torments, is what we have no business debating here. We reproduce the main articles of this posthumous document:[51]

CONFESSION OF MESSIRE LOUYS GAUFRIDY, *Prince of Magicians, from Constantinople to Paris.* – I confess that the Devil appeared to me and I made a pact with him. I confess that I read the grimoire to make him come. I confess that the Devil promised me that by the virtue of my breath I would inflame with love all the girls and women I wanted, provided that this breath reached their nostrils and from then on I began to blow out all those who came to me at will. I confess that I frequented the house of M. de la Palud and that I longed for Magdeleine; but her mother held her so closely, that it was because of this that I breathed on her mother, so that she brought her to my room and she took confidence in me; so that, finding myself with Magdeleine, I kissed her and more… I confess that I gave her a devil named Eumodes to assist her, to serve her, and to warm her up to my love; that I married her to Belzebuth who appeared as a gentleman, and that after the marriage she signed a pact. The Devil says he would make a racket if I burned these promises. I confess that I burnt the grimoire. I confess that sorcerers, witches and wizards are marked with the Devil's little finger and that the marked parts are insensitive. I confess that when I wanted to go to the Sabbath, I would stand at my window and Lucifer would take me there. I confess that the Devil is worshipped, each according to his degree; that the masks all worship him lying on the ground; the sorcerers on two knees and the Wizards, as princes of the Sabbath, only on one side on their knees. I confess that

---

49 Paris, de Bure, 1751, 2 vol. in-12 (tome I, p. 146).
50 Lyon, 1611, in-8, pages 40-43.
51 We reproduce these summarised confessions as given by Garinet, in the supporting documents of his *Histoire de la Magie en France* (History of the Magic in France). M. Baissac, in his book *Les Grands jours de la sorcellerie* (The Great Days of Witchcraft), gives them in extenso.

HUMAN JUSTICE 139

I abused Magdeleine, a princess from Friesland, and other girls, on whom I blew. I confess that the Devil is a real monkey of the Church; that they baptise on the Sabbath in the name of Belzebuth, Lucifer and others; that there are twelve priests there who say Mass in turn and that the Devil serves the Mass; that the torch they raise when the Mass is at consecration is very bright and stinking. I confess that the bell of the Mass is made of horn and the staff is made of wood to ring it. I confess that there are some masks who are in charge of bringing a cat from their farmhouses, to make it eat communion, which the others don't want to eat."

Here, before my very eyes, is a curious collection of the time,[52] One can never imagine the turpitudes and foolishness that abounds in this trial. There is no doubt that Gaufridy was the lover of the young lady de la Palud; it is also certain that he used occult means to seduce her. Moreover, he was a publicly scandalous clergyman, and all the ferocity deployed against him by the judges and inquisitors failed to make him interesting.

I will give up describing the phases of this unprecedented affair; the possession of Magdeleine, afflicted with Belzebuth, Leviathan, Asmodeus, Baalberith and Astaroth; and of another young nun, named Louise Cappeau, in whose body the *Prince of the Synagogue* sent the demons *Verrine*, *Grézil* and *Sonneillon*; the exorcisms of Fathers Domps and Michaëlis, the very edifying sermons of the devil Verrine, sent by God (sic), to convert and denounce Gaufridy, that is to say to make him burn in this world and save him in the other; the convulsions of the possessed, embellished with vile details, obscene poses of the whole body, spasmodic tresses interspersed with revelations to make a one-eyed courtesan blush.

I think that my reader is sufficiently edified by all these scenes, where the burlesque rub shoulders with the filthy; I think his curiosity is satiated to the point of nausea. If I am wrong, let him refer to the book in-8 published by Father Michaëlis, under this title: *Histoire admirable de la possession et de la conversion d'une pénitente séduite par un magicien, ensemble la Pneumatologie* (An admirable story of the possession and conversion of a penitent seduced by a magician, together with Pneumatology.).[53]

The whole first half of the XVII century is infested with possession and exorcisms, and each time the executioner gives the epilogue, torch in hand, on a pyre! – Sad times! Everywhere the horizon is filled with bloody reflections; it looks like a land of plunder. But this land covers thousands of leagues; the people are at peace and the glimmers of fire testify that the sovereign courts do "good justice in the name of the King".

On July 8, 1617, the wife of the famous Marshal of Anchor, the beautiful Eleonore Galigai, appeared before the Parliament of Paris, where she was beheaded and burned for crimes of bewitchment and evil spells. In addition to what was found in her room (amulets, books of magic characters and "rolls of velvet constellated to

---

52 *Histoires tragiques de nôtre temps* (Tragic stories of our time), by F. de Rosset. Paris, 1614, in-12.
53 Paris, Chastellain, 1613, in-8.

dominate the minds of the greats"), it was established that she had brought from Nancy two Ambrosian monks to celebrate the sacrifice of a black rooster; not to mention other spells that were detailed; it did not take so much to lose the marshal's wife. It was she who, pressed by President Courtin with questions, nailed his mouth shut with such a proud reply. As he asked her by what charm she had bewitched Queen Marie de Medici, she had the audacity to reply

"My spell has been the power that strong souls will have eternally over weak souls."

We have reported above,[54] on the subject of possessions, the pitiful trial and dreadful torture of the parish priest of Saint-Pierre de Loudun, Urbain Grandier, guilty of having displeased the great cardinal. Eliphas Lévi suggests in his *Ritual* that the Minister's anger may have been more than resentment of the libel imputed to Grandier: "The Cardinal of Richelieu, who had ambitions for all powers, sought all his life, without being able to find it, the transmission of the *wand*".[55] His cabalist Gaffarel could only give him the sword and the talismans; perhaps this was the secret motive for his hatred of Urbain Grandier, who knew something of the Cardinal's weaknesses. Laubardemont's secret and lengthy conversations with the unfortunate priest a few hours before his last torture, and the words of a friend and confidant of the latter on his way to his death: "Sir, you are a clever man, do not get lost," give much to think about.[56]

After the nuns of the Sainte-*Beaume*[57] and the Ursulines of Loudun, it was the turn of the Franciscan nuns of Louviers.

The devil was in the convent. The nuns were relirious, convulsing and accusing two priests of having bewitched them; one was still alive, Boullé; the other, named Picard, died in 1642. The scandals began in the first days of the following year, 1643.

These two clergymen were most certainly guilty of spells,[58] in the same way as the infamous David, the oldest Director of the convent, and the first, apparently, had instituted a permanent Sabbath in this religious community. But as always in such a case, intrigues, the wild-eyed fanatics charge the authors of their sad state without measure and without discernment; they attribute to them everything that happens, even that which they could not foresee and combine. This is the common rule and the case of all the possessions I mention in this chapter, and so I have only recalled for the record that of the Ursulines of Loudun, which is worthy of being classified separately. In Loudun, the only sorcerers are the exorcists, whether or not they are conscious of the disorders that break out: Urbain Grandier is innocent.[59]

---

54 Chap. I, pages 50-56.
55 This is the Wand of the Magicians.
56 Eliphas Lévi, *Ritual*...
57 It was at the Sainte-Beaume that the exorcisms were performed, in the case of Magdeleine de la Palud.
58 Today it seems guilty of suggestion with criminal intent.
59 This is certainly not the case of Picard and Boullé, nor of Gaufridy, nor especially of Father Girard. – All these cases have therefore been classified as witchcraft trials in this fourth chapter, whereas the Loudun case had previously been told in the first chapter as a case of pure and simple possession.

HUMAN JUSTICE

It is apparent that Magdeleine Bavent copies the part of Magdeleine de la Palud;[60] only she does less well, since her confessions and the filthy tales she spices them up with make her forever locked up in the oozing and icy shadow of an underground dungeon.

But she had achieved her goal at that price; the decision of the Parliament of Rouen, dated August 21, 1647, condemned the living and the dead to fire. The sepulchre of the Picard priest was violated, and Boullé, garroted to the same post as the corpse of his accomplice, perished in the same flames, after having been dragged on the same rack... And their ashes are thrown to the wind!...

Possessions multiplied around this time, mainly in the convents. In France, England and Flanders, only demonic and exorcist people were heard. However, to be moved by the echoes of a great trial like those of Loudun and Louviers, one must reach the third of the XVIII century. In 1730, the Devil set off again on a fresh start; he made a great fuss in the convent of Oullioules, near Toulon, with the famous adventures of the Jesuit Girard and the beautiful Catherine Cadière, his mistress. It is always a new version of the same scandals, but this time the ignoble one reaches the proportions of a nightmare. The sadism grows worse, and in spite of ourselves, we think of the poet's *Femmes damnés* (Damned Women):

> Those whose throats love the scapulars,
> Who, concealing a whip under their long clothes,
> Mix in the dark night and lonely woods,
> From the foam of pleasure to the tears of torment.[61]

When Baudelaire wrote this stanza, he had probably just reread the voluminous file of the Court of Aix.

It was, in fact, before the Parliament of that city that the parents of La Cadière, in terror, brought a criminal lawsuit against Father Girard...

Girard had many friends in the very heart of the Parliament; the influence of the company was exerted, sovereign, and the magistrates were divided. When it came to the vote, twelve of them condemned Girard to the stake or gallows; the other twelve shared the acquittal, the disciplinary penalties and the declaration of incompetence. The Jesuit, benefiting from the equality of votes, was simply referred to the church judge, who acquitted him (1731).

And Catherine was returned to her mother.

As we have seen, these trials rarely had such a lenient outcome. Moreover, it must be said that the judges were often disgusted, ill-disposed to be debonair. So many scandals and disgusting scenes! How much mud stirred up, waiting for blood!

In the presence of such abuses, one can almost imagine the exasperation of Jules Garinet, who allows himself to be carried away by the opposite fanaticism: "The only way –he says–, to completely free ourselves from possessions and sorcer-

---

[60] It is known that hysterical people often lie, or at least amplify and embroider the truth with the best faith in the world.
[61] Charles Baudelaire, *Les Fleurs du mal* (Femmes damnés) (The Flowers of Evil (Damned Women)).

ers, is to send to the hospital the hysterical sanctimonious people who will claim to be possessed in the future... As long as the exorcists are not sent to prison, the race will continue to exist. The remedy is Violent, I admit it; but it is the only one that is suitable. To great evils, great remedies"[62]

This chapter could be closed here; but we ask the reader to pay more attention, and to go back a few hundred years with us. We are about to witness a terrible drama...

Trial and Revenge of The Templars

We are at the beginning of the fourteenth century: the half-religious, half-military Order, established in the East around 1118 by Hugues des Payens, has prospered prodigiously. The Knights Templar had nearly ten thousand Lordships in Europe, and their opulence, which had become proverbial, centralized an almost unlimited power in their hands.

On the other hand, although they affect to bow respectfully before both civil and religious authorities, their projects show an ambition bordering on madness. Heirs –they flatter themselves– of this Johannite tradition[63] which constitutes the esoteric marrow of Christianity, they perform, in the shadow and silence of their Commanderies, strange and secret rites... In short, the popular voice, which incriminates them with witchcraft, also denounces their morals as infamous. This last accusation was never established on irrefutable evidence; but if the Order's apologists were able to claim the benefit of the doubt in favour of the Templars, they were never, at least, able to rehabilitate them in the great day of the historical controversy, by washing their memory of all suspicion.

Jules Garinet sums up the grievances brought against the Knights Templar in this way: "It was said that at the reception in the Order, the recipient was taken to a dark room, where he would deny Jesus Christ by spitting three times on the crucifix; that the one who was received would kiss the one who received him at the mouth, then *in fine spinæ dorsi and in virga virili*; that the Templars, in their general chapters, worshipped a golden wooden head with a long beard, bushy and hanging

---

62 Garinet, *Histoire de la Magie de France* (History of the Magic in France), page 292.
63 I would ask to those who doubt this assertion to examine carefully the curious and rare book published in 1831 under this title: LEVITIKON, or *an exposition of the fundamental principles of the early Christian-Catholics*. Paris, in-8. In this work, in addition to the summary of a pseudo-Johannite dogma, we find a version, called authentic, of the Gospel according to Saint John, the only one adopted by this Church, and the *list of the Johannite pontiffs* from Christ and Saint John to the present day, including all the Great Masters of the Temple. That the pseudo-Johannites of the XIX century were, as Clavel claims (*Histoire pittoresque de la Franc-Maçonnerie* (Picturesque history of Freemasonry), 1884, grand in-8, figures), mystifiers who pretended to rekindle an extinguished flame and revive a dead cult, is what I do not want to debate; what seems certain, according to the conscientious examination of this work, is that this cult really existed in the past, in an esoteric and latent state. The M*anuel des Chevaliers du Temple* (Manual of the Knights of the Temple). Paris, 1825, in-12, can still be consulted.

moustaches; instead of eyes, two large carbuncles shone, sparkling like fire.[64] They were still accused of taking a vow of sodomy, and of refusing each other nothing..."

"In Languedoc, three Commanders of the Order, who were tortured, confessed that they had attended several chapters of the Order; that in one of these chapters, held in Montpellier, and at night, as is customary, *a head* had been exposed; that the devil had immediately appeared in the form of a cat; that this cat was adored and spoke kindly to all; that afterwards several demons came in the form of women, and each brother had his own."[65]

Whatever one may think of these astounding accusations, which caused so many brave Knights to be burned at the stake, it is impossible for us not to note, in passing, what resemblance, if not absolute identity, such scenes (whether we want them to be real or false) bear to the Sabbath of the sorcerers on the one hand, as we have described in Chapter II, and on the other hand to those orgiastic and mystical meetings all together, which have always been attributed to the sectarians of dissident Gnosis by contemporary authors who deal with their rites and mysteries.

The Marquis of Saint-Yves, in a book that is remarkable in so many respects, glorifies what he calls the *Mission of the Knights Templar*. In them, he salutes the orthodox of traditional esotericism, the proponents of social peace, the founders and inspirers of those States General –a veritable outline of synarchy– which were, throughout our history, the intrepid and moderate organ of popular demands, and as a great voice, firm and respectful, coming from the very bowels of the nation.

If this is the case, the Estates General of Tours (May 1308) showed themselves to be parricidal by denying the Temple and abandoning the Templars to the fury of their executioners. Moreover, with his customary loyalty, M. de Saint-Yves himself proclaimed this unimpeachable fact, which would be one of the stumbling blocks of his hypothesis for the superficial ones: "The unanimity of the Three Orders gave Philippe-le-Bel iron and fire...", we read on page 216 of *La France vraie*[66] (volume I).

This does not matter. It is not without precedence to see the son following the traditions of the father, after having condemned him; the worker living again in his work, after having died by it. And without going so far, St. Peter, who denied his master Jesus Christ three times, was nonetheless the first head of the Christian Church. It is therefore not with such arguments that we will oppose the illustrious Apostle of the Missions.

No matter how noble the thesis he supports, we would like to see it founded in history on some proven fact, so that it may be acceptable. Without going into the discussion in this field, we shall say why, in terms of pure metaphysics, this thesis seems to us at least risky.

---

64 "...Each chapter –says Henri Martin–, had an image: it was a human head with a long white beard, *having, in place of the eyes, carbuncles shining like the brightness of the sky*, with a human skull and human skin: some of these idols were three-sided and mounted on four feet; one of them had been seized at the Temple of Paris." (Henri Martin, *Histoire de France* (History of France), t. IV, p. 473).
65 *Histoire de la Magie en France* (History of Magic in France), pp. 78-79.
66 *La France vraie* (The True France), Mission des Français, Paris, 1887, 2 vols. in-18.

The Knights were custodians of a social and religious doctrine. This is historically certain. It remains to be seen which one.

That the Temple possessed the Orthodox tradition is hardly sustainable. This famous Order remains dogmatically tainted with Manichaeism. Mignard, in particular, has brought together overwhelming evidence in support of this opinion. The emblematic figures carved in relief on the Essarois stone casket, an evidence[67] (among a thousand) which he details with perfect skill and sagacity, are of such a nature as to leave no doubt. The character of obscene mysticism that is characteristic of these diarchical symbols even seems of a precision typical enough, to serve as a hyphen in the species, between the two great grievances stipulated against the Templars: Manichean gullibility and impure vice.

Let's retain only the Manichaeism in the charge of the Knights Templar. This is more than enough to refute the attribution made to them of a traditional doctrine of tri-unitary syncretism, mathematics, or (as M. de Saint-Yves excellently calls it) a synarchic tradition.

The primordial, absolute antagonism of two incompatible principles is the essence of Manichean dogma; it excludes the synarchic Ternary and the Monad from which this Ternary emanates.

Manichaeism is the radical negation of the principle of return to Unity. Go and build a synthesis on such a basis! A chimerical project: we might as well want to restore Babel...

The Templars, as we have said, did not pass for simple heretics.

Apart from the imputation of Manichaeism –exclusive, in our opinion, of the attribution that M. de Saint-Yves generously gave them of his own doctrine– the knights were still accused of black magic and sodomy.

These were capital crimes in the jurisprudence of the Middle Ages. They were so serious, moreover, that they seemed to the XIV century judges to be nothing more than a deception, an excuse for the coup d'état of 1307. It has to be said. What an excellent opportunity for the King of France and for the Pope, his creature, to abolish in one fell swoop the power of these superb defenders of the throne and the altar, a thousand times more dangerous than their worst enemies, and what a natural pretext for sharing their prodigious spoils!

The successor of Peter and the heir of Hugues Capet had already prepared this master-stroke for a long time;[68] only waiting for the right time to act in concert...

---

67 *Suite de la monographie du coffret du duc de Blacas*, or *Preuves du Manichéisme dans l'Ordre du Templet* (Continuation of the monograph of the Duke of Blacas, box set, or Proofs of Manichaeism in the Order of the Temple), by Mignard. – Paris, 1853, grand in-4, figures.

68 It was thanks to the protection of Philip the Fair, that Bertrand de Goth, Archbishop of Bordeaux in 1300, came to the papal throne in 1305, under the name of Clement V. In order to buy the monarch's complacency, the future pope had to subscribe by oath to six formal conditions, the last of which, kept secret, bound him to pursue the destruction of the Templars until the Order was abolished.

This means that Clement V's protests, so soft, so obviously made for the form and the edification of the gallery, were nothing but an odious comedy on his part. It was evident from his haste, which he then put to ratify everything after some semblance of investigation in Poitiers.

HUMAN JUSTICE

That hour finally dawned. Several formal denunciations, including those of two apostate Templars, made it possible to crack down on the Knights at a moment's notice and to wrap all the Knights in a single network. The net was cast in the night of November 12th to 13th, 1307, when all the king's governors and officers received the fatal order in a sealed envelope.

In the morning, the Knights Templar were arrested by the whole of France and their property was sequestered. – In Paris, one hundred and forty knights were in irons; they were proceeded against with unusual rigour. The question was never more cruelly inflicted. The R.P. Imbert, inquisitor of the faith, led the interrogations, assisted by commissioners appointed by the king. At their head was Guillaume de Nogaret, an angry man whose fanaticism was bordering on delirium.

In the provinces, the inquisitor sub-delegates the ecclesiastical commissioners and the interrogations begin.

Of all the proceedings brought against these unfortunate people, only eight authentic relationships remain: those of Caen (where 13 Templars were in irons); – of Pont-de-l'Arche (10 Templars); of Cahors (7 Templars); – of Carcassonne (6 Templars); – of Beaucaire (45 Templars); – of Troyes (5 Templars); – of Bayeux (5 Templars); and finally of Bigorre (11 Templars).

In Caen, the accused were promised total mercy, but those who resisted were nevertheless tortured.

While the case was investigated in his own state, Philippe-le-Bel invited the other potentates of Europe to imitate him in his rigour.

Germany did not hasten to answer his call, but Sicily, Italy, Castile, England and Aragon followed France's example.[69]

In Flanders, less rigour was deployed. In Cyprus, the power of the Order made the task of the persecutors arduous and delicate; Amaury, regent of the kingdom for the young Hugues IV, was forced to postpone the repression in the face of the threatening attitude of the Knights, fortified in Nimove.

The trial dragged on everywhere, with alternative confessions and retractions; the court clerks have altered several depositions, leading to long, dead-end debates.

However, under pressure from the King of France, who reminded him of his commitments, the pope issued bull after bull to speed up the process, and he ranted and raved about it up to seven times (1308). New procedures entrusted to the bishops did not produce better results. Provincial councils were held...

But it is impossible to specify all these details.

In short, Pope Clement V issued a final bull in 1310 to order the final judgement of the Knights Templar. A small number denied; others confessed; many, as I have said, retracted their confessions. The Councils of Sens and Rheims made four categories of accused: some of them (classes 1, 2, 3), repentant and reconciled to the

---

69 We are speaking, for the time being, only of the arrest and the proceedings, for in several places these led to the acquittal of the Knights, as in Ravenna, Mainz and Salamanca (1310). Whatever happened to these individual sentences, the Order, which was abolished by the Council of 1311, did not exist anywhere, at least openly and under its real name. In Portugal, the Order of Christ rose from its debris.
In Aragon, the Templars had proudly organised armed resistance, not without success.

Church, were released for ecclesiastical penance or life imprisonment; others (4th class), who had been declared relapsed, were handed over to the secular branch and executions began.

On May 10, 1311, in front of the Abbey of Saint Anthony, the first condemned man was burned alive, in the hope of intimidating the others who had recanted and reducing them to the letter of their first confessions. But they were unshakeable.

Eight days later, fifty-four of them went up on pyres built on the same site. This execution, slowed down at pleasure, so that death would come more slowly and atrociously, shatters the constancy and high bravery of these martyrs, who take heaven as their witness that they die innocent. The following days, fifteen Templars, who refuse to say they are guilty, are burned in two groups.

In the provinces and in Piedmont there had been several similar executions.

However, the great master, Jacques de Molay, was still languishing in irons with his great priors; he did not climb the scaffold until March 18, 1313,[70] in the company of the Prince-Dauphin, who followed him in the solemn retraction of his first confession. Both were burnt at very low fire, on the island between the gardens of the king and the Augustinians, at the precise place where the equestrian statue of Henry IV stands today, on the terrace of the Pont-Neuf. The next day, the Chevalier Aumont and seven Templars, *disguised as masons*, piously collected the ashes from the pyre. The Order of the *Freemasons* was born...

As early as September 1311, the Council of Vienna, where more than three hundred prelates were seated, had abolished the Order of the Temple; the immense properties of the community, passing to the Knights of St. John of Jerusalem, recently established in Rhodes, was to benefit only indirectly,[71] to the iniquitous heir of Hugues Capet. More clearly fortunate, the Spanish monarchs managed to get all the property that the Knights Templar owned in their states.

Whatever reservations we may have had in qualifying the crimes attributed to them, we cannot avoid one last question, which touches too closely on the subject of this book: Were the Knights Templar sorcerers?

It is a matter of agreeing on the words... Will the reader forgive us for digressing?

It is a rule of prudence, always beware of categories that are too clear-cut and labels that are too exclusive...

An occultist of our day has condensed, in a double and excellent formula, the distinctive definition of the hierophants of Light and Night: "The magician has a power he knows; the sorcerer tries to abuse what he does not know...". The Devil (if

---

70 Many authors, notably Henri Martin, *Histoire de France* (History of France), tome IV, page 503); Bouillet, in his *Dictionnaire d'Histoire et de Géographie* (Dictionary of History and Geography); and Coilin de Plancy, in his *Dictionnaire Infernal* (Infernal Dictionary), give a different date: March 18, 1314. – We shall see that Masonic traditions say the same.
This apparent contradiction has no other cause than the reworking of the Calendar under Charles IX, by the Edict of Roussillon (1564). The year which only began at Easter went back to 1st January. Jacques Molay's ordeal therefore took place on the date of 1313 or 1314, depending on which system was adopted: the old or the new.
71 Transfer fees, taxes, fines and royalties of all kinds, – barely disguised confiscation.

it is permitted in a book of science to use this decried and vulgar word), the Devil gives himself to the magician and the sorcerer gives himself to the Devil.[72]

That's called being taken at face value. The Janus of occultism is superiorly pencilled there, in the antithesis of its double nature: of these two faces, one smiles, imbued with a serene and gentle authority; the other grimaces, withered with the twin stigmata of final impotence and envy. Everything seems to be indicated in each of them by the effect of repulsion; what they are, what they *know*, what they *want*, what they can, what they *dare*.

But, however judicious they may be, these kinds of absolute formulae are marred by a redhibitory vice. The best of them, which state the universal which is the rule, not only neglect, but deny the particular which is the exception.

This is the pitfall against which all generalisers come up against, stubbornly stubborn in their laconic sentences; for having navigated in their waters, Eliphas Lévi could not avoid the reef where they all end up capsizing.

He who has given himself to the Devil –they will object to Eliphas–, can pull himself together, if only for a minute. The Devil, slave of a mortal, can also take back his rights for a moment and dominate his everyday dominator for once. This has been seen.

With all due respect to the infallible sticklers of indelible labels, the intractable awarders of final qualifications had to cry out; nothing is absolutely detestable or perfect in this relative and sublunary world. – The Wise Man, like any other, can sin by mistake or by malice,[73] and if he has earned the name of Wise Man, it is because in him evil is the exception. And so it is with the wicked man; a generous feeling can sometimes blossom in the heart of the most criminal, and if one is right in saying that this man is evil, it is because good thoughts are the exception in him.

Let us be more precise, the sorcerer who, having acquired the intelligence of a law, applies it to the good, acts as a wizard. – In the same way, the magician, guilty, even once, of prostituting science to evil, obviously does the work of a sorcerer.

This is what destroys these convenient categories, these masterful divisions so dear to your drawer brains, countless Joseph Prud'homme of psychology and morals!...

This is certainly very unfortunate. But the few principles already explained will find their justification in a little-known example, whose crucial and decisive importance no one will doubtless dispute.

In the course of a chapter entitled *Human Justice*, this example is doubly relevant because, after having seen the courts of fanaticism at work, accumulating hecatombs of sorcerers of the lowest level, pell-mell with innocent victims, we will see high-ranking insiders split into two hostile sects, a gloomy epilogue to the Templar tragedy! One of these sects, diabolically and criminally greedy for exclusive sovereignty, will proscribe the other, and, prostituting to the lowest works the effective science and the august powers of High Magic, will do the work of sorcerers, in the strictest sense of the word, and above all the most terrible.

---

72 Eliphas Lévi, *Dogme*....
73 The Holiest, says the Scripture, sins seven times a day.

We shudder just now at the quick summary of the trial of the Knights Templar, at the picture of their inexpressible torment. Were they sorcerers? – I leave it to you to judge. Hear ye.

Rich and powerful, above all ambitious, endowed with surprising and fearsome powers, conferred on many of them by a partial and relative initiation into the mysteries of an often contested science, sometimes ridiculed, but always outlawing priests and absolute governments, the Knights Templar could obviously, in the political and social order, determine sudden and unforeseen upheavals, of such a nature as to change the face of Europe and even the world... This is what the Pope and the King of France vaguely suspected.

Beware only of the superficial logic of the events questioned in their apparent significance, Clement V must have seen the Knights of the Temple as valiant defenders of Catholicism and zealous supporters of the pontifical throne; Philip the Fair, as subjects full of loyalty and fervour for the dynastic cause. But a singular intuition, awakened in the heart of these two potentates, protested against these appearances.

Frightened, the monarch and the pontiff (the latter even before his election) resolved the total destruction of the Order, and pursued this result *per fas et nefas*,[74] in defiance of all the voices of conscience and humanity. They were in turn perfidious and violent, hypocritical and ruthless.

Idolatry or witchcraft! What did they really care about?.... What they tried hard to bury under the ashes of the pyres from 1311 to 1313 was the possibility of a political revolution and the still undecided plan for social and religious reform.

But they had not taken into account the laws of repercussion and balance. They did not know that an idea, even a germ, is not drowned in the blood of those who made themselves the apostles and legatees. This ferocious and illusory prudence and the infamous ambush that resulted lost them both immediately – and what is more, it caused a shock in the future, almost five centuries apart, which must have shaken the earth again; a late shock that immediately caused the most sudden and colossal collapse in the history of mankind. *Seventeen hundred and ninety-three*[75] was a lightning reply to the iniquitous stop of *Thirteen hundred and twelve*!

Clement V and Philip were undoubtedly clairvoyant when they felt the living threat that the Templars posed to them, despite all imaginable protests of fidelity and love, but they were blind in their stubborn barbarity, if they could flatter themselves with the hope that an auto-da-fé, so complete and so swift that it could be carried out, would reduce to nothing the Templars, their power and the Word they carried within them.

Once they had been adjourned to *appear before God* –the Pope within forty days and the King within a year– history shows us both of them to be lugubriously faithful to the appointment...

Of the two apostate Knights, denouncers of the Order, the first one, involved – one does not know how–, in an obscure trial, was hanged by a court order; the other was found bathed in his blood...

---

74 Literally: *Through right or wrong*. It refers to unfair disputation.
75 In the middle of the French revolution the French king was executed in January 1793.

Like the Grand Master's companions in captivity, these two pusillanimous Knights who, during the Grand Master's torture, had dishonoured the Temple by persisting in their confessions, died no less miserably...

An immense secret society had been secretly formed out of the debris of the Order.

Henceforth, vengeance was preparing in the shadows the mines and counter-mines whose explosion would terrify us four hundred and fifty years later; while waiting for this dreadful and belated retaliation, it decimated, one after the other, all the assassins of Jacques Molay. "By breaking the Templars' sword, they had made daggers out of them, and their proscribed trowels only built tombs".[76]

With the ruin of the Temple decided on both sides, the pope and the king lost no time in accomplishing it. Never before had the execution of a larger plan been carried out more comprehensively and perfectly and with greater promptness. In less than six years, the dreadful Moloch with two heads, one crowned with shame, the other with infamy, had devoured the ancient Order of the Temple in its reddened bronze bowels... It only half this time, the revolutionary Moloch, born from the ashes of the Knights of the Temple, was to take only three years to devour the ancient world!

But giants grow slowly... It will take this one four centuries of childhood to reach the age of strength and puberty.

The hourglass has emptied little by little; the cup has filled up drop by drop: one more tear..., it will overflow.

Then the flood!...

The four centuries are over. Now he is an adult, the collective giant of bloody claims, and out of his cave he will begin his work in broad daylight.

In what way and from what perspective? We shall see. He shows himself in the sun, but covered with a mask.

It will bear the name of *Illuminati* for another fifty years, before suddenly bearing the name of the *French Revolution!...*

In fact, from the second half of the 17th century, secret societies multiplied in a surprising way; they buzzed about in all directions; it was like a multitude of swarms that could be seen coming out of the earth, vibrating in the sun in the effervescence of unaccustomed labour.

The ominous hour has come –the noon of punishment– and the industrious bees of vengeance were preparing their sting for the great battle. Already the century has tasted their heady honey, whose aroma rises to the brain, a subtle poison that blinds and makes one delirious... Listen a moment longer and what you have mistaken for a buzzing of insects is the rumble of a distant but approaching storm; it is the confused and growing rumour of millions of human voices, shouting Vengeance and Freedom!

Germany seems above all to be the nursery of the Enlightened Ones, the rallying point of the sects.

---

76 Eliphas Lévi, *Histoire de la Magie* (History of Magic).

Powerful lords, eager for revelations from beyond the grave, fill with blessings some mystics of good faith who say to them: *my son!* And above all many charlatans who deceive and exploit them.

Then mysterious societies were formed and recruited from all sides: *Weisslzaupt*, a professor at the University of Ingolstadt, founded his *Areopagites*; public curiosity became involved and they became fashionable for a while.

Swedenborg dogmatises in Sweden; *Schrœppfer* evokes in Leipzig; *Yung-Stilling* vaticin on the other hand. *D'Eckartshausen* teaches in Munich the highest speculations on the numeral magic of Pythagoras; *Lavater*, the theosophist from Zurich, travels to Copenhagen to participate in the mysteries of the Northern School. These are nothing less than "*physical* manifestations of the *active and intelligent Cause*" (the Word!). At intervals, as if they were doing each other by hand, Danish theurgists evoke St John, Moses and Elijah, without mentioning other less know characters from either Testaments. Finally, the "followers" abound, and it would be madness to pretend to list them all. Of all these *Enlighteners*, there are few good ones (with the exception of Eckartshausen), many mediocre ones (such as *Yung-Stilling*, *Swedenborg* and *Lavater*), and even more detestable ones (such as *Schrœppfer*, *Weisshaupt* and many others). Nor can we say that the best were free of faults or did not make fools of themselves.

This School of Theurgy, where such seductive wonders are performed, has its analogues almost everywhere. Unheard of, a letter from the Baron of Liebistorf to Claudius of St. Martin (dated December 1793) tells us that there was a Northern Court other than that of Copenhagen,[77] has long since governed according to spiritualistic inspirations. His cabinet *does not take a step* (textual: *ne fait pas*) without consulting ghosts!

Readers who are curious about a systematic count of secret societies in Germany and elsewhere will refer to the many books that have appeared over the last hundred years to denounce or defend them; they can learn the pros and cons. However, one should be careful not to give a verdict on insufficient evidence in a trial as exceptional as it is complex, and which one can only judge in the first instance; for the time has not yet come for the final verdict that impartial history will render some day, in the belated and solemn silence of all appeased passions.

For us, our goal is to show the daughter of the proscribed Temple, this *occult Masonry*, disguised, elusive and multiform, behind the thousand sects of the Enlightened One that she has been able to group around her, and preparing in the shadows, *–per fas et nefas*, too– the vengeful and sovereign reply to the bulls of Clement V, as well as to the ordinances of Philip the Fair.

We have before us the original edition of a book published in 1789, under this title: *Essai sur la secte des Illuminés* (Essay on the sect of the Enlightened (S.L. in-8). The Marquis de Luchet, anonymous author of this prophetic lampoon, describes throughout the works of the Enlightened Ones, the work of their circles, the trials

---

77 This is undoubtedly that of Prussia, as a letter from St. Martin to the same Liebistorf, dated March 6, 1793, leads us to believe. It reads: "I know that Germany is full of these initiations, I know that the Berlin Cabinet conducts itself and its King only by these initiations."...

and oaths of their followers; he unveils the *Berlin Nocturnals*, lists the various mystical sects that we have briefly mentioned, from the Order of the *Knights of the Apocalypse*, founded around 1690 by Gabrino, the adventurer who had taken the title of Prince of the Sevenfold (pp. 129-131), to the *Order of the Knights and Friars Initiates of Asia* and the sect of *Saint Joachim* which derives from it. However, after having titled two of its chapters: *That the sect of the Enlightened must necessarily destroy the kingdom where it will be protected* (pp. 80-94); and *That the kings are most interested in destroying the new sect* (pp. 95-107), M. de Luchet did not fail to recognise the central knot of so many threads, branched out throughout Europe: "I will not give up, he said, to present a great reform of Masonry as a remedy." (P. 163.)

Then, foreseeing the upheaval of the old world with a lucidity that would seem apocryphal, if his book, published in 1789, had not been criticized at the time of its appearance, he specifies the work of the lodges and the aspirations of the acolytes in the declamatory style of the time: "All believe they are called to make a revolution, all are preparing it ... The Earth is suffering; a new scourge is tormenting it, Nature is groaning, Society is decomposing... This is how the sect of the Enlightened Ones will end. How many evils would prevent the one who would suffocate it in the cradle, and justify a moment of violence by the laws imposed by the past!" (pp. 137-138, *passim*).

It is indeed a partisan of the old world who is thus frightened away, isn't it, reader? Does he feel the ground beneath him clearly enough?

Alas! When one evokes in a retrospective mirror all the horrors of a revolution that was just and generous in principle; when one calculates what the vengeance of the Knights Templar cost France and the world in blood and tears, does has one the right to reproach the Marquis de Luchet for his enigmatic terrors, and can one at least deny him this testimony, that standing on Atlantis close to being engulfed, he knew how to foresee and predict the rising tide of the waves that were to submerge it?

"Oh my fellow citizens –he exclaims in his preface–, believe that we do not spread false alarms; we have written with quite a lot of courage and we are far from having said everything... (p. IV); it is all about consideration, gentleness and politeness with men of iron, who, dagger in hand, mark their victims (p. XV)."

Further on, after unveiling the mystery of the initiations and transcribing *in extenso* the formula of the dreadful oath imposed on the acolytes, whatever their rank, he adds (p. 156): "The mysteries are celebrated today in secluded and almost unknown places; in twenty years' time they will be celebrated in the temples". Still four years after this prediction were not over when Hebert's friends inaugurated the cult of the goddess Reason on the metropolitan altar of Notre-Dame...

Strange encounter! The man whose acute intuition was able to foresee so many events to come, still seems, in the last pages of his book, to glimpse Napoleon and his despotism in the shadows of a more distant future: "Oh you, fill the earth with great deeds and virtues, Oh Fame, carry your harmonious trumpet elsewhere!.... Never publish that a captain, even more carried away than valiant, counts for nothing the victims immolated to his ambition, as long as their blood makes the laurels grow...[78] Spread a thick veil over the odious intrigues spun by men who have conspired to shame sovereigns; unworthy manoeuvres that leave service without reward, virtue without honour, talent without protection, truth without homage, Homeland without glory, Throne without support, genius without employment, Society without harmony..., the unfortunate without asylum, the wise without hope, and the Kings themselves without security." (Pages 174-175, *passim*.)

Cagliostro

But independently of the great theosophical movement of which Germany was the centre, a number of extraordinary figures, dressed in secret missions, travelled all over Europe, astonishing its capitals, and almost all of them transferred their enigmatic magnificence and suspicious popularity to Paris. The Count of St. Germain and Joseph Balsamo (later Count of Cagliostro) are worthy of being mentioned in the front line. Both of them, ambassadors, following Cadet de Gassiourt, or, if you like, international missionaries, were specially charged with the task of establishing an efficient correspondence between the various chapters. Saint-Germain was the envoy from Paris; Cagliostro, the one from Naples.[79]

Everyone knows the vogue enjoyed by these characters, and the enthusiasm which they had the skill or science of raising with the dust of their splendid resources.

That they were acclaimed by illiterate people, naive admirers of all men of prestige –from the shanty dentists at fairs to the gallant generals on parade– is noth-

---

78 M. de Luchet is undoubtedly thinking of Lafayette, but what does it matter? The most lucid are often mistaken, their prophecy is no less striking. This is the case here.
79 *Tombeau de Jacques Molay* (Tomb of Jacques Molay), Paris, year V, in-12 (p. 34).

ing that can surprise us; but that in the middle of the XVIII century, the sceptical and mischievous world of which Voltaire, d'Argens and Diderot were daily delights, welcomed, pampered and adored men who were obviously superior, but who only walked around surrounded by equivocal wonders, and whose manners, however beautiful and gallant they were, still had an aftertaste of candid charlatanism and singular audacity – that is what seems unheard of!

Nothing could be further from the truth, however. St. Germain's melodious and ever-equal voice, recounting his conversations with Pythagoras, Virgil and Jesus Christ, was certainly not to displease; and when his ring-laden fingers, running over the keys of a harpsichord, awakened chords of a strange and poignant archaism as if at the heart of the instrument: If, when tacitly questioned by some beautiful duchess, he gave the most natural answer to this at the very least bizarre: "This, Madame, is an aria I wrote around the year 2008 B.C., in the town of Erech, to woo a young princess of Chaldea", everyone marvelled, but no one had the bad taste to question the truthfulness of the storyteller.

What can we say of those famous Cagliostro's dinners, where the most illustrious lords of the Court fought over invitations; of those fantastic dinners, where the voice of the *Grand Cophte* populated the room, at the moment of dessert, with visible souls with shivering wings, and made the Duke of Richelieu, Semiramis and Cleopatra sit down to the right and left, resurrected in all the magic of their legendary beauty?

Enchantment, prestige, necromancy, what do I know!... Oh, sorry, I forgot that you, dear reader, knew: *suggestion*, didn't you? So the most sceptical, haughty and polite society in the world was docile to the *suggestions* of Cagliostro and St. Germain.

And yet, while intoxicated, lulled by the charm of these great lords of the Occult, Parisian high society abandoned itself in their arms, with the defeated gesture of the woman who gives herself, Saint-Germain, the first, silently organised the noisy clubs of the next day and fertilised the future riot with his inexhaustible gold –capable of shaking the power of a king by violence; on the other hand, and then, the infernal foresight of the *divine* Cagliostro warped the intrigue of the necklace– capable of ruining the honour and prestige of a queen through suspicion.

All Grand Cophthus had to do to enter the world of the Court was to create his *Egyptian Masonry*, of which the little princess of Lamballe agreed to be the master, by express order of Marie Antoinette. Poor Queen! His confidante, his close friend, was already marked and stigmatised with Cagliostro's secret sign: L.P.D., initials whose interpretation, as if it were a hieroglyph of the Kabbalah, had three meanings. Contrary to the normal exegesis of esoteric symbols, the hierophant willingly gave the two higher meanings: the superlative[80] –*Freedom of Thought* (in French it is *Liberté de Penser*: LDP)– is the affirmation of independent initiative in the intelligible order; the comparative –Freedom, Power, Duty (in French *Liberté, Pouvoir, Devoir*: LPD)– is the ternary in the moral order. But it carefully conceals even the existence of the inferior, positive meaning: this was the very secret of the Order, the

---

80 Following the Masonic inversion: L.D.P.

political and social arcane of the Neo-Templars, the sentence pronounced for almost five centuries against the heirs of Philip the Fair: *Lilia pedibus destrue*: treads upon the lilies.

Let us report a truly convincing historical anecdote about this regicidal motto and in support of his seniority: "The deputy Grégoire presented the Convention with a medal minted in 1642. On one side it shows an arm sticking out from the clouds, harvesting three lilies with a sharp sword. The legend is: *Talem dobit ultio messem* (this is the harvest that revenge will bring). On the reverse, another arm throws lightning on a broken crown and sceptre, with the words *Flamma inetuenda tyrannis* (at the appearance of these fires, the tyrants will tremble".[81]

A PROPHECY OF PARACELSUS ON THE BOURBONS

---

81 *Tombeau de Jacques Molay* (Tomb of Jacques Molay), page 3.

Among the Prophecies relating to the Great Revolution, the 32 pantacles of the Paracelsus Pronostication should be mentioned in the first line, as well as several of the enigmatic engravings attributed to Abbot Joachim of Flora (or Calabria). I have two Latin editions of Abbot Joachim: one, from 1589 (Venice, in-4), with a frontispiece, an engraved title and 33 intaglio figures of often astonishing prescience; the other edition is also from Venice (1600, in-4), decorated with a frontispiece and six engraved figures in the form of wheels. As for the Paracelsus Pronostication, I also possess two copies: one is the edition of 1536, S.-L. in-4, Latin text, with 32 even more astonishing figures. Here is the exact title: *Prognosticatio eximii Doctoris Theophrasti Paracelsus (ad illustrissimum ac potentissimum Principem Ferdinandum Romanorum Regem*, etc. anno 1536). The other copy is a very beautiful original manuscript, containing an unpublished French translation by Christallin (librarian of the Count of Charolois), written in his own hand (Latin text opposite), with a pseudo-key which consists of 32 notices of reckless adaptation to the events of the reign of Louis XIV. This precious manuscript is dated 1712 (three years before the death of the Great King). Format in-4, bound in an antique calf binding, decorated on the covers with the coat of arms of the Prince de Condé; the spine, strewn with fleurs-de-lys and radiant suns, marks the period and takes us back to the reign of Louis XIV.

" Sun-King, fertilising the lilies in full bloom"

Also a facsimile specimen of the prophetic engravings of Paracelsus and Joachim.

HUMAN JUSTICE

He whose power brings forth from the earth the Flower that is more illustrious than all the others, makes it arid and rotten in time and place; this is what is happening to you, Oh You who are today a Lily of the Field, tomorrow as Christ says. You will be thrown into the oven... which means that you will emigrate into loneliness, ruin and exile; and in this universal lowering of yourself without example, you will be humiliated in memory of the years that have passed. By prudence and the fear of the Lord, You could have made your affairs stable and prosperous; but Your own cunning has brought about Your ruin, and now You must leave the place where You entered.

(PROGNOSTICATIO EXIMII DOCTORIS PARACELCI, S. 1, 1536, IN-4. FIG. 11)
A PROPHECY BY JOACHIM DE FLORE CONFUSIO AND ERROR VITIABITUR.
(VATICINIUM XIX)

On two cottons of unequal size rise the Symbols of the two Pontifical and Royal Powers. From a third column (lower than the other two, an armed arm emerges from a scythe that threatens both Powers.

*How can we fail to recognise the blind and impersonal Power of the people, attacking the Crown and the tiara?

I don't care which pope in particular has been able to apply this prophetic figure to any particular commentator. For me, this hieroglyphic figure, already so clear in itself, and which has as its epigraph: It will be EVERYWHERE ONLY CONFUSION AND ERROR, IN CORRUPTION, expresses a state of affairs which reached its apogee in 1793-1794, under the Reign of Terror.

This medal can be seen at the National Library, where it has been kept.

Here again, according to Cadet de Gassicourt, is the translation of a ciphered Masonic message, which was spread by Cagliostro, in France as well as in England: *"To all true masons, in the name of Jehovah! The time has come when the construction of the new temple of Jerusalem* MUST *begin. This warning is to invite all true masons in London to gather in the name of Jehovah, the only one in which is a divine trinity,* to be at Reilly's Tavern, Great Queen Street, tomorrow evening, the 3rd of the present

1786, on the 9th of this month, to form a plan, and to lay the foundation stone of the true temple in this visible world... CAGLIOSTRO.[82]

For those who know the Masonic symbols of the temple of Solomon, of the death of Adon-Hiram and of his future resurrection, I think this message is clear.

Enough of Cagliostro and the travelling followers; the anecdotes and commentaries that their history would require would fill half of this work...

Now, if I go into all these details in a chapter that should only deal, it seems, with the trials of witchcraft, it is because I want, by multiplying the documents, to bring out the evidence of a titanic struggle between followers of two different initiations; a struggle whose mysterious preliminaries have been symbolised and the necessary outcome predicted by Saint Martin, following all the rules of the most exquisite esoteric art, in an epico-magical poem, in one hundred and two songs: *Le Crocodile ou la guerre du Bien et du Mal, arrivée sous le règne de Louis XV; œuvre posthume d'un amateur des choses cachées* (The Crocodile or the War of Good and Evil, which arrived during the reign of Louis XV; posthumous work by a lover of hidden things.).[83]

This formidable war –the reality of which I make a point of proving, without promising to reveal its history, here at least– this war falls, in various ways, within the object of a chapter entitled: *Human Justice*; and only superficial readers could see in it a sterile and unjustified digression; a living symbol of our human claims, the French Revolution, doubly just and legitimate in principle, has proved doubly iniquitous in its application; and it is in what way human justice differs from that of God.

To do Evil on the basis of a just law is more revolting to a right conscience than to do Evil by virtue of a principle of iniquity.

Every tree must bear its fruit, according to its race the evil tree bears evil fruit, that is the order of things; the day will come when the evil tree will be uprooted, sawn down and thrown into the fire. But the good tree can only bear bad fruit if it degenerates, if it degenerates, and the spectacle of such an alteration is always distressing; it can only be carried out in Satan's laboratory and by the *law of the Binary*, that is to say, of irremediable antagonism.

We have seen, and we shall verify again, that the Regime of Terror is the fruit of an impure Binary.

Truly enigmatic and astounding, this long delirium of the noblest and most civilised of peoples has baffled the sagacity of all historians. Who would not be exhausted by impotent conjecture, at the appearance of these periodic tides of national bloodshed, where France, metamorphosed into a bacchante, takes pleasure in wallowing with these frenetic and sublime cries all together, which seem imbued with a feverish lyricism of fierce joy and despair?

To shed a sudden light on this strange period, so fertile in cataclysms, a few lines from Abbé Constant (Eliphas Lévi) will suffice: "We remember the strange speech that the president of the Revolutionary Court, his colleague and co-initiate, made to Cazotte himself, condemning him to death. The terrible knot of '93 is still

---

82 *Le Tombeau de Jacques Molay* (The Tomb of Jacques Molay), pages 36-37.
83 Paris, year VII de la Rép., 1 vol. in-8 of 450 pages, small text.

hidden in the darkest sanctuary of secret societies; to the followers of good faith who wanted to emancipate peoples,[84] other followers, of an opposite sect which was linked to older traditions, made a terrible opposition by means similar to those of their adversaries; they made the practice of the great arcane impossible by unmasking the theory. The crowd did not understand anything, but they defied everyone and fell back down in discouragement, lower than they had wanted to elevate it. The Great Arcanum remained more unknown than ever, only the neutralised followers could not exercise power to dominate others or to deliver themselves, so they condemned each other as traitors and dedicated themselves to exile, suicide, dagger and scaffold.[85]

For the time being, let us leave Cazotte and his trial; we shall give this episode the attention it deserves, happy to be able to provide the curious with details of unquestionable authenticity, which, though of the strangest importance, seem to be generally ignored.

Reserving, therefore, without losing sight of this scene, so revealing of the great revolutionary drama, let us consult the author of an interesting and conscientious work published in 1819 under this title: *Des sociétés secrètes en Allemagne, de la secte des illuminés, du Tribunal secret* (Secret societies in Germany, the Illuminati sect, the Secret Tribunal), etc.[86]

This essayist –who could not have the competence of Father Constant in matters of Illuminism– enveloped all the followers in the same reprobation. Between the two schools, all distinction is unknown to him.

It is however surprising to see him write, forty years before the publications of Eliphas Lévi, sentences of this kind:

"To find the key to the Revolutions, from the torture of Charles I to that of Louis XVI, one must always return to this intractable sect…. The red cap, which we saw in 1793 become the emblem of the Jacobins, was the ornament of the British Independents when Cromwell rose to power. Without going any further, isn't it quite singular that at the height of our Revolution, the leading roles were filled by *Pache, Marat, Clootz, Lazouski, Buoncirotti* and *Miranda*, all Swiss, German, Polish, Italian and Spanish members of the Illuminati!… (page 179).

We have already seen that there are three degrees in the Order of the Illuminati. The highest rank was that of the Grand Master; the Duke of Orleans had it on in France a few years before the Revolution…. (p. 226).

The emperors Joseph II and Leopold, who had penetrated the secrets of the Enlightened Ones, were victims of the *Aqua Toffana*. The members of the insurrectional movement of October 5th, June 20th and August 10th were arrested in meetings of followers and initiates, at the *Social Contract Lodge*, rue Coq-Héron, I got it from an eyewitness. Robespierre played a role, but he was not initiated;[87]

---

84 Constant here speaks of the Neo-Templiers.
85 Eliphas Lévi, *Dogme de la Haute Magie* (Transcendental Magic Its Doctrine and Ritual).
86 Paris, Gide fils, 1819, in-8.
87 The writer is mistaken here, Robespierre was perfectly initiated; he was even among the leaders of the second degree.

that is why he was overthrown. He wanted to isolate himself from the sect of which he was the instrument: his head fell on the scaffold...

Never before had the Enlightened Ones seen themselves so powerful; in 1793 they had the executioner's axe at their disposal... Genius, value, talents, virtues, opulence, all passed under the fatal level of the guillotine; Bailly, Custines, Malesherbes, Delaborde, Lavoisier, Westermam, Élisabeth and Vergniaud; all them were executed. Nothing was spared and all that was majestic and sublime disappeared under the scythe of the triumphant Enlightening; only the *black band* remained...

One will ask me, in this hypothesis, why the Grand Master of the Paris Chapter[88] and his acolytes, after having overthrown the throne, perished themselves on the scaffold! I will answer by a fact that is proved after their triumph, THE ILLUMINATI ARE SPLITTING;[89] *one party withdrew to the Jacobins and the other to the Convention. The Jacobins dominated until the Thermidor 9th; it was then that Camille Desmoulins, Hébert, Chaumette, Clootz and the Grand Master of the Chapter were dragged to the torment.* The latter denied his father at the Jacobins' tribune, and protested that his mother had prostituted his bed; it was known where his vows were aimed at; it was betrayal of the sect; he was delivered to the executioner... (pp. 181-183).

The earth would be nothing but a vast heap of rubble and ruins, had not Providence suddenly raised a man whom fortune called to the highest destinies, and whose fall, however much it might have been desired, plunged Europe back into an incalculable series of revolutions. The famous day of Brumaire 18th dealt a terrible blow to the sect of the Enlightened Ones; it saw the fifty-year-old work destroyed in one day by the power of a soldier (p. 184).

The fall of *Napoleon Bonaparte*, due in large part to the Enlightened Ones, resuscitated their influence on all points; it led us in a few years to this false situation which we take for rest (p. 203).

This league of the Enlightened Ones, of Invisible *Seers*, threatens our property and our lives more than ever; *the book of blood is open*, names are written on it, and a hundred thousand assassins, who have sworn to spare neither their relatives nor their friends, are on the move. The unfortunate Fualdès died under their blows (p. 256)."

Will we be forgiven these long quotations? They were necessary. The opinion expressed by the writer of 1819 is a singular guarantee of the truthfulness of Eliphas

---

88 Philippe-Égalité.
89 The 1819 writer is not alone in his opinion: "Philip (said on his side, the Cadet of Gassicourt) had exhausted his coffers and his ambition lost him. After the king's death, for which he himself had voted, he thought he had seized the reins of state; he would have succeeded, no doubt, BUT THE INITIATES SPLITTED. *The loss of the Bourbons, sworn by the Knights Templar, only allowed him to govern by losing his name*; he thought it would be enough to renounce it. He denied his father at the Jacobin tribune; he protested that his mother, a prostitute, had received a coachman in her bed, and that he was the fruit of these shameless loves. And he humbly begged that his name might be taken away from him, and he took the name of Equality. But Robespierre already had a party..." (*Tombeau de Jacques Molay* (Tomb of Jacques Molay), p. 47-48).

Lévi's allegations in 1855. And when the revelations of Cadet de Gassicourt, dated 1796 (*Tombeau de Jacques Molay*, year V) are included, there is little room for doubt.

Moreover, the very facts of the Revolution bear their Templar stamp, and plead in favour of our thesis.

The name *Jacobins* comes from *Jacobus Molay*, and not, as is commonly believed, from the church of the Jacobin monks, a meeting place that the occult sect of Masonry had to choose in preference to any other, even by nominal coincidence. These conspirators had previously founded, in rue Platrière, a *Jean-Jacques* Rousseau lodge, in the house of the famous writer whose theories Robespierre's party was to realise. When this famous lodge was inaugurated, *Jacobinism* had already been named for a long time. But knowledge of this name, which was too significant, was reserved for the masters alone. Let us listen to the Cadet de Gassicourt:

"In order to admit only trustworthy men to their vast projects, they (the Neo-Templiers) invented the ordinary Masonry lodges, under the name of Saint-Jean and Saint-André. These are the ones known in France, Germany and England; societies without secrets whose practices only serve to achieve change, and to make known to the real masons the men they can associate with their great conspiracy. These lodges, which I could call preparatory, have a purpose of real usefulness; they are devoted to charity, they have established between different peoples bonds of brotherhood infinitely estimable; therefore one sees the most virtuous men eagerly seeking such societies. The *true* TEMPLARS or JACOBINS do not hold a lodge; their assemblies are called CHAPTERS. There are four Chapters, one in each city designated by Jacques Molay[90] and each composed of twenty-seven members. Their motto is Jakin, Booz, Mac-Benac, Adonaï 1314, whose initial letters are those of *Jacobus Burgundus Molay beat anno 1314*".[91]

Cadet de Gassicourt adds to these details other revelations about their words and signs of recognition, their philosophical doctrines and their emblems. I have to refer to his work, I cannot transcribe everything, but everything has its value.

There are some very eloquent coincidences, the observation of which is singularly thought-provoking! Thus the heirs of *Jacobus* or *Jacques Molay*, the descendants and successors of those bandits whom the Middle Ages named the "Jacques,[92] *after having established their residence in the very house of Jean-Jacques* (the philosopher par excellence of the Revolution), ended up settling in the *Jacobins*; it was under the name *Jacobinism* that they exalted and propagated their incendiary doctrines.

To those whom such similarities (already noted by Eliphas) bring a smile of compassion, how can one suggest that there may have been something strange and significant in the choice of the premises designated by the Jacobins to receive the poor fallen king? It was Luxembourg, which the National Assembly, in view of the emergency repairs to the Tuileries, had assigned to Louis XVI as his residence, after

---

90 "From the depths of his prison he created four mother lodges: for the East, Naples; for the West, Edinburgh; for the North, Stockholm, and for the South, Paris (*Tombeau de Jacques Molay* (Tomb of Jacques Molay), p. 17.
91 *Tombeau de Jacques Molay* (Tomb of Jacques Molay), pages 21-22.
92 The peasants who revolted in the 14th century against the lords where called the Jacques, since Jacquet was the former nickname of the French peasants.

the day of August 10. But the Jacobins could not tolerate that the successor of Philip the Fair should find in this palace a decent asylum for his little-known majesty. In Luxembourg, the captive king would still retain the appearance of his freedom; perhaps the Assembly would be tempted to return the ghost of power to him... It is a prison they need for their revenge; and what prison? – THE TEMPLE! Irony of an inexorable destiny! It was at the Bastille[93] that Jacques Molay and his people were thrown out on the iniquitous order of a king of France, when the king of France was the strongest! – At the Bastille, then a simple city gate, flanked by two towers... After four and a half centuries of patient and dark struggle, the King of France, defeated in turn, outlawed, humiliated, fallen..., and the heirs of Jacques Molay, all-powerful at that time, relegate him to the damp shadow of their old tower; a sinister place, once both barracks and convent, today a simple prison: *Et nunc, Reges, intelligent; erudimini, qui judicatis terram!*

With the Monarchy desecrated, brought down and brought to nothing, the Jacobins turn against Catholicism. Chaumette, Anacharsis Clootz, the year before, had opened the persecution; under Robespierre, it reached its paroxysm. The hatred of the Neo-Templars was not satisfied by the spectacle of Philip the Fair punished in the person of Louis XVI; poor Pius VII had to pay in his turn the terrible debt contracted by Clement V...

– Fictitious comparisons! A special coincidence of events that are all fortuitous and in no way supportive! It is easy to establish afterwards a causal link between facts which have no other correlation than a vague analogy!... – We are making no secret of the fact that the majority of our readers will keep to this language, despite the notable number of rather singular clues, which we have taken it upon ourselves to group into a compact cluster. If nevertheless, opening a book *printed before the great revolutionary cataclysms,* we were to show the double plan of this Revolution (anti-Bourbonnian and anticlerical), stopped for a long time in the lodges of a Masonry that proclaims itself Templar, what would those who accuse it of being chimerical and paradoxical object to our thesis?

The trial of Cagliostro, who was sentenced to death by order of the Inquisition, and whose sentence was commuted by the Pope to life imprisonment, is well known. Let us look at the *Vie de Joseph Balsamo, comte de Cagliostro, extraite de la Procédure instruite contre lui à Rome, en 1790, traduite d'après l'original italien imprimé à la chambre apostoliquelife* (Life of Joseph Balsamo, Count of Cagliostro, taken from the Proceedings against him in Rome in 1790, translated from the Italian original printed in the Apostolic Chamber) (Paris, 1791, in-8, portrait). Pages 129-132 give us the detailed account Cagliostro gave to his judges of his initiation into the mys-

---

93 "It was with the taking of the Bastille that the Revolution began, and the initiates pointed it out to the people because it had been the prison of Jacques Molay. Avignon was the scene of the greatest atrocities, because it belonged to the Pope and because it contained the ashes of the Grand Master. All the statues of the kings were demolished in order to remove the statue of Henry IV, which covered the square where Jacques Molay was executed. It was in this same square, and not elsewhere, that the initiates wanted to erect a colossus trampling at the feet of the crowns and tiaras, and this colossus was only the emblem of the body of the Templars." (*Tombeau de Jacques Molay* (Tomb of Jacques Molay), pages 42-43).

teries of the Illuminati. The scene takes place in a country house three miles from Frankfurt in Main in 1780. We will transcribe this textual confession:

"...We went down fourteen or fifteen steps into an underground passage and entered a round room, in the middle of which I saw a table; it was opened, and underneath it was an iron box which was opened again and in which I saw a quantity of papers: these two people[94] took from it a handwritten book, made in the form of a missal, at the beginning of which was written: WE, GREAT MASTERS OF THE TEMPLARS, etc... These words were followed by a formula of oath, conceived with the most horrible expressions, which I cannot remember, but which contained the commitment to destroy all despotic rulers. This formula was written in blood and had eleven signatures, in addition to my number, which was the first, all written in blood. I cannot remember all the names of these signatures, except for the names N., N., N., etc. These signatures were those of the twelve Grand Masters of the Enlightened Ones; but the truth is that my number had not been made by me, and I do not know how it was there. What I was told about the contents of this book, which was written in French, and the little I read of it confirmed that *this sect had determined to strike its first blows on France*; that after the FALL OF THIS MONARCHY, it was to strike Italy, and ROME IN PARTICULAR; that Ximenes, of whom we have already spoken, was one of the principal leaders; that they were then at the height of the intrigue, and that the Society had a great quantity of money scattered in the banks of Amsterdam, Rotterdam, London, Genoa and Venice[95]..." (P. 180-181.)

To insist on the value of this deposition would be an insult to the reader's sagacity. So when the throne was abolished, the altar was attacked; the churches closed and devastated; the priests reduced to betraying their oaths; the goddess Reason enthroned under the living emblem of a prostitute on the metropolitan altar of Our Lady; all ecclesiastical goods sequestered or distorted: these things and a thousand others were only the first effects of the Jacobin resentment. And when Bonaparte, sixteen years later, insulted the majesty of the pope captive at Fontainebleau, and, pale with rage, pushed the violence (it is said) to the point of splitting the pontiff's white robe from top to bottom with a blow from his steel spur, this enemy of all sects became, without suspecting it for sure, the late executor of the Templars' vengeance.

How many similar comparisons could be made, if this were our main topic!

Let's borrow from Eliphas Lévi, who narrates them so well, another one of those terribly eloquent anecdotes of the French Revolution. – The year is 1792.

---

94 Two enlightened people who accompanied Cagliostro.
95 One reads in this same *Life of Cagliostro*, published on the documents of the Holy Office (Italian edition, 1790; French translation, 1791), this significant sentence, about the sect of the Enlightened Ones, known as the High Observance: "This one professes the most resolute irreligion, *will use magic in its operations*; under the specious pretext of *avenging the death of the Grand Master of the Knights Templar*, its main aim is the *total destruction of the Catholic religion and the monarchy*" (page 90).

"The king was captive in the Temple and the elite of the French clergy in exile, or in the Abbey. The cannon was thundering on the Pont-Neuf, and threatening signs proclaimed the Homeland in danger. Unknown men organised the massacre. A hideous, gigantic, long-bearded figure was everywhere where there were priests to be slaughtered. – He said to them, with a wild sneer: this is for the Albigensians and the Waldensians! This is for the Templars! This is for Saint Bartholomew's Day! This is for the outcasts of the Cévennes!... And he struck with rage, and he always struck, with the sword, with the blade, with the club. The weapons were broken and renewed in his hands; he was red with blood from head to toe; his beard was all stuck to it, and he swore with appalling blasphemies that he would only wash it with blood.

It was he who proposed a toast to the nation to the angelic Miss Sombreuil...

After the death of Louis XVI, at the very moment when he had just died under the axe of the Revolution, the man with the long beard –that Wandering Jew of killing and revenge– climbed on the scaffold in front of the terrified crowd; he took royal blood in both hands and, shaking it on the heads of the people, he said in a terrible voice: *French people, I baptise you IN THE NAME OF JACQUES and of liberty!*".[96]

Another quotation from the scholar Eliphas will take us back to the person and the trial of the initiate Jacques Cazotte, whose strange adventure we have chosen to conclude this chapter.

We know under what conditions the Kabbalist Pasqualis-Martinez came to offer the initiation to the novelist of the *Diable amoreux* (Devil in Love); it is a mysterious legend to which we will no doubt have to return elsewhere. – In any case, Father Constant, after having sketched the story, followed his account with the following reflections:

"The initiation of Cazotte was to make him a devoted supporter of order and a dangerous enemy for anarchists; and, in fact, we have seen that there is talk of a mountain on which one rises to regenerate oneself, following the symbols of Cagliostro; but this mountain is white with light like Tabor, or red with blood like Sinai and Calvary. There are two chromatic syntheses, says the Zohar, the white one, which is that of harmony and moral life, and the red one, which is that of war and material life: the colour of the day and that of blood. The Jacobins wanted to carry the standard of blood, and their altar was already erected on the red mountain. Cazotte had placed himself under the banner of light and his mystical tabernacle was placed on the white mountain. The bloody mountain triumphed for a moment and Cazotte was proscribed Cazotte had prophesied his own death,[97] because his conscience was committing him to fight against anarchy

---

96 *Historie de la Magie* (History of Magic), pages 443-444.
97 The density of this chapter forbids us to reproduce *in extenso* the most astounding prophecy ever uttered by the human mouth. Anyone can read it in the first volume of the posthumous works of LA HARPE, an eyewitness and ear witness, who has preserved it for us in its smallest details.

HUMAN JUSTICE

to the death. So he continued to obey his conscience, was arrested again[98] and appeared before the Revolutionary Court; he was condemned in advance. The president, after pronouncing his judgement, gave him a strange speech, full of esteem and regret; he urged him to be worthy of himself to the end and to die as a man of heart as he had lived."[99]

It was at a table, at the home of the Duke of Nivernais, at the beginning of 1788. The company, as numerous as it was illustrious, was composed of great lords and ladies, courtiers and people of the legal profession, and finally academicians and poets. The negative and libertine philosophy of Voltaire and Diderot was then a strict obligation, even for the Ladies; one had therefore disparaged the priests, then told gravely anecdotes, interspersed with dithyrambic exclamations in honour of the future Revolution which would abolish prudery, of this Revolution which all wished for.

Cazotte had supported this apology only with an impatient uneasiness. Suddenly he stood up, pale and with his eye lit by a enigmatic flame; in front of all those guests feverishly looking forward to the future, he suddenly tore the veil of future time. – Ah, rejoice, gentlemen, for all of you will see this sublime Revolution which will kill you all in the very name of Fraternity and Reason. – You, Mr. de Condorcet, you will die proscribed by it, you will die in a dungeon of the poison that the happiness of that time will oblige you to always carry with you; – you, Mr. de Champfort, also proscribed, you will die of twenty-two razor blows; – you, Mr. de Vicq d'Azyr, you will have the same death; – You, Aymar de Nicolaï, I see you climbing the steps of the scaffold; – you, Mr. Bailly, will die on the scaffold; – you too, Mr. de Vicq d'Azyr, will die on the scaffold; – you too Mr. Roucher, on the scaffold!

Here I quote verbatim: – *Oh, it is a challenge* –shouted from all sides–, *he has sworn to exterminate us all.*

NO! IT IS NOT ME WHO HAS SWORN!

Who then has sworn all these arbitrary sentences? Who did? – The Jacobins, the Neo-Templars!... it's all too clear.

Let's start again. – Fortunately (here it is La Harpe speaking), you do not put me for nothing in all these wonders! – You will be there, Mr. de La Harpe, and for a miracle at least as great; you will then be a Christian. – If our heads –they cry out–, are not to fall off until that day, we are all immortal!

– Are we happy, we women –says the Duchess of Grammont– to have had nothing to do with your revolutions? At least we never attack our sex.

– Your sex, this time, will not defend you. Yes, Madam Duchess, you too will get on the scaffold. The hangman will take you there in his cart. Ah, at least you will leave me my carriage draped in black... No, no, and bigger ladies than you will do without... Blood princesses, then... Bigger ladies still... Here; Madame de Grammont thought it prudent to break the dogs... You will see that he will not even leave me a confessor! – You will not have one, for the last one to be granted one, by grace, will be... – Speak up!

– The King of France.

Everyone stands up; one finds that the joke becomes too strong and above all that it extends beyond the limits of propriety. The master of the house runs to Cazotte, and in a penetrating tone of voice, begs him to abandon this gloomy joke. But Cazotte believes what he said. As he was about to leave, Madame de Grammont, eager to divert him, questions him:

– Mr. Prophet, you have told us our good fortune, but yours?

– Have you read, Duchess, about the siege of Jerusalem in Josephus? During the siege, a man went round the ramparts seven days in a row, shouting with a gloomy voice: 'Woe! Woe to Jerusalem, and woe to myself!' On the seventh day a huge stone thrown by the enemy machines reached him in the middle of the front line and smashed him to pieces.

Without further explanation, Cazotte curtseyed and went out.

98 He had been arrested once, and saved by his daughter as Sombreuil, during the massacres of September.
99 *Histoire de la Magie* (History of Magic).

This page of Eliphas piqued our curiosity, so much so that we decided to learn more, at length, about the last hours of Cazotte. Chance served us well, by making fall into our hands a brochure that was undoubtedly not much sought after and little known, but which was a precious revelation to us. It is the trial *in extenso* of Cazotte, published under the Directory, probably by order, under this title: CORRESPONDANCE MYSTIQUE DE JACQUES CAZOTTE *avec Laporte et Pouteau, intendant et secrétaire de la Liste civile, pendant les années* 1790-1791-1792, *suivie de son interrogatoire et de son jugemenet* (MYSTICAL CORRESPONDENCE OF JACQUES CAZOTTE with Laporte and Pouteau, Intendant and Secretary of the Civil List, during the years 1790-1791-1792, followed by his interrogation and judgment).[100]

The title is a little misleading, at least in form. Apart from eight pages of notes and one page of epilogue, it is, as we have said, the minute of the trial that filled the hearing of 24 September 1792: the Revolutionary Court condemns Cazotte to the death penalty for crimes of high treason and conspiracy against the constituted authorities. However, almost the entire hearing was devoted to the reading of the letters that Cazotte had written to Laporte and especially to Pouteau, to be placed before the eyes of the king by them.

From time to time, a few fragments of interrogation slip in between two letters; the accused is questioned with consideration and moderation; he answers with calm, gentleness and firmness:

D. – *You may be tired: the Tribunal is ready to give you as much time as you think you need, to take food, refreshment or rest?*

R. – *I am very sensitive to the Tribunal's attention. The fever that I am in at the moment puts me in the position of supporting the debate; moreover, the sooner my trial is over and the sooner I will be free of it, as well as the judges and the jurors.*

When the accused refuses to answer, the President passes without insisting. Not a word of reproach or blame. What a courteous trial!

To awaken the reader, truly charmed by this polite discussion, where one can feel the mutual esteem piercing under each word, all that is needed is for the terrible sentence from earlier to come back to his memory: *Cazotte was condemned in advance!*

In the midst of unbridled political passions and great hatred, this gentleness painfully detonates, this courtesy seems to be affected; finally –to use a vulgar expression– this trial is chilling.

Condemned in advance! A dreadful word… and rigorously true. So true, in fact, that the Court of First Instance, without any consideration, *rejects an application for jurisdiction* raised at the bar by the defendant Julienne; and if ever jurisdiction was declined, it was that day.

"The accused based his protest on the fact that, having been tried on 2 September by the sovereign people and by municipal officers in their sashes, who had released him, it was impossible, without infringing the sovereignty of that

---

100 Paris, Lerouge, Deroy et Maret, year VI of the Republic, I vol. in-12 of 182 pages, with portrait.

same people, to pass judgement against him on the facts for which he had been arrested and then released." (p. 19).

Non bis in idem. – The axiom is well known everywhere and uncontested and dominates all legislation . What does the Tribunal do?

"The Tribunal, without stopping or having regard to the protest lodged by Mr. Cazotte, *orders that it shall be disregarded…*" (p. 17).

It added that "a copy of the said protest and a copy of this judgment shall, at the National Commissioner's request, *be sent to the Minister of Justice, to be communicated by him to the National Convention, if necessary…*" (p. 17). (*Ibid.*). However, as the death sentence pronounced during the day was executed that evening, at about seven o'clock, this restriction served a great purpose. What barbaric irony!

Moreover, it must be admitted that Cazotte's correspondence was, under the circumstances, as compromising as possible.

Like Saint-Martin, a disciple of the same Martinez, then posthumous pupil of Jacob Boehme; like Dutoit-Mambrini, the theosophist of Geneva, who published in 1793, under the pseudonym Keleph-ben-Nathan, an admirable work[101] despite some errors; like Fabre d'Olivet, whose initiation dates from this period; like others, Cazotte belonged to the oldest tradition; he belonged to the Orthodox initiation mentioned above. But less cautious than Dutoit and St. Martin, he was one of those who actively worked, on the astral, moral and intellectual levels, for the counter-revolution.

L. C. DE SAINT-MARTIN   J. CAZOTTE

Adept, he was one of the first victims of the Jacobin or Neo-Temple Gentlemen.

---

101 *La Philosophie divine* (The Divine Philosophy), S.-L., 1793. 3 vol. in-8. Dutoit was the spiritual son of the theosophist Saint-Georges de Marsais.

One must see how the judges of Cazotte want him to speak on the chapter of his initiation. Listen to the insidious question he is asked:

D. – *Which sect did you join? Is it that of the enlightened ones?*

R. – *All sects are enlightened, but the one I am talking about in my letter is the sect of the MARTINISTS. I remained attached to it for three years; various causes forced me to resign; nevertheless I have always remained a friend of it* (p. 45).

Cazotte responds with a rare presence of mind. He himself had sensed, at the moment when the struggle between the two rival initiations was about to begin, how dangerous the shock would be; everything leads one to believe that he had wanted to avoid it in the first place. – Let us refer to the catalogued letter N., dated 4 April 1792:

"The spades will turn against the spades, my dear friend; have a little patience... You are not initiated? Applaud yourselves for it! Remember the word: *Et scientia eorum perdet eos.* If I am not safe, I whom divine grace has removed from the trap, judge the risk of those who remain in it.

The safety of the cows' floor has long been praised. THE KNOWLEDGE OF OCCULT THINGS IS A STORMY SEA FROM WHICH ONE CANNOT SEE THE SHORELINE" (pp. 94-95).

And yet he has changed his mind. – If the terrible struggle is inevitable, let him throw himself into it. He feels so strongly that it is a matter of life and death for all of us that he, that excellent man, that orthodox theosophist, that gentle old man, after shouting out to the foreigner in France to restore absolute power to the king, cries out: "The king must be on guard against one of his inclinations, and that is clemency..." (pp. 94-95). Let him beware of stopping the sword; let him reflect on the punishments suffered by the leaders of the Israelites who spared the victims designated by the Lord. *Man does not know what he is doing when he wants to spare this blood; his compassion degenerates into cruelty... The greatest happiness that can happen to a criminal is to be tortured on the earth,* BECAUSE WE DO NOT PAY TWICE[102] and that it is terrible to fall guilty and unpunished into the hands or under the justice of the living God" (pp. 64-65).

There are so many lessons to be learned from this book, so many instructive and unpublished details about men and the occult causes of the great Revolution... Alas, we have to limit ourselves. Already too dense, this chapter goes beyond its normal framework. Let us now move on to the end. Let us listen to the end of the indictment of Réal, the public accuser:

"...And you –he said to the accused–, why do I have to find you guilty, after seventy-two years of virtue? Why must the two who followed them have been employed in meditating on projects all the more criminal in that they tended to re-establish despotism and tyranny? Why must you have conspired against the freedom of your country? It is not enough to have been a good son, a good

---

[102] *Non bis in idem!* Poor Cazotte! This unquestionable principle will for once be contested at his trial, and it will cost him his life.

husband and a good father, you must, above all else, be a good citizen..." And further on: "He could not excuse himself for a lack of ignorance, he who was a philosopher and INITIATED; he who, in the ice of old age, kept the fires of a boiling and enlightened youth..." (p. 173-174).

Following Julienne's plea, Lavau, president of the Revolutionary Court, assisted by the citizens Dubail, Jaillant and Naulin, judges, read the death sentence.

After pronouncing the above-mentioned judgement, the president addressed the condemned man with the following speech[103]:

"Weak toy of old age, unfortunate victim of the prejudices of a life spent in slavery! You, whose heart was not big enough to feel the price of a holy freedom, *but who proved, by your security in the debates, that you knew how to sacrifice your very existence for the support of your opinion, listen to the last words of your judges! May they pour into your soul the precious balm of consolation! May they, in determining you* TO COMPLAIN FOR THE SORT OF THOSE WHO HAVE CONDEMNED YOU, inspire you with that stoicity which MUST preside over your last moments, and *imbue you with the respect which the law has inspired in us...*

YOUR PEERS HAVE HEARD YOU, YOUR PEERS HAVE CONDEMNED YOU; *but at least their judgement was as pure as their conscience;* at least no personal interest came to disturb their decision by the heartbreaking memory of remorse. Go, regain your courage, gather your strength, contemplate death without fear; THINK THAT IT HAS NO RIGHT TO ASTONISH YOU: IT'S NOT A MOMENT THAT SHOULD FRIGHTEN A MAN LIKE YOU!

But before separating yourself from life, *before paying to the law the tribute of your conspiracies,* look at the imposing attitude of France, in the bosom of which you were not afraid to call out loudly the enemy, what am I saying?... The wage-slave! See your ancient homeland oppose the attacks of its vile detractors with as much courage as you supposed cowardice. *If the law could have foreseen that it would have to pronounce against a guilty man such as you,* out of consideration for your old age, it would not have imposed any other penalty on you; but be reassured, if it is severe when it pursues, when it has pronounced the sword falling from its hands. She (the law) groans over the loss even of those who wanted to tear her apart. What she does for the guilty in general, *she does especially for you.* Look at her shed tears on that white hair, which she thought she had to respect until the moment of your condemnation; *may this spectacle bring repentance within you; may it commit you,* WRONG OLDER MAN, *to take advantage of the moment that still separates you from death, to erase even the slightest trace of your plots, with a regret that is rightly felt.*[104]

Another word. You were a man, a Christian, a philosopher, an INITIATE; know how to die as a man, know how to die as a Christian; that is all that your country can still expect from you!"

---

103 This speech is of such a nature and scope that I do not think I have the right to delete a single word; I transcribe it in extenso (pp. 178-181).
104 Here, the fanaticism of the Neo-Templar touches the sublime of tenderness! It is the sectarian who would like to convert his enemy before killing him.

The author of the booklet continues: "This speech, which struck part of the audience with astonishment, made no impression on Jacques Cazotte. Afer the words: *go, regain your courage, gather your strength, contemplate death without fear, think that he has no right to astonish you, it is not a moment that should frighten a man like you*, he raised his hands and shook his head, raising his eyes to the sky with a serene and determined face. Taken to the criminal office, he told those around him that he regretted only his daughter... The execution of the judgement took place on the Place du Carrousel at around seven in the evening: the condemned man showed admirable presence of mind and composure along the road and on the scaffold" (pp. 178-185, *passim*).

I do not know what impression the trial and sentence has left on the reader, but I protest to him that he has just witnessed a solemn and formidable drama; he has felt, without a doubt, that this is more than just a criminal trial.... I would be afraid of distorting his emotion by mixing in the expression of mine. I will end with a few noble words of Eliphas:

"The Revolution, even in the courtroom, was a civil war, and the brothers greeted each other before they killed each other. On both sides there were sincere, and therefore respectable, convictions. He who dies for what he believes to be true is a hero, even when he is mistaken, and the anarchists of the Bloody Mountain were not only bold enough to send others to the scaffold, they themselves climbed it without turning pale. – Let God and posterity be their judges".[105]

---

105 *Historie de la Magie* (History of Magic).

Chapter V
The Sorcerer's Arsenal
ה

The Pope = the Quinary = the Will, its instruments... *The Sorcerer's Arsenal*

We have seen Satan enthroned in his temple of ignominy, and the Black Magician, supreme pontiff of his cult, officiate there in great pomp.[1]
    It was curious for us to visit all the corners of a building which is both the pantheon of Fanaticism and the Basilica of Folly.
    Nothing typical escaped the patience of our investigations; not that we looked at every pillar, but finally –if only for a minute– our gaze wandered everywhere, attentive and scrutinising.
    The infamy of the sanctuary is known to us; the abomination of the idol, the shame of the servant, and the turpitudes of the cult.
    It would remain for us to complete our examination by a visit to the sacristy. – Satan's sacristy is the sorcerer's arsenal.
    Let's go to work and make an inventory of the objects there.
    One more word, before we begin our task. Since we have little space at our disposal, we have had to neglect the scrupulous, methodical counting of the numerous rites and interminable ceremonies in which the three twin sisters who legislate in this place indulge: Superstition, Malice and Stupidity.
    The Liturgical Summa of the Sorcerer is composed of massive folios and in-quarto, which we have very superficially leafed through together, reader friend, stopping only at the most decisive pages.

---

[1] According to the ancient, traditional, archaic rite. – In Chapter VI: *Modern Avatars of the Sorcerer*, we will again surprise the Sorcerer in the exercise of his priestly duties, but according to the new rite and dressed in a costume in fashion of the day.

The Inventory which we are about to undertake will provide us, from time to time, with a pretext for returning to them.[2] It will only be incidental, for sure; descriptions and information will be delivered in a jumble. No systematic division is to be expected...

And even, to shorten this chapter –avoiding transitions that would not connect anything, and comparative clarifications that would not elucidate much– we will (like a bailiff) proceed in alphabetical order. Light will emerge, if possible, from the possible clash of ideas.

Let us blindly trust the logic of chance!

Grimoire Lesson

Inventory of the sorcerer's arsenal
(Grouping of subjects in alphabetical order)

A

ADRAMELECH. – Syrian idol; the Middle Ages made him a devil. – See ch. I.

---

2 Much of the information which would be included here has already been given in the course of the preceding chapters, sometimes in sufficient detail.
We consider it unnecessary to produce them again, but, when it is possible to do so, we shall take care to refer the reader back to them, in order to avoid repetition.

AGGARATH. – One of the wives of Sammael, in the Pneumatics of the Talmudists. – See ch. I.

AIGUILLETTE. – It is, in the pictorial language of Sorcery, the name of the *Phallus* that is to be paralysed, to this end to prevent the young spouses from fulfilling their conjugal duty. This is called *nouer l'aiguillette*[3] (see chapter III, p. 105).

ALBERT LE GRAND (ALBERT THE GREAT). – From the works of this theologian, bishop of Regensburg (1196-1280), fragments have been extracted from which two grimoires (see this word), even more stupid than famous, have been composed:

1° *Le Grand-Albert* (The Grand-Albert) (or *the admirable secrets of Albert the Great*) was printed many times, in the formats of in-12, in-18 and in-24. – It is divided into four books: the first deals extensively with the mysteries of animal generation, conception and seed; the second deals with the virtues attributed to plants, stones, animals, astrology and the wonders of the world; the third offers our meditations a treatise on the virtues of droppings and excrement, the properties of several unfortunate insects, and ends with a rich collection of so-called natural secrets; the fourth book is a banal treatise on *Physiognomy* and also concludes with a list of recipes. – One of the best French editions is that of *Lyon*, 1775, in-18 with figures.

2° Even more extravagant, the *Petite Albert* (Little Albert) (or the solid treasure of the) contains black magic formulas which are impertinent and baroque, but which are even more successful on the lips of our shepherds and village sorcerers; they have put all their confidence in this lampoon, which is for them the Alpha and Omega of kabbalistic science, and if they have any natural disposition, faith crowns them sorcerers. – See preferably the edition of *Lyon*, 6516, in-18, "enriched with mysterious figures and the way to make them".

Under the title of *Albert-Moderne* (Modern Albert), collections of scientific recipes have been published, with the laudable aim of modifying the prevailing ideas among the rural populations, and of substituting for the superstitious formulas dear to them some notions of positive science. Nevertheless, the incorrigible shepherd always comes back to his solid treasure.

ALMANACH DU DIABLE (DEVIL'S ALMANAC). – Semi-prophetic and semi-facétieuse publication, directed against the Jansenists, during the reign of Louis XV. Some of the predictions contained in this work may have seemed a little reckless to the authorities, who diligently removed the copies they were able to seize. As a result, the two *Almanacs of the Devil* for the years 1737 and 1738 (in the Underworld, in-24), became rare and climbed quite high in book sales.

AMULETS. – The Amulet is an object of superstitious devotion, which people carry on themselves to protect them from some misfortune, to ward off some accident or to escape some epidemic.

---

3 A spell that was believed to have the power to prevent the consummation of the marriage. This is indeed an old impotence spell. The counter-spell was *dénouer l'aiguillette*.

The Amulet is protective, a shield; it is attributed a passive and preventive virtue; this is how the Amulet differs from the Talisman (see this word), which is commonly believed to have active and acquisitive properties.

Amulets have infinite variations: from the living toad carried in a horn box (see chapter III, p. 101), as guarantee against bewitchment, to the *Agnus Dei*, to the blessed medals, scapulars and other pious objects, whose use the Church authorises and even advises.

Mascots and other *Lucky charms*, which have been so fashionable in recent years, are magical objects of a bastard nature, between the Amulet and the Talisman.

ANDRODAMAS. – A sort of fabulous magnet, which has the property of attracting silver, iron and bronze.

ANDROID. – This was the name given to certain metal statuettes, masterpieces of mechanics, to which the property of thinking, speaking and moving was attributed. All automatically.

Albert le Grand was considered to have made an *Android* who reasoned metaphysically with unfailing rigour. As this quibbling automaton accumulated syllogisms on dilemmas inexhaustibly, Saint Thomas Aquinas, weary and impatient with his deafening dialectic, smashed it to pieces with a blow of his stick.

Some sorcerers went about it in other ways to obtain an Android, or rather a *Homunculus*. – Christian excerpts this amazing recipe from a handwritten grimoire: "Take a black hen's egg and squeeze out a quantity of mucus equal to the volume of a large bean. Replace this mucus with *sperma viri*, and fill the crack in the egg with a little virgin parchment, slightly moistened. Then put your egg in a layer of manure on the first day of the moon of March, which you will know from the table of pacts. After thirty days of incubation, a small monster with some semblance of human form will emerge from the egg. You will keep it hidden in a secret place and feed it with aspic seed and earthworms. As long as it lives, you will be happy in everything." (Christian, *Histoire de la Magie* (History of Magic), p. 450-451).

And this is how the odious marries with the ridiculous. – (See the word *Mandrake*.)

ANTICHRIST. – Incarnation of the diabolic Word, as opposed to the divine Word in Jesus Christ (See the very curious explanations I give on this subject in the first chapter).

APPLE. – The sorcerers, wishing to go to the Sabbath, greased their whole body with a certain ointment based on narcotic drugs: then the Devil appeared to them at "midnight", and took them to the "place" of these assemblies. – See our chapter II, in the *Key to Black Magic*, we shall return to the composition of these ointments.

ASTROLABE. – This is the instrument used by Astrologers to determine the state of Heaven on the day and at the hour desired, and to draw up the *Genethic Theme* of which the *Horoscope* is the commentary.

The *Astrology* of the ancient sanctuaries was a real and profound science; unfortunately, it has become depraved by being vulgarised, to the point of becoming unrecognisable.

Judicial Astrology,[4] which was so honoured in the Middle Ages and which still has fervent supporters today, is one of the most illusory and ridiculous things imaginable. - See Fabre d'Olivet's excellent essay on the Astrology of the Ancients; it is a page as deep as it is substantial: *Vers dorés de Pythagore* (Golden Verses of Pythagoras), Paris, 1813, 1 vol. in-8 (pp. 269-278, sixteenth review).

ATTRACTIVE PLANT (by *Van Helmont*). - On page 708 of the complete works of this spagyric theosophist (published in Frankfurt MDC LXXXII, in-4) we read: - "Noui herbam passim obuiam, quæ si teratur et foueatur manu, donec intepuerit, mox alterius manum detinueris, quoad et illa tebescat amore tui, ille totus continuo ardet, ad aliquot dies. Detinui pedem cuiusdam catuli, hic confestim peregrinum me secutus adeo, quod noctu ante cubiculum ejularet quo eidem aperirem, renunciata hera sua. Adsunt Bruxellæ mihi huius facti testes." (*De Magnetica vulnerum curatione*, chap. XXVII, p. 708).

This famous plant, whose knowledge is traditional among the Brothers of the Rose + Cross, is none other than *Verbena rustica*. Its use has never been within the reach of black magicians, although its vulgar name can be read -among a thousand others- in all the pages of their Grimoires.

If I speak so without hesitation or ambivalence, it is because first of all -I repeat- the *attractive plant* is designated by its real name in the worst collections of witchcraft. It is above all because its effectiveness depends entirely on the exact astronomical time when it must be picked, and on the essential rites for the preparation of the lightning philtre of which it provides the basis.

By insinuating that it is enough to warm the Verbena in his hand to develop its virtue, Van Helmont gives distorts the conditions required for its authentic use. He is silent on this point; we must be silent like him.

AVATARS. - This is the name given to the many and varied forms in which a being is incarnated in turn. (See, in Brahmanic theology, the incarnations of Vishnu). I speak, in chapter I, of the typical Avatars of Satan.

B

BAMBOO, BLACK. - A magical plant from the West Indies, used by black sorcerers for their love potions. It can be substituted for *Van Helmont's Attractive Plant* (see this word).

BAPHOMET. - This is the idolatrous figure, or rather the occult symbol, which the Templars were accused of worshipping (see details in ch. IV.).

BASILISK. - A fabulous animal on which the most incredible tales have been told. "Just as -says Boguet- that ... the mule born of a donkey and a mare: is the

---

4 Birth chart astrology.

Basilisk, born of a cock and a toad." (*Disc. des Sorciers* (Discourse of the sorcerers), Lyon, 1610, in-8, p. 84).

The same demonologer disputes seriously if the Basilisk kills with his gaze, as is notorious for "the Serpent Catoblepas, which makes its home around the Nigris Fountain in Ethiopia, which many believe to be the source of the Nile." (*Ibid.*, p. 187.) Needless to say, Boguet decided in favour of the affirmative.

In our countryside, it is still believed that old cocks lay an egg (!) from which the basilisk comes out.

The Basilisk was one of the familiar faces of the Sabbath... Today there is a small snake of that name, but it seems to be of a different breed, you suffer its look without dying –at least at once– and the natural crown, gemmed with a carbuncle, which made a heraldic crest on the forehead of this singular reptile, has completely disappeared...

BAT. – This nocturnal and silent animal, which is not a bird, but neither looks like a mammal, figures prominently in Satanas' classic menagerie.

Vespertilian blood is used in the composition of a host of spells and charms (see *Evocation*).

Some people consider the Bat to be the protective deity of houses, the *genius loci*, who we must be careful not to destroy or even frighten.

These kind of flying penates[5] are particularly revered in the Caribbean. The unwary person who, at home, would kill one of them, would risk her life.

BEAST OF THE APOCALYPSE. – Fantastic and hieroglyphic animal from the vision of Patmos. Saint John sees it rising from the sea. (Refer to chap. I.)

BEAU-CIEL-DIEU (GOD). – This is the name of a magical poisoning charge, the composition of which was revealed during the memorable trial of the shepherd Hocque. Read in chapter III of our book the history of this trial and the discovery of this charm.

BEELZEBUB. – Idol of Syria, which I describe in chapter I. The Middle Ages turned Beelzebub into a demon.

BELL. – Bells are commonly attributed with the natural virtue of repelling lightning.

This belief has given rise to a strange practice among devotees. They fight over small silver bells, blessed by the pope, and which Home exports annually by the thousands. When a storm threatens to strike the trees and chop the harvest, the devotees come out with the bell they brandish on the threshold of their farm or house, and –God willing– they ward off lightning and hail, which will fall on the land of the neighbours, ungodly enough not to have procured, in good time, a small silver bell blessed by the Holy Father.

For the Black Mass Bell, which is made of horn with a wooden clapper, see chapter IV, Gaufridy's posthumous confession.

---

5 Penates: They were the household gods, who presided over families, and were worshiped in the interior of every dwelling, by the Romans.

THE SORCERER'S ARSENAL 175

BELPHEGOR. – Another idol of Palestine, which the Christians also made one of the companions of hell.

BEWITCHMENT. – The purpose of this spell is to strike an enemy from a distance. – Sorcerers thus sow death, consumption, disease or any other scourge that Hell has made them dispensers of. – See chapter III for the different modes of bewitchment.

BIRDS. – Some mystical shepherds still derive from the flight of the birds –both lucky and ill-fated–, fateful omens, in the fashion of the ancient augurs.

The universal symbolism of the magicians, which once established connections from one world to another, had attributed bird hieroglyphics to certain cosmogonic powers. Thus the Dove expressed the plastic and configurative virtue of the celestial wife *Ionah*; the Raven, the devouring and compressive force of *Hereb*, the occult agent of the return to essence. The Phoenix was the emblem of substantial homogeneity under the illusory transformations of matter. The Eagle represented the pure Spirit, etc... But soon everything became confused and the tide of general materialisation invaded the science of symbols.

For the Sorcerer, the Eagle is nothing more than a bird whose brain, mixed with food, would cause a certain delirium; the Dove spills its blood in the flask where impure potions are elaborated; the Raven gives a stone that would have the virtue of reconciling enemies, etc... – The Pelican, the Blackbird, the Owl, the Kite, and finally the Hoopoe (already mentioned) are prostituted by the Sorcerer for such ridiculous uses.

BLACK COQ. – The sacrifice of the black rooster is part of the ceremonies of evocation, according to the *Grimoire d'Honorius* (see this word).

In this grimoire we read: "After sunrise, a black rooster shall be killed and the first feather of the left wing shall be taken and kept for use in its time. The eyes, the tongue and the heart shall be plucked out, dried in the sun, and then ground into powder. At sunset, the rest of the rooster will be buried in a secret place, etc... On Tuesday, at dawn, he (the necromancer) will put the feather of the rooster on the altar, which will be carved with a new penknife, and he will write on clean white paper, with the blood of Jesus Christ (consecrated wine), the figures represented, etc..." (pages 8 and 9 of the alleged edition of Rome, 1760, in-12, with coloured figures).

The theosophist *Amaravella* teaches us that the *sacrifice of the Black Rooster* is part of the rites of trial observed by the *Heung-te* (brothers) of the *San-hohwuy* Chinese society, whose followers are punished by an imperial edict with death. These Heung-té are black magicians, united to do evil (see the *Lotus*, 2nd year, volume IV, n° 22).

BLACK MASS. – An obscene and blasphemous sacrifice, which the Devil and his acolytes celebrated on the Sabbath (See chapter II).

BLOOD. – Blood has a plastic and powerfully expansive virtue, which makes it very suitable for all the operations of the Goetia. But if the magicians of antiquity seem to have spread it in the evocations, only sorcerers nowadays disgrace their rites with these abominable libations.

The spilled blood abundantly engenders the larvae and serves to objectify them.

"Blood is the great sympathetic agent of life; it is the motor of imagination, it is the animated *substratum* of magnetic or astral light, polarised in living beings; it is the first incarnation of the universal fluid; it is materialised vital light. It is made in the image and likeness of infinity; it is a negative substance, in which billions of living and magnetised globules swim and agitate, globules inflated by life and all the vermilion of this elusive fullness... The visions are the delirium of the blood... No one would invent the monsters that his over excitement brings forth; it is the poet of dreams; it is the great hierophant of delirium." – Eliphas Lévi, *La Science des Esprits* (The Science of Spirits).

See, at the word *Carcass*, Porphyry's masterly opinion. See also, in chapter III, the evocation of Tiresias Odysseus.

The blood of the doves entered most of the *Philtres*. (See this word.)

BOWL, FATEFUL. – Divination instrument, made of an alloy of the seven mystical metals, with all the letters of the alphabet engraved around the circumference. A ring full of theurgic signs is suspended by a wire above the bowl supported by a tripod – and one evokes the Sibylline geniuses.

This was at least, if we are to believe Ammian, Marcellin and Zosimus, the rite celebrated by some of the courtiers of Emperor Valens, under the direction of the magician Pallade.

The latter pronounced the evocations aloud, standing in the heavy cloud of consecrated perfumes. A laurel wreath girdled his forehead, in the style of the Delphic priests, and a branch of verbena was waving on his right... We saw the ring quivering and swaying at the end of the wire. Suddenly a metallic note tinkled, plaintive; then another, then two more: the ring had struck the Θ of the zodiacal band; then the E, then the O, and finally the Δ. – Théodore! Cried one of the assistants, and it was not considered useful to continue the operation any further that day. (The request made to the Geniuses Rectors of Destiny concerned the successor of Valens Augustus, whose first reply from the Invisibles had prophesied a violent death).

Fatal prediction! Caesar, who had spies everywhere, soon found out everything. His anger was great, made tenfold by his fear. He had Pallade arrested and dragged him to the torture chamber, together with the suspect whom the oracle seemed to have crowned for the scaffold: Theodore. The first syllables of this name sounded to imperial ears like a sacred threat... But where to stop, on the slope of mistrust? Other names also began with the four letters ΘΕΟΔ... and this fateful arrest had struck the tyrant's mind. Anxious that it might be another candidate of Fortune, the Emperor successively condemned to death all *Theodosius, Theodore, Theodat...*

It was a lost cause. The future made it well known that it is possible to evade Caesar's edicts, but not to evade the decrees of Fate. Valens died in a war against the Goths: he was burned at the bottom of a thatched cottage, where he thought he would find an asylum after the defeat – and his successor was in fact Theodosius (the son of one of those whom Valens had killed). The emissaries of death had not been able to discover this young man in Spain, where he was living in seclusion.

Thus the oracle of Pallade was fulfilled, the man with the theurgical bowl (378).

BROUCOLAQUES. – Name of the Vampires of Greece; the name alone has changed, the stories are the same (see p. 74).

C

CAMAIEU. – Gaffarel, author of *Curiosités inouïes sur la sculpture talismanique des Persans; Horoscope des Patriarches et lecture des Étoiles* (Unheard-of curiosities on the talismanic sculpture of the Persians; Horoscope of the Patriarchs and reading of the Stars) (Rouen, 1631, in-8, with two planispheres), – Gaffarel names *Gamahez* or *Camaïeux* the stones spontaneously imprinted with certain hieroglyphs, to which he attributes admirable virtues, and which he classifies among the natural talismans.

According to his theory, renewed by Oswald Croll –*Livre des signatures* (Book of Signatures)–, these imprints, often marvellous in their finesse and sharpness, are the signatures of the Elemental Forces that manifest themselves in the three lower kingdoms.

Long before Gaffarel and Crollius, the great Paracelsus knew the Gamaea, whose marvellous virtues he used for his occult medicine. In his works, he dealt with them in great detail and on several occasions, particularly in volume II of his *Opera omnia* (Geneva edition, 1658, 3 vol. in-folio). See, among others, volume II on page 172, column 2e.

CANDLES. – The sorcerers make candles out of tallow of hanging, to garnish the *Hand of Glory* (see this word).

For the black candles of the Sabbath, read Gauffridy's confession, which I report in chapter IV. The guests of these assemblies must hold one of these lights in their left hand, when they bend over to kiss the back of Leonardo.

Jérôme Cardan speaks in his works of a *Magic Candle* for the search for treasures. It is also made of human fat; it is adapted to the concave part of a black crescent made of elbow wood, so as to depict the Hebrew Shin (ש), symbol of the elemental fire, or the Sabbath flame between Leonardo's two horns. When, armed with this strange object, one approaches the place where some treasure is buried, the candle begins to spark; this phenomenon is accentuated as one approaches, and the flame goes out when one touches the treasure.

CANTHARIDES. – Flies of a metallic and shiny green colour, which owe to an extremely poisonous alkaloid –Cantharidin– aphrodisiac properties, which sorcerers knew how to take advantage of in the composition of their ointments and their electuaries, to determine the direction of erotic dreams.

See chapter II of our book. – In the *Key to Black Magic*, we will give, in the chapter on ointments, all the details we may want to know.

CARCASS. – However careful I may be to avoid the dogmatic theories of High Magic for the time being, I cannot bring myself to pass over in silence a page of

Porphyry, which is in the first place revealing the profound meaning attributable to the bloody rites of evocation by the sword. Listen to what this theurgist says in substance: "The soul, remaining bound to the body, even after physical death, by a strange tenderness and an affinity all the more narrow as this essence has been separated more abruptly from its envelope, we see souls in great numbers fluttering, all disoriented, around their earthly remains. Moreover, we see them diligently searching for the remains of foreign corpses, and, on all things, for the freshly shed blood, whose vapour seems to restore to them for a few moments certain faculties of life.

"Sorcerers therefore abuse this notion in the exercise of their art. None of them knows how to evoke these souls by force and compel them to appear, either by acting on the remains of the body they have left, or by invoking them in the vapour of the spilled blood." (Porphyry, *Des Sacrifices* (The Sacrifices), chap. II of True Worship).

I summarise without comment.

CAT. – Transformation of women into cats (see ch. III). Berbiguier's antipathy to this animal (see chap. I).

CATOBLEPAS. – It is, according to the demonologist Henry Boguet, a kind of dragon, whose gaze kills, like that of Basilisk (see this word).

Gustave Flaubert gives a completely different description of this fantastic animal: "The Catoblepas, a black buffalo with a pig's head falling to the ground and attached to its shoulders by a thin, long and flabby neck, like an empty gut. He is sprawled completely flat, and his feet disappear under the enormous hard mane that covers his face." (*La tentation de saint Antoine* (The temptation of Saint Anthony), Paris, Lemerre, 1884, small in-12, p. 247).

CHARACTERS. – These are, in Magic, the manifest signs of a verb, or simply expressive signs of an idea. – Isolated, they are called *hierograms*; grouped according to the occult laws into a symbolic whole, they are called *hieroglyphs*. When the hieroglyph appears as a plastic symbol, a painting or a drawing that in itself has an apparent meaning, it becomes an *emblem*. Finally, it is best to call it a *pantacle* if it affects a geometric shape (circular, triangular, stellar, etc.).

The Grimoires are full of strange signs, representative of demons and planetary spirits, and which seem at first glance to be completely indecipherable.

This is not the case with most of them. These characters, originally composed according to the rules of an invariable art, have no doubt been altered to the point of becoming unrecognisable at times; no doubt also mystifiers have introduced into these works new signs, scribbled at pleasure, in the absence of any rules, and which it is necessary to know how to recognise and reject at first sight. But for the other characters, it is only a question of finding the key. The Brothers of the Rose + Cross have published this key in a very strange mystical work: *Chymica Vannus* (Amstel., ap. J. Janson., 1666, in-4, fig.). See, for example, pages 55, 62 of the Complement, entitled *Commentatio de pharmaco catholico*; we shall see how the authors,[6] by the methodical combination of radical signs, form hieratic syllables, and compose words

---

6 These authors are called: – "Pro-authoribus Immortalibus Adeptis", seen at the bottom of the title.

by the marriage of these syllables with each other. The adaptation is purely spagyric in *Chymica Vannus*; but this adaptation is only an example proposed; and the rule, remaining identical, can be applied, in a similar way, to the formation of characters in the field of the other sciences which are branches (like the alchemical branch) of the universal strain of Hermes. It is only rarely useful to go very far in the analysis and synthesis of characters. In most cases, the list of zodiacal and planetary signs together constitutes a very passable primitive alphabet, the combinations of which explain and justify the hieroglyphs which seem to be the most rebellious to any interpretation.

In this matter, the *Stéganographie* (Steganography) of Abbot Trithème, especially his *Polygraphie* (Polygraphy), will be fruitfully consulted. Trithème is the great master of secret writings.

See also the *Monas hieroglyphica* of John Dee (in volume II of the *Theatrum chymicum* of Strasbourg, –Argentorati–, 1659).

The characters of the Grimoires are said to be the signatures of certain demons. In order to evoke them, care is taken to trace these characters around the *Magic Circle* (see this word).

CHARM. – A magical preparation, which is dealt with at length throughout chap. III, (see also chap. I.

CHILD'S SKULL. – Sorcerers attribute to the skull of a murdered child the virtue of rendering its bearer invisible. Collin de Plancy, in his *Dictionnaire infernal* (Infernal Dictionary), recounts the trial of a man named Vautrin, sentenced to death by the court of assizes of the Haute-Marne, in February 1857, for having coldly cut the head of a breastfeeding child. He intended to compose a charm of invisibility.

CLAVICLE. – King Solomon is credited with this very strange treatise on the evocation of the Spirits, although no doubt it was written much later, but which was evidently the work of an initiated Rabbi.

It must be said that printed editions of the *Clavicle* are uniformly detestable and uninteresting.

As for the manuscript copies, there are also many notoriously altered and ridiculous ones; but sometimes one finds good copies, studded with a large number of coloured characters and pantacles.

For those who have the key to its hieroglyphics, it is an infinitely precious work; for others, if they believe the text to be deliberately mystifying, they will only be able to get the most false idea of what the Kabbalist master claimed to teach there.

I possess a very beautiful manuscript of the *Clavicle*, translated from Hebrew into French in 1641, and riddled with curious pantacular and talismanic figures. This copy comes from the library of Eliphas Lévi, who took from it the plate he gives (in his *Rituel*), as a revelation of the composition of magnets and the circulatory law of lightning. More complicated in the manuscript, the figure is drawn in red, yellow, blue and black ink and is called the *Great Pantacle*.

COCA OF PERU. – Quite recently introduced in our pharmacopoeias, this vegetable substance is the leaf of the *Erythroxylon coca* (*Malpighiaceae*). The singular property that we know about it, to calm the most stubborn hunger and even to support the body in the absence of any food, made it considered as a tonic and a restorative, moreover rather harmless.

It is certain that Coca, taken in the right dose, acts as a powerful condenser of the vital forces.

On the other hand, this strange product has a sedative property, which it owes to its alkaloid, *Cocaine*: a crumbly, white, bitter and crystalline powder. Cocaine hydrochloride suppresses the most nagging physical pain; the action is sovereign, immediate and absolute: without struggle, the pain gives way and goes away. It is majestic. Neither Chloroform, nor Morphine, nor even Atropine or Hyosciamine offer anything comparable. Awful toothache subsides within a minute. It is to the point where, just by sprinkling Cocaine on the gums, crossed out tooth could be extracted, without the patient even suspecting that the dentist's forceps were there.

It would be expected that innovative practitioners were quick to equip the medical field with such an agent. Coca took its place among the nutritive tonics, stomachic and reconstituting tonics, and its alkaloid was put at the head of the sedatives. Coca wine rivalled that of cinchona itself, and cocaine shots became fashionable.

Unfortunately, the beneficial properties that I have said cannot forbid to classify this plant as one of the most perfidious and dangerous specimens of the plant kingdom.

It is well said that Peruvians, who chew it like betel, can endure twelve hours and more of continuous work in the mines; that they can support the longest and most tiring walks without food, with a load of 100 pounds on their shoulders; but it is not said that Coca takes them to the grave in less than three years. The natives, who have made a habit of this diet, hardly exceed this limit. This is why the Spaniards have made every effort to eradicate in Peru a habit that is so detrimental to their interests, and the Second Council of Lima condemned the use of Coca as early as 1567.

The Peruvians consider the properties of this leaf to be magical, and the wizards of South America make it part of all their evil spells. At the risk of being booed by the positivists, I dare to claim here that Peruvians are not wrong.

Coca, like *hashish* (see this word), but in other ways, exerts a direct and powerful action on the astral body; its customary use loosens in man certain compressive bonds of his hyper-physical nature, bonds whose persistence is a guarantee of salvation for the greatest number.

If I were to speak without hesitation on this point, I would not be believed, even among occultists.

I must confine myself to one piece of advice. – You who value your life, your reason, the health of your soul, avoid hypodermic injections of Cocaine like the plague. Not to mention the habit which is created very quickly (more imperious, more tenacious and more fatal a hundred times than any other of its kind), giving birth to a particular state.

A door has been crossed; a barrier has collapsed. Abruptly introduced into an unknown world, one finds oneself in contact with beings, whose existence was unknown until now.[7] In short, a *tacit pact* has been made.

How did it come about? – By the virtue of blood… This will seem clear, if one has grasped the significance of the few translated lines from Porphyry, about the word *Carcass* (see this word). Blood, as this theosophist suggests, is a magnet for the spiritual powers, for it provides them with the means to objectify themselves and to regain for a moment some of the faculties of life.

It is known that behind all substances, even mineral ones, there are latent virtualities, good or bad, and more or less eager for fleeting objectification.

Cocaine is extraordinary in this respect; but I would not advise anyone to bring, even transiently, to the state of nature those beings who escape from the state of essence behind its crystalline veil. The configurative and plastic power of the blood can react on these potential beings and manifest them *outwardly*; but this theurgical mixture has the value of a pact: it will be good to take care of it.

COLOURS. – In practical magic, this is the name given to certain preparations which are applied to the eyes to give the view of spiritual things. – See what Nydauld says about them (*De la Lycanthropie* (About Lycanthropy), Paris, 1515, in-8).

In the *Gnome irréconciliable* (Irreconcilable Gnome), a facetious tale in its form, long attributed to the Abbot of Villars, but which is in fact the work of Father Androl, we find a page in which the occult eye drops are discussed. We will transcribe it in its entirety, as it offers amateurs several other details of precious interest: "… I returned to the ceremonial without disgust. I took back the tunic and the mysterious hat; the characters, the fumigations and the lustrations were not forgotten. On my knees, with my face turned to the East, I recited the Enchiridion of Pope Leo; an eye drops made from certain herbs that Psellus used to see the spirits were applied to my eyes; and finally, after I had been made to swallow a few drops of an elixir extracted from an exalted and purified earth, Magnamara sat down on a philosophical chair, and commanded the Prince of the Underground Peoples on behalf of the great God of the Universe, and by virtue of his most holy, august and adorable name, to go to his chamber at that very hour. He obeyed the voice of the philosopher and introduced himself. Magnamara then raised his eye-drops, and I saw the Prince of the Gnomes clearly before me." (*Le comte de Gabalis, ou Entretiens sur les sciences secrète* (The Count of Gabalis, or Interviews on the Secret Sciences), new edition, London, Vaillant, 1742, 2 vols. in-12. – Volume II, pp. 141-142).

COMETS. – Comets have always been considered as harbingers of the most lamentable tribulations: wars, devastation, plagues, famine, calamities of all kinds.

CROSS. – Boguet had a woman named Françoise Secretan burned as a witch because the cross of her rosary was chipped. This, it seems, was an extremely serious and revealing clue for the judge (see *Discours des sorciers* (Discourse of the Sorcerers), p. 295).

---

7 If one wants to know this world, it is better to enter it through another door than this one.

D

DECANTER. – A forecasting tool, from which Cagliostro in particular has benefited greatly. Either a decanter full of crystal-clear water, or a magnetised crystal ball; it was in such environments, very refractive for astral light, that he made his *Doves'* eyes float for a long time. He named young boys who were still innocent, or girls who played the role of *passive seers*, while he held them under the irradiation of his magnetic will. These little beings then saw the chain of future contingents unfold in the form of a series of images that were obviously sibylline, a sort of concrete prophecy, which was only waiting to be translated into demotic language. The Doves expressed themselves with exclamations. Suddenly Cagliostro, with an inspired and vibrant voice, improvised an oratory or dithyrambic commentary, and the most mocking souls and the most sceptical minds were then subjugated.

It is said that in the early years of her marriage, Marie-Antoinette of Austria, still being Madame la Dauphine, wanted to consult the oracle, persisting in her whim, despite all the objections of the Magician, who finally complied only to obey a formal order. – What dreadful mirage did the Dauphine see condensed in the dazzling crystal? – She never says; but it seems certain that the spectacle was terrible, for she fainted in that place.

This is only a legend, perhaps greatly embellished by passing from mouth to mouth. In any case, after 93, her memories were brought together, and once upon a time she was enlightened. It was said that Cagliostro showed the daughter of the Caesars a scaffold erected in the midst of a tumultuous rabble; an executioner whose hand, already stained with august blood, struck a queen at the foot of a log; then a metal triangle falling like lightning, and a head –that of the unfortunate spectator herself– a blond and charming head rolling in the basket of her!

DEMON, BEARDED. – The alchemists of the Rose+Croix school attribute the success of the Philosopher's Stone to the intervention of a *bearded demon*.

This demon, a symbolic representation of the *Anima mundi*, is none other than the *Baphomet* of the Templars (see this word). It is the living ⚥, born from the fecundation ☿ of the philosopher's with the golden ♀.

DEMONS. – Jean Wier, in his treatise *de Lamiis*, gives a very complete and detailed list of the infernal hierarchies, under this title: *Pseudo-monarchia Dæmonum*. – Princes and great dignitaries, Ministers, Ambassadors, Justiciers, Officers of the House of Lucifer, Master of Ceremonies, nothing is missing, – even the steward of small pleasures!

The good Wier certainly wanted to use the ridiculous as a terrible weapon against the champions of Anthropomorphic Demonology.

DEVIL. – See our entire chapter I, and in chap. III.

DIVINATION (instruments of). – They are innumerable; the *Tarot* must be placed at the head (see this word).

Let us also mention birds, egg whites, coffee grounds, clear water, fire, earth, and a thousand other objects that diviners flatter themselves to ask questions about.

THE SORCERER'S ARSENAL 183

In the words *Decanter and Bowl, fateful*, we will find details on two very curious kinds of divination.

For the rest, I refer to Gaspar Peucer, whose work, translated into French by Simon Goulard de Senlis, is the most complete work of its kind: *Des Devins, ou commentaires des principales sortes de divination* (Diviners, or commentaries on the main kinds of divination), divided into XV books, in which Satan's tricks and impostures are discovered, etc... (in Antwerp, by Hevdrick Connix, 1587, 1 vol., very large in-8, of 700 pages).

DIVINING ROD. – It is a forked branch of beech, alder or hazel, stripped of its bark; one of the branches of the forked end is held in each hand, and the divining rod inclines itself towards the ground, to indicate the underground presence of a spring, a treasure, or the hiding place of a criminal.

Physique occulte (Occult physics), by the Abbot of Vallemont (La Haye, Moëtjens, 1690, 2 vol. small in-8, frontisp. and peculiar engravings), is entirely devoted to the study of the divining rod. It gives a theory of physics, the refutation of which R.P. Lebrun endeavoured at length in his *Histoire critique des Pratiques superstitieuses* (Critical History of Superstitious Practices) (Amsterdam, 1737, 3 vol. in-8, fig.). Two out of three large volumes are devoted to it.

DOVE. – This charming bird, once dedicated to Venus, plays a great role in the making of the *Philtres* (see this word).

For the flock of pigeons that flew around the pyre of Grandier and which once gave rise to so much commentary, see chap. I.

DRUM, MAGIC. – It is used by Siberian Tatars to make the Devil appear. It is a type of Basque drum, scribbled with hieroglyphic signs; it is called *Kamlat*. A deafening cacophony prefigures the evocations; the sorcerer capering, gesticulating and shouting accompanies his sound instrument. Finally, the Devil appears in the form of a monstrous bear, running from parts of the North: but it is most often to beat the evocator.

E

EGG (White of). – Configurative and refractive material for astral light. Many modern sibyls successfully practice divination by egg white.

ELVES. – Demons or genies, spirits of light or darkness, in the mythology of the Edda. Demonologists want to see devils.

ENCHANTED ROD. – This rod, also called lightning rod, gives power over the infernal hierarchies. At least that is what the grimoires ensure.

To prepare this rod, a forked stick of wild hazelnut is shod at both ends, with the iron of a cutlass that was used to gorge a *kid* (a small child). Care is taken to magnetise these two frameworks, to reserve the skin of the victim, which is cut into a single circular strip; and to draw the *Circle* (see this word), this strip is fixed to the ground with nails torn from the coffin of a child who died without baptism, etc.

ENCHIRIDION. – One can say of the *Enchiridion* what I have already said of the *Clavicles of Solomon*. All the printed editions are deliberately altered, as are most of the manuscripts bearing this title. However, it is not impossible, with perseverance, to discover a good manuscript copy of this collection, rich in mysterious formulas, and above all in pantacular figures, where the entire interest lies, for the bibliophile as well as for the occultist.

It is claimed that Pope Leo III, who received from Charlemagne the territory on which the popes' subsequent claim to temporal power was based, thought he was paying homage to the monarch with usury in this cabalistic book.

One of the least bad Latin editions is that of Rome, 1670, in-12: *Enchiridion Leonis Popæ, serenissimo imperatori Carolo Magno in munus pretiosum datum, nuperrimè mendis omnibus purgatum*.

The French editions, especially the so-called Rome edition, by Fr. Angelo de Rimini, S. D. (c. 1850), vol. in-12, fig., are unspeakable speculations from the low bookshops.

EPHIALTES. – Smothering incubus for the Greeks; *Insultor* of the Latins. See the words *Incubus, Succubus* and chap. III.

EVOCATION (Instruments necessary for). – In the *Rituel* of Eliphas Lévi we read: "One must choose a solitary and deprecated place, such as a cemetery haunted by evil spirits, a dreaded ruin in the countryside, the cellar of an abandoned convent, the place where an assassination was committed, a druidic altar or an ancient temple of idols.

"One must be equipped with a seamless, sleeveless black robe; a lead cap studded with the signs of the Moon, Venus and Saturn; two candles of human tallow, planted in black wooden crescent-shaped candlesticks; two crowns of verbena; a magic sword with black handle; a magic fork; a copper vase containing the victim's blood; a incense holder containing the perfumes, which will be camphor, aloe, ambergris, storax, incorporated and kneaded with goat, mole and bat blood; four nails, torn from the coffin of a victim; the head of a black cat, fed with human flesh for five days; a bat drowned in its blood; the horns of a goat *cum quo puella concubueritit*, and the skull of a parricide.

"All these horrible and rather difficult to gather together objects, are put together for the evocation."

F

FARFADETS.[8] – Familiar, mischievous and good-natured elves, to whom the legend attributes a rather beneficial influence. But Berbiguier, diverting this term from its traditional meaning, immortalised it by applying it to demons and especially to the invisible sorcerers who persecute them.

Berbiguier is the type apart. In chapter I you can read about this facetious undertaker of the occult world.

---

8   Farfadets are creatures of French folklore. The word translates variously as "Sprite", "Imp", "Brownie", or "Leprechaun", though they also resemble the Pixies of Britain's West Country.

THE SORCERER'S ARSENAL 185

But I have promised to say a word about the weapons he uses to put these rascals on the run. One could write a long chapter on the magical arsenal of the Berber alone. His means of defence are very similar to the means of attack used by those under the jurisdiction of Lancre and Boguet.

LES TRAVAUX DE BERBIGUIER
Il extermine ou capture les Farfadets, ses persécuteurs

(Fac-simile d'une gravure du livre DES FARFADETS)

The "Works" of Berbiguier

He exterminates or captures the Goblins, his persecutors. (Facsimile of an engraving from the book *Des Farfadets*).

"Jesus Christ was sent to earth to wash mankind of its sins. I am perhaps destined to destroy the enemies of the Most High."

This is the clear and laconic epigraph of the book of the *Farfadets*. – Let us see how the new Messiah proceeds to destroy these monsters vomited by Hell. I will summarise his compelling explanations:

The first thing to obtain is an ox heart, which will be boiled in a pot, with two pints of water. When the heat has sufficiently softened it, pins, nails and wooden splinters will be put in it, exclaiming in a terrible voice: "Let everything I do serve as payment: I am sorry for the worker of Beelzebub". Then this viscera will be nailed to a table with three stab wounds, repeating the imprecations;

Salt and sulphur will be thrown into the fire which boils the pot;

When you feel the Farfadets, in various forms of invisible animals, entering at night into the mystery of the alcoves and walking, jumping, getting familiar with even the most intimate attitudes, in a deplorable tête-à-tête, you will prick them sharply on the sheets with a punch or bacon;

Or else tobacco may be thrown in their faces, and while they are rolling blind and dizzy, they will be collected pell-mell with the tobacco powder, and enclosed in hermetically sealed jars, where a few pinches of fresh tobacco and cayenne pepper, with a little good vinegar, will be added from time to time. – What a salad! "Tobacco is their food and vinegar quenches their thirst. So they live in a state of discomfort, and they will witness my daily triumphs; I place my bottles so that they can see every day what I do against their comrades..." (See *Les Farfadets*, Volume III, p. 227).

"Another way of waging war on the Farfadets is to kill all the toads that can be caught in the countryside: toads are acolytes of the spirits of hell." (Volume III, p. 229.)

We know Berbiguier's defensive weapons.

Let us conclude by examining his telescope: *"My revealing bucket* is a wooden vase, which I fill with water; it serves to reveal the Farfadets when they are in the clouds..." (Tome III, p. 229). This bucket... placed on my window, repeats to me in the water all the operations of my enemies: I see them crossing, arguing, jumping, dancing and flying, much better than all the *Forioso* and *Saqui* of the earth. I see them when they ward off the weather, when they pile up clouds, when they lighten lightning and thunder. The water that is in the bucket follows all the movements of these wretches (*sic*). I see them, sometimes in the form of a snake or an eel, sometimes in the form of a monkey or a hummingbird... – Unbelievers, look at my bucket, and you will no longer upset me with your denials!" (Pages 225-226 of Volume III.)

Berbiguier describes all these fine operations in a seductive phrase: *my works*.

It is thought that the bad jokers, seeing the good man in these dispositions of mind, would take pleasure in having him skimmed from the Inferno of the apocalyptic letters, which he has conscientiously collated among the supporting documents.

Let us conclude with some of these extracts: – "*The ambassador of the Evil Spirits, Rothomago, on the fifth day of the moon, to M. Berbiguier, exterminator of the infernal cohort.*

"Berbiguier, will you stop tormenting me and all my colleagues? Miserable that you are! You have just killed fourteen hundred of my subjects, and I was almost a victim on the day of your work, when I was in the pipe of your stove! If you would be more lenient with us, we would call you our sovereign.... You would be the head of all minds; you would enjoy not only this great advantage, but also the advantage of possessing all the beautiful women who would be in your palace; for you must know that we have here all the queens, the princesses, and finally all the most beautiful women who, for 4800 years, have made the delights of all the greatest heroes of this world! ... See and consent, and you will be the happiest of all mortals; otherwise... we will come en masse to fight you with torches, to exterminate you in the course of the summer...

The extraordinary ambassador: ROTHOMAGO."
(Volume III, p. 417, passim.)

Other epistle:
"Of the infernal and invisible Committee...

Farfaderico-parafarapines! Tremble, Berbiguier... It is we, Moreau, the Vandeval, who write to you; we, whom you lacerated yesterday with seven mortice pins, we whom you denounced to the priest.... You also enjoy, from time to time, revealing the sacred mysteries of the *Opoteosoniconigamenaeo* to the first to come. – Tremble with fear!... Nothing will protect you against our revenge, neither your fat Levite of a robe, nor your left side pocket where you put your coins, which will always be full of our claws, nor your voluptuous puddings that serve as a throne for love, and from which the line that wounded the heart of our tender Feliciadoïsca started. What had she done to you, wretch!... An old Rodrigue[9] like you, whom a sixteen-year-old girl wanted to take with her, is there anything to cry for help?..."

(I stop in time; it becomes indecent...)

"If you want to enter our society, all you have to do is say yes aloud on the 16th of February at 3.13 p.m.; then you will be well received; you will be taken away in a zephyrean gondola, which will take you to a place of delights where you will enjoy *ad libitum*.

"Farewell. – Signed: MOREAU and VANDEVAL." (T. III, pp. 309-310, *passim*.)

Poor Berbiguier!...

FLUIDIC FORM. – It is the astral body, the ethereal double of the physical body, capable of projecting itself outwards and acting at a distance, while the body rests motionless. – See chapter III, and chapter VI.

FLYING PISTOL. – It is a diabolical coin, endowed with a singular virtue: faithful to its first owner, it returns of its own accord to its original owner, to the great detriment of the unfortunate innkeeper to whom it was given as payment. The next day, the innkeeper only finds a dry leaf, of alder or birch, in the place where he put the coin.

FUMIGATIONS. – It is the fragrant smoke of the consecrated perfumes, which are burnt in ceremonial magic operations, and by name in the theurgical evocations (see the word *Perfumes*).

---

9 Rodrigue is a character from Corneille's play *le Cid*, a dashing hero torn between passion for Chimène and duty towards his family and country.

G

GHOULS. – The Ghouls are the witches who devour unspeakable carrion on the Sabbath, and who dig up the dead in the cemeteries to feed on their shreds. The Salic law condemns them under the name of *striges*; it fines them (see chap. III.).

GNOMES. – Elemental spirits. – See Paracelsus and the *Comte de Gabalis* (Count of Gabalis), by the Abbot of Villars. The Gnomes haunt the underground chasms.

GOAT FOOT of the *Sabbath*. – What they do in these assemblies. – See chapter III.

GRIMOIRES. – As a general rule, this is the name given to all the books of superstitious magic, all the collections of abominable recipes, interspersed with blasphemous formulas. In the past, the Grimoires were carefully searched for in order to destroy them, and often the unfortunate ones found with these kinds of manuals were punished with death.

Le grand Grimoire, avec la grande Clavicule de Salomon, la Magie noire et les forces infernales du grand Agrippa (The Great Grimoire, with the Great Clavicle of Solomon, the Black Magic and the infernal forces of the great Agrippa), etc. S.L.N.D. in-18, is undoubtedly one of the most curious; but no one is as famous as *Le Grimoire du pape Honorius, avec un recueil des plus rares secrets* (The Grimoire of Pope Honorius, with a collection of the rarest secrets), Rome, 1670, in-16. Coloured circles and figures. (Now almost impossible to find.) – "This Grimoire is not unimportant to the curious of science. At first glance, it seems to be nothing more than a web of revolting absurdities; but for those initiated into the signs and secrets of the Kabbalah, it becomes a veritable monument to human perversity; the Devil is shown as an instrument of power... The doctrine of this Grimoire is the same as that of Simon and most Gnostics; the passive principle substitutes the active principle, passion, therefore, is preferred to reason; deified sensualism; woman put before man, a tendency that is found in all anti-Christian mystical systems; this doctrine is expressed by a pantacle placed at the head of the book. The moon of Isis occupies the centre; around the selenic crescent are three triangles which form a single triangle; the triangle is surmounted by a double-crossed ansate cross; around the triangle which is inscribed within a circle, and in the interval formed by the three segments of the circle, on one side is the sign of the spirit and the Kabbalistic seal of Solomon; on the other, the magic knife and the initial letter of the Binary; below, an upside down cross, forming the figure of the lingam, and the name of God אל also upside down; around the circle, one reads these words traced in the form of a legend: *Obey your superiors and be submissive to them, because they are careful to do so*." (*Historie de la Magie* (History of Magic), by Eliphas Lévi).

These lines of Abbé Constant say more than I can add. This excellent magician was very busy in his works of the Grimoire d'Honorius; one must read –*Clef des grands Mystères* (Key to the Great Mysteries)– the magnificent and sinister story of the priest Verger, preluding, by infernal evocations and assiduous reading of the Grimoire, to the furious mania which was to make him a murderer.

I have already transcribed a page from the *Grimoire d'Honorius*, about the *Black Cock* (see this word).

The copy in my possession –allegedly an edition of Rome, 1760, in-12; in reality a modern reprint from Lille, Blocquel ed.– bears on its last page four diabolical signatures (enclosed), bloody characters which have been traced neither with a pen nor perhaps with a brush:

These are the most notoriously satanic and blasphemous hieroglyphics I have ever seen in my life:
1. A stick with three forked crosspieces, with two square dots at the base;
2. A black triangle, between two baphometic horns;
3. An inverted Shin (*w*);
4. An opaque hand, the five fingers extended, under the inverted *w*; this hand symbolizes the negation of the pentagrammatic dogma.

I had the colouring matter (reddish-brown) that was used to trace them analysed: it is blood.

The paper is yellowed all around, or rather scorched like a candle flame.

Without going any further into my inductions, I conclude that this Grimoire was the property of a witchcraft adept.

Among the most singular and rare Grimoires, one must also mention the work entitled *La Sexte-Essence dialectique et potentielle, tirée d'une nouvelle façon d'alambiquer, suivant les préceptes de la sainte Magie et l'Invocation des Démons* (The Dialectic and potential Sixth-Essence, drawn from a new way of convolution, following the precepts of Holy Magic and the Invocation of the Demons (Paris, 1595, in-8.) – Highly peculiar; particularly recommended to lovers of ambiguous mysticism.

H

HAND OF GLORY. – Sorcery described in chapter III.

HASHISH. – This is the name given by Orientals to the fatty extract of Indian hemp (*Cannabis indica*), prepared with the flowering tops, which is reduced to the consistency of an ointment by a special process.

The same hemp, smoked like tobacco, is called *Kief.*

The smoke of the kief, and especially the assimilation of hashish (taken pure in the form of a bowl, or mixed with a date preserve), gives a particular, otherworldly intoxication, which is prized by certain natures, mystical and sensual all together, as a foretaste of the heavenly happiness of the chosen ones.

One must read Baudelaire's *Paradis artificiels* (Artificial paradises), where the poet's style surpasses, in precise erudition and didactic firmness, the usual language of scholars. It is marvellous to see with what wisdom Baudelaire decomposes the psychic action of this strange ingredient, which has the power to exalt joy or exacerbate pain,[10] bringing to the superlative the feeling that dominated the soul the minute it was ingested. It is an expansive director of passions and latent ideas; through it, the Unconscious manifests itself to the amazed Consciousness – and the soul, contemplating itself in its own mirror, reveals itself positively to itself.

In this way, we meet a friend from within, whom we never suspected; we talk with our guardian angel, or, if we prefer, with the instigator of perdition that each of us carries within.

Before the fall of Eden, the universal man had the almost divine faculty to objectify all his ideas. If he thought of beings, he created them by dreaming. Now it seems that hashish restores for an hour to the individual man that ineffable power to effortlessly exteriorise everything whose image he carries within him. It seems that the creative verb is returned to him, as he possessed it before his sin.

Thus, by the virtue of hashish, man evades or seems to evade the sentence that was pronounced against him, in the person of Eve, his volitional faculty: *I will multiply your labours and your conceptions. In pain shall you give birth...* and that the agnostic Bibles render with these words: *I will multiply the evils and the groans of your pregnancies; you will give birth in pain.*

In the second book we will develop an explanatory theory of this prodigy. Suffice it to say here that hashish always favours and sometimes spontaneously determines the exit from the astral body.

Indian hemp is a magical herb, in the first place.

HIGH-HUNT. – In some parts of Lorraine and the northern provinces of France, the air transportation of sorcerers on the Sabbath is known as the "High Hunt". – See chapter II.

HIPPOMANES. – Singular growth which, according to some authors, grows on the head of foals. This fleshy substance, used in a large number of philtres and charms, is said to be highly endowed with aphrodisiac virtues. This is, in any case, what demonographers are unanimous in claiming.

HOOPOE. – Common bird especially in Asia Minor: it is said that one sometimes finds in its nest a miraculous stone whose possession confers supernatural powers. – It is this stone which must be set as the stone of a ring, to make it a ring of invisibility.

---

10 The exaggeration of painful feelings only manifests itself in experiences made unexpectedly, blindly and without preparation; for hashish, taken in full knowledge of the facts, on the contrary heals the wounds of an ulcerated soul. It is enough to concentrate one's will on the senses; for the exercise of will, abolished or at least blunted in the region of physical activity, becomes all-powerful in the internal and virtual sphere.
Nevertheless –to take an example– there can be no doubt that among the pusillanimous, hashish extends terror to the borders of delirium. The temptation to commit suicide is frequent; one is asked to flee, in death itself, the fear of death.

I

IDOL. – Material representation of a Divinity, taken by the vulgar profane for that very Divinity. Idols can be considered as incarnations of Satan. (See chap. I.)

ILLUMINATI. – It is treated at length in our chapter IV, and in our *Seuil du Mystère* (Mystery Threshold) –*De deux sociétés secrètes* (Of two secret societies) en 1890 and *Discours d'initiation Martiniste* (Martinist Initiation Discourse) in 1890.

IMMORTALITY (Elixir of). – The alchemists were said to have composed, with the philosopher's stone, a universal medicine or Elixir of Life, which, according to some, prolonged existence beyond normal limits, and according to others, ensured immortality to all those who agreed to regulate its use. Read *Zanoni*, the superb magic novel by Sir E. Bulwer Lytton. See also the very curious revelations published in the *Lotus*, 1st year, N° 2 and 3, under this title: *L'Élixir de Vie*, under the signature: a *Chela*. – Who is not familiar with the traditional and symbolic legends of the Fountain of Youth and the water of eternal youth? Cagliostro and St. Germain were said to have the secret. (See chapter IV.)

INCUBUS. – Unclean ghosts of the male sex who rape women in their sleep; as opposed to Succubi (see this word), female ghosts who abuse men and disappoint their dreams. By extension, Incubi and Succubus have been named *Incubus* and *Succubus*, all invisible, supposed to have a love trade with mortals (see *Ephialtes*). Please refer to chapter I, and ch. III, and ch. VI.

INFIDELITY. – The use of ordeal potions (unnamed mixtures, frequently used in the Middle Ages and served to the suspected wife in the *Chalice of Suspicion*) dates back to the best times of Israel.

The wife who persisted in claiming to be innocent was subjected, by order of the Great Consistory, to the trial of the *Waters of Bitterness*. A priest carefully collected dust from the tabernacle, mixing a pinch of it with the juice of bitter herbs in a little water. This was the drink that the unhappy person had to swallow in one gulp, at the very door of the Holy of Holies.

If guilty, she died, says the Legend, her eyes rolling and in horrible convulsions; if the drink had no effect on her, the young woman was honourably dismissed: her innocence could no longer be disputed.

K

KALI. – Goddess of murder, among the Hindus. Her followers constitute the formidable secret society of the *Stranglers* or *Thugs*. See chapter I.

L

LACES. – They were used for ligatures of all kinds, especially for the *Aiguillette* knot (see this word). Read in chapter III.

LAMPS. – A thousand tales have been told about the marvellous and perpetual lamps. One of them is said to have thrown a strange light in the sepulchre of Tullia, daughter of Cicero, after so many centuries.

Gosset published a very curious dissertation on sepulchral lamps, following his work entitled: *Révélation cabalistique sur la Médecine universelle* (Kabbalistic Revelation on Universal Medicine), 1735, 1 vol. petit in-8.

LARVAE. – Inconsistent fantastic substances, but real, devoid of their own essence and living a borrowed life. They attach themselves to those who gave birth to them and who, in the long run, exhaust themselves in feeding them. (See chap. I, and chap. VI).

LEMURES. – Larvae with perverse instincts. It was thought that they could be the damned souls, who have returned to this world to help the demons in their infernal task of proselytism.

LEONARD. – This is the demon who presides over the Sabbaths, most often in the form of a monstrous goat (see Chap. II.).

LEVIATHAN. – The Talmudists give this name to the androgynous Spirit of Evil. Considered in its male incarnation, it is Sammael, (see this word) or the *Insinuating Serpent*, and in its female incarnation it is *Lilith* (see this word).

LILITH, – or the *Tortuous Snake*. Lilith is the wife of Sammael (see this word) and the female incarnation of Leviathan (see this word). See chapter I.

M

MAGIC CAKE. – Cakes baked on the kidneys of the Queen of the Sabbath were distributed at the Black Mass. The *Confarreatio* is the devil's communion (see ch. II.).

MAGIC CIRCLE. – It is a circumference traced on the ground and in the centre of which one stands, in ceremonial magic experiences, especially when evoking spirits; a protective barrier that cannot be crossed without falling into the power of the fantastic beings who have been able to respond to the evocation. As long as one remains sheltered by this mysterious rampart (symbol of the collective will, good or bad, with which one is in communion), one runs no risk.

At least that is what the sorcerers ensure. They add that if one strikes with a magic *wand* (see this word), one of the demons that crowd around the circle, under the appearance of screaming monsters, he is immediately forced to enter the circle and obey the wizard; he can only regain his freedom after having been discharged.

As for these circles of thick and dark greenery, which one finds in the meadows, and which stand out in force against the uniform colour of the surrounding grass, the peasants call them *Fairy Circles* (see what I say about them in chap. II).

MAGIC MIRROR. – The story goes like this: the Sagas of Thessaly used to trace their cryptic formulas in blood on these mirrors: the moon –another mirror– would immediately reflect these bloody characters and the answer would then be printed on its silver crescent. This is how the Oracle was rendered.

Later, mirrors were made from the seven metals of Hermes. The most common mirrors are made of pewter, studded with devilish signs or pantacles. These objects only had the name of the mirror. They were not polished, but in the long run, when you looked at them, your imagination became excited; a halo blurred the contours of the enlarged disc, and prophetic images were confusedly drawn on it.

The Baron du Potet's mirror consists of a circle sprinkled with small coals – a favourable medium for the refraction of images.

All these mirrors impress the sensitive by virtue of the same law. Cagliostro's *decanter* (see this word) is itself, all in all, a magical mirror of another form.

In the ceremonial operations of Theurgy, concave mirrors are placed on the four walls of the occult cabinet.

MAGIC PLANTS. – The attractive plant is not the only one endowed with occult properties of marvellous energy. The ancient magicians knew XXII plants, whose virtue corresponded to the esoteric meaning of the XXII arcana of the Absolute Doctrine. Verbena referred to Arcanum VI (the lover of the Tarot).

The magicians of the Middle Ages had only been able to collect the wrecks of these traditions. Late heirs of a science that had fallen, though still real,[11] they reduced the list of sacred plants to sixteen names. Again the numerical order of the normal classification was inverted, and unfortunate substitutions further altered an already unrecognisable nomenclature.

According to César Longin, the sixteen sacred plants are:
1. Heliotrope (*Ireos* of the Chaldeans), the herb of sincerity;
2. Nettle (*Roybra*), the herb of bravery;
3. Virga pastoris (*Lorumborat*), the grass of fertility;
4. Celidoine (*Aquilaris*), the grass of triumph;
5. Periwinkle (*Iterisi*), the grass of fidelity;
6. Catnip (*Bieith*), the herb of vitality.
7. Dog's Tongue (*Algeil*), the grass of sympathy;
8. Henbane (*Mansesa*), the herb of death;
9. Lily (*Augo*), the grass of manifestation;
10. Mistletoe (*Luperax*), the herb of salvation;
11. Centaury (*Isiphilon*), the herb of enchantment;
12. Sage (*Coloricon*), the herb of life;
13. Verbena (*Ophanas*), the herb of love;
14. Lemon balm (*Celeivos*), the grass of comfort;
15. Rose (*Eglerisa*), the initiatory herb;
16. Serpentine (*Cartulin*), the herb of fluids.

MAGIC WORDS. – The sorcerer prefers them incomprehensible, because his Creed is none other than that of Tertullian: *quia absurdum*. – On the reason and virtue of barbaric words and unintelligible names, see chapter III.

MAGICAL POISONING CHARGE. – This is the name given to the charms composed to kill cattle; they are buried at the threshold of stables or sheepfolds. – See Hocque's trial (p. 97-98) and the details I provide in chap. II.

---

11 The Science of the Neo Magi of Chaldea.

MAGNET. – Once thought to be a magical poison, sorcerers used to pound it and make it part of their charms (see this word).

The *wand* of the Magician (see this word) was hollow and contained a magnetic steel rod.

According to Marcellus Empiricus, the magnet cured headaches.

The Basilide sectarians used it as a talisman (see this word) against the power of evil spirits.

MAGNETISM. – It is the art of physiologically influencing a person (who takes the name of subject), of substituting the subject's own will; in a word, the art of sovereignly taking over his organs, so as to make him do what he does not want to do and to prevent him from doing what he wants. This habitual fact of the intrusion of a foreign will, which replaces the will of the subject, should be called subjection. The isolated phenomenon of transmission to the subject of a particular will, to which he will obey, is called suggestion.

Hypnotic sleep is one of the most banal manifestations of magnetism; while the subject sleeps, he is, so to speak, like soft wax between the fingers of the magnetiser. But it is a mistake to believe that suggestion can only be practised during sleep, and in many cases it works wonderfully on perfectly awake subjects. See our chapter VI.

Magnetism, conceived in its broadest sense, embraces a very large part of the phenomena which can be realised; its domain extends far and wide, in the sphere of practical magic.

MALEFICES. – In general, any spell or superstitious operation, with the aim of harming one's neighbour. Our entire chap. III deals in detail with spells.

MANDRAKE. – The Mandrake (*Atrope Mandrogora*) is a narcotic and poisonous plant, of the *Solanaceae* family, very close cousin of the Belladonna (*Atropa Belladona*).

It is well known that all the toxic Solanaceae, such as Morella, Belladonna, Datura, etc., were used in the same way as Hemlock, Oenanthus and Hemp in the preparation of magic ointments. But the Mandrake offers other titles to our curiosity. Its root, bristling with tufted filaments, most often affects the figure of the thighs or genitals;[12] it also sometimes displays the outline of a human head.

According to an old tradition, man first appeared on earth in the form of monstrous mandrakes, animated by an instinctive life, and that the breath from above ever-greened, transmuted, disintegrated, and finally uprooted, to become beings endowed with their own thought and movement.

Also, in the Middle Ages, it was the dream or the delirium of certain followers, aspiring to the *Vital Mastery*, to find the composition of the original-principle, in order to make mandrakes grow; to react and be aroused to the mental life, by the infusion of the *Archon*.

---

[12] Which has made it appear to be an aphrodisiac, according to the theory of natural *signatures*, already touched upon in the word *Camaieu*.

THE SORCERER'S ARSENAL 195

Others, less ambitious, were content to obtain false *Teraphim* (see this word), by evoking a *larvae* (see this word), in a mandrake cut in human form; a hideous idol that they conjured up to make oracles... It is hard to imagine the furious madness to which superstition led them! It was from under the gallows that they went to fetch the mandrake; to pull it out of the ground, they tied a dog's tail to its root and hit it with a mortal blow. The poor beast in agony, struggling, uprooted the mandrake. Then (they believed) the sensitive soul of the dog would pass through the mandrake and, out of sympathy, attract the spiritual soul of the hanged man...

Other sorcerers forged a metallic *Android*, hoping to confer on him the gift of speech.

By extension, Mandrakes, *Androids, Homunculus* and *Teraphim* were called Mandrakes; they even came to name any magical preparation capable of rendering an oracle in this way.

See the words: *Android* and *Teraphim*.

MARKS. – Stigmata imprinted by the Devil on the bodies of his acolytes.

Leonard has his *controllers*, who stamped wizards and witches, just as metals are stamped at the Mint. The mark most often affects the features of a toad, a hare, a mouse, etc... The place is insensitive to stings, and pinpricks do not make even a drop of blood spurt out. The mark is sometimes on the forehead or in the eye, more usually at the folds of the mucous membranes and in the most secret parts of the body. (See chapter II.)

The surgeons are therefore charged with visiting the accused, and with planting needles in all places of the body where it is supposed that the Devil's signature can be concealed. And woe to the poor accused who neglects to cry out every time the sharp point touches his flesh. He is lost in advance.

Often, like Lancre in the land of Labourt, the judge charges the repentant witch (who saved her skin by a spontaneous confession) with this long, barbaric and meticulous search, on the person of all the accomplices denounced by her. I would suggest that the unfortunate witch is displaying an abominable zeal, in order to buy, as far as she is concerned, the clemency of the magistrate.

Pierre de Lancre was gallant by nature; so all the witches who knew they were passable had only one dream, to dodge the scaffold and escape through the alcove, stepping over the judge's bed.

Lancre's favourite was a fifteen-year-old girl called the Murgui, a fierce denunciator of her former friends, who, having been sent by the judge to find the *stigma Diaboli* on them, preferred to martyr the prettiest – her possible rivals of the next day!

This is what Michelet (*La Sorcière* (The Sorceress), p. 221) and M. Jules Baissac (*Les grands jours de la sorcellerie* (Great days of witchcraft), p. 401) suggest; it is what seems to emerge from Lancre's own narrative.

MELICERTES. – The *King of the Earth* (root: טואדלמ); bloody deity, whose idol was raised in Tenedos (see chap. I.).

MENDES (goat of). – Raised in the temple of God, his mission was to sacrifice the modesty of the young Egyptian girls (See chap. II.).

MOCHLATH. – One of the four wives of *Sammael* (see this word), in the Cacopneumatics of the Kabbalists (see chap. I.).

MOLE. – The blood of the mole was used in a great number of philtres and electrical goods.

MOLOCH. – The devouring idol of Moloch stood wherever the Phoenicians had settlements and colonies. (See chap. I.)

MONSTERS. – They were said to be born of the Devil's impure trade with Witches.

Miserable followers of Goetia sometimes obtained nameless monsters, by throwing, according to the energetic word of Eliphas Lévi, human seed into animal soil. A small number of these monsters come to term, but almost all of them expire a few days after birth. As for the very few that become adults, they have no chance of coming of age – being blasphemous blasphemies of Nature, which lies to itself, always with regret.

N

NAGUAL. – Mexican Nagualism is not without analogy with European Lycanthropy. It is a pact of tacit solidarity, of offensive and defensive alliance, between a man and an animal: the sanction of such a pact is in the reality of the occult bond that unites them.

The Nagual is a crocodile, a lion, a snake, a bird, or any other animal, to which the native has been attached, since childhood, by an indissoluble fluidic bond. The ceremony that consecrates this bond is very similar to an initiation...

Therefore, for each *initiated* native, the Nagual is an *alter ego*; and all his life, man remains coupled to this beast that cherishes and protects him, sharing his adventurous existence, his good and bad luck, his sorrows and joys, suffering from the evil from which he himself suffers. This strange solidarity cannot be doubted; the facts of Nagualism are certified by the most honourable and least suspicious testimonies.

Example of Nagualism, guaranteed by the R. P. Burgoa:

A huge crocodile attacks the R.P. Diégo, as it was riding a horse on the shore of a lake. Skilful and vigorous enough to break free at once, this priest spurs his horse, and, brandishing his shod stick, charges the monster, which is still trying to drag him to the bottom of the lake. The mount's kicks are no small help to the missionary, during this duel of a new kind. In short, he can go his own way, leaving the crocodile for dead on the shore.

But back at the Mission's headquarters, the first news Father Diego is told is the inexplicable agony of a young Indian boy, whom he had punished a few days before, with extreme rigour... Once checked, the Indian was wearing all the wounds made to his *Nagual*. This young man died – and at the same time the crocodile was breathing out at the water's edge. (Detailed details of the adventure can be read in chapter LXXI of the *Description géographique de la province de Santo-Domingo* (Geographical Description of the Province of Santo Domingo), by R. P. Burgoa).

I note incidentally for occultists how *Nagualism* differs exactly from *Lycanthropy*. The *werewolf* is merely the objectification of the erratic astral body of a sorcerer in catalepsy; whereas the *Nagual* is a being perfectly distinct from the Mexican sorcerer, a being of inferior species, but to which he is bound by a chain of solidarity which have clear consequences and seems unquestionable.

On the subject of repercussion phenomena, see our chapter VI.

NAHEMAH. – Queen of the Striges, in the Cacopneumatic of the Rabbis, and one of the four wives of *Sammael* (see this word). See also Chapter I.

NENUPHAR. – The anaphrodisiac properties of white nenuphar (*Nymphea alba*) are certainly magical; for they come precisely, like those of *Oak Mistletoe* (see this word), from the influences of stars in effective conjunction, at the hours when the plant is gathered and the philtre is prepared.

By itself, nenuphar is only endowed with banal emollient and sedative virtues, due to the mucilage it contains in abundance. But the charmers, experts in the works of ☽ and ♄ knew how to make ice-cold and frosty drinks, whose penetrating acuity numbs the most unbridled senses.

The Mystical Lotus of the Hindus, symbolising to a certain extent the blossoming of the Spiritual Essence in the silence of appeased passions, is a kind of nenuphar (Padma).

NUMBERS. – There is a science of numbers, whose mysteries are due to the most sublime arcane of transcendental magic. The language is lost for the modern man. But there are also many superstitions relating to numbers, and these are related to witchcraft (see any *Grimoire*).

O

OAK MISTLETOE. – Mistletoe is a parasitic plant which attaches itself like a plant polyp to the branches of certain trees, especially oak, pumping out the superabundant vitality of the sap.

The Druids harvested it with a golden serpent at certain times and composed a prodigiously powerful elixir from its juice, rich in magnetic qualities. Mistletoe performed miracles in their hands, for they were magicians. – In the hands of sorcerers, who wanted to exploit it in their turn, this vampiric plant never gave anything but harmful or derisory results.

Fabre d'Olivet tells us that Ram, the theocrat of the migrating Hyperboreans, owed to a divine revelation the art of extracting a remedy from oak mistletoe, which cured Elephantiasis, that terrible evil, the exterminating scourge of the Celtic races, for a few days, and which was then considered incurable (see the *Hist. philos, du genre humain* (Philosophical history of mankind), volume I).

M. de Saint-Yves, who confirms this tradition, adds that the true Mistletoe, already very difficult to discern from similar parasites, only displayed its marvellous virtue when harvested under certain conditions, at a precise astronomical hour –see the *Mission des Juifs* (Mission of the Jews).

The progress of magnetism will one day lead to the discovery of the absorbent properties of Oak Mistletoe. The secret of these spongy growths, which attract the unnecessary luxury of plants and become overloaded with colour and flavour, will then be revealed; mushrooms, truffles, tree galls, the different species of mistletoe, will be used with discernment by a new medicine by dint of being old. Paracelsus will no longer be laughed at, as he used to collect the *usnea*[13] from the skulls of the hanged men… But one must not walk faster than science; it only moves backwards to better advance." –Eliphas Lévi, *Historie de la Magie* (History of Magic).

OBI (Mandigoës). – Formidable occult power, which is decimating the population of the West Indies. – See what I say about it in chapter III.

P

PACT. – It is a contract, express or tacit, but freely consented to by both sides, between the Devil and the Sorcerer. – See chap. I, and chap. II.

PEGS. – Sorcerers used wooden or metal pegs, which they stuck, with imprecations, into the wall nearest the victim chosen as target for their evil spell. The rather unexpected effect of this operation was, it is said, to provide urine retention. People sometimes died from this spell, according to Wuecker.

The Grimoires said that to obviate this spell, one only had to spit in one's right shoe before putting it on!

PERFUMES. – Perfumes, says Agrippa (*Philos, occulte*, book III, chap. LXIV) attract spirits "as a magnet attracts iron." They are used in cult ceremonies and in magical operations.

This is why the Sorcerer, always trying to imitate the priest and the magician, does not fail to use it for his evocations. Since sweet perfumes have an evocative virtue in the sphere of pure Spirits, it seems analogical to him to evoke impure Spirits by the effusion of the most unfortunate odours. He preferably uses the stinking fumigations of Saturn, which according to Eliphas Lévi (*Rituel…* (Transcendental Magic Its Doctrine and Ritual), chap. VII) are Dingridium, Scammonaeus, Alum, Sulphur and foul Asyssa. – See the word *Evocation*.

PHANTOM. – A generic name, designating any visible aggregate of molecules previously elusive to the eye, and suddenly compacted into the shape of a living being.

The classical Phantom is none other than the Ghost, that is to say the appearance of a deceased person, objectified from scratch: *Simulacrum vita carens*.

Ghosts are, for the most part, nothing more than aromatic coagulations, dead or dying, – residues of astral shells in the process of disintegration in the fluidic ocean; perispirits[14] devoid of all consciousness, and which an external force has reacted to only for a fleeting existence.

---

13 Usnea is a genus of mostly pale grayish-green fruticose lichens that grow like leafless mini-shrubs or tassels anchored on bark or twigs.
14 In Spiritism, perispirit is the subtle body that is used by the spirit to connect with the perceptions created by the brain.

When they manifest themselves, it is preferably around burials, slaughterhouses, amphitheatres, or even sewers and solfataras.

See the case of Cideville in the chapter V, and the description of spiritualist phenomena. – In The *Key to Black Magic*, we will deal in detail with the question of the ghosts.

PHILTRES. – In Black Magic, philtres are drinks to disturb the psychic balance and to inspire delirious passions. – See chap. III.

PHYLACTERIES. – See *Amulets* and *Talismans*.

PYTHONS. – Sacred serpents of Apollo, which coiled up on the arms of the Pythias, when they prophesied. Pythons were also called the Inspiring Spirits of the Sybil.

For the Pythoness of Endor, see chap. IV.

Q

QUEEN OF THE SABBATH. – She was usually the most beautiful. She had to be a virgin and sacrifice her modesty to the *Stinking Goat* (*sic*). See the description of the Sabbath, Chapter II, pages 154-163, especially.

QUESTION. – Preliminary torture inflicted on defendants, to extract from them the confession of their crimes or the names of their accomplices.

See the description of the different modes of torture, taken from Dr. Regnard, chap. IV.

R

RED DRAGON. – I have in front of me an obviously modern edition of this memorable grimoire. It is a clumsy reprint of the 1521 edition, and claims to pass for print the following year (1522).

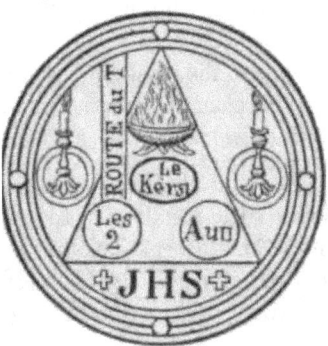

THE RED DRAGON
Magic Circle

The *Dragon rouge* (Red Dragon), or the art of commanding celestial, earthly, infernal spirits, etc. S. L., 1522, small in-12. (Decorated with a strangely naive frontispiece, printed in red, like the title).

The work will be judged by these lines, which open the first chapter. This great book is so rare, so much sought-after in our lands (sic) that, for its rarity, it can be called, according to the Rabbis, the true GREAT WORK; and it is they who have left us this precious original, which so many charlatans have wanted to forge needlessly by trying to imitate the real one, which they have never found,[15] so that you can catch money from the simple people who address the first person, without looking for the real source.

THE RED DRAGON
Frontispiece

This one was copied from the true writings of the great King Solomon, which were found by pure chance, etc...

This is the first page of the Red Dragon. – *Ab una, disce omnes*.

RHOMBUS. – A sort of magic spinning top, with a monotonous humming, whose magnetic action is most powerful.

Hecate's Rhombus was one of the most famous among the witches of ancient Greece. It is mentioned in the oracular fragments attributed to Zoroaster: "Operare circa Hecaticum turbinem" (*De dæmonibus et sucrificiis*).

RINGS. – If it were a question of High Magic, I would speak of the *Ring of Solomon*, made of the seven mystical metals and provided with two kittens (one of moonstone with the star of the Macrocosm, the other of cornelian with that of the Microcosm), engraved with two hallmarks of gold and silver. For the details, I simply refer to the l'*Historie de la Magie* (History of the Magic) of Eliphas Lévi.

---

15 This is what some people of bad company *call spitting in the air, so that the spit falls back on your nose...*

THE SORCERER'S ARSENAL 201

The *Ring of Gyges* or of invisibility, whose legend everyone knows, should not occupy us either.

A thousand extravagances are told about the wedding and engagement rings. Wizards advise husbands, when exchanging rings in front of the priest, to deliberately push the ring down to the root of their wives' fingers. For if the ring does not go lower than the second phalanx at that very minute, the wife takes ascendancy over her noble husband, whom she will turn into a fool and probably into a cuckold. Whereas, if the ring encircles the very root of the ring finger, the man will be the master of the house. Therefore, the Spell casters give young girls who feel a vocation to wear panties and relegate their master and lord to the third degree the perfidious advice to bend and stiffen their fingers during the ceremony.

It seems that superstitious, but far-sighted husbands could parry this manoeuvre by passing a ring of a monstrous diameter on the marital finger. – Unfortunately, the case is foreseen by the wily master of all prestige. The too wide ring is also symbolic of a disadvantage that husbands like to avoid. My modesty forbids me to say more. The rings are a kind of amulet or talisman, depending on the case.

S

SABBATH BOILER. – It is in an iron cauldron where the sorcerers and their companions reduce the broth of small children to a jelly-like consistency, with enchanted herbs and the venom of reptiles. – See Shakespeare (*Macbeth*, Act II).

SABBATH GOAT. – Favourite form borrowed by the prince of these congregations, whose name is Leonardo (see our chap. II).

It was reputed to be the fatal animal goat and sorcerer. Its blood was used in special compositions, in order to provide some terrifying visions.

This animal sometimes played the role of incubator. Thus we see in the Bible that some women of Israel abandoned themselves to the goats.

SABBATH. – Assembly of sorcerers and demons, which I have described throughout, from chapter II. – See also chapter III.

SACRAMENTS OF THE DEVIL. – Black Magic, this reverse religion, also has its sacraments, where one can distinguish, as in those administered by the Church, matter and form. This is discussed at length in chapter III.

SACRIFICE. – Human sacrifices were universally accepted and passed into the mores of all the peoples of antiquity. I speak of this in chapter I, and especially in chapter II.

SALAMANDER. – A sort of lizard that lives in water, and was once considered to be endowed with the singular privilege of frolicking in the flame as in its element, and to stay there for a long time without the slightest discomfort.

It is on the basis of this tradition, which was once universally widespread, that the neo-kabbalists named Salamanders the Elemental Spirits of Fire.

SAMMAEL. – This is, according to the Talmudists, the male incarnation of *Leviathan* (see this word); they also qualify it as the *sinuous Serpent*, see chap. I.

The Zohar attributes the sin of Eve to the seductions of Sammael. From the latter, the demonologists have made one of the princes of Hell.

SATAN. – The fallen angel, the Devil. Our whole first chapter deals with it explicitly, and our whole work with it implicitly. See especially chapter I.

SATYRES. – Country deities of the heathens.

The first Fathers of the Church speak of them as real beings, in flesh and blood. St. Anthony (St. Jerome tells us), met a Satyr in the desert who offered him dates and asked him for prayers.

There has been much dispute over the question of the Satyrs. The controversy was fierce at all times. Some want to see monkeys; others claim that the Satyrs were only men of the woods, savages. Read the very curious work by F. Hédelin, unfortunately quite rare:[16] *Des satyres brutes, monstres et démon* (About satyrs, monsters and demons), of their nature and worship, against the opinion of those who considered Satyrs to be a species of men distinct and separate from the Adamites. (Paris, Buon, 1627, in-8.).

Needless to add that the Satyrs (goat-feet) are part of the menagerie of the Sabbath.

SECRETS. – Occult remedies, composed of words and gestures, to cure all kinds of diseases.

Wonderfully stupid formulas. Often the stingy peasants pay dearly for them. They are the verbal expression of an influence that is transmitted, from father to son, in certain families. It should be noted that if the owner of the secret gives or sells it, he loses it for himself.

When it comes to witchcraft, faith does everything... However, the peasant, who has paid twenty coins for some foolish recipe, will never doubt the efficiency of such an expensive treasure. If the secret has cost him nothing, it is much less valuable to him, and therefore less likely to work a miracle in his hands.

I have seen shepherds "heal from the secret", in five or ten minutes, a cow, a pig, a horse, suffering from desperate illnesses, and which the vet considered lost. – Curiously enough! The "healer of the secret" never accepts a coin for the price of the cure he performs. He works for glory.

The *Grimoire of Honorius* contains a number of recipes for "healing secrets". As it is very rare, I think it would be curious to copy one of them:

"Against the flow of the belly. – I entered the Garden of Olives and met St. Elizabeth; she spoke to me about the flow of her belly, I asked her for mercy for mine, and she ordered me to say three *paternosters* in honour of God and three *Hail Mary* in honour of St. John (*sic*)... Say three *paternoster* and three *Hail Mary*, as it is said above, and you will be healed." (*Grim. d'Honorius*, Rome, 1760, in-12, p. 62).

This is a secret for healing oneself; but all the formulas for healing other men or animals are more or less of this kind.

---

16 Reprinted by Lisieux, but in very small numbers.

THE SORCERER'S ARSENAL 203

See also the word: *Strings of the winds*.

SHIRT OF NECESSITY. – We must not forget here the shirt nicknamed "shirt of necessity", which the Germans call *Nothembd*, so celebrated by our ancestors and which they used to wear during the war against the blows of stings, balls and cannonballs... Fat women used the same shirt to give birth more fast and more comfortably.

"It had to be made on one of the nights of the Christmas week; so much so that the virgins spun the linen in the name of the Devil, they unwound it; they wove and sewed the shirt. They tied two heads to the chest: the one on the right side had a long beard and was like a morion with a head; the other on the left side was terrible to see, and had a crown like that of King Beelzebub. On each side of these two heads there was a cross and the whole shirt covered the man from the collar to half the body with the sleeves." (Jean Wier, *Hist., disputes et disc. des illusions et impostures des Diables* (Histories, disputes and discussions of the illusions and impostures of the Devils), etc., with two dialogues by Erastus, Geneva, 1579, in-8, book V, chap. XVIII.)

SIGNS. – The sign is, in Magic, the point of support required by the will to project towards a prefixed goal. The adequate is the sign is to the inner verb, the more perfect and therefore effective it is. The countersign is a parry, by means of an occult shield, which sends back to the aggressor the shock in return for the blow he has dealt.

I cannot say more in this first septenary. During the second one (*Key to Black Magic*), I will develop this theory.

SNAKE EGGS. – The snake, primarily a magnetic animal, lays eggs very rich in a mysterious substance, which the alchemists of a certain school called mercurial cerebrin. This substance cannot be used in metal work, because the ☿ is specified for the Animal Kingdom; but its presence, explaining the occult properties of snake eggs, justifies the sagacity of the Druids, who collected them with care.

The adepts of Black Magic are not unaware of these exceptional properties; they take advantage of them for their evil spells.

SORTILEGES. – Operations of Black Magic. They are seen throughout chapter III.

SPIRITISM. – Sort of religion, founded around the middle of the century, by Allan Kardec (pen name). Spiritist practices consist mainly in the evocation of the beloved dead. The ceremonial used for this purpose has nothing of that indelible stamp of greatness that still saves, in the eyes of the artist, the most sacrilegious rites of priestly antiquity. If our modern necromancers make the oracle of the tomb speak, it is through the ministry of sibylline hats, talking occasional tables and *revolving tables* (see this last word).

See Chapter VI, where mediums and Spiritism are discussed.

SPIRITS. – This is the name given to the invisible agents that manifest themselves by knocks in seances (see chapter VI.).

STILETTO, MAGIC. – The *Clavicules de Salomon* (Clavicles of Solomon) (Manuscript of 1641, in-4, already quoted) want you to make it yourself. The handle must be, like the blade, made of fine steel, studded with magic characters. The consecration of the "Stiletto" is the same as that of the *sword* (see this word). The scabbard will be made of a brand new piece of red taffeta.

STRINGS OF THE WINDS. – "... The peoples of Fionia, before their conversion to Christianity, sold the winds to the sailors, giving them a cord with three knots, and warning them that by untying the first knot, they would have a gentle and favourable wind, at the second knot, a more vehement wind, and at the third knot, an impetuous and dangerous wind." (*Olaüs Magnus*, translated by Dom Calmet, *Traité sur les apparitions des Esprits et sur les Vampire* (Treatise on the Appearances of the Spirits and on Vampires), Volume I, p. 250).

SUCCUBUS. – Demon or female ghost, which provokes dreams of lust in young men; read in chapter III the summarized story of Goerres. See the words *Incubus* and *Ephialtes*.

SWORD. – The Magic Sword, says the Manuscript (already quoted) of *Solomon's Clavicle*, must be brand new; having washed it well with wine, in which you will mix a little of the blood of a white dove which will have been killed one Monday, at six o'clock in the morning, and after having wiped it with clean cloths, you will wait until Tuesday, at six o'clock in the morning, to take it in your hand, and say these words with great attention: *Agla, On, Pentagrammaton, On Athanatos*, etc. (follows the conjuration).

Afterwards you shall engrave or make to be engraved on it, with the chisel of art, at the same hour of six o'clock in the morning, the following characters and words:[17]

araritha

"And when you have done so, you shall cast incense that has been blessed, and say the prayer *Agla, On*, etc. (shown above), and then you shall put it in its sheath, which must be new, and keep it for the time of need."(p. 13 of the *Clavicle*).

SYLPHS. – Elves, or Elemental Spirits of the Air (doctrine of the neo-kabbalists, followers of Paracelsus and modern rabbis).

T

TACITURNITY (charm of). – When a sorcerer or witch denied his crime, he was laid bare; then, shaving or depilating all his body, a meticulous investigation was carried on it.

---

[17] We have a specimen of the strange characters which fill these kinds of works; but it seemed good to us to leave it there, for this kind of reproduction.

THE SORCERER'S ARSENAL 205

Why was this done? – First, to find the *stigma Diaboli*, the Devil's signature... In these places, the skin, completely insensitive, could be perforated without flinching. This was no small task (see *Marks*).

Above all, however, before inflicting the *Question* (see this word) on the defendants, they tried to find out if they did not hide the *Charm of Taciturnity* in some fold of the flesh or nail; it was a sort of diagram, which had the occult virtue of suppressing all pain, to the point that the exhausted torturers asked for mercy before the patient had flinched.

See what is said about this charm in chapter III.

TALISMAN. – It is a sign, a character or an image, consecrated according to art, in order to bring good luck in a given circumstance.

There are talismans for the acquisition of wealth, marked with the sign of ☉; talismans for Love, composed under the auspices of ♀; talismans of ♃, to dominate men and constrain fortune; talismans for bravery and victory, studded with the sign of ♂, and so on.

Some talismans claim to be of the high Kabbalah; others, like the *Devil's scapulars*, are of the lowest Goetia.

See also the word *Amulet* in chapter II.

TARANTULA. – This very poisonous spider is quite common in Southern Italy. It is said that those who are bitten by it, rush, it is said, in an interminable outburst of frenetic dance. The venom of the Tarantula was once part of some Neapolitan sorcerers' compositions.

TAROT (or BOOK OF THOTH). – Hieroglyphic instrument of the ancient Wise Men, later to become the instrument par excellence of *divination* (see this word); finally degenerated into a simple card game. Court de Gébelin, in his great work (*Le Monde Primitif* (The Primitive World), 1777, 9 vols. in-4), attributes the invention of the Tarot to the magicians of Egypt. Others trace it back to the primitive cycles of India, this ancient teacher of Mitzraim: a constant tradition among certain tribes of nomadic gypsies from the high Himalayan plateaus, who passed on –from time immemorial and from father to son– the divinatory art, inseparable from his prestigious instrument.

The Tarot is essentially composed of twenty-two magic keys, figurative of the XXII Arcana of the Absolute Doctrine; and of for suits of fourteen cards, each one marked with a tetragrammatic sign: of the *Staff* (י, Yod ♃, Male Principle, Common *Clubs*); – of the *Cup* (ה, He ☿, Female Faculty, Common *Hearts*); – of the *Sword* (ו, Vav ♃, lingamic union of the two combined virtues, Common *Spades*); – finally of the *Sicle* or *Denarius* (ה, second He □, or ⊖ fruit of this union, Common *Diamonds*).

Every suit of fourteen cards is made up of the *Pythagoras Denary* (⊖ or θ, or 10, ספרות *Sephiroth* of the Kabbalists), and a Quaternary[18] of emblematic figures, representing the application of the great Name or Scheme יהוה to each of the dynasties (the King is י ♃, the Queen ה ☿, the Knight ו ♃ and the Valet ה ⊖).

---

18 Tetractys of Pythagoras.

For further details, please consult Papus' very rich and complete work, the *Tarot des Bohémiens* (Tarot of the Bohemians).[19] Of all the occultists who have dealt with Thoth's book, Papus is the first to have the boldness and talent to scientifically deduce the law that governs the march of the Tarot. No one has gone further along this fruitful path.

Many editions of the Tarot are known; some of them are fundamentally altered in the figures, to the point of being unrecognisable. Examples: the German and Chinese Tarot cards, and the so-called Eteilla's corrected deck. Several others offer very notable variants. The most recommendable editions, with regard to the Magic Synthesis, are the so-called Besançon and Marseille editions, especially the last one. However, they cannot be said to be satisfactory...

It was expedient to rebuild at least the authentic edifice of the XXII Keys. Mr. Oswald Wirth bravely undertook this arduous task: by substituting correct drawings for the shapeless colourfulness of the old Tarots, this young initiate did a most meritorious job.[20] All lovers of Theosophy are now familiar with the Tarot de Paris, where the symbolism of the XXII Keys has been restored to its original purity by Mr. Wirth.

In the hands of the magician, the Tarot is a philosophical machine, revealing an absolute Synthesis. In the hands of the gypsies and the card-pullers, it is a mediator of divinatory lucidity; and since, through a dark alchemy, perverts know how to spoil the best things, *–optimi corruptio pessima–* the Tarot degenerates only too frequently, in the hands of modern sorcerers, into a very lucrative instrument of blackmail and even crime.

By inverting the four letters of the hierogrammatic word Taro, one obtains the sacred words: *Ator, Rota, Tora.*

TAUROBOLY. – Mysterious sacrifice of Mithraic origin; referred to the cult of Cybele by the Romans.

The priest immolated the sacred bull with a single blow of the priestly sword and, rushing under the warm fountain he had just opened, dipped his lip first of all in it, invoking the gods; then he stretched his shoulders to the mantle of living purple, which the sacramental sprinkling was going to cover it.

When the Emperor Julian wanted to make himself present and propitious to the gods of his old-fashioned Olympus, he consumed the sacrifice of the Tauroboly. Then, blinded by the blood that flooded him and suffocated by the fetidity of his steamy vapour, he saw the dethroned larvae of ancient Polytheism appear when he got up; pale and silly ghosts, fearful shadows that flee in light volutes at the sole sign of the cross, like those inconsistent morning mists, suddenly vanished at the first ray of sunlight.

TEETH. – The *Teeth* compete with hair and nail clippings for priority in the composition of spells (see chapter III).

---

19 Paris, Carré, 1889, large in-8, fig. – See; on Papus and his works, our *Seuil du Mystère* (Mystery Threshold) (2nd edition).
20 See the *XXII Clefs du Tarot de Wirth* (XXII Keys of the Wirth Tarot) (Poirel, publisher, 1889).

TERAPHIM – This is how the hieroglyphic and priestly oracle of the ancient Hebrews was called. This oracle answered the questions of the high priest with *Urim* אורים and חוסים *Thummim*; toda we would say by tossing a coin. For the false *Teraphim*, see the words *Android* and *Mandrake*.

TEUTAD (or TEUTATES) and THOR. – Two fierce deities of the ancient Celtic. Human blood was annually shed as a sacrifice on their altars, lost in the sacred depths of the sounding forests –*luca sonantia late*. See chapters I and II.

THUNDER. – See in chapter III, the role of thunder in the Wonder.

TOAD. – One of the animals most often cited in the Grimoires. We have dealt with it in chapters II and III.

It is certain that the mere sight of a toad produces a rather intense magnetic effect on impressionable people; it is believed in the countryside that it is enough to be fixed by this animal with a little persistence to fall into syncope.

Sorcerers seek for their charms the *Crapaudine*, a kind of stone which is said to be found in the heads of some toads.

TRANSPORT (FOR THE SORCERERS TO THE SABBATH). – This is what, in the East of France, is called *High-Hunt* (see this word). Refer to chapter II.

TURNTABLES AND TALKING TABLES. – This is modern witchcraft: I mean Spiritism and Spiritualism.

What, in reality, is *Spiritism* (see this word)? – It is the art of getting in touch with vampiric entities, elementals, larvae, etc…, which swarm in the inter-sidereal space and sometimes give a fleeting appearance of life to empty and dying astral shells, aerial corpses in the process of disintegration.

Does this mean that we deny any possibility of relations with higher Spirits, and even souls reintegrated by death into the kingdom of ethereal cosmogonic substance, of which our world is the material excrement? – Certainly not. Only it seems to us that, within the species, the Spiritists or Spiritualists, with the best will in the world, evoke nine hundred and ninety-nine times out of a thousand ambiguous, evil, stupid and brutal beings.

But this comes under the discussion of occult theories. We shall return to it in the second septenary: *The Key to Black Magic*.

In chapter VI of this tome we shall see how spiritists use tables, pedestals and other furniture to make their so-called spirits speak.

See also the *Seuil du mystère* (Threshold of Mystery).

U

UNDINES. – Elemental spirits of water, according to the eclectic doctrine of the neo-cabbalists. See what the Abbot of Villars says about it, in his *Comte de Gabalis* (Count of Gabalis).

UPAS. – From this tree (very common in the Maluku and Sunda archipelagos), the naturals know how to extract one of the most fearsome poisons known.

Generally, the poisonous preparation itself is given the name *Upas*. There are two Upas, also toxic: *Upas antiar*, extracted by incision from an Urticea (*Antiaris toxicaria*), and *Upas tieuté* (*Tsettick* of the Javanese) which is prepared by reducing the bark of a liana (*Strychnos tieuté*) to the consistency of an extract. – Monographers have mistakenly confused these poisons with the famous Curare.

Muslim tradition says that the Upas trees miraculously came out of the soil of Java, under the curse of the prophet, and for the punishment of the infamous vice so common in Malaysia.

In the tormented centuries of the Middle Ages and the Renaissance, the adepts of poisonous magic, Genoese or Florentines, made these poisonous and subtle juices from tropical vegetation come back at a high price: they had the use of them.

URINE. – Sorcerers agree in proclaiming that the urine of a little boy or a young virgin is a marvellous specific for all kinds of illnesses, such as ringworm, mumps, rheumatism... – See, in chapter VI, the strange mixtures that a modern sorcerer elaborates for the healing of the sick and the exorcism of demons.

The marvellous virtue of urine, beaten according to the rite, to excite rain and storms, can be seen in ch. II.

USNEA. – Paracelsus, who has done wonders with the *Usnea*, defines it as a *kind of extremely spongy and tenuous tartar*, which is found on certain woods and on certain animal substances after decomposition. Legend has it that he would even collect it from the skulls of the hanged men; it was used to make up sympathetic remedies of incomparable virtue.

V

VAMPIRES. – Astral entities which, surviving the mortal remains of certain individuals, delay indefinitely their molecular disintegration. These pseudo-animal entities, united to the corpse by an invisible umbilical link, become erratic and attack the sleeping living. Vampirism is, so to speak –a posthumous, hereditary, often epidemic disease–. See for more details, our chapter III.

VITZLIPUTZLI. – The God-snake of the Aztecs, whose idol is periodically sprinkled with bloody libations. See chapter I.

VOLT. – Wax figurine, modelled in the resemblance of the one you want to bewitch. By extension, any spell that is intended to bring death or illness, by virtue of magical execution.

This topic analysed in chapter III, with all the details it contains. See also chap. IV, *Men of Menh*; and chap. VI.

VOODOO. – Wizards of the West Indies, fanatical sectarians of the snake-god, Voodoo. – See chap. III.

# W

WAND. – It cannot be a question here about the *Wizard's Wand*, a magnetic steel rod, imprisoned in an almond tree branch, which carries a small crystal lance at one end and a small resin lance at the other. In addition, Eliphas Lévi treats them knowledgeably in the *Rituel de la Haute Magie* (Transcendental Magic Its Doctrine and Ritual). – See our chapter IV.

Sorcerers also have their Wand, with which they draw the *magic circle* (see this word) and claim, in their overconfidence, to dominate the elements. "This wand must be of hazel –says Collin de Plancy–, and of the shoot of the year. It must be cut on the first Wednesday of the Moon, between eleven o'clock and midnight, while pronouncing certain words. The knife must be new and kept above, when cutting. Then the wand is blessed; the word AGLA + (אגאלא) is written on the large end, in the middle ON + (און) and TÉTRAGRAMMATON + (יהוה) on the small end; and it is said: *Conjuro te cito mihi obedire*… etc….."(*Dictionnaire Infernal* (Infernal Dictionary).

Other wizards, more astute, rim the branch at both ends, with the steel of the blade used to cut the branch; then they magnetised these two ironed ends. Finally, they rub the small end with blood, and soak the big end in urine where they have extinguished a firebrand. – These various rites, observed by the witch rabbis of Alsace, are extremely remarkable from an analogical point of view; they bear witness to a real science, deviated to the left.

WATER. – Witches have been accustomed to beating the water with rods; summoning demons. This small operation is intended to excite storms and hail, or to make heavy rain fall (See chap. III, p. 109, where I tell the story of a young girl, precocious with the most ambiguous arts, and who always carries with her the water she intends to use for this conjuration).

Water was once used for trials. People suspected of witchcraft were thrown into the river. If they drowned, they were considered innocent; if, on the other hand, they were found floating, it was an infallible indication of their guilt. In this case, they were burned. An attractive alternative!

Boiling water was also used for trials. The accused had to plunge his hand into a boiler placed on an inferno, and bring back a blessed ring, suspended by a wire between two waters.

WEREWOLVES. – "In Sorcery, men and women who have been metamorphosed or who metamorphose and transmute themselves into wolves, are called Werewolves" –Collin de Plancy, *Dictionnaire infernal* (Infernal Dictionary)–. See our chapter III.

WHITE MICE. – Some sorcerers, and notably a miserable renegade priest who has passed away, with weapons and baggage, in the service of Satan, still consummate spells, by slitting the throats of white mice, which they feed with consecrated hosts.

This mode of *bewitchment* (see this word) is traditional among a corrupted fraction of the Roman clergy. – On such priests, see chap. II.

END OF INVENTORY

We have not pretended to examine everything in detail; nevertheless, we hope that this chapter, compared with the three preceding ones, will leave little to be desired in terms of the essential information on the Wizard's Religion.

It remains to hunt down the character in his modern costume. We will make our efforts in Chapter VI.

Chapter VI
Modern Avatars of the Sorcerer
ו

The Lover = the Senary = Opposition = Reciprocity
Medium term = Product... *Modern Avatars of the Sorcerer*

Sorcerers in the 19th century? Real sorcerers? The thesis is untenable
– Mr. Father, I am not afraid to support her.
– Are you scoffing? In this day and age! Wizards.... Under the smock and under the tailcoat?
– Under the cassock itself and under the frock.
– Come on, you're almost making up words; I like it better that way.
– I'm the most serious person in the world and I hope to prove it to you.
– The demonstration is all right, but you will have some difficulty in convincing me. I won't hide from you that I am very sceptical by temperament... It was, you see, our great fault, we Church people, to take this pitiful spawn too seriously in the past. The gallows and the pyre, come on! We should have administered some cold showers to these lads. That is my feeling. Who doesn't know, moreover, that the sorcerer died in the Middle Ages?
– You begin with an unfortunate assertion, Mr. Father! You give credit to a common cliché, I concur with you, but agree with me that it is wrong. It was not a hundred years ago that the Inquisition of Rome condemned the Count of Cagliostro to the last torment.[1]
– As a freemason!
– And as a sorcerer. The judgement makes a clear accusation of "*Superstitious Magic*". In any case, Mr. Father, we depart from the question. Would you please grant me an hour's interview? Proofs in hand, I'll do my best to convince you.

---

[1] The death sentence was commuted to that of life imprisonment, without hope of pardon.

It was two o'clock in the afternoon. We went up to my house and the Father *** did not leave until nightfall, but he was doubtless over-convinced of the reality of magical powers, and of the current multiplicity of cases of witchcraft.

I must admit that I had enough proofs in my hands to change his mind: several cases of a unique order and of a truly unimpeachable character. I have the deepest regret that I can only produce short fragments of them. Not to mention the demands of my setting, certain highly suitable motifs impose a reserve on me that perhaps one day I will be able to put aside.

These files relate to the religion of the famous thaumaturge Eugène Vintras, and more particularly to the deeds and gestures of one of his spiritual heirs.

But many other objects will be offered for our examination, before we approach the heretic Vintras and the followers of his Gnostic sect. It is with them that I will end this speech.

Do we believe that magnetisers, spiritists and mediums are not sorcerers...? They do witchcraft, like Mr. Jourdain of prose – without knowing it. More than one does it knowingly!

That if one were to ask me for a quarrel of words, arguing from common opinion, which distinguishes Hypnosis and Spiritism from Black Magic and its spells, I would answer that opinion is wrong. But without beginning with a contentious thesis, and anxious to get to the very heart of my subject, by recounting phenomena on the character of which one cannot be mistaken, I thought it preferable to open this chapter on an unexpected setting: the presbytery of Cideville, in 1851.

Perhaps there is not a single criminal trial in the annals of Magic where prodigies are more positive and more firmly established than in this modest affair, which took place before the Justice of the Peace in Yerville (Lower-Seine) at the beginning of 1851.

This trial will not be to the taste of amateurs of decorative witchcraft, accustomed to the majestic display of judicial dramas with great spectacle. They may feel obliged to wrinkle a disdainful lip, and to lend only a poorly attentive ear to the result of an investigation conducted with such a meagre apparatus, and which came to lead to a simple police hearing; we will not complain less about these false curiosities, for wanting to sacrifice the peremptory substance to the theatrical form, and to ignore the so powerful interest which is attached to formal facts attested under oath by such a number of unimpeachable witnesses.

What makes remarkable the case is its indelible originality, distinguishing it at first glance from all similar trials, is that the complaint, far from being filed against the sorcerer, instead emanates from him.

It was the shepherd Thorel who, before the cantonal justice of the peace, sued the parish priest of Cideville for damages for the three blows this clergyman landed on him with his cane.

The origin of the case goes back to the imprisonment of a certain G***, a village witchdoctor, famous throughout the surrounding area for his claims to occult medicine. This strange man had politely led his patients to the cemetery, under the pretext of infallible treatment; other clients were on their way to join them. Con-

MODERN AVATARS OF THE SORCERER

demned on the denunciation of the priest Tinel, G fulminated some vague threats and swore to take revenge.

The shepherd Thorel, plaintiff at the bar of Yerville, is, by his own admission, only the occult agent of G**, the faithful executor of the supreme will of a master of whom he claims to be a very humble and respectful disciple.

The following is a summary of the facts, certified in a unanimous voice, under oath, by more than twenty witnesses.[2] I have before my eyes the very meticulously detailed narration of the Marquis de Mirville[3] himself, one of the eyewitnesses to the phenomena.

Two young boys, twelve and fourteen years old, who were destined for the priesthood, were brought up by the priest in the presbytery of Cideville. It is on them that Thorel's vengeful fury was unleashed, as he took care to establish fluid communication beforehand, by approaching the younger one, in the course of a public sale.

From then on, a veritable storm of phenomena descended on the presbytery, shaken to its very foundations by the blows struck in its thick walls and partitions, to such an extent that the cracked building threatened falling down. On several occasions and for hours on end, hundreds of curious people came running to search the place in all directions, without managing, at the height of the gust, to unmask the cause of these blows, which were multiplying on all surfaces of the house. Yet they came from two kilometres away (here, I suspect that such distance is exaggerated), and really nothing was neglected in the explorations, both outside and inside. But the noise remained inexplicable.

In the meantime, the mysterious agent deigned to show his intelligence by setting the rhythm of certain tunes, which it has the courtesy to vary at the whim of the assistants.

Mr. de Mirville ran up unexpectedly, according with the Invisible the conditions for a dialogue by different numbers of knocks: one knock meant *yes*, two knocks meant *no*; more than two knocks corresponded, in normal progression, to the number of each of the letters of the alphabet.

Thanks to this ingenious procedure, which perhaps was abused since then, the Devil –for Mr. de Mirville does not flinch at this masterly appellation– the Devil replies with infallible sagacity, a most spiritual appropriateness and an imperturbable aplomb to all the questions he is asked, such as the name, age, domicile, the quality of a crowd of foreign and unknown people in the country. Never has a demon showed more complacency....

Then, the inert objects that started dancing, the tables tumbled, the chairs to wandered through all the rooms; and the knives, the brushes, the breviaries, flow out of one window to enter through the other!

---

2 I speak, of course, only of the witnesses heard in court; for to count them all, one would have to count in hundreds.
3 *Des Esprits et de leurs manifestations fluidiques* (The Spirits and their fluidic manifestations); volume I of the great work, pages 331-363.

The shovel invited the fireplace) tongs to a mazurka, and as soon as it was executed; the irons moved back to the back of the room, followed by the flame of the hearth, which unfolded, sinuous, like a snake.

The glass panes shattered; the heavier pieces of furniture rose up and remained suspended in the air. An enormous desk, loaded with books, rushed forcefully towards the face of Mr. R... de Saint-V..., then, stopping abruptly a few millimetres from his forehead, fell down at his feet without making more noise than a feather.

All these things were observed and affirmed by an ever increasing number of honourable witnesses, who came from the surrounding area: among others, Messrs. de V..., householders in the town of Eu, Doctor Mr... de Bacqueville, the Father L..., vicar in Saint-Roch, and finally the mayor and the municipal authorities of Cideville.

As for the child that Thorel touched, he constantly saw behind him the shadow of a stranger dressed in a blouse. A few days later, Thorel was shown to him, and without hesitation, he cried out, "*There's the man!*".

One of the priests present said that he could clearly see a greyish column of steam moving, undulating, behind the obsessed child. Several others saw this kind of steam snaking around, which condensed and expanded in turn and then disappeared with a whistle through the slits in the door.

The child was terrified; his nervous state was a cause for serious concern; convulsions soon followed. Suddenly he saw *a black, hairy hand* coming out of the chimney; everyone heard the sound of a vigorous bellows. The child shouted, and everyone could see with amazement the mark of five fingers, perfectly stamped on his cheek. He jumped out, the poor child, in the false hope that the hand, which has disappeared into the chimney, would come out through the upper hole!

However, one of the clergymen permanently resident in the presbytery timidly makes a *bold* proposal. He confessed that once read, in a book of witchcraft, that the Invisibles dread the point of swords. Why not take the chance? – As soon as said and done; so much so that after several negative tests (the Magic Agent is so quick to evade!) there occurred an incident of capital importance for occultists, and our readers are asked to take good note of it, because it is revealing in the first place... The attempt seemed fruitless and was about to be abandoned, when one last stroke of the spike caused a crackling flame, accompanied by a high-pitched whistle. A white smoke spread immediately, so thick and foul that the windows had to be opened until it had dissipated...

This unforeseen phenomenon gave the actors confidence in their duel with the Invisible; the experience was repeated again and again.

Suddenly, a word resounded in the room, weakly but clearly articulated: *Sorry*, said the voice. Everyone heard it positively.

The swords were laid down, to resume the dialogue, stated above:

– Pardon...

– The gentlemen reply: *yes, we will forgive you and we will do better: we will spend the whole night in prayer, so that God will forgive you in turn... but on one condition, that tomorrow, whoever you are, you will come yourself to ask forgiveness of this child.*

– *Do you forgive us all?*
– *Are there many of you?*
– *Five, including the shepherd.*
– *We forgive all of you...*

As soon the dialogue ended, all phenomena ceased as if by art of magic, and everything went silent in the presbytery, until dawn, when the first light of which illuminated a group of priests on their knees.

In the afternoon, a man came to the presbytery. It was Thorel, with his eyes downcast, his attitude constrained. His face, which he can't hide behind his cap, was covered with scratches and bleeds in several places...

– *This is the man who has been persecuting me for two weeks!* Shouted the child, who started to shake with all his limbs.

Asked by the priest why he had come, Thorel replied that his master had sent him to fetch the little organ.

– *No, Thorel, you have come for something else. But where did you get all these scratches?* –The shepherd wants to avoid the question. Father Tinel insisted:

– *Be frank; you have come to ask forgiveness of this child. This is what brings you here... On your knees, Thorel!*

– *Well... Sorry! Yes, sorry!* –cried the wretched man, and he crawled on his knees, towards the child, on which he lays his hands. Since this touching, everyone saw that the poor little one's condition was getting worse and that the phenomena were redoubling in intensity!

A second meeting took place at the town hall between the clergyman and the shepherd. The shepherd, in front of many witnesses, fell on his knees as he had done the day before:

– *Excuse me, I beg your pardon...* –but this time he crawled towards the priest...

– *What are you apologising for, Thorel? Explain yourself!* –But Thorel was still moving forward, almost touching the priest's cassock...

– *Don't touch me, for God's sake, or I'll strike you!* –It was then that the priest of Cideville, drove into a corner of the common house, struck on the arm of the sorcerer the three blows of the cane which are the basis of the trial...

The phenomena that I have omitted in this summary cannot be counted. I know of no case richer in findings of any kind. There is nothing to be desired; neither the sharpness, nor the frequency, nor the variety of the prodigies, nor the spontaneous cooperation of the most serious witnesses and the perfect concordance of the most solemn attestations.

The Justice of the Peace of Yerville was astonished; never before had such allegations astonished the echoes of his courtroom. His verdict, rather vague and obscure, at least gave evidence of the unanimity of the testimonies. The defendant priest was dismissed; Thorel, whose case was dismissed, was ordered to pay all the costs of the proceedings. (*Judgment of the Tribunal de simple police d'Yerville*, dated February 4, 1851).

This is therefore, in the narrowest sense of the word, a contemporary and perfectly qualified example of *Black Magic*.

The Sorcerer, Thorel has the same titles as a Hocque[4] or a Gaufridy.[5] The purest purists would be ill-advised to deny him this qualification, which his works justify both in substance and form.

Others are no less deserving, in fact, they are modern necromancers.

I have defined witchcraft as: *the use of the occult forces of nature for evil*. Magnetism falls under this definition in most cases; *Spiritism* in almost all cases.

Indeed, let us try to confine the notion of these two arts in a general formula.

What is *Magnetism*, according to the magnetisers themselves? – The subjugation[6] of a thinking being to the will of another being. Or more clearly: the annihilation of free will.[7]

What is *Spiritism* or *Spiritualism*, according to its apologists? – The evocation of the dead. Or more clearly: the temporary retrogression, towards an inferior mode of existence, of souls in the process of evolving towards a more perfect mode.[8]

So, *unless there is a higher goal, pursued* (and then achieved), *which legitimises the present evil, in view of a greater good to come*, I say that the work of magnetisers and spiritists is in principle a harmful work.

As for the *forces of any kind* put into action by them in order to obtain these results, no one will seriously dispute that they can be qualified as occult.

Hence it follows that, in principle and with few exceptions, magnetists and spiritists, using occult force to accomplish *an evil work*, are, knowingly or unknowingly, *sorcerers*.

And I reach this conclusion, starting from their own premises!

What would it be, in truth, if I were to take as my starting point the principles laid down in the traditional science of the magicians in another field? – Without encroaching on the developments in Book II, I can give an idea of the conclusions that such premises would lead us to.

The state of *magnetic subjection* is nothing other than the *temporary alienation* of a being, previously free and *now possessed*. This more or less despotic and more or less lasting possession is the fact of a *daimon*[9] (vampiric and parasitic existence), which the magnetiser has incited against the person of the subject.

---

4   See the trial of Shepherd Hocque in chapter III.
5   See the case of the parish priest Graufridy, accursed of sorcery, in chapter IV.
6   Do not confuse *Subjugation* and *Suggestion*. See the distinction made to the word *Magnetism* in the small dictionary in our Chapter V. Subjugation is the state of beings who habitually obey suggestions.
7   Not all magnetisers proceed in this way. Those who limit themselves to therapy by the infusion of invigorating fluids are the followers of the vital Mastery; their work is healthy and praiseworthy, generous and beneficial. But from biological transmission to the use of suggestion, the slope is very slippery. What magnetiser can flatter himself that he has never crossed it?
8   I am well aware that not all Spiritists would admit to this paraphrase. To hear them, the aim of their science is to break down the barrier which separates earthly man from posthumous man. However, they teach the progressive evolution of beings. Doesn't making a being on the way up temporarily return to a stage that has already been reached, make him or her retrograde? But the Spiritists not always are consistent.
9   I give the word Demon the Greek spelling (δαίμων) so that one should not be misunderstood to the point of assuming that it is the *Devil*, when I use this word –demon– in the sense in which Porphyry and Jamblique understood it.

It is true that the cases differ. – If the suggestion is limited to compelling the subject in a specific case, in order to accomplish an isolated fact, the daimon remains potential until the desired time, and perishes on the spot, when it passes from power to action. – But if the suggestion is prolonged, in order to determine a series of similar acts, often in the long term, the daimon which constitutes the virtual link, the living substratum of these acts determined in potential, and whose realisation is staggered on the road to the future; this daimon, I say, then seizes the subject, and possesses it by direct reason of the determinism that drives the latent life of these acts, necessary in the future.[10]

So much for *Magnetism*.

As for *Spiritism*, let us only say that the alleged evocation of so-called spirits has no other effect, as a general rule, than to make present or even to create beings no less lemurian[11] and parasitic, always useless, very often harmful, sometimes irreparably fatal.

Mrs. Blavatsky was farsighted when she predicted that the ultimate consequence of the spiritist invasion in the West would be, in the short term, the assured loss and total ruin of thousands of souls, unconscious victims of Allan Kardec and his subversive doctrine.

Many were surprised to hear me express such an unfavourable opinion of Spiritism and to fight stubbornly against a kind of religion which counts among its apologists a number of respectable writers and even true scholars. I will say more: such spiritists (Louis-Michel de Figanières, for example) astonish occultists by the power of their intelligence and the boldness of their intuition. Their works, a chaos of light and shadow, is full of bold and profound views; it may be useful to study them under the light of occultism.

It is clear that I do not deny the value of the spiritists. I am severe with a doctrine which is altogether most remarkable, only because of the terrible consequences to which it fatally leads: psychic promiscuity and spiritual anarchy.

What the Doctors of Spiritism lack is the discernment of spirits.

I have said and I maintain that it is not impossible to establish, without falling into the traps of the Enemy, direct relations with the Superior Intelligences and even with the Souls that are free from carnal fetters. The cult of the Ancestors, in China and elsewhere, consecrates the reality of these relationships; but these relationships can only be established on a hierarchical scale. It requires a science which not even the followers of Spiritism suspect, and the use of procedures whose secret can only be conferred by initiation.[12]

One should not believe that Spiritism was a new invention. The Lemurian forms, which from time immemorial have seemed to take pleasure in passing them-

---

10 Any one can identify within himself such beings, true cancers of the soul, whose life, all borrowed, seeks to develop at the expense of the life of the soul which nourishes them. What we teach here is more terrible than one might think. Thinkers will find in our theory (which will be deduced in Book II) the key to imperious and sometimes unbreakable habits.
11 The lemures were shades or spirits of the restless or malignant dead in Roman mythology, and are probably cognate with an extended sense of larvae.
12 This science is Theurgy, and these procedures are related to the art of Psychurgy.

selves off as souls from beyond the grave, disappointed men long before the striking Spirits, emigrating from the new world, encumbered the old with their noisy presence; long before Allan Kardec formulated his Spiritist Gospel and the Baron of Guldenstubbé obtained the phenomena of direct writing of which he proved so glorious.

The evocation of the beloved dead and of the geniuses of the Cosmos was a custom familiar to all ancient peoples: it is not even the mode of communication that has become de rigueur –revolving and talking tables– that has not been in use since ancient times. The whole of the East had recourse to it many centuries before our era, and without leaving the classical domain of Greco-Latin scholarship, Tertullian guarantees us that it was no more common under the Empire than the oracular tables –*menæ divinatoriæ*– which responded to the consultor by a system of striking knocks. The same author also mentions the sibylline goats –*capellas divinatorias*– whose forked foot beat the retort, by means of a percussive alphabet also known in advance.

In Ammianus Marcellinus we also read of the violence that the zeal of the first emperors converted to Christianity displayed against the devotees of these kinds of oracles.

When the American method of spiritualist communication invaded in Europe around 1853, with all the apparatus of turntables, talking pedestals and oracles by knocking and rapping, it was a fury, a delirium... First of all, the tables had cracked, jumped, waltzed, under the imposition of hands, then without, contact. The emulation won, afterwards, hats, chairs and pedestal tables.

But the dance of the furniture soon became banal; the marvellous went *crescendo*; the pencils wrote of their own accord; luminous hands, like the angel's at Balthazar's feast, appeared in their turn; they were seen, touched and felt... Finally, the Invisible, familiarising itself with the guests of the material world, was seen, compacted, materialised: ghosts appeared, in precise and living forms.

What was needed, in the final analysis, what is still needed today, to see all these marvels accomplished? – There is only one condition that is always and everywhere invariable: the presence of an intermediary, a *medium*.

When asked what a medium essentially consists of, we would define him as a man (or a woman) suffering from vital incontinence, and exhausting himself by feeding from his fluid substance (too expansive and complacent to borrow), a crowd of parasitic larvae, which swarm and multiply in his astral atmosphere, in his occult nimbus.

If this definition seemed obscure, we would beg the public to wait until our second septenary is brought to light, where the last details will be given.[13]

Any esoteric comments here would be out of place – and, what is worse, premature. We feel that there is all too much of a tendency to colour this first, purely documentary, book with explanatory interludes that are hors d'oeuvres.

---

13 May he wish to refer, from now on, to the *Mystères de la Solitude* (Mysteries of Solitude), published in numbers 5 and 7 of the *Initiation* (2nd year, pages 101-125 and 23-37). We have cleared up many mysterious questions there.

Therefore, the *sine qua non* condition for the wonders in which spiritists want to see the direct action of disembodied souls is the intervention, strictly passive, of a good medium. Around him torrents of phenomena burst forth, all similar to those of Cideville, described above.[14]

Do the so-called spirits communicate by means of striking knocks? It is by means of an alphabet similar in every way to the one imagined by Mr. de Mirville in the presbytery.

Do they manifest themselves through apparitions? It is in a form very similar to that of the ghost who, following the young seminarian, was constantly standing behind him.

For the spectators, everything happens in the same way as in Cideville; some, like children, see a human form; others, like the clergymen, see only a moving, vaporous column; and finally, there are some who perceive nothing at all, as was the case with several witnesses who came from the surrounding area.

The analogies are not limited to this. Heavy objects move around, fly away, wander around, return to their starting point, or, having risen several feet above the ground, fall back without noise.

Cloudy shapes become clearer, condense; hands appear... (how can we not think of the hand that struck a strong slap on the poor boy's cheek).

Most often luminous or flesh-coloured, these hands come out of a moving fog. Their contours, clearly accentuated, become indecisive towards the wrist area; the line then hesitates, trembles in a halo, and ends up being lost by insensitive damage in the vaporous swirl of the forearm.

These hands are palpable; those who have touched them readily compare them to skin gloves inflated with warm air,[15] and if, having grasped them, one wants to hold them by force or pull them on oneself with authority to discover the arm to which they are attached, the whole thing becomes a vague outline, an aggregation of problematic substance, inconsistent and melting under the fingers... Sometimes the hands still appear black and hairy, as in Cideville. In any case, they act with absolute freedom and perfect ease, so that there is no doubt that they are attached to a living, normal, albeit invisible, human body. When the hand is well defined, alone and without apparent support, it is not rare to see the invisible body objectify itself in its turn; total or partial, these coagulations dissolve as easily as they are compacted.

It is clear that these exteriorizations exhaust the medium; the more they multiply, the more weary it appears. Feeling the need to supply nervous strength, he grabs the hands of a young and healthy person, who immediately feels the fluidic suction of this parlour vampire. It is a delicious sensation of languor, accompanied by shivers. And in fact, the room temperature drops by several degrees in less than a minute. Icy breezes run in all directions, like a wind. These atmospheric phenomena are preferably accentuated at the precise moment of the important objectivization by their volume and sharpness.

---

14 It can be said, from a certain point of view, that in Cideville, the youngest of the seminarians had become a medium, manifest not only of the larvae that Thorel the shepherd used, but also of the sidereal form of this magician, itself envisaged as a lemur and parasitic entity.
15 See Eliphas Lévi, *Clef des grands Mystères* (Key to the Great Mysteries).

Mediums are more or less integral to all these spectra. Let me explain.

When it happens that a misguided spectator strikes or injures the luminous or condensed apparitions in human form, which appear around these sickly beings, they immediately suffer the repercussion of the wound made to the ghost. If the weapon used is sharp, the scratch, or at least a mark that looks like a scar, soon marbles the medium's skin.

This repercussion phenomenon is usually not serious, when the aggressor has harmed only a larvae evolving in the occult nimbus of the medium; the accident is much more serious, if the blow of the spike has damaged the very substance of the experimenter at the exit of the astral body.[16]

In a public session in New York by Z…, a powerful materialization medium, a Yankee thinks it's witty to try his *bull-dog*[17] on the ghost, which he hit with a bullet at close range. Immediately, a cry of distress was heard several steps backwards from the poor medium, who had fallen unconscious and whose chest was stained with a deep bruise; and yet he could not have received the bullet, which was stuck on the wall, in the opposite direction, because the American, sitting right in the space which separated the condensed spectrum from the medium, aimed straight ahead, and therefore at the opposite of the medium. The medium was repercussionally affected and remained suspended for more than a month between life and death, and healed only with great difficulty.

This fact, which is truly typical, was certified to me by one of the most serious people, who himself had it from an eyewitness of this sad scene.

It is not wrong to make a new connection with the case of the shepherd Thorel, whose face shows all the scars of the blows he received the day before in his astral form. This leads us to mention one more of the thousand details that we had to omit, in summing up the Cideville affair. Father Tinel had loaded a gun with dust-shot to shoot sparrows. At the height of the mysterious gust, he fired in the direction of the noise. The child, who alone saw the shepherd's shape clearly, declared him to be suffering from two pellets in the face. The next day, Thorel's face is checked to see if the mark of the two pellets is perfectly distinct!…

The identity of the phenomena is undeniable, whether it is Spiritism or Sorcery; and we have no need to multiply examples and testimonies here. However sceptical and ill-disposed our readers may be to agree on such wonders, let them take the trouble to attend a few sessions of Spiritism, and their disbelief will fall before the eloquence of the facts.

There are mediums of all kinds, some of which are said to cause *physical effects*, that is to say, phenomena such as striking, moving objects, levitation, etc… Others are said to *materialise*: visible and tangible forms condense in their presence, some-

---

16 The phenomenon observed at Cideville, of a spark followed by smoke, indicates the complete and definitive dissolution of a fluid coagulate; as Thorel survives, it is because the point has dissolved only one larvae: such a blow reaching the astral body itself would have been fatal to the sorcerer.
In this case, Thorel would have been found dead in his house the next day, and no doubt a peremptory label would have been affixed to the accident: rupture of aneurysm.
17 The British Bull-Dog was a popular type of solid-frame pocket revolver.

MODERN AVATARS OF THE SORCERER

times luminous and diaphanous or coloured and opaque forms, sometimes of living beings, or even inanimate things, sometimes of stable and perfectly evolved objects, or of fleeting and dissolvable aggregations. – Finally, there are those who are called *incarnation* mediums.

The case of the latter is not the least surprising, nor above all the least worthy of examination.

They offer for a time the hospitality of their body to beings who incarnate in it, and who, taking possession of the organs, activate and govern them at their whim. In this order of phenomena, we have witnessed strange, astonishing scenes... In a few seconds, the voluntarily possessed is modified, corrected, transmuted from top to bottom, to the inner model of the daimon that has taken possession of him.

Circe's wand was certainly no quicker, nor its effects more prodigious. – The medium is unrecognisable; his posture, his voice, his gaze, his gestures have changed abruptly; his features are themselves transformed. It is a sudden metamorphosis of the whole person...

Another man is in front of you. And (a frightening thing!) it sometimes seems as if *He who is there* is a being known to the spectator, a loved one, who has been dead for many years... suddenly resurrected in the skin of a stranger, in a *borrowed body*, the first to come, who, at this very hour, is unaware even of the name, even of the fact of the past existence of the dead man who lives again in him!

How can we doubt, however? The resemblance bursts out, positive and paradoxical all together, all the more impressive as it is psychic, super-mundane and *spiritual* rather than plastic and material, for it must be adapted to the basic features of the medium; the skeleton does not change, in fact, and only the soft and fleshy surfaces are modelled on the morphogenic pattern of the internal sculptor, whose instantaneous art is practised with an influence from the inside out!

It is a self-exteriorization; through the carnal *bark* of the evocative, the evoked inner self *transpires*. The passing soul imprints its own effigy on the face of the medium who undergoes its intimate, virtual, hyper-physical embrace...

It's done: the physiognomy of the being who incarnates has been placed on the passive model of the intermediary who offers himself for incarnation.

And it is a moving, unforgettable spectacle!

You will find the gestures, the attitude, the vocal inflections of your loved one; through the medium's mouth, he speaks to you of things of yesteryear; he stirs up the ashes of old memories buried deep in your soul, and whose secret he alone shared with you!

Tears wet your eyes; an invincible emotion hugs your heart. No more doubts, it is He!...

And you return home shocked, sure that you have seen Him again, in fact mystified and disappointed by an elemental, or even a larvae of the second atmosphere.

This equivocal being, a pseudo-psychic mirror, has reflected the image of the deceased, still alive in the tabernacle of your memory. Everting and clearly, in order to reproduce the imprints of yesteryear about to fade away in you, this larvae told you about your soul...

One can imagine the terrifying scope of such mystifications... Elementals, like all ambiguous and semi-conscious beings of the Negative Light, are magnetised by perverse instincts.[18] The morality of those they usually haunt cannot resist.

A great number of mediums have slid down this slope to the swamp where souls are rotting in the most abject depravity. Onanism is in more than one person the least consequence of this moral degeneration. I know many who feed *humano semine*; this disgusting habit has passed into a state of furious mania. To the point where they go from door to door offering their shameful services at home.

I know some of them who carry the indelible stigma of this profound disturbance of instincts on their faces. There is even one, which is one of the most powerful and well-known, that nature has designated in advance for strange destinies. Far from following his colleagues in the path of sexual aberrations, this one has only one dream: normal love. She is, with a male head and a conquering moustache, the best-built woman in the world. This androgynous woman is perfectly regulated and in a very gallant mood. Two of my friends know something about her...

But enough about that.

In chapter one, we read about the more than indecent exploits that are familiar to the elusive and protean beings who move around professional mediums. *Table dancing*, even when performed in the family, presents no less alarming dangers for the honour of women, the chastity of young girls and the innocence of children. Mothers and fathers (exclaims a scholar who is very expert in matters of spiritism, Mr. Bonjean de Chambéry), *mothers and fathers, who do not wish to develop premature feelings in their daughters; husbands who wish a respite from their wives, beware of the magnetic chain in general, and of table dancing in particular!*

It will come as no surprise to anyone that magnetism has had equally disastrous effects in the hands of reckless experimenters, imperfectly initiated, or lacking in high and severe morals.

Seven years ago I saw this criminal experiment succeed; a doctor, whom I shall not name, suggested to a young sleeping Israelite that a glass of water, which she would find near her when she woke up, was full of a terrible poison. She was nevertheless ordered to drink it in one gulp.

–*But Salomé will die*, the girl objected (this young subject manifested two distinct individualities in his sleep: she used to talk about herself as a perfectly indifferent third party).

–*Salome will die*, replies the Doctor, a sinister echo.

The young girl wakes up and empties the glass without hesitation. Immediately, her face decomposes:

---

18 We know the gloomy adventure of a blameless and most devout widow, who lost herself to all the senses, for having surrendered with abandon to the so-called spirit of her husband, who had died recently, and whom she adored. She was only too happy to find him again in the paradise of spiritist phenomena.
The problematic being who gave herself for the soul of her soul, persuaded her that marital relations could restore between her and him the intimacy of yesteryear. At the present time, this unfortunate being has completely sunk into the depths of the incubic abyss. Her body is dying, her soul is dead.

–It's fire, what I drank there! Help me, help me!

The unfortunate girl, having not kept the slightest memory of what had been prescribed to her in her sleep, thought she had acted spontaneously.

Six minutes after swallowing this clear water, she vomited an abundance of vermilion blood between two convulsions.

The terrified Doctor only had time to put her back to sleep again, and to put to naught, by a new suggestion, the old one.

It was not difficult for him to do so, but what he could not repair were the traumatic consequences of this unspeakable experience. The poor child saw death at close quarters; a round ulcer had opened in her stomach, and the slow healing of such a serious illness sapped her robust youth. And the young practitioner, who had not a bad heart, was completely cured, I imagine, of the itch of reckless experiments.

I also saw a young and pretty working-class girl, most modest and honest, getting naked and dancing –under such kind of influences– a very nimble dance. Eleven people were present, including three young doctors, four students, a pharmacist, all young men!

To obtain this sacrifice of his last modesty, it had not even been necessary to put her to sleep. Taking her hand and staring her in the eyes, and twice repeating the order to take off her dress, had been enough… She was literally bewitched, the demon of the impure dance possessed her.

When she was dressed and out of the state of enchantment, she was told what she had done, she blushed up to her neck, but did not want to believe it.

That was the plan. – The inventor of this gallant escapade –who should have been very surprised if it was qualified as a little infamy–, had seized a piece of evidence, the most insulting for the poor girl, but also the least contestable… On presentation of this material and peremptory proof, she cried her eyes out.

And when she was returned to the too gullible father who had, for a coin, entrusted his daughter to the Dr. ***, no one dared to boast of the success of such a cowardly breach of trust. She herself remained silent, burning with the outrage that she had not been able to forger, although more than six years have passed since then!

Finally, I saw, with my own eyes, a young boy striking his mother, in the heart region, with three violent stab wounds (using one of those theatrical weapons, whose blade slides into the handle, with a skilfully arranged trigger). The subject, who was seventeen years old, was perfectly alert, but under the despotic rule of suggestion.

Those who know how frequent are the cases of recurrence, in the internal imperative act which determines the accomplishment of the suggested will, can understand all the temerity of this third experience.

What a scourge is Magnetism in imprudent or unscrupulous hands! Again, the authors of the three exploits described above were not evildoers; their aim was not criminal. At most, they obeyed an unhealthy curiosity, which in their own eyes was decorated with the respectable name of scientific zeal; they would, if need be, claim the privileges of experimental frankness, which are considered imprescriptible in the court of modern conscience.

But let us suppose a criminal educated enough to bend the classical procedures of hypnotism to the accomplishment of his evil designs. If he comes across sensitive subjects, he will use them as occult arms, to strike anyone who is an obstacle to his ambition; while, smiling and huddled in the shadows, without danger of being discovered, he will wait for his victims, shot one after the other, to litter with their corpses the path which they obstructed with their cumbersome personalities.

Let's be careful with this; I affirm that not only will the wretched man be able to steal, murder and the rest by proxy, but he will also be able to protect himself from any indiscreet suspicion.

It has been said that learned psychologists, coupled with skilful physiologists, were able, in one such case, to unmask a scoundrel, by unravelling the complex web of his hypnotist tricks; but I maintain that they were misguided. Providence had permitted this man, considering it impossible for suspicion to be aroused in the first place, to omit something in the precautions he took. And in fact his calculations had gone beyond what would have been necessary to foresee in any other circumstances. He had said to himself: "I know my sleepwalker; he has no memory of the things suggested to him during hypnosis when he is awake. I will therefore put it in his head to beat N... to death; by committing this crime, he will believe he is acting freely. To be on the safe side, I can persuade him again that he hates N..., guilty towards him of some supposed injustice; he will therefore confess to the magistrates that he killed N... out of vengeance. And everyone will believe him." This ruthless man had reasoned perfectly; everything he had planned was carried out to the letter...[19] Unfortunately for him, by a providential coincidence: 1° the examining magistrate, who had for some months been studying hypnotism, should turn his mind in this direction; 2° and he should somehow have learned that the accused usually served as a subject for the real culprit. It did not take more than that to lose him. The magistrate immediately sniffed out the truth; having taken the advice of a competent friend, he took it upon himself to put the man to sleep, who, moreover, persisted, as had been foreseen, in maintaining that he had acted of his own free will, out of vengeance. As soon as he had fallen asleep, the memory from his previous sleeps returned to him, and the odious web of darkness spread out by itself in broad daylight.

But the hypnotist could have foreseen this improbable hazard. It even seems astonishing that, criminally determined as he was, he did not take the precaution of suggesting immediate suicide to the author of the material fact.[20] Everyone would have said: "He killed out of vengeance; he killed himself out of remorse! ..."

---

[19] Where did we read the account of this case? This is what we were unable to find. We therefore give it only with express reservations. – In any event, no experienced experimenter will dispute the possibility of these facts, nor the logic and plausibility of their sequence: as they stand, they can serve as a basis for argument.

[20] Let us not be accused of recklessness and lightness, under the pretext that we show how the real culprit could have foiled the prosecution, or even ensure his impunity forever by a new crime. No doubt, we would be unforgivable to use it in this way, if the theory of suggestion had not become commonplace, even among the ignorant. Thank goodness we are not guilty of having thrown this terrible weapon into the hands of the first to come; but, since this disclosure is a *fait accompli*, let us not be told of any measure to be guarded against. Reluctance, at the point we have reached, would be a hypocritically vain precaution, a parade of foolish prudence, an unbearable coquetry of virtue.

Even admitting that such a wretched man was looking at two corpses instead of one – but was he a man to back away from yet another crime? At least he could suggest to his sleepwalker that he should not remember anything in his later sleeps, or even persuade him that he could never be put to sleep again.

All suggestions on a sensitive subject, are carried out in a mathematical way. Coming even from different sources, they are bound and chained together with an inflexible logic. The soul of the sleepwalker is a soft wax, which hardens under the fingers of the kneader; the magnetist's task is to arrive first at the modelling.[21] The following experiment, which I can vouch for, provides a peremptory demonstration of this.

A young doctor, a friend of mine, without putting Miss B. to sleep, contracts her hand muscles by suggestion. I tried immediately, but in vain, to get in touch with her, to restore the hand to its normal state.

Passes, breaths, suggestions, orders formulated in every way, all were useless.

Weary of my efforts I said "Sleep!" to the girl. She fell asleep on the spot, standing up. I was careful to make sure that her whole body was under my control, except for the clenched hand, which resisted and persisted! An idea crossed my mind: "I am breaking –I cried out– any link, any relationship between the doctor and you!" All was in vain; the contracture was rebellious to these efforts. Late convinced of my impotence, I finally woke up Miss B..., and the doctor approached her to destroy his first suggestion. To the amazement of all of them, I had severed all suggestive ties between her and him, so that also he failed. This is the curious and, I think, rather new point of the experiment. I had to put Miss B. back to sleep and restore the relationship between her and my friend, so that he could finally relax that stubborn hand.

When one thinks of the relative omnipotence which, thanks to Mesmer, can be acquired by the first to come on certain passive or timid natures, one is sometimes tempted to pass a severe judgement on this man to the point of injustice. It is a sad gift, it is said, that this famous doctor, a dazed populariser of a science that would like to be practised like a priesthood, and that religious antiquity taught its followers only in the crypt of mysteries, in the shadow of an altar where the gods manifested their effective presence שכינה *Schechina*, in the very heart of the Light of glory אין סוף אור *Ain-Soph-Aor*. In this sacred atmosphere, the dragon of the Lower Astral did not penetrate. The mirages of the illusory עשיה *Ashiah* were unknown here – and even outside the sanctuary, the greedy larvae fled in fear of those who had once crossed the fourfold mystical circle of the Covenant. These had a sign on their foreheads; the baptism of the fire-principle had regenerated them. From then on, they could leave Memphis or Thebes, return to their homeland... Therapists of

---

21 The theory of suggestion has been thought to be ruined, in its absolute nature, by insisting on the prodigious and sometimes insurmountable resistance than an honest conscience –shaped from childhood by good ideals–, would offer to immoral or criminal suggestions. The objection is easy to overcome. What, in fact, is education (this moral orthopaedics), if not a whole *edifice of previous suggestions*, not only patiently superimposed, but also artfully cemented? This edifice should be abolished first of all, before claiming to replace it with a scaffolding of reverse suggestions. In short, to take up our first comparison, with such natures, *the instigator of evil did not come first in modelling*; the wax had hardened under fingers other than his own.

the soul and doctors of the body, they felt missionaries from Above, to spread to the profane world the ever pure and beneficial irradiation of this flame, whose tutelary focus was concentrated, invisible, in the depths of the tabernacle.

Alas! Today... the ubiquity of the astral lie surrounds us with its tumultuous influx; the caduceus of Hermes and Aesculapius is changed –in the hands of the evil ones– into an exterminating sword, when it does not become the wand of the lowest and most abject gulp. Oh miraculous wand! The scholars who picked you up handle you awkwardly and go so far as to deny your existence when you still shine in their hands...

This magnificent power, once the prerogative of the highest initiates, after having –very recognizable and sublime until its lowering– lit up the athanor in the secret pantries of the Rosicrucian alchemists of the Middle Ages and the Renaissance (those as Jechiel, Abraham the Jew, Paracelsus, Fludd and Van Helmont), prostituted herself entirely through Mesmer, who delivered her, by popularising her, to the ignorant, clumsy and perverse hands.

Was Mesmer an intuitive or an insider? That's the question. In the first case, in spite of the gaps and inconsistencies in his system, he was a remarkable inventor; he can hardly be held responsible in court for the abuses that his discovery must have entailed. In the other case, he was a great criminal, a traitor and a defiler.

Magnetism, in order to be beneficial, had to remain hidden. But at this point there is no turning back; perhaps the initiators would have done better not to make such a disclosure, but in the end they have said too much or too little, so let them speak, since they have not been able to keep silent.

If Magnetism, at the present time, is not revealed in its true light, it will inevitably determine a terrible crisis in the moral order; the eternal problem of free will seems to be solved by the negative, and the psychic compass will panic and lose its normal orientation. Finally –a harbinger of the great cosmic cataclysms– the notions of Evil and Good will be confused again.

This extreme peril would have been avoided, like the hierophants of Thebes and Eleusis, by reserving such power for the followers of a hierarchical teaching, under the guarantee of initiation. This is all too true. But is it opportune to insist so much? It is better to say a word about the modern theorists of Magnetism and their certainly generous attempt to save it from the hatreds of charlatan exploitation by assimilating it to the other sciences.

Honour therefore to those as Deleuze, Puységur, and du Potet, who loved Magnetism with a rather noble love, to aspire to grasp it in its essence. For lack of full success, at least their stubborn sagacity, practising to guess the great laws of nature, received as a reward the unshakeable faith that they exist. These laymen intuitively perceived certain reflections of truth-synthesis.

Honour even to the magnetizing psychologists of the Braid school. If, unable to penetrate the nature of a great agent and the mysterious laws governing astral tides, they have taken the decision to deny these things, at least they have constructed a theory which is superficial, but perfectly rigorous, and which gives an exact account of phenomenal appearances. The Suggestion is an excellent method for the grouping and classification of facts; nothing more, nothing less.

The most accredited doctrine in this day and age rejects a priori the hypothesis of the *fluid*, instinctively and one can say almost blindly supported by the empirical disciples of Mesmer and the diffuse theorists of his school. This dogma is on the index of the University and no one is unaware that its professors monopolise the vogue.[22]

Still, one must distinguish in the camp of the Braidists. Parisian hypnographers are perhaps not to be cited as models.

Those of the Salpêtrière school, in particular –with Mr. Charcot in mind– are in fact making a big fuss; and it will be seen that I speak literally and figuratively. The name of amphitheatre, which they decorate one of the scenes of their exploits, is a word that is half too long. They take care of the staging with paternal solicitude.[23] No display repels them; no orchestral accompaniment is foreign to them, neither the Chinese tam-tam and gong lavished in their experiments, nor the most dithyrambic and noisy one, granted by the greatest number of them, not to say encouraged by all of them.

On the other hand, they do little work. Not only have they discovered nothing, but they hesitate to sanction and promulgate, even under a new name, the most indisputable principles, formulated in lucid terms by the teachers of Nancy. – Less turbulent, this School of Nancy; less theatrical, but more conscientious and daring as a whole, and recommendable in so many respects; hostile to all uses of the gong

---

[22] I have done justice to the theory of *Suggestion*, which the Braidists developed, if not constructed from scratch; I mean at this time the less noble side of these academics.

Since these gentlemen of the Faculty, having shamelessly installed themselves in Mesmer's house, had the bad taste of attaching the epithet of charlatan to the name of the innovator whose scientific heritage they were squandering (and moreover distorting), the *question of the fluid* has become for them, no doubt in hatred of the master, the touchstone of the hypnographers. You are a serious man, a *good young man*, a physiologist of the future; you are a *dignus intrare*, and as a result you will be awarded the academic certificate of *hypnotist...*; but if you have the impudence to believe in the *fluid*, you have become a master juggler, acrobat, showman, etc. These bad words are synonymous with the apostles of magnetism.

It should be understood, however. The Braidists profess to believe that suggestion is transmitted without an intermediary; that its mechanism is a purely internal phenomenon, in the absence of any agent external to the subject. I believe, with all occultists, in a plastic mediator, a transmitter to the material organs of the orders of will; I have defined, in the *Seuil du Mystère* (Threshold of Mystery), this Agent of convertibility of voluntary thought into accomplished act, this omnilateral substratum of all phenomenal reality. I believe that sound, heat, light, electricity, those *nescio quid* that the old physicists called imponderable fluids, are the manifest modalities of this agent, which is their correlation, their synthesis to all. I shall give proof of what I am saying in my *Key to Black Magic*.

Having said that, I would add that since the idea is dearer to me than words, I have no objection to renaming the *fluid*, as *Magnetism* has been renamed. One has to be conciliatory. I therefore offer to renounce the *word* –fluid– if it is true that this word has the magical virtue of making hydrophobic the irreconcilables of hypnotism.

[23] Are they not the foster fathers of official somnambulism – a child by adoption, which they have had the glory of renaming, substituting the flattering name Hypnotism for the impertinent term Animal Magnetism?

and the tuning fork, the drum and the tam-tam; concerned above all with the true and the useful: rational induction in theory, experimental therapy in practice. His learned and modest doctors, those as Liébeault, Bernheim, Beaunis and Liégeois, verified, clarified, extended and consolidated this beautiful theory of suggestion, interviewed by Father Faria, and which the Englishman Braid reduced to a scientific formula. Achieving the point of perfection to which the teachers of Nancy brought it. It is a flexible and marvellous theory, giving an account of everyday and normal phenomena with a rigour that would be called mathematical; not going (as we have noted) as far as the hyper-physical laws of magnetism, but unassailable in its apparent mechanism, in the field of strict positivism and experimental realism, gaining in lucidity what it lacks in depth.

Experience has not yet brought the masters of Nancy back to the consciousness of a biogenic agent. The *psychic force* of the scientist Crookes remains unknown to them.

Except for Mr. Liébeault, undisputed founder of the School and fervent of old date (when there was courage and almost temerity in claiming and displaying his opinions as a cockade). Mr. Liébeault, deeply shaken in his scepticism by the conclusive eloquence of the cures he obtained, notably the cure of children with udders, in whom the hypothesis of any suggestion is self-refuted, all the honourable practitioners of Nancy vigorously deny the doctrine of the fluid. A fatal reaction against the assertive enthusiasm of so many magnetists, who had alternately moved themselves from candid empiricism to silliness and from obvious charlatanism to scandal. These unscrupulous hounds, the hawks of public meetings, whose presumptuous ignorance was complicated by a suspicious morality, are the ones that, by exploiting Magnetism almost lost it…

Mr. Liébeault distinguishes himself from his Braidist colleagues by his disregard of old academic routines, the radical absence of prejudice in science and the absolute disdain of what is said about it. He goes much further in his findings than anyone else from the same School.

One day –it was in May 1885– Mr. Focachon, a pharmacist in Charmes, brought to Dr. Liébeault a most sensitive subject (Miss Élisa N…), on which they succeeded in the most memorable experiment that had been attempted since those of Crookes[24], the application of a vesicatory by suggestion.[25] The vicissitudes of the experiment, carried out in forty-eight hours, under rigorous conditions of scientific evidence and experimental control, are recorded in a report written by Dr. Beaunis, and initialled as witnesses by Messrs. Liébeault, Focachon, Bernheim, Liégeois, Simon, etc… One understands the crucial importance of such a result, in the presence of which it is no longer possible to question the stigmatisation phenomena, so

---

24 We reserve the phenomena attested by the scholar Crookes for our second septenary: *The Key to Black Magic*. These facts are so extraordinary, that it seems prudent to deal with them only when it will be possible to provide us with a parallel explanatory hypothesis.

25 Read the letter from Mr. Focachon to Mr. Félix Fabart (5 July 1885) inserted on pages 332-337 of the latter's book: *Histoire de l'Occulte* (History of the Occult) (Marpon, 1885, in-12). It contains all desirable details.

frequent among ecstatic people. Has the self-suggestive mechanism of this alleged miracle not now been demonstrated?

Eight months later, one morning when we attended Dr. Liébeault's consultation, we suggested to him at once that he try on one of his patients, taken at random, an experiment of mental suggestion, or rather of transmission of thought, that is to say, one of these as yet unexplained phenomena, which Dr. Regnard, Mr. Charcot's pupil and friend, described as a rather cavalier feather: "These things are not a matter of science. We don't talk about them at the Sorbonne. Our hospices at Bicêtre and Charenton, the various chambers of our correctional courts are the only places where from time to time it can be discussed." (Lecture given at the Sorbonne,[26] on March 5, 1881).

Dr. Liébeault, full of audacity and loyalty, accepted our proposal from the outset and, when the experiment was over, did not hesitate to sign the Minutes as follows:[27]

MINUTES relating three facts of MENTAL SUGGESTION obtained by Messrs. Liébeault and Guaita at the home of Dr. LIÉBEAULT, 4, rue de Bellevue (Nancy).

"We, the undersigned, LIÉBEAULT (Antoine), doctor of medicine, and DE GUAITA (Stanislas), man of letters, both currently living in Nancy, attest and certify having obtained the results that we are about to read".

1

"Miss Louise L…, asleep in magnetic sleep, was informed that she would have to answer a question that would be asked her mentally, without the intervention of any word or sign.

Dr. Liébeault, with his hand resting on the subject's forehead, paused for a moment, concentrating his own attention on the request: 'When will you be cured', which he intended to make. The sleepwalker's lips suddenly moved: – 'Soon' she whispered distinctly.

She was then invited to repeat, in front of everyone present, the question she had intuitively perceived. *She repeated it in the same terms in which the question had been formulated in the mind of the experimenter.*

---

26 This lecture was reprinted by Dr. Regnard, in his book already quoted: *Sorcellerie, Magnétisme* (Sorcery, Magnetism), etc… (Paris, Plon, 1887, large in-8, fig.). See pages 282-285.
27 We learn that Dr. Liébeault published these Minutes in his book *Le Sommeil provoqué et des états analogues* (Induced Sleep and Similar Conditions), Paris, Doin, 1889, in-18 (pages 305-306). Earlier, Professor Beaunis would have given it already in his book of *Somnambulisme provoqué* (Induced somnambulism), Paris, J.-B. Baillière, in-18.

This first experiment, undertaken by Dr. Liébeault, at the instigation of Mr. de Guaita, was thus fully successful. A second test gave less rigorous results, but perhaps even more curious, as we shall see."

2

"Mr. de Guaita, having contacted the magnetised woman, mentally asked her another question: *'Will you come back next week?'*.[28] *'Perhaps'*, was the answer of the subject; but invited to communicate to those present the mental question,[29] she replied: – *'You asked me if you would come back next week'*.
This confusion about a word in the sentence is very significant: it seems to me that the girl stumbled, reading the magnetiser's brain."

3

"To avoid that an indicative sentence would be pronounced, even in a low voice, Dr. Liébeault wrote on a note: – *'Mademoiselle, when she wakes up, will see her black hat transformed into a red hat.'*
The ticket was passed in advance to all the witnesses, then Mr. Liébeault and de Guaita silently put their hands on the subject's forehead, mentally formulating the agreed sentence. Then the young girl, informed that she would see something unusual in the room, was awakened.
Without a moment's hesitation, she immediately looked at her hat, and with a great burst of laughter, she cried out: – It wasn't her hat; she didn't want it. It had the same shape, but the joke had gone on long enough; she had to get it back... – But in the end, what do you see has changed? – You know it well; you have eyes like mine. – What else has changed? They had to insist for a long time before she would agree to say what had changed in her hat: *'She was being laughed at...'* In a hurry of questions she finally said: *'You can see it's all red!'*
As she refused to take it back, they had to put an end to the hallucination, telling him that it would return to its original colour. The doctor blew on the hat, and once it had become hers again in her eyes, she agreed to take it back.
These are the facts that we certify that we have obtained together. In witness whereof we have drawn up these minutes."

Nancy, this June 8, 1886. (Made in duplicate.)
Dr.-A.-A. Liébeault. Stanislas De Guaita.

It goes without saying that Dr. Liébeault, extremely sceptical about the *transmission of thought*, was not counting on the success of such an attempt.
We have cited this experience and the even more astonishing experience of the vesicatory, to show how little the Dean of the École de Nancy allows himself to be disconcerted by the most unexpected proposals, and with what courageous frank-

---

28 Double question, therefore more complicated (author's note).
29 Need it be said that each time they were informed in advance of the question that would be asked? (author's note).

ness he vouches for the most unorthodox academic facts, when he has seen them and verified them for himself.

The despotism of the scope of our work forbids us to stay longer in the paths of Allan Kardec and Mesmer.

That the contemporary apostles of Magnetism and above all of Spiritism usually stumble and slip into the rut of witchcraft – this is what we feel we can demonstrate by reasoning and examples.

As for the mob of low-class enchanters –bonesetters with ambiguous gestures; midwives with suspiciously skilfulness bending to the elaboration of potions, as well as to the tricks of abortion; card-pullers with viperine eyes, a honeyed voice, a slavish attitude, with impertinent nuances, and whose double entendre sentences warn, solicit, encourage all confessions (for it is remarkable that the client, who has come to hear himself told his fortune, ends up telling it himself, nine times out of ten)–, these companions of crude witchcraft are of only secondary interest, both because of their relatively small number and because of the even smaller circle of their influence. We will not say anything about them.

It would remain for us to introduce the reader to the cohort of doubtful mystics, those are much less rare and less harmless. We think their study would certainly not lack interest or usefulness. There would be books to be written on the absolute perversion of the moral sense, which is revealed in most of them, in the most varied and sometimes most picturesque forms.

Unfortunately, we have a duty of public health to fulfil, which forbids us the comparative table that we would have liked to draw. The task of denouncing one of the lowly idols of the mystical Sodom is a task that requires a certain number of pages; we have taken on this task, and we are forced to sacrifice the last pages of this chapter to the only sectarian whose mask we wish to tear off.

But our false pontiff belongs to a school of thought, and it is necessary to say a few words about it: a few notions about the master Eugene Vintras (Eue); and we shall move on, with the turpitudes of John the Baptist, to the distressing but instructive display of the promised revelations.

The Carmel of Eugene Vintras
And The Present Grand Pontiff of the Sect

"*...An abominable association, dressed in a hypocritical ostentation of virtue.*" H.H. Pius IX.
(Briefly condemning the sect of Vintras, February 10, 1851).
"*It's out in the sun, provoking all the examinations, that we do the work of life*".

(Le Cri du Salut, by John the Baptist, page 22).
"*They have raised an altar to the demon of impurity and made it their God.*"
(Epig. of a brochure by Mr. Gozzoli, revealing the mysteries of Tilly-s.-Seules.

On August 20, 1842, the criminal court of Caen sentenced the founder of *Carmel* or the *Work of Mercy* to five years' imprisonment, a fine of one hundred francs and costs,[30] as a swindler: Elijah himself reincarnated in the person of a prophet worker, *Pierre-Michel Strathanaël*, of his angelic name,[31] – and of his vulgar name, *Eugène Vintras*.

The Giver Of The "Supreme Blessings Of Light And Life."

The new pontiff opposed this sentence, which was nonetheless upheld, on appeal in Caen (November 20, 1842) and in *cassation* in Paris (June 3, 1843).

Moreover, the accusation of fraud was not the only one he was charged with. We are asked to take note of these few lines of Father Constant: "Vintras, whom his sectarians pose as the New Christ, also had his Iscariotes: two members of the sect, a certain Gozzoli and one named Alexander Geoffrey, published the most odious revelations against him. If we are to believe them, the sectarians of Tilly-sur-Seules (that was the name of their residence) engaged in the most obscene practices; they celebrated in their particular chapel, which they called the cenacle, sacrilegious masses in which the chosen ones attended in a state of complete nudity; at a certain point, all of them gesticulated, burst into tears crying out love! love! and threw themselves into each other's arms; we will be allowed to suppress the rest.

---

30 Swindling seems to be a virtue of tradition in the Holy-Carmel; for the present pontiff of the sect, to whom we shall have the grace to silence his name, was also sentenced on this account to three years imprisonment, towards the end of the Second Empire. Quoting the exact date of the judgement and the court that handed it down would be tantamount to naming the figure. Finally, he was condemned and suffered his sentence.

31 One of the dogmas of the sect attributing an angelic origin to men before sin, the prophet liberally distributed names ending in "ël" to all the followers of Carmel. This inflection constitutes the corporate name of the establishment. It is to be believed that the nominal statistics of the incarnated angels appear in the Archives of the Work.

"Because I have always believed that I would only be at peace and in true triumph, when I could wear on my hat the news of the trials I have gone through. My wicked adversaries therefore tried to make my trials known. I have the will to wear them on my hat."

(Letter from Batiste to Miss Maria M***, Sept. 25, 1836)

These were the orgies of the ancient Gnostics, but without bothering to switch off the lights. Alexander Geoffrey assures us that Vintras initiated him into a kind of prayer that consisted of Onan's monstrous act, performed at the foot of the altars; but here the denouncer is too odious to be taken at his word.[32]

We shall see in a moment how these accusations against Vintras coincide with those against his successor. Not even the master's "private chapel" makes one think of the disciple's "secret oratory". Only the first one, even in his worst follies, keeps a certain appearance –haughty, primal, lyrical and paradoxical– to which the other would vainly aspire.[33]

Eliphas Lévi wants to doubt the last accusation he relates... His reserve is understandable and he honours it, in the absence of any decisive evidence. But did the famous magician know that on August 25, 1842, Vintras wrote to Geoffrey (under his angel name Jehoraël):

"To the angel worshipper, to the sweet Jehoraël, I will lend assistance. Love to your sacrifice will always unite you..."[34] (Enigmatic!)

And on September 6 of the same year, these lines, which seem less obscure, are still in the dark; it is therefore feared that they will not be understood:

"*My beloved Jeho, when my affections seek your affections, everything is on fire and I am near you! I then plunge into a sea of flames, each wave of which is a boiling blade.* Heavenly pleasures, seeing us freed from our senses and their harshness, descend upon us; they intoxicate us with a holy and divine voluptuousness".[35]

Language usual to the prophet. See what he writes to the Countess D*** (*Dhocedoël*), about a pretty boy (*Azzolethaël*), the Angel of the Tropics, for whom the great lady seems to have had a crush – in God:

"Our Azzolethaël is burning with affection and thoughts; he is beautiful with all the beauty of a proud and timid candour. His gaze is as deep as his beautiful soul; his heart hangs on his lips... He loves you: in his prayer, he calls you to God, his *burning mother*, or to Jesus, in his *mystery of love* (????), his Eucharistic sister". (November 8, 1846).[36]

---

32 *Historie de la Magie* (History of Magic).
33 See Vintras' style, often ridiculous, he always runs away from platitude. That of the present pontiff is uniformly fetid and slobbery.
34 *La France mystique* (Mystical France), by Alexandre Erdan, Coulon-Pineau, 1855, 2 vols. in-8, figures. – Volume I, page 244.
35 *La France mystique* (Mystical France), volume I, page 244.
36 Ibid, volume 1, page 245.

"What could I tell you now, except something that will once again set your noble affections for the Angel of the Tropics on fire (text!). I asked to read in his heart: the Word told me to press him on mine and to breathe on his soul (!!?). I did it, Dhocedoel! He fell down, crying out grace and thanks (here we are informed): then a new life that physically surprised our leaders (sic!) became his life. His eyes cast fire; the sky of his eyelids hides lightning..."(of 14 December 1846).[37]

We did not think it inappropriate to recall these bits of correspondence, which Alexandre Erdan quotes in Volume I of his *France Mystique*. Thus the reader is introduced to the secret mysteries of Carmel, and perhaps he will find that the letters of the Pontiff are in their place, as an introduction to those of his spiritual heir;[38] these two series of letters seem to shed light on each other; they are mutually a most pungent and instructive commentary.

Moreover, we cannot hide the fact that Eugene Vintras was not a common impostor, or some vulgar and perverted devotee. Abbot L.-F. André, who stigmatised the man in the name of religion and morality, confessed that "we cannot deny him a true genius and an astonishing power of sympathetic attraction".[39]

This Vintras, one of the most prodigious mediums who ever manifested the great book of hyper-physical atmospheres, built a whole pseudo-magical synthesis, a hustle and bustle of neo-Gnosticism, seasoned with a precious devotion to the Virgin and to Saint Joseph; the sublime and the grotesque meet and marry there.

It is remarkable that this worker without letters, suddenly seized by the Spirit like the Albigensian prophets, struck down by grace and now overflowing with revelations under the divine impulse –like a cup too full in a feverish hand– was able to produce in a few years a work as massive as the sum of a Thomas Aquinas; a work in which astonishing pages of eloquence and intuition stand out, drowned in the most indigestible hodgepodge of platitudes and absurdities one can conceive of. He could have reissued the famous word *Plenus sum sermonibus* (for he speaks Latin willingly, without knowing the first word of that language). It is even fair to observe that his manuscripts abound in quotations from Fathers, Doctors, biblical texts, etc., references which are generally exact and which he threw on paper at random and without concern for verification. Witnesses to his ecstasies unanimously affirm that he had no books in front of him when he scribbled his incoherent revelations.

Very curious in sum, this heterogeneous mixture is worth examining. The only list of the books of which it is composed would fill several columns. And those which remain as manuscripts are even more numerous.

But what made Vintras famous in the circle, already important at that time, of lovers of the marvellous, were the prodigies that exploded around him, and on all things, the appearance of bloody hosts, wherever he went up to the altar.

---

37 *La France mystique* (Mystical France).
38 Frosty, stinking and dogmatic, these seem to expose in cold blood the doctrine of which these –burning and passionate– seem to offer a living adaptation.
39 *Affaire Rosette Tamisier*, preceded by a note on P.-M. Vintras and his sect. – Carpentras, 1851, in-12, page 4.

Strange drawings and unknown signs appeared in crimson characters on immaculate hosts a few moments earlier; a delicious wine streamed from the chalices, in front of many witnesses without a pause for thought; blood flowed, red and alive, from a painting depicting a descent from the cross, to the great astonishment of the magistrates in charge of an investigation[40] the bells were ringing by themselves, etc…

Rosette Tamisier

We cannot doubt that Vintras was a powerful thaumaturge. We will not need to repeat the extremely peculiar, precise and complete details that Father Constant provides on Pierre-Michel, in his *History of Magic* and especially in his *Key to the Great Mysteries*. Nothing is better established than the perfect authenticity of the phenomena, if not the mediumnic and by no means celestial origin of these prodigies. Eliphas Lévi is not very tender with the pontiff, and he is right.

A few years ago, our eminent friend, the Father Roca (who, while firmly rejecting the anarchic and inadmissible part of the dogmas of Vintras, admired the power and depth of intuition that this strange prophet manifests at intervals), Abbot Roca had us hold four pages handwritten by the hand of an old priest, who was one of the most faithful sectarians of Tilly-sur-Seules. This is obviously an erroneous account

---

40 This is the case of Rosette Tamisier, in Saint-Saturnin-les-Apt (1850-1851). We reproduce the portrait of this ecstatic woman and the sketch of the miraculous painting, which attracted so many curious people and pilgrims to the chapel of the château.

On November 10, 13 and December 16, 1850, with Rosette Tamisier praying in the chapel, the painting was seen covered in blood. This mysterious liquid (which doctors –notably Dr. Clément– have analysed with a test tube and a microscope, and whose chemical and physiological identity they certify), this liquid seems to have come from the Saviour's right flank. Mr. Grave, sub-prefect of Apt, ran to stop what he considered a masquerade, verified the miracle in such obvious conditions that he signed the minutes. The mayor and the parish priest of Saint-Saturnin had long ago declared themselves convinced. Other agents of authority –municipal officers, gendarmerie captain, etc.– have also been convinced. When the phenomenon was about to take place, the chapel bell, spontaneously shaken, without any human hand having touched the rope, summoned the faithful to the verification of the prodigy.

The same events occurred again on December 19 and 21.

The emotion was immense; pilgrims rushed in from far and wide; they crowded into the country's inns, which were full to bursting point and were never empty. Finally, the Episcopal authority intervened, declaring that there was no miracle (it was enough, of course, that Rose Tamisier was suspected of affiliation to the church of Vintras, for them to obstinately deny the facts despite all evidence). In short, the religious cabal prevailed, and Rose, arrested, was brought before the Criminal Court of Carpentras. Despite all the efforts of the Public Prosecutor's Office to establish the fraud, despite the pressure exerted on the witnesses, absolutely no evidence against "the saint" could be discovered, this was the name given to Rose by the fanatical province. The Court, which, moreover, believed without evidence in the bad faith of this poor girl, declared itself incompetent (judgement of September 3, 1851).

Incredible! The big argument of the Public Prosecutor, to establish that there is juggling and not miracle, is that, in the last observed phenomenon, the blood seemed to be dance from bottom to top, against the laws of gravity. Thus this profound logician –putting down in principle the possibility of a miracle– starts from the fact that it is even more surprising than was supposed, to conclude that there can be no miracle!

PAINTING OF THE CASTLE'S CHAPEL

of various circumstances that signalled a visit to Vintras in May 1861 by Eliphas Levi. This factum records the so-called remorse of the magician, suddenly filled with divine grace and greeting, in the most sublime Work of Mercy, the most sublime of the providential manifestations, and it is obviously an erroneous account of various circumstances that signalled a visit to Vintras in May 1861 by Eliphas Lévi.

At the bottom of the fourth page, we read this note from Chanoine Roca's pen: "Please ask Mr. de Guaita to verify whether the critical judgement made by Eliphas Lévi on the doctrines of Carmel is prior or subsequent to this *conversation*, and whether the pamphlet in question, *which Eliphas himself condemns* (!), is not confused with the said judgement, as it remains in his writings. This point is very important to me."

At this hour Eliphas Lévi is dead; it is easy to make him speak.

Unfortunately for the narrator of the famous interview, the *Key to the Great Mysteries*, where Vintras was masterfully painted, was published in 1861, the same year in which Father Constant, passing through London with his Polish disciple, Count Branitzky, could not resist the temptation to show him a prophet: they had both gone to see Vintras. Father Roca can also read on page 203 of the *Science des Esprits* (Science of Spirits), published in 1865, this decisive sentence: "A voice comes out of the wall; it speaks to us. We do not know where it comes from. 'It is Saint Michael!' said poor Vintras; 'It is the Devil' cried the wicked Mr. de Mirville, who was indignant to be called good, *and both wrote big books*. But what was that voice saying? – *Poor people, and then it's not Saint Michael*; vulgarities, and then it's not the Devil."

It is difficult to be more formal; but we will better offer our friend, Father Roca, even more conclusive evidence.

In 1886, at Baillieu's home at 53 Quai des Grands-Augustins, we unearthed a copy of *Le Glaive sur Rome et ses complices* (The broadsword on Rome and his accomplices) (London, Dulau, 1855, in-8). This volume, one of the most dithyrambic that Vintras wrote, comes from the occult library of Eliphas Lévi. Its margins

MODERN AVATARS OF THE SORCERER

are riddled with curious signed notes. On the back of the false title, ten verses, also in the hand of Eliphas, are written; we believe them to be unpublished, and it is our pleasure to offer them to the public.[41]

What do you say, my dear Abbot? Please take note of the date: 1864. – This is how, in 1861, Vintras converted Constant.

Do you want more? – I can, for your special instruction and the edification of all occultists, pick up some of the marginal notes with which Eliphas has strewn this book. They are pungent enough to merit the honours of printing.

Several pages of the *Introduction* bear this approving mention: *Good.* – On page 1, this sentence: *Here begins the galimatias.* – Pages 11 and 12: *Impiety, ignorance, stupidity and delirium... This satire of the most beautiful of all cults is vile and foolish.* – On page 17, where the author speaks of "rich tripods" where "disinfectants" burn, Constant sneers in the margin: *Camphor and phenol Bobœuf.* – Page 23: *Stupid fury against a dogma he proclaims himself.* – Vintras saying, on page 36, "that God did not have recourse to any molecules" to create the world, one reads in the margin: *Oh Mr. Prudhomme!... Ex nihilo nihil.* – Page 37: *Double Galimatias.* – Page 179: *Doorman gossip.* – Page 215: *This, better written, would be very beautiful*[42] – Page 249: *What an abominable frenzy!* – Page 290: *Prose in blank verse... This is not a style, it is a saw.* – Vintras exclaiming (same page): "the life of the prophets, belonging to all, is really heavy only for them," Eliphas emphasizes and observes that *their prose is heavy for others!* When he came to invoke "the Eternal born of God (sic)", Eliphas exclaimed, like the terrible child he sometimes is, *Nose of God! N... of God!* – On page 296, he adds: *Nothing is hideous like these sketches, or rather these debaucheries of sacred poems, and these white verses, truly cadaverous, which make a grimace and flatten themselves, like badly preserved foetuses.* Page 302: *How he hates priests, this false pontiff of pride and folly!* – Page 304 presents this fine marginal appreciation: (*There is beauty in this jargon: it is like the sun through a muddy window!* – Vintras vaticine (page 320): "You would have seen the name of Ezekiel on his forehead"; Constant counteracts quick as a flash: *and his banalities in his prose.* – On page 325 (this is very curious), Eliphas noted: *portrait of the author*; yet, here is what it says: "Stories that spend their lives akin to greatness, and that exhaust the blows of their vanity and the sweat of their pride in playing celestial scenes, without it being possible for them to conceal from the eyes of those who stare at them their devilish heart and soul...". Page 335: *And*

---

41 As Eliphas Lévi was, at our discretion, one of the greatest intelligences of the nineteenth century, we do not want to lose such a wonderful opportunity to provide such peculiar specimen of his writings.
42 No bias, as we can see.

this man accuses the priests of lacking charity! This page is odious and foul. – Page 336 *(in fine): Referred to Raoul Rigault.*[43] *–* P. 337, the signature "Peter of the Lord" lights up the verve of the mischievous Constant: *say rather "Infernal Peter", and it will still be too much of a pretension: you are only the Devil's Pierrot. –* Page 352 *(in fine): Pearls in the dunghill. –* Page 364: *Crazier and prouder than Simon the Magician! –* Page 368: *Quite right idea of the Devil. –* Page 429 *(in fine): This is true, but then why insult the Pope? –* Page 443, Vintras exclaims: "No more blind faith!" His opponent is apt enough to hammer his nail in his face: *Why then do you want them to believe that you are Elijah, and that St. Michael spoke to you? etc.*

Well, my dear Canon, what do you think? And do you find the answer of a disciple of Eliphas to the factum of a disciple of Peter Michael peremptory?

We were anxious to absolve the memory of the great magician from such a suspicion of infamous resignation. Once this duty was accomplished, we are happy to record a fact which cannot be disputed, it is the irruption, wherever Vintras stayed, of a veritable whirlwind of madness, dragging everything along with it, men, beasts, and even inanimate things; uprooting the strongest convictions, frightening away the most beautiful intelligences, making the most austere and tried Doctors deviate from the Catholic faith.[44]

M. Madrolle, a famous and very articulate theologian and Father Charvoz, the parish priest of Montlouis-les-Tours, are not the only noisy defections in the Catholic party. Father J.-F. André, author of the *Affaire Tamisier* (Carpentras, Sept. 1851, in-12, fig.), explains this with terror: – "Little by little –he says–, the sect, one of the most attractive that ever appeared, has crept everywhere like a cancer. Honourable men, esteemed clergymen, got drunk from the dangerous chalice. Father Léopold Baillard, from the diocese of Nancy, has trained a prodigious number of proselytes. Mystical society produced all the so-called saints bearing bloody stigmata –there are now more than three hundred of them in France– the visions, apparitions, incidents of Beelzebub and Behemot and more." (Page 5.)

And further on: "The magnetic influence of the Organ is boundless; in a word, it turns heads." (Page 7.)

The Duke of Normandy –in other words, Naündorf, the so-called Louis XVII– had converted all the more easily to the new sect, as his membership was important. The prophet predicted that God would sit him on the throne of France, and that he would be the *Great Monarch*.

---

43 This note, which seems to relate to the execution of the hostages by the insurgents of the Commune (1871), would suggest that Eliphas Lévi (died in 1875) traced these critical assessments, or at least some of them, well after the time when he wrote the note on the back of the false title. Here is the passage to which this note refers: "The courtiers' livery, which blushes on the pale black chest of the anti-pontiff of Nancy and Toul, will not serve as a shield against the exterminating angel; the golden cross will be hidden then, but alas! it will never be the cross of grace". Let us not forget that this sentence, printed in 1855, seems strangely prophetic all in all.

44 It is no doubt on the basis of this general rule that the author of the fanciful factum just mentioned unscrupulously puts in the mouth of Eliphas this incredible phrase: *I was told – don't see Pierre-Michel, because he will seduce you; I assure you that I am perfectly won over!*

MODERN AVATARS OF THE SORCERER

For it must be said that there is a job for a great monarch, in the sacred shop of "Elijah". Apart from the *angelic names* attributed to all the chosen ones of Carmel, apart from the ministries that make each one enter into the spirit and virtue of a great figure from the holy books (Abraham, Melchisedec, Daniel, Elijah, John the Baptist and even Joseph and the Blessed Virgin); there is a profusion of titles, qualities, surnames, first names, nicknames, etc., in the Work of Mercy, which are dizzying. It is well known that false mystics do not hate to be distinguished by glorious names:
One cannot make too much of a favourable opportunity.

In short, without even thinking of sketching out a classification, however general it may be, I shall quote a few elitist titles in a jumble. At the top of the list is the great heroine of Carmel, the *Joan of Salvation*, who "will introduce the Great Monarch" (*sic*). There are also three mystical *Joan* of Mysticism: *Joan of the Whip*, who casts out demons; *Joan of the Star*, whose role is to show the way to the *Marian*; and finally *Joan of the Lily*, whose mission is to unite in pure love with the greatest saints. There are also three *Josephine*. Then come the pontiffs of *Cordial and Holy Effusion*, of *Cordial and Holy Unification*, of *Prudence, Adoration, Wisdom, Regeneration*, etc. Finally, the categories of souls, which the prophet knew how to divide by angelic origin: the *Glaivataires* (*sic*), the *Virginaries*, the *Voxataires*, the *Donataires*... These are some specimens of the sacred repertoire of the *Sons of Mercy*. The rest will be forgiven...

Suffice it to say that the Blessed Virgin lives in Loches, and that Melchisedech goes every evening to smoke his cigar on the bridge of the Guillotière.

Enough is known at this time about Eugène Vintras and his sect, to make it possible to come to the doctrine and works of the infamous sorcerer who prides himself on succeeding this grandiose adventurer of mystery.

The task I take on as Rose + Cross is as sad as it is repulsive; but I consider it a duty.

The Kabbalistic Order of the Rose + Cross[45] did he not inscribe at the head of his concordat the mission that he recognises himself and that he proclaims, to fight witchcraft wherever he encounters it on his way, to ruin it in his works and to annihilate it in its results.

The Brothers have undertaken with honour to pursue the followers of Goetia, the so-called *magi* whose ignorance, malice and ridicule decry our mysteries, and whose ambiguous attitude, no less than their scandalous doctrines, dishonour the universal Brotherhood of High and Divine Magic, to which they brazenly claim the glory of belonging.

Since they have the audacity to call themselves our own (that is magicians), we shall have the audacity to tear off the masks of devout virtue with which they clothe themselves, and, revealing them to all in their hidden hideousness, to drag them out into the great sun: We have condemned them to the baptism of light! Let no one come and speak to us of Christian leniency and charity about them: we would

---

45 The Kabbalistic Order of the Rose + Cross should not be confused with the *Third Order of the Catholic Rosicrucians*, recently instituted by Josephin Péladan. – There is no link between them.

certainly lack it if we allowed these Satans to make new fools in peace and swell the pestilential torrent of all mystical abomination.

Don't charge us with exaggeration: we will be reticent!

Let no one suspect us of slander; slanderers are accustomed to naming the one they denounce, and their denunciation remains anonymous; as for us, on the other hand, we will not give the real name of a Goetian of the worst kind, but it is without fear that we will sign our own: *Stanislas de Guaita* ℵ.

So let the pontiff of infamy keep the domino of the pseudonym, we will not leave him any other.

Our aim is not to debase a man, however miserable and criminal he may be. Our aim is to denounce to the Inquisition of Public Contempt an abominable doctrine, which, alas, has seduced too many naive people... Our aim is to confound a shameful sect,[46] which today has too many proselytizers, most of them lost, and members, almost all of them irresponsible...

The present disciple of Eugene Vintras, who gives himself for the spiritual legatee of the prophet, the continuator of his mission and the heir to his supreme pontificate,[47] is a defrocked man in his sixties, doctor of theology, formerly one of the torchbearers of casuistry.

Just as Vintras claimed to embody the spirit of Israel's most illustrious nabi and signed Elijah! His disciple thus boasts of embodying the precursor of the Christian law and willingly signs John the Baptist!

But there are also cases where, convinced that, by virtue of the rather convenient principle of spiritual unions, he hypostatically merges with a number of other characters, he signs: John the Baptist, Elijah, Gabriel, Daniel, Abraham...

He is no longer a man: he is a consistory incarnate!...

---

46 It should not be believed that the sect of the Carmel de Baptist –a sort of mystical lupanar– constitutes an isolated fact, an anomaly in the contemporary history of religious associations.

We read on page 183 of Dr. Gibier's remarkable work, *l'Analyse des choses* (Analysis of things), that "A talented English writer... had succeeded in founding a community in the East, where there were a number of English and American girls and women of good society."

"The community –the author continues– had, and still has, at the time of writing, adherents in Europe, even in Paris and America; I know some of them, of both sexes. Well, behind the pietism and refined mysticism of the followers there were, and still are, the most disgusting obscene practices, elevated to the level of a principle and a cult *ad mojorem Dei glariom*.

After the death of the false prophet, his disciples were preparing to spread, by occult initiations, the doctrines that had been secretly entrusted to them, and after the precautions that one can guess; a convoy of young men of both sexes, some of them married, were preparing to leave for the Levant, when a young neophyte of the new Onanic Priape had her eyes opened in time; the charm of the suggestion was broken. With great abnegation, she did everything possible to repair the evil done and prevent it from happening again. Thanks to her, today the association is disintegrating."

47 It must be added, to be true, that our hierophant is only the *schismatic Sovereign Pontiff of the Carmelite convent of Elijah*. Most of the Carmelite Churches have separated from him, at different times and under different pretexts; the great majority of the Pontiffs have formally disowned him...

In these circumstances, it seems prudent not to generalise our accusations, and although any inheritance from Vintras is rightly highly suspect, *we affirm nothing about other association than John the Baptist and his school...*

John the Baptist was condemned, from the beginning of 1887, as a sorcerer and a perpetrator of a filthy sect, by a court of honour, secretly constituted to hear his works and doctrines.

This condemnation, which brought to light certain documents, was immediately notified to him by a letter from Oswald Wirth, dated May 24, 1887. The guilty party was given time for reflection and repentance... Despite the warning, he did not stop proselytizing and victimizing.

Today, therefore, some of his dark works are revealed, but without debasing him by name. All that is needed is to put on their guard possible future dupes and victims.

The figure is not totally unknown in the world of the occult. In order to avoid giving his real name, while at the same time naming him in such a way that he is easily recognised by all those he would henceforth try to seduce, we will give him the pseudonym of Doctor Baptist. Moreover, in order to conform fully to the Catholic tradition of rigour towards works, without prejudice to moderation towards people, we will keep silent about the place where the Carmelite convent of the accused pontiff stands. Let us simply say that this dogmatist lives in one of the great cities of France.

Dr. Baptist's case was very carefully and meticulously investigated. The voluminous files[48] of depositions, evidence and (the exhibits are deposited in the archives of the Rosicrucian; if published, they would easily fill two folio volumes....

This means that we will only be able to cite minute extracts from them; at least we will try to choose them in a meaningful and probative manner.

First of all, let us specify what the great arcane of Carmel consists of, its mystery of shame and iniquity. We will then prove it, authentic pieces in hand. This method has a great advantage: it will dispense us with explanatory comments at the end of each line of our quotations, so that the reader will understand everything effortlessly.

As we have seen. The man to whom the doctor flatters himself to succeed him was not the first to come, neither as a miracle worker nor as a mystic.

Vintras, whom a penetrating intuition enabled him to plunge into certain mysteries –the notion of which he then disguised, by bringing them to life, according to his sickly imagination, in the most incredible outfits– Vintras had understood very well the *law of biological gradation* which, welding together all the links of mineral and vegetable existence, animal, hominal, celestial and spiritual, makes

---

48 These files, which are in our hands, contain in particular: 1° a collection of autograph letters from the pontiff (more than 1500 pages of in-4 and in-8 formats): correspondence with Miss Maria Mr. with Oswald Wirth, with René Caillié; – 2° a very large number of brochures, most of them handwritten or autographed, some of them printed; – 3° forty-one or so in-4 pages of Miss Maria's depositions. – 4° a few letters addressed to ourselves, as well as to several of our friends; – 5° notes on Baptist, from various sources; – 6° books and manuscripts of sacrifices and liturgy of the cult of Elijah, etc.

Nearly all the letters condemning the Doctor are in his own hand and signed by him; others are in the pen of Mr. Mr... (the generous host who practises Scottish-style hospitality in his favour), but commented by the Doctor. We have all the original letters. So, no error is possible.

the uninterrupted and progressive chain of universal life rise up from the chasms of matter (where the most minute instinct languishes in unconsciousness), from reign to reign, from sphere to sphere and from hierarchy to hierarchy, to finally end up at the foot of the very throne of Unity.

Vintras knew little of the mechanism of *Involution*, or the descent (by sub-multiplication) of the Spirit into Matter; but it seems certain, I repeat, that he had understood the mechanism of repercussive *Evolution*, or of the synthetic return of fallen spiritual sub-multiples, freeing himself by successive efforts from material fetters, in order to reintegrate himself into the bosom of the celestial Unity, which has the name of the Eternal Word.

With this in mind, it is conceivable that the work of salvation, in the doctrine of Carmel, consists:

1. In the *Individual Redemption*, which is none other than the ascent of the human monad, evolved through the stages of an indefinite progress, until the perfect restitution of this monad to the bosom of the Mother Unity, from which it once emanated;
2. In the part that each one takes in the *Collective Redemption*, by assisting the other Adamic monads (either human or elementary – i.e. not yet evolved to the hominal stage), to this end "to make them climb, step by step, the ascending ladder of life", and finally to assume them with oneself, in one's own rise towards Unity.

These views are correct; but let us see how Dr. Baptist adapts such orthodox principles to religious ontology, to morality and particularly to the celebration of the neo-Christian cult of Elijah.

The supreme and secret dogma of Carmel, as we shall reveal it here, is already virtually derived from the primitive doctrine of Eugene Vintras; John the Baptist only brought it to its full development. This doctor is logical; he is even a serious theologian of his own kind.[49] If he does not have the genius of his master, he was able to deduce the most extreme conclusions from the premises he set out.

Be that as it may, it seems idle to debate here the responsibility attributable to each one. Whether Vintras-Elijah was more or less far away is of little importance to us. Whether he has stopped there, whether his disciple has pushed this far, we cannot dwell on these distinctions, for us it is of no interest. Let us set forth the Carmelian doctrine, as taught by Doctor Baptist, under the guarantee of an oath of absolute discretion. Let us denounce the rites of his Church, as his faithful celebrate them: in the most inviolable secrecy.

The Carmel of the cult of Elijah thus admits the redemptive ascent of beings –from the most infinitesimal to the most glorious– on the progressive ladder of life.

This ascent, as we have said, can be seen from two points of view: individual and collective.

Everyone must therefore: 1° work on his own ascent; 2° participate to the extent of his strength in the general ascent of beings.

---

49 He was, it seems, once considered one of the masters of exegesis.

But in what way? And first of all, how to go about it? Let us lay down some principles.

It is an absolute rule that *one can only give what one has.*

Therefore, one must acquire before wanting to give; one must "celestify oneself" before claiming to help one's neighbour to put on the celestial nature.

Thus, collective ascension is subordinate to individual ascension, which is the first duty.[50]

How is this duty to be fulfilled? We touch on the great secret of Carmel.

It is through an act of guilty love that the Edenic fall took place; it is through acts of religiously accomplished love that redemption can and must take place.

Note: Doctor Baptist, accepting to the letter the ingenious allegory of the Talmud (reproduced in the book of Zohar),[51] teaches that humanity has been degraded by a double adultery, in the persons of Adam, defiled by the caresses of Lilith, and of Eve, debased by the kiss of Sammael; thus the bodily vitality of the first couple was infected at its very source, by the leaven of concupiscence, which mingled with it... Proof of this is in the sentence of repression fulminating in the Eternal One. Did he not say to the woman, "You will give birth in pain?" And so Eve was punished, according to the proverb –and literally– by which she had sinned.

Let us continue our presentation of the Carmelite Doctrine.

The union of the sexes, the restitution of the androgynous state (which was the Edenic state) has as its eternal symbol the very tree of the Science of Good and Evil.

It is the key to ascent, as well as to decline.

The right or perverse intention divinises the union of the sexes or the mark of an infernal stigma; the consequences of this act are, depending on the case, life or death. Abnormal or contrary to the laws of sanctity, the union of love constitutes an infamous and degrading crime; normal or conforming to these laws,[52] it is for man the only way of reintegration into the primordial rights of his nature: it is the *Sacrament of the Sacraments.*

Sexual intercourse can therefore take place in an *infernal mode* (as in earthly paradise, where the fall of Adam and Eve is accomplished) or in *heavenly mode* (as practised in Saint Carmel, whose name alone means: *flesh lifted up in God*).

The Baptist Doctor and his faithful are united in love on all levels and with the beings of every hierarchy: 1° with the higher spirits and the chosen of the earth, to "celestify" themselves, to acquire virtues and to *ascend*[53] individually; 2° with the profane and the inferior spirits, elementary, animal, to this end to "celestify" these poor fallen natures, to make them participants in the acquired virtues; finally to make them climb, degree by degree, the ascending ladder of life.

---

50 It is from this principle that we conclude that purification is necessary, before engaging in life-giving acts (see below).
51 Allegory exposed in our chapter I, page 43.
52 We shall see in a moment that these laws are marvellously elastic.
53 We would say ascend, if we did not want to offer the public a sample of the vocabulary used in Carmel. – With his doctors, one must be used to all surprises.

This is what John the Baptist calls the *Right of Procreation*, a sacred privilege, which he considers the most sublime prerogative of the initiation to Saint Carmel.

All the kingdoms of nature are open to the neophyte, who, by entering this religion, receives the investiture of the delegatory right of procreation; his role is henceforth to lead all beings in the process of evolution up the stairway of universal nature. He fully enjoys the *holy freedom of the children of God*.[54]

Outside unions there is no salvation. All men in the sect possess all women, and vice versa. This communism of love is an integral part of religion, the altar is a bed; the holy hymn is a universal epitaph song; the kiss is a priestly act which extends to all beings; it multiplies and blossoms like a perennial flower through all the concentric spheres of the visible and invisible natures.

The problem, it cannot be over-emphasised, is therefore as follows: 1° to unite in love with superior beings, with the egregorees of the luminous hierarchies, with the chosen saints, in order to ascend with oneself, and these are the unions of wisdom; 2° to unite in love with beings of an inferior nature, with elementary spirits, with *humanimals*, in order to make them ascend with oneself, and these are the *unions of charity*.

The whole thing is to make them climb the ladder, without risking oneself going down it...

We can see where this doctrine leads, in morals and in religious sociology: 1° to promiscuity without limit, to the ubiquity of shamelessness; 2° to adultery, incest, bestiality; 3° to incubism and onanism, which are erected as acts inherent in worship, as meritorious and sacramental acts.

Here then is the dogmatic basis of this religion, whose temple appears to be a sacred brothel, and whose redemptive cross is erected as a lingam of flesh!

The many extracts we are going to provide, and whose perfect authenticity we attest on honour,[55] will bring to light several fundamental dogmas of Carmel, which are linked to the right of procreation –the central axis around which everything revolves–; let us mention, among others, the curious theory of the *glorious bodies*...

The reader is now in a position to understand everything; he has no more use for our explanations. From now on, our role will consist mainly in bringing the texts closer together. It is the Pontiff himself who will speak; it is he himself who will betray himself.

But before moving on to the excerpts, we must give the public an account of the circumstances that have placed all these pieces of evidence in our hands; they must understand their unquestionable authenticity, their value and their significance.

When we came across the Pontiff of Carmel on our occultist's road, he presented himself to us frankly –some would say shamelessly– as an adept of the highest ranks, an heir of the Masters of Kabbalistic Wisdom. First of all, there was no men-

---

54 This freedom is the right of the elect; but it is formally taught further on that the right of the neophyte is that of the elect. Shouldn't "learning" be made possible?
55 When the slightest doubt is possible, we hasten to make it known.

tion of Vintras. Baptist had only the "Orthodox Tradition of the Divine Sciences" in his mouth.

For some time we believed in his good faith, as did many of our brothers who were initiated into the same school as us and who, around the same time, came into contact with the doctor. As for his initiation, it was not long before it inspired a singular distrust. The man still seemed sincere to us, although we were already disillusioned about the chapter of the adept; it seemed to us that he was deluding himself. And now that his character is well known to us in so many deplorable aspects, some doubts have remained on this point. It is certain that he had hours of weakness, when he cried out: "But why then does God not confirm my mission[56] by the slightest sign? For I have nothing, absolutely nothing, that is proof of my great mission." But at other times, he got worked up, he strove to do something, and we did not consider it impossible that he may come to believe in his science, his *mission* and his followers.

It is because of this doubts that we thought it appropriate to conceal his name and even the name of the city where he resides. We would not have this last regard for a simple and pure charlatan, a vulgar impostor. He certainly deserves these epithets in more than one respect; but perhaps his soul of a false prophet lights up intermittently with a glimmer of sincerity...

As long as our relations were limited to the exchange of a few letters, all went well. The "missionary of Heaven" hid behind the meanders of a language that is the one used by certain mystics, bombastic, stringy and vague, parabolic and devout, often enigmatic and always diffuse. When one proceeds by general ideas and avoids any precise controversy, it is easy not to betray one's ignorance. Have we not said, moreover, that he is not lacking in elementary education, and that he is even, in his opinion, a fairly good theologian?

In short, if we still had some illusions at that time, they soon fell away, when we had the opportunity to see the prophet and talk with him. His conversation did not support the examination.[57] He was notoriously fleeing from the solid ground of controversy. At the foot of the wall, he hid either behind the impossibility of dealing with such subjects in a casual conversation or behind the reserve imposed on him by the prudence and mysterious traditions of his school. He finally confessed to us that he was the successor of Eugene Vintras; we had to suppress some awful grimace, for he took our repugnance into account, adding "that we could agree on another ground: that of traditional occultism". We immediately told him how pleased we were with this statement, for Vintras was well known to us and we never had greeted such an authority.

---

56 Dossier n° 4 – Deposition of Miss Maria Mr..., supplement, p. 43.
57 As he had interpreted "according to a revelation from Above", the constituent symbols of the detailed Pentagram (as given by Eliphas Lévi), we one day had Baptist observe that he translated by Spirits of Water and Spirits of Fire "two signs which were simply the names of Adam אדם and Eve חוה in Hebrew. Without the least doubt, he gave us this memorable reply (we still have his letter): – *You are perfectly right in the philosophical sense, but from the point of view of the meaning of the divine Order, I am no less right on my side!*

However, serious suspicions were emerging in our minds. Cautiously questioned, two followers of the sect had betrayed something of the arcana of ignominy... As for us, eager to know more, we made our efforts to provoke new confidences. The most serious revelations were made to us, a few days later, especially by the prophet's host, a brave and dignified old man, misled by the best faith in a shameless world, who let us penetrate mysteries whose gravity he could in no way imagine. When we left the city of X... we were strongly awakened, if not enlightened on the character of this individual.

It was then that certain sudden and unforeseen events, in which the Baptist Doctor was directly involved, make manifest to us his presumptuous ignorance on the one hand, and on the other his vain audacity and cold perversity. His soul was uncovered as was his spirit: both were revealed together, marked by the fourfold stigma which is the very signature of Satan: pride, impotence, stupidity, envy.

This happened in February 1887. An investigation was opened by a vehmic court.[58] Its debates do not belong to the public, but the present revelations are executive of the sentence that was then pronounced.

Suffice it to say that one of our Rose + Crosses, (head for Paris, of the 2nd degree of the Order), Mr. Oswald Wirth, gave us a voluminous correspondence, which lifted the last doubts, touching on the mysteries of Carmel.

Mr. Wirth had met the Doctor in August 1885, through a friend from Châlons, who was once still a fervent Carmelite sectarian, Miss Maria M. Relationships were established on both sides and many letters were exchanged.

Put on his guard, on the one hand by such a half-confidence Miss Maria M. escaped, and on the other because of certain ambiguous and two-way phrases which he had found in the correspondence of John the Baptist, Mr. Wirth was quick to guess the infamy of the sanctuary and the immorality of the Pontiff.

From then on, he conceived and took on a double mission, which he subsequently carried out with the same rare moderation and prudence, disabusing Miss Maria M. and put a spotlight on John the Baptist.

He therefore played his part with the disciples of the old rock next to John the Baptist, and did not reveal his true feelings until December 1886, when the Carmelite convent no longer held any secrets from him. Miss Maria M., whom he had had no great difficulty in convincing or restoring to the path of duty and reason, was a precious help to him in this discipular comedy, which he conducted for fifteen great months. He gently led the Doctor to betray himself with his own pen. These letters are in our possession, all written and signed by the character's hand.[59]

The former are of no direct interest to us. That of June 8, 1886 already contains data which, although still vague, nevertheless seem worthy of finding their place here.

---

58 The vehme or vehmic courts, was a secret court established by Charlemagne to hold the Saxons in Christianity and obedience. Later, as a continuation of this court, but with a different character, the holy vehme, a secret association also known as the frank judges, was implemented in Germany. Guaita seems to use this word to mean a kind of secret tribunal of adepts.
59 They even bear, amalgamated together, the Doctor's mystical name and his real name.

"The delegation of science to empower and make all beings ascend, which is only a co-participation in the creative power, to make beings from below climb the ladder to have a more and more perfect life, should be the prerogative of human nature; and it is by this that man is, by right of procreation, and must in fact be, through Initiation, clothed with royalty, which is an association, by delegation, with the rights and the sovereign power of the creator..."[60]

It is here, as you can see, that the logical law brings us to the question of the fall, by which human nature is deprived of this royalty... It is necessary for every man to admit and confess that apart from Initiation, not only is he ignorant of the ways and means of making beings ascend, but that he himself is under the domination of the laws which make him a slave to vices and passions.

Here he is placed in a terrible alternative, which offers him no way out, this king of nature. *If he listens to the doctrine of Roman Catholicism, he is obliged by law to absolute continence, and then nature in revolt inflicts upon him the most terrible denials, refusing –more or less–, to accept such constriction, which human nature feels is not in conformity with the laws of its creative origin.*

But if he ceases to listen to this Catholic doctrine, he has nothing but corruption before him, which leads him down the path of vices and passions.

All this had attracted my thoughts, and this problem, similar to that of the sphinx, weighed on my conscience like a nightmare. I shouted to heaven, in order to receive the solution to this enigma?

You don't have to go very far in the initiation, to see that *the solution only polluted the way of love.*

Here, then, the law of the sexes, an essential condition of any law of love, according to the constitutive laws of human nature (sic), arose in its turn.

Why did God divide the sexes? – Moses states the fact, but he is absolutely silent about the reason for it. *This was reserved only for the initiated.*

Man, then, is in the presence of A NEED WHOSE NATURE MAKES A LAW, and he knows nothing about it, neither about the cause of the need that dominates him, nor about *the divine laws to be followed.*

Society opens the doors of marriage to him; but there are many social obstacles to this condition, which RESOLVES NOTHING, *so to speak, about the terrible problem.*

This brings us to the heart of our subject, this is where true initiation begins. *We are in front of the generations who have left the earth* and who inhabit this army of worlds that roll in the immensity of space... *How can we establish living relationships with the beings of these worlds?* And then some live in the light; others, on the contrary, are plunged into darkness. How can we reconcile some and avoid others?...

And those who live on earth, is it not possible to establish living relationships with those who are in the same difficulties than we are?...

Oh! The initiation must solve this vast problem!

---

60 Let us apologise to the reader for subjecting him to such a jargon: he must make his own mind.

Surely this problem is solved. – Dear son, you are worthy to know it and to receive these secrets which I have paid for through the most terrible trials! But may I have the joy of being able to transmit them to you through Initiation.

Be blessed with the supreme blessings of him who is life, light, life-giving and regenerating love, to transform beings!"

† Jean-Baptist… (Dossier 1 – Letter of June 8, 1886, *passim*)

Six days later, a long letter brought Mr. Wirth new revelations.

The Doctor repeats himself in every way. His incontinent style –a stringy, brackish liquor with a nauseating spread– his style is as slimy as his thought. We give only epistolary excerpts, yet we are obliged to decant them constantly[61]:

"Dear blessed son of heaven…, the right of procreation should not be confused with that of generation, for it is absolutely distinct from it, and procreation is different and independent above all of the right and power of generation.

Since human nature has been divided into two sexes, the right to procreation can only be exercised BY THE FERMENT OF LIFE OF BOTH, IN THE IMAGE OF THE POWER OF GENERATION…

It is the *Ferment of Life*, produced in the state of purity and light, which Initiation teaches us to attain, which makes beings ascend, through the Right of procreation delegated by God.

It is evident that in the exercise of this right and power of procreation, both beings, raised through initiation to this kingship, find themselves in the holy Freedom of the Children of God.

The society has established laws for marriage, and rightly so. But with respect to the right to procreate, it cannot be so. Nevertheless, if legitimate spouses were initiated, it would only be easier for them to exercise the right to procreate: BECAUSE THIS IS EXERCISED EVERY DAY, *while the generation is subject to the laws of nature…*

These principles are remembered, it remains to be established that the *right and power of procreation is lawful for insiders, that it is in conformity with divine laws and rules,* AND THAT IT WILL NOT BE PERMITTED TO ANYONE TO INCRIMINATE THE EXERCISE OF THIS RIGHT, IN ANY CASE AND UNDER ANY PRETEXT, *because God legitimizes it in favour of the initiates…* TO EXERCISE THIS RIGHT IS THE MOST MORAL ACT that it is possible… in order to make the beings of the three kingdoms of nature ascend, *through the ferments of life of which they*[62] *have made themselves capable of making an effusion,* in the light, purity, sanctity and blessing that they have been able to acquire…

This power of procreation, the essence of the Royalty of human nature, with the right of generation, cannot be recovered without preparation. And this is where the greatest difficulty of my mission has been…

---

61 We prune out useless or redundant phrases, but without ever changing an iota.
62 THEY are "the Initiates", not "the beings", as one might think from the construction of the sentence. Moreover, the general meaning is obvious.

Doctrine, in theory, is possible by letter; for it is a path of science; but *experimental science demands and requires to be placed under the aegis of a master who supervises the paths followed....*"

(DOSSIER 1. - Letter of June 14, 1886, *passim*)

"Initiation by pure theory would be vain and even dangerous. To know the ways and means of this right of procreation... and not to apply it in favour of the beings of whom we are kings by initiation, would be the *crime of crimes*, the infamy of infamies. That would be the crime against the Holy Spirit, who is not forgivable either in this world or in the next! Therefore, to avoid this misfortune, God does not allow perfect Initiation to those who would only accept it in theory and not in practice."

(DOSSIER 1 - Letter of June 23, 1886, *fragment*)

Two interminable homilies, dated August 10 and 13, 1886, call for Mr. Wirth's unfailing discretion. As Mr. Wirth had to visit Father Z*** -a new conquest of Carmel, or at least the sectarians were deluded by this illusion- the Baptist was not at rest, he was very much afraid that a careless or premature word might arouse scruples in the conscience of the excellent priest, whom he intended to lead to the unions gently and without rushing him. Already too quickly one had been in business with this ecclesiastic, the object of all the Doctor's solicitude. What he writes on this subject has its merit:

"...In front of the dazzling clarity of the Doctrine of Life, the brain of our friend (Father Z**), although so admirably gifted, was shattering; he was bothering himself, saying: 'Stop, I don't want to stop; my brain is bursting'. *Now, if the exposition of the doctrine produced such effects, you understand that it was impossible, before sufficient preparation, to pass from doctrinal theory to implementation*... So, as you can see, we haven't even touched on *the question of acts*, of the way of operating..."

(DOSSIER 1. - Letter of August 13, 1886, *passim*)

Whatever happened to these apprehensions and repugnance, the Baptist Doctor, judging Father Z*** to be well on the way to taming himself, added, towards the end of this same epistle:

"This is the state of our friend... He is preparing himself, disposing himself, and this is the indispensable condition for the power of procreation, for his works and his operations of life. He does not go beyond that at the moment.

For you too, there is no obstacle to this preparation; *if you want it, say yes,* AND I WILL PREPARE AND SETTLE YOU UP, *like our friend, if not better still... I will wait for your correct answer...*"

(DOSSIER 1. - Letter of August 13, 1886, *in fine*)

I will see to it that you are prepared for it! What did our Pontiff mean by this? - A letter addressed by him to Miss Maria M. tells us that this Carmelite initiate, as we have seen, lived in the same town as Mr. Wirth. Now, here is what the Doctor wrote to her, about the same time:

"I am going to lay down here the principles of eternal law which dominate the question which concerns us.

First principle. – The Holy Freedom of the Children of God exists only in the Glorious Kingdom, and no one is in the Glorious Kingdom except by faith and the doctrine of Carmel;

Second principle. The apprentices, that is to say, those who are called, have the same rights as the chosen ones, some to learn, others to do; but this presupposes the acceptance of Carmel;

Third principle. – The law of the Unions is the tree of the science of good and evil. *Those made according to the laws of decay lead to the abyss; those made according to the divine rules open the paths of destiny...*

It is easy, according to these principles, to know the line to be followed, concerning the *pretender of the appeal* (one guesses that it was Mr. Wirth!). If he accepts the Elijah's faith, if he regards the doctrine of Carmel as true and divine, *he enters into the rights of the apprentices, which are those of the chosen ones.*

It is good to proceed with prudence, reserve and wisdom, AND NOT TO EXPOSE OURSELVES TO BE MAL JUDGED. You have seen how successful we have been here with Mr. X... and Miss Z...; but it is because we have not been too hasty.

To tell you the truth, IT WOULD seem GOOD TO ME THAT HE (Mr. Wirth) KNOW THE TRUTH BY YOU, AND EVEN THE PRACTICE, but you know under what conditions, for the good and honour of Carmel!..."

(DOSSIER 3 – Letter to Miss Maria M., dated Sept. 7, 1886)

So this is the kind of thing Dr. Baptist wanted to "have prepared" Mr. Wirth. But Miss Maria M. did not enter into this way of thinking. She had constantly refused *the unions*,[63] and practised the Carmelite religion, except for that. The Doctor always hoped that she would come to his sights, and often he would get very angry with her, telling her "that she would never get anywhere unless she complied with passive obedience. *Out of union, he cried, out of union there is no salvation!*

(DOSSIER 4 – Deposition of Miss Maria M., pages 24-25)

Another letter from the Doctor to Miss Maria M. proves abundantly that this lady, an excellent sleepwalker, whom he considered to be in communication with the Spirits of Light, was opposed to the regime of unions.

One day when the *celestial mothers* (*sic*) had, through Miss Maria M., severely debased these practices, the Doctor, very perplexed, wrote to the Seer a priceless letter, which we shall transcribe almost in its entirety:

"I thank you, beloved Eve, for the reply of our dear heavenly mothers.

Allow me to put before your eyes my double situation, as a missionary to myself, for my personal ascension, and as a missionary to the other chosen ones.

There seems to be an opposition between these two missions, and yet I must reconcile them:

---

63 In French, the word *union* has many meanings, besides "union", being one of them "coupling" or "mating".

I must take care of everything that concerns my ascension. It is an absolute duty, because I will only be able to give what I have acquired;

– But John the Baptist must also multiply himself by ten[64] (*sic!*) and if he does not multiply himself, he will do nothing and obtain nothing.

But then, dear Eve, you see the problem to be solved for John?

– If John is concerned only with his own ascension, he may well go the way of his own perfection. But, in that case, he will not multiply himself by ten;

– If he wants to multiply himself by ten, as is his absolute duty, otherwise he will not achieve anything; in this case, how can we reconcile the rules that are so perfect for John's ascent with the need to multiply himself by ten?

This is what embarrasses me. *I would like to follow the will of our celestial mothers in everything, because I know that the rules they give are perfect.*

But, I confess to you, I would also like to multiply myself by ten…

Dear Mrs. S., in the name of Elijah, he did not prescribe rules as strict as those of our dear heavenly mothers!…

Open your heart to these great problems; pray well and see what either Elijah or our heavenly mothers will say to you…

JEAN-BAPTIST…

(DOSSIER 3 – Undated letter to Miss Maria M.)

Nothing is more foolish than the blissful perplexity and the contained bad mood that this kind of epistolary consultation breathes. On the contrary, the soft and hypocrite tone, the bland and prolific style, the abundance of rehearsals –all disgusting things everywhere else– seem on the contrary to increase tenfold the comedy of this cheerful play… So we were anxious to produce it, constrained as we are to pass over in silence a host of the most curious details. Indeed, our setting refuses to accept such developments. We are forced to come to the conclusion of the correspondence with Mr. Oswald Wirth.

This young occultist who, on many questions, knew infinitely more than the Doctor,[65] was beginning to grow weary of giving him the titles of "sublime and venerated Magus, supreme depositary of the Holy Truth, celestial Initiator of the children of the earth to the divine arcane of Light and Life!" or those of "Sublime and illustrious Master, Missioned from Heaven for the redemption of the Earth, august and powerful Hierophant of the mysteries of the Holy Carmel".[66] For Mr. Wirth, having resolved to "make John the Baptist speak", had felt, with just sagacity, that he could only conquer the citadel of his blind trust by bombarding the dungeon with his immeasurable pride…

In short, Wirth had had enough of this ambiguous role; he decided to end it by the end of November 1886. So he wrote to the prophet:

---

64 Put 1 in the 0, – the phallus in the cteis.
65 From that time, in fact, Mr. Wirth had already penetrated some of the esoteric truths, which are still perceptible, though distorted, under the symbols of Freemasonry.
66 We are not exaggerating; these titles are textual. Mr. Wirth, who varied them with art, never failed to make a pompous display of them at the head of each of his letters to the pontiff. And the fool to fall for it, like a jay trapped by birdlime.

"...On the subject of the sublime doctrines of the divine Carmel, I believe that I am receiving at this moment as a revelation of this supreme initiation, whose investiture I so ardently desire to receive. *I hope at least that I am not the plaything of an illusion, or of the manoeuvres of evil spirits...*

According to the intuitions that come to me, the Initiate can only enter into the plenitude of his theurgic power by his union with a person of the opposite sex to his own? But this union is not the ordinary marriage, whose purpose is generation. Here it is only the religious act par excellence..., but it requires a preparation, a preliminary purification which is much more serious than that required for ordinary communion; for this is the *Sacrament of the Sacraments, the one which gives all life, or all death.*

This act is, moreover, essentially free, that is to say, absolutely independent of the physical conveniences required for generation... *All men are the husbands of one woman, and likewise all women become the wives of one man.*

The affections are not individualised, but become collective; all the initiates are now one man and one woman, and in this they are made in the image of God..."

The question was boldly asked and the answer had to be decisive. It was not long in coming. The hierophant was thus placed at the foot of the wall and did not hesitate to give his entire thought:

"Dear beloved Chosen One! *You have understood very well the divine ways in which Heaven has invited you and where Heaven is leading you!...*

You have clearly seen the condition of the supreme right of procreation... In the exercise of this divine right, to the highest degree, we are what the scriptures call gods: *Ego dixi, dii estis!*

This is the sixth sense, which has been lost in decay, and *which must be regained (sic!).* This is the exercise of hominal royalty over the beings of the three kingdoms of nature, on earth and in the worlds.

It is the Ferment of Life, which, grafted on to the principle of life of the beings of the three kingdoms, makes them climb, step by step, the ascending ladder of life.
THIS IS THE SACRAMENT OF THE SACRAMENTS, AS YOU SO APTLY PUT IT.

But no one can be alone, in the exercise of this right of procreation, *only one has fluids. The leaven of life is the combination of fluid heavens.*

But it is, therefore, of absolute necessity, that the two operators should be in the condition of elevating the Royalty of human nature.

The logical law makes it clear why the freedom of the sons of God is, under these conditions, an absolute right: HE IS LIKE A KING WHO CAN MARRY WITH ALL, *but only if his wife is of royal race.*

This freedom, which seems so great at the present time, when royal daughters are so rare, is, as you can see, not very extensive.

But it will be extended, in proportion to the Initiation into the Divine Order.
YOUR CONCEPTION IN THIS RESPECT, AND THE STATEMENT YOU MAKE OF IT IN YOUR LETTER, IS PERFECTLY ACCURATE.

It is obvious that the question of generation is subject to other laws...

MODERN AVATARS OF THE SORCERER

You will be the first disciple of life in the male order;[67] you will be the first in this election, which is the expectation of all the beings of creation...
Receive the holy and living kiss of the brotherhood of life. Be blessed, etc.
† JEAN-BAPTIST...
(DOSSIER 1 – Letter of November 24, 1886, *fragment*)

A few days later, feeling that he had shown insufficient enthusiasm, Baptist returned to the supposedly inspired letter from Mr. Wirth. The Pontiff has had time to stretch the strings of his guitar: listen to the ardent and triumphant hymn vibrating under his fingers:

– "Dear Son of Heaven, blessed by my heart and the hearts of the elect! If, in the ten years that I have known the divine Carmel, my heart has known many of the joys of the heavenly order, the one that has flooded my mind and soul, reading your precious letter, (placed in the front row)...

Now, dear Chosen One, you are the true Son of Heaven. – When I gave you this name, it seemed very strange to call Son of Heaven a being who lives on this earth. But I spoke thus in the law of your calling, *and behold, this title is the one I must give you at this hour, if I am to speak in the light of truth, according to the will of my heart.*

You say with perfect accuracy: 'I now await the opportunity to pass from scientific knowledge to life-giving acts; for science acquires value only through its applications'. You are right: *we, too, are ready; we have been waiting for a long time for the blessed day to come.*

The first among the chosen ones, you are about to begin *the chain that will raise the ladder of life* (*sic!*); welcome that Heaven is ready, and that the Star that has shone in your eyes leads you among us!

You will be ahead of all the others, and first you will enter the true and eternal kingdom of human nature. You ARE NO MORE MY DISCIPLE, Dear Chosen One, YOU ARE ANOTHER MYSELF. How beautiful is your destiny, and what consolation it brings to my heart!

At last this problem which will make the children of the earth true Sons of God has been solved, no longer in my conscience and in my personal experience, but in the heart of a free and independent being!

NO ONE, AROUND ME, IS AS ADVANCED AS YOU: *I want to speak in the male order.*

IN THE WOMEN'S ORDER, I HAVE ALREADY,[68] as your letter says. COME AND PUT AN END TO YOUR INITIATION, BY THE LIFE-GIVING ACTS OF THIS SACRED KNOWLEDGE, BY COMING INTO OUR MIDST. YOU ARE AWAITED WITH JOY, FOR YOUR ELECTION IS KNOWN HERE TO THOSE WHO HAVE BEEN CHOSEN BY HEAVEN TO ENTER INTO THESE VIRGINAL WAYS...

---

67 Although the other chosen ones of Carmel are less advanced than Mr. Wirth, it will be seen further on that the Baptist does not only let them procreate; no doubt as *apprentices*...
68 Listen to the leno, who proposes his daughters! In a little while he will let them speak, so that they may offer themselves.

Our last letters have remained a secret around me. *The reason for this is that each one must remain the master of the application he can make, of the science that is given.*

It is a rule of prudence to avoid treacherous blows; for there are beings for whom the secrets of conscience of others are not sacred.

I want them to be sacred, for they are sacred before God!

Jean-Baptist
(Dossier 1. – Letter of December 2, 1886, passim)

Here is now the secret: a letter of December 5, signed by three young girls initiated into Carmel, countersigned by their mother (!) and apostilled with a pontifical approval of the Baptist:

"Blessed Son of God, loved by Heaven and our hearts!.... We have admired the heavenly action of the light in you, *for, without having had the opportunity to study Elijah's doctrine in depth, you have nevertheless been able to understand the deepest of mysteries.*

CARMEL MEANS FLESH RAISED UP TO GOD, AND THE LIGHT FROM ON HIGH HAS MADE KNOWN TO YOU HOW ONE IS CELESTIFIED HERE BELOW, BY THE VERY ACT WHICH WAS AND STILL IS THE CAUSE OF ALL MORAL DECAY... (This is clear.)

ALSO, HOW MUCH WE DESIRE TO SEE YOU IN OUR MIDST! We have so often prayed at the Holy Altar, that we may be granted to see a chosen one as Heaven wills, and as you are about to be!

Heaven has made great promises to the head of the divine Carmel, for the day when he will have true disciples around him... *Our wish would be to see you next to the Father, as the first chosen one, to make the chain of life...*

IF YOU COME, YOU WILL BE ABLE TO RECOGNIZE OUR GOOD WISHING, FROM THE WAY OF SCIENCE, YOU ARE PERMITTED TO ARRIVE TO THIS EXPERIENCE; *for God does not judge beings by their lights, but only by the acts of life of which they prove themselves capable...*

The one who has a cordial affection for you: Nahelael.

We greet the Son of Heaven, as she who held the pen, in the blessing of the election into which he enters: Idhelael. Anandael.

I approve the doctrine of this letter, signed by the angelic names of the Trio, and by the mother: Shephael.

Jean-Baptist
(Dossier 1. – Letter of December 5, 1886, passim).

It seems that this collective epistle sets out the points on a few I's, which had not been well received until then, in the Elijah's text.

It is the only one whose *original* is not in our hands, it was requested and returned. But we had the foresight to keep its imprint, which amounts to the same thing...

So this was the state of Baptist's mystical correspondence with Mr. Wirth, when the *"Master of Wisdom"* was warned that his disciple was mocking him!

MODERN AVATARS OF THE SORCERER

Then he thought he could turn back and deny all his earlier teaching, and protested that he had not been understood.

One hesitates to read the Doctor's last letters; yes, one really hesitates, not knowing what one should admire more, of the audacity[69] duplicity which this man made appear, or his inconceivable blindness.

It was on December 2 that he wrote this enthusiastic letter (overflowing with both triumphant joy and naive abandonment), which reads: "*You are no longer my disciple, dear Chosen One, you are another myself!*" It was on December 5 that he approved the collective letter from the three girls and their mother, a choice piece in which we mark the following sentence: "*Without having had the opportunity to study Elijah's doctrine in depth, you have nevertheless been able to understand the deepest of mysteries...*".

Well, we have before us two letters from the same John the Baptist to the same Oswald Wirth, one dated December 11, 1886, in which these lines are found:

"*I have given you the names, which were not due to you, but which can only be deserved after long years of meritorious deeds...* You HAVE ONLY HAVE SEE THE PARVIS OF THE PROFANES AND NOT THE SANCTUARY...*"

The other, dated December 13, says:

"In the views I had of your spirit, I must tell you that *you appeared to me in an increasingly unfavourable light...*

---

69 The Doctor's bad faith is no less blatant on other occasions. It bursts out particularly in the case of the Marquis of Saint-Yves. As long as Baptist believes that this illustrious theosophist will be able to bow to his mission, he makes him a great prophet.

In his letter to Mr. Wirth, dated February 8, 1886, he speaks of "...the great initiate, the enlightened seer Saint Yves". – "Ah –he continues–, how moved I was when I read the pages which set out the main thrust of Mr. Saint-Yves's work: *The Mission of the Jews!* This chosen one did not receive the initiation of a living person from earth; he received it from heaven. But what a science is in him, and how much he appears above his contemporaries! *How sweet and good it is to read these pages, inspired by the light from on high!* At last, I am no longer alone... You see who we are. Oh! reread the writings of Mr. Saint-Yves, and at this school you will learn what an enlightened *clairvoyant is, who has received what I call initiation!...*"

(Dossier 1. – Letter n° 11)

To the same Mr. Wirth, the Doctor wrote on July 7, 1886, that is to say, five months after the eulogy which has been read: – "The Light of Prophecy... is a necessity; without it, one takes for history what is only seen from the future, *and then all is confusion. This is what happened to Mr. Saint-Vues*".

(Dossier 1. – Letter n° 20)

In a long epistle –a masterpiece of overconfidence– addressed to Mr. Barlet, dated August 20, we read: – "*His authority will crumble in the face of a scholarly and profound criticism of his work*: The Mission of the Jews"

(Dossier 6. – Copy of a letter to Mr. Barlet)

Finally, in a letter addressed to Mr René Caillié, dated November 20, 1886, Doctor Baptist speaks of two occultists of the Western School, and he says: "*Mr. Saint-Yves had opened a false path for these workers*; but there is a very strong movement, which tends to bring them back to the true path".

(Dossier 5. – Letter 11.)

On December 7, I resolved to submit you to the Criterion of the Light from Above... *I appealed to your spirit; it came hesitant and all dark.* The test showed what you were; the letter we ask for,[70] YOU WERE KNOWN, NOT AS AN INITIATE, BUT AS ONE WHO DOES NOT UNDERSTAND WHAT WE HAVE VIEWED...

When the sun shines in the firmament, those who live in darkness cannot stop its rays. (textual!)".

Thus, the pupil who has become a master in his turn, the most advanced of the followers, the chosen one from heaven who has known how to discover by his own strength the Great Arcanum of the Arcana, this one becomes, in less than a week, a blind man who has seen nothing, a fool who has understood nothing... This is what our amazed Pontiff maintains! Ah! certainly, it is to master hypocrisy, charlatanism and imposture – stupidity too. Indignation rises to the throat in the presence of such stupid audacity: *Peccatum est stultitia...*

In any case, these few excerpts may give an idea of the voluminous correspondence that Mr. Wirth made available to us in the last days of February 1887.

Moreover, we already had several books of documents that were no less significant. Another Rose + Cross of the 2nd degree, Mr. René Caillié, an engineer in Avignon, had, around the same time, deposited in our hands his own correspondence with the Doctor.[71]

On the other hand, a holy priest, who had spent a great deal of apostolic eloquence, to bring this wretch and his numerous escorts of dupes and victims back to the path (we are scrupulous in naming this ecclesiastic, because, having pleaded with us the irresponsibility of the Baptist, he may not approve of tearing off the mask of a man in whom his charity wants to see only a madman), the holy priest wrote to us on January 7, 1887:

– "...On the eve of my retirement, Mr. M*** made some revelations to me, the seriousness of which he did not understand, and the significance of which escaped him completely. A word will make you understand.

The character has a secret flat, which consists of a so-called oratory, where he locks himself up alone twice a day, and a small room where he sleeps stealthily from time to time, in order to track down the Spirits who try to kill him and who, he says, are unaware of this place. This flat is next door to the dwelling where the G... family lives...[72]

Two days before, Mrs. T.., returning to her occult, so-called spiritual unions, finally revealed this frightening mystery to me. THE UNFORTUNATE WOMAN IS OBLIGED TO RECEIVE CARESSES AND EMBRACES, NOT ONLY FROM THE SPIRITS OF LIGHT, BUT ALSO FROM WHAT SHE CALLS HUMANIMALS, STINKING MONSTERS THAT STINK UP HER ROOM AND HER BED, AND WHO UNITE WITH HER TO RISE THROUGH HUMANIZATION.

---

70 The letter of the girls, which was returned, in fact, after copying it.
71 He begged us to save six ladies of Turin, his friends, innocent swallows of the ideal, who had caught, like so many others, the hideous glue of the false prophet. – May we have helped to open their eyes!
72 This family is composed of three members of the work: two of the young girls who signed the collective letter and their mother.

She assured me that they knocked her up several times, and that during the nine months of this gestation, she experienced all the symptoms, EVEN THE EXTERNAL SIGNS OF THE PREGNANCY. – *The term has come; she gives birth without pain and it escapes* AS A WIND[73] *from the orgone[74] from which the children come out, when deliverance takes place for the woman.*

It is worse, as you see, than what the Abbot of Villars says about sylphs, salamanders and elves. The Count of Gabalis is out of date, and a great deal.[75]

I tell you exactly what this poor hallucinated woman told me; I certify it on my honour AND I DO NOT TELL YOU ALL."

An investigation was opened, to gather new documents. It lasted about two months. Before closing it, it was decided to appeal to the frankness of this young Carmelite woman, whose eyes had been opened by Mr. Wirth, who was given the task of collecting her detailed statement. To this end he left for Châlons (May 1887). Mademoiselle Maria M., disillusioned and confused at having been fooled by an impostor, had the courage to say everything. She bravely signed her statement, which was immediately countersigned by Mr. Wirth (May 18, 1887). She also gave him a huge file, which, in addition to the Doctor's autograph letters, contained books on the liturgy of the cult of Elijah, numerous revealing manuscripts, and finally autographed works and reproductions of bloody hosts – all of which are related to the secret mysteries of John the Baptist's Carmel.

As soon as Mr. Wirth returned, after examining the new documents, the occultists gathered in a court of honour unanimously condemned Dr. Baptist (May 23, 1887). It was served on him the next day.

But before bringing to light the works of this person, he was given ample time to make amends. The sentence, which remained suspended for almost four years on this guilty head, is being carried out late today. K.O.P.

May the false prophet enter the path of repentance! This is the vow of the initiates who have judged his conduct in the face of Heaven and their conscience.

It remains for us to leaf very superficially through the depositions of Miss Maria M. and the files we have on her.

We shall not disgust the public by over-emphasising the nature of the obscene practices which Baptist erected as sacraments, and we shall take care, in all things, to exclude the many personalities whose names are more or less directly involved in the circumstances of this deplorable affair. Moreover, decency will compel us to translate into Latin a few overly technical phrases.

---

73 These are, according to Baptist, the *Glorious Bodies* which will be spoken of later.
74 A vital energy or life force.
75 Baptist seems, indeed, to have taken the symbolic and paradoxical theories of the Count of Gabalis to the letter (*Entretiens sur les Sciences secrètes (Conversations on the Secret Sciences), London, 1742, 2 vols. in-12*). *Nothing resembles more his way of* making humanimals ascend, *than the Count's procedures for* immortalising gnomes, wads, salamanders and sylphs*.

Maybe the Doctor Baptist believed that the Abbot of Villars meant, by Philosophical Marriages, acts of incubation analogous to his *wisdom unions*.

Beata simplicitas! I would one be tempted to say with Jean Huss, if it were no longer about to exclaim with Tertullian: *prava maleficorum stultitia!*

FRAGMENTS OF THE DEPOSITION OF MISS MARIA M.
(May 18, 1887).[76]

"In May 1871... He (B***, *or the Doctor Baptist*) *began to talk to me about long-distance unions**, saying that all I had to do was to call Jean-Baptist from Chàlons, to feel him at once close to me in my bed. I was curious to experience this; but I could never perceive the slightest trace of John the Baptist, in spite of my repeated calls.

Mrs. T*** had already told me about these long-distance unions; she even claimed to be pregnant in this way... (Pages 7-8.)

I soon realized the relations that Baptist had with all the members of Carmel. One day when he was locked up with Mrs. T***, I had to warn her of an urgent visit. He came to open the door and I saw that he was wearing a shirt.

I learned that in the time of Elijah (Eug. Vintras) similar things were happening, but Elijah reserved his favours for people of the great world, and did not compromise himself in the midst of the vulgar people, whom Baptist delights in. It was more hidden, more decent in appearance; he did not compromise the families and only spoke to women who were free of themselves, such as the Marquise of *** the Countess of ***, whom Mrs. Vintras called *female monkeys*, or *b...* who came to take her man. (Page 11.)

Baptist having consulted me, asleep, on the theory of the glorious bodies which Mrs T*** gave birth to and which were to serve the spirits of dead people for their ascension, I shattered this way of seeing, by demonstrating that imperfect beings could not, by their own means, bring others to the state of perfection. (Page 13-14.)

In March 1883, "*Carmel was in all its action*". The Father granted very frequent favours to Miss J.G*, while *Mr. L*** was violently in love with Miss C.G**. But, on the other hand, Madame L did not find sufficient compensation for the loss of her husband in the few favours granted to her by the Father. Her jealousy became terrible, and Baptist had to fear that she would divulge the secret of Carmel... The affair between L** and Mademoiselle C.G** had to be broken off. *The latter had to beg forgiveness on her knees from Mrs. L***, while this lady, lying with her husband, performed a heavenly union. This rupture cost a lot to Miss C.G***, who turned it into an illness. (Pages 15-16.)

The Baptist gave to Mademoiselle J.G**, "*his consolation*", to gradually bring all the other members of Carmel to her; she was responsible for making confidences to them, committing them to surrender themselves to the *Father*... (Page 17.)

Since the G*** family, had only two beds, the *Unions* took place in one, where the *Father* slept with both daughters at the same time. (Page 19.)

---

76 We do not for a moment doubt the absolute sincerity of Miss Maria M., who dictated a deposition so fully in accordance with what, on the other hand, we already know about Carmel. However, it is our duty to point out that this deposition has only the value of a testimony, and not that of material, overwhelming proof, as are the Doctor's autograph pieces, extracts of which we have so far given.

From what I have seen, Baptist must be suffering from satyriasis, as his Unions with both of them were so frequent that they would have exhausted men younger than him.

Imo, quod pessimum est, ex ipsius ore accepi eum, si quando solus cubuerit, quod quidem raro accidit, sese ipsum polluere.

In ventrem ergo cubans, manu stupratur. Tunc fœminei crebro Spiritus vocati apparent, quorum formas modo simul, modo alternis vicibus sibi submissas sentit. Flammeæ e mentula ejus micant scintillæ..., etc.

Ab ipso præterea me doctam esse testor, nullo sanguinis vinculo prohiberi, quin et fideles coëant invicem: nec patrem cum filiâ, neque cum filio matrem, neque cum fratre sororem unquam rite misceri fuisse nefas...

Etiam et in vasibus indebitis confitebatur mulierem cum viro aliquando jungi decere, si præsertim fuerit mulier veneri minime idonea.

Huic præcepto nempe Doctor libenter indulget: creatum est os ad edendum, creata sunt genitalia ad coëundum. Attamen interdum licet communionem in vase buccæ sub omnibus speciebus fieri: vitæ etenim coitus Sacramentorum Sacramentum iuncupabatur apud nos. (Pages 23-24, *passim*)

In February 1886 Miss M*** had a dream which seemed a bad omen for her father.[77] The Baptist, having consulted the spirits, *found* that a magical operation had been directed against Mr. M***, and was to be fatal to him on an appointed day.

Baptist made the *countersign*, and on the day in question it is said that he was forced to make sacrifices. Thus Mr. M*** was saved, and the *victory of Carmel* was complete over the opposing forces. (Page 30)

Carmel was still waiting for the *Great Monarch*.[78] Baptist set out on the journey from Frohsdorf. – The money was given to him by Mrs. L*** (the Holy Virgin of Loches), who dedicated for this purpose the sum she had intended first of all for her burial, a sum which became superfluous, since she was never to die, or rather to rise again[79] after three days.

Baptist saw Henry V and told him that his mission was to be the Great Monarch, and as proof, he announced the resurrection of Mrs. L***.

At the death of Henry V, Baptist was very disappointed, for he had promised so many things to his followers for the day of the coming of the *Great Monarch!*

He was not embarrassed for long, and threw himself on the so-called descendants of Louis XVII.

---

77 Mr. M**, the host of the Baptist. – Please do not confuse his daughter, Miss M**, with Miss Maria M.
78 This is, as we remember, one of the prophetic *hobbies* of Carmel.
79 This reaches the sublime of the odious. – The prophetic account of this resurrection exists in the Dossier 3, in an autographed document from 1877, which ends with a proclamation "*to the pontiffs of the cult of Elijah and the elected consecrated women consecrated to the Marian of Carmel*":
"We ask the pontiffs and the elected women..., who would have received the attached autographed text, to be kind enough to keep it carefully, until the day of the expected miracle. It will serve to attest that they have been called to bear witness to the truth and to certify how everything has been accomplished, in this prodigy which opens the era of the blessed times of the Third Revelation, etc..."
Come on! Come on! That's what we call selling the bearskin when it's still running!

He himself was to give me to the Great Monarch for the unions, saying that this time, at least, I would not refuse. (Pages 34-35)

Baptist often spoke to me of Black Magic; in my sleep he sought to discover the secrets of certain magicians...

His supreme means were poultices of faecal matter,[80] prepared according to his own rites...

He spoke to me of white mice, fed with consecrated hosts;[81] but he claimed that it had been done by another person, whom he did not name. (Pages 39-40, *passim*)

I acknowledge that I have dictated the preceding 40 pages, and affirm the exact truth of it. Châlons-sur-Marne, May 18, 1887."

Signed Maria M. Countersigned: Oswald Wirth.

Let us complete this statement with some extracts from an additional letter from Miss Maria M. to Mr. Wirth, dated May 28, 1887.

"Dear Sir, since your departure from Châlons, I have still found in my memory various facts relating to Baptist.

He takes statuettes of saints, baptises them in the name of the people to whom he wants to make something happen (*sic*)... The statuettes are consecrated to some devil, but the formula of consecration is a prayer addressed aloud to a saint; in his mind he is addressing the Devil, the evil Spirit.

There are also animal hearts pierced with pins. The person (object of the spell) feels stung in the heart and sometimes the operation results in death.

There are still the *supreme commandments*, written on blessed parchment, with ink and blood... The commandments are read aloud, with a certain ceremony, then sealed, always in a separate way, and burnt. This burns, the Spirit to whom it is destined reads it (*sic*), and is forced to do what the commandment requires...

He can boast that he has caught me in his sad nets... I still have in my possession a certain vial that he had sent to me to obtain *Unions of Life*: it was Mr. Ch. who uncorked the vial; he wanted to taste it, but he thought he had been poisoned. The sperm could be recognised in this balm."

(DOSSIER 4. – Appendix)

It seems useless to point out that all these practices are closely related to the ugliest taste. The reader, to be convinced of this, need only reread our chapter III, where the evil spells of traditional witchcraft are detailed.

---

80 To those who would doubt these Panurge's dishes, we will recall that during the Second Empire, during a trial in which he was condemned as a swindler to three years in prison, Baptist confessed to practices which were all similar, and that he declared before the judges "*in conformity with his faith*". As an exorcism, he spat in the mouths of the possessed, but his universal panacea consisted, in addition to poultices of faecal matter, of an elixir composed of his blessed urine, mixed in certain proportions with that of Sister C***.
We can see after more than 20 years, Baptist has not changed!

81 When in 1886 we spoke of John the Baptist to a young man of letters from our friends, in whose family the Pontiff had long been known, our friend assured us that Baptist practised this unholy spell, but he gave us no proof of it.

Miss Maria M. ends her letter by asking Mr. Wirth to be always at her disposal to defend her, in case Baptist wanted to harm her. She can rest easy; the hierophant no longer has any control over her. Moreover, it can be said, in principle, that the sorcerer is only to be feared by those who are afraid of him. Baptist knows this well, and he abuses it.

The fact is that this sad sire has brought mourning and discord, sometimes death, to more than one family from which he was expelled after being welcomed. In this connection we can quote a fragment of a letter addressed to us on March 7, 1887 by the same priest mentioned above:

"It is true that on the weak spirits, and especially on two women... he succeeded in frightening them in such a way that they died. *One of them, in Le Havre, from the hour he pronounced his death sentence, had him constantly before her eyes, threatening, terrible, with a coffin under her arm, and beckoning her to lie down in it.* His delirium lasted several days and nights, and death followed.

I will later put this relationship before your eyes, as it was transmitted to me by Mr. P., from Le Havre.

I will also tell you what he went to do at Frohsdorf, to Henry V, whose head he troubled for a long time..."

It may seem interesting at this time, before we finish with this lamentable character, to transcribe here and there a few sentences from the manuscripts and autographed brochures in Dossier 3. The secret doctrine of Carmel is betrayed here, but expressed in vague terms, usually intelligible only to the initiated – like you and me, dear reader! As they are, these various booklets are only communicated in the sect under the cloak: they belong to the esoteric liturgy or the occult archives of John the Baptist's Carmel.

Declaration Concerning the Seven Mysteries
whose Key was brought by J.-Blissful Elijah Gabriel, at St-Carmel

"It is up to the ministry of John the Baptist to give us the key to the seven mysteries which constitute the set of truths of the Third Revelation.

First Mystery. – Adam, of his glorious body, made himself a body of penance, through his own fault, with Eve, in their fall; and we, through Jesus Christ, the new Adam, can form on this earth an Edenic body, which we will call the *Glorious Spiritual Body*, or our body of immortality, which is the *nuptial robe* of which the Gospel speaks...[82]

---

[82] This is the (misunderstood) theory of the *Plastic Faculty*, which constantly generates an *Astral Body* adequate to the present situation of the being in question, and suitable for the environment in which it is temporarily immersed.
This magnificent theory of the *Plastic Faculty* has never been brought to light in a correct aspect. The astral body has been much and authoritatively dissected, but the nature of the *Astral Body* and even the existence of its substratum, the plastic potential of the soul, seems to be misunderstood. This problem will be discussed in Book II: *Key to Black Magic*.

Second Mystery. – We can also regenerate on this earth the glorious spiritual bodies of those who died without possessing this wedding robe...

Fourth mystery. – Here we are going to touch on the Mystery of the Mysteries of the Holy Carmel. Saint John summed up his entire teaching in this motto: *Let us love each other*. We must understand, in fact, how and by what means we can help our brothers and sisters to make themselves worthy of being generated in their glorious spiritual body..., how and by what means we can open the way of ascension for them. If they are the living, how and by what means can we help them to leave the path of sin to make the old man die in them... And if it is a question of the spirits who have not yet entered into the laws of their humanisation, how can we prepare them? – It must be possible for us to penetrate into the worlds of repression... and to wrest from the Prince of Darkness the victims who are subjected to the punishment of sin... In the same way, we must be able to open the paths of ascension...; and what we do for those beyond the grave, we must also attempt for those who live on earth..."

The brochure from which we have detached these lines was written by Baptist on February 4 and 5, 1881. – Following it we find a curious prayer, traced on a rag of paper, by his papal hand. It is easy to read it:

Prayer
To celestify our spirit, to angelise our soul and body and to sanctify our heart

"Oh Father, Oh Son, Oh Holy Spirit; Oh Jesus, Oh Mary, Oh Saint Joseph! Deign to send us the spirits of the heavens of glory, the spirits and souls of the worlds of light and of the divine worlds, our heavenly patrons, Elijah and all those who love us; so that the action of divine grace in us may celestify our spirit, angelise our human nature, soul and body, and sanctify our heart, through the life-giving operations of pure and holy Love in us, to be Christs and Maria-Christs in spirit and in truth.

In the name of the living God, one and triune in persons, and in five ways of life: *Elohim, Sabaoth, Adonai, Verona, Jehovah*. – Amen. Hallelujah." (September 24, 1880)

On the other hand, we read a few sentences, at least suspicious ones, in the autographed explanation of the so-called *Impériamaëlique* Host:

"The beings who want to transfigure themselves and become Christs and Maria-Christs must not remain in isolation. But as it says in the Sacrifice of Glory, they are electrified and revived by the sacred principle of true and pure love.

But it is not enough to form a *duo* on this earth, it is also necessary to unite with a *duo of life*, which is in the spiritual and celestial worlds..." (Page 3)

This kind of *wife-swapping party* is, alas, still only expected by the chosen ones. The author continues:

"The Sacrifice indicated by this host will be offered in the Carmelite convent: it is the evening sacrifice; the woman's sacrifice precedes the divine sacrifice, which is offered in the morning. Thus the end and the beginning embrace each other and become one... (Page 5)

Those who have ascended Mount Carmel are transformed, regenerated, transfigured: they are spiritual-heavenly. In this case, they have recovered the androgynous state of creation. (Page 13)

But it is the Sacrifice of Divine Glory that will give us the most important and significant expressions.

This Sacrifice is not autographed; our copy, written in its entirety in the hand of Mr. M***", bears the following mention:"This is the first copy, begun on Monday 1 March at nine o'clock in the morning and completed on Friday, March 5, at eleven o'clock in the morning: Signed: † JEAN-BAPTIST ELIJAH GABRIEL."

SACRIFICE OF DIVINE GLORY
29 pages in-8. – March 1880

"... Love them (men), love them without measure; love them so that they may be a constant cry of grace before my father. – Love them while they *remain a man* and give yourself perpetually to them. (Page 7)

We confess it before heaven and earth, in the very word of Elijah: TRUE LOVE, BE IT IN SKY OR ON EARTH, APPROACH ALL, JUSTIFY ALL, SANCTIFY ALL. The Word has proved what love is. *It is he who made man; without ceasing to be God for this reason.* (Page 8)

The Word was made flesh; HE WAS NOT MADE AS A SOUL, HE WAS NOT MADE AS A SPIRIT, HE WAS MADE AS A CHILD! Oh, that all the chosen ones of Carmel strive to be like the divine Word, whose heart says his love. (Page 12)

We must be the high priests of love, THE DELEGATES OF ALL THE POWERFUL LOVERS OF DIVINITY, to soar over all spheres. We must hold in our hands the bonds that link the mineral, vegetable, animal and spiritual worlds, and cross all the circles, *set them on fire* and triumph.

We will eat the bread and drink the wine of the sacrifice of Glory, and nourished by the glorified consubstantiality, we will no longer be us. OUR FLESH, WHICH HAS BECOME EUCHARISTIC, WILL MAKE US PENETRATE INTO THE INTIMACY OF THE SECRETS OF THE ETERNAL SPOUSE... (Page 19-20)

We must love, we must love sovereignly: our strength, the strength of all of us, is love...

Let us hear the words of Elijah: *"If you tremble, you are lost"*. IF YOU ARE NOT, YOU DO NOT KNOW LOVE! *Love undertakes, it overturns, it rolls, it breaks.* Rise up! BE GREAT IN YOUR WEAKNESS. FEAR HEAVEN AND HELL, YOU CAN...

Yes, Elijah's pontiffs, who are transformed, regenerated, transfigured on the mountain of the. Carmel, say with Elijah: TO US THE LADY! TO US HELL! TO US SATAN!..." (Page 25).

So much for the *Sacrifice of Divine Glory*.

In another office, also manuscript, also occult, the *Josephic Sacrifice of Glory* (43 pages in-8), we note the following sentences:

"May our *communion of life with the sacred symbols of the black Josephic Sacrifice*, which have been *changed into a sacrament* by divine omnipotence, bring about divine unification in us!

May our hearts, born of the old Adam, see the great mystery of love in them; may they be reborn anew..." (Page 33).

This manuscript bears a long mention in the Doctor's own hand: "Collated and certified to be true to the original written by John the Baptist..." (Page 33). " March 1881. Signed: Jean-Baptist Elijah Gabriel..."

Let's stop there, because it would be idle to go further into these huge files, which we would not learn anything new from examining them now.

As additional information, a few book titles will suffice: *Le Sacrifice provictimal de Gloire du marisiaque du Carmel d'Élie* (The Provictimal Sacrifice of Glory of the Marian of the Carmelite convent of Elijah) (45 pages, small in-4, manuscript); – *Le Sacrifice provictimal de Marie* (Le Sacrifice provictimal de Maria) (printed, Lyon, grand in-8, 27 pages); – *Le Sacrifice provictimal du chrétien* (The Provictimal Sacrifice of the Christian) (printed, Lyon, S.D., large in-8, 32 pages); – *La raison de nos espérances aux jours de deuil où nous sommes* (The reason for our hopes in the days of mourning where we are) (printed, Lyon, 1878, large in-8, 70 pages); – *Le Cri du salut* (The Cry of Salvation) (lithog., January 1877, in-8, 32 pages); – *Aux pieux adhérents de l'Œuvre de la Miséricorde* (To the pious adherents of the Work of Mercy) (lithogr., Sept. 7, 1877, in-8, 32 pages); – *Vision d'Élie à Bruxelles* (Vision of Elijah in Brussels) (lith., large in-8, 6 pages); – *L'hostie du sanctuaire de la redoute de la Sagesse* (The host of the sanctuary of the redoubt of Wisdom) (autogr., 1878, in-8, 8 pages); – *La consécration au Sacré-Cœur* (The consecration to the Sacred Heart) (printed, Lyon, 1884, in-8, 64 pages); – *Les sept lettres du 9 septembre* (The seven letters of September 9) (lith., August 1878, in-8, 20 pages); *À quels signes nous pouvons reconnaître si nous sommes transformés* (What signs we can recognise if we are transformed) (autogr., August 1878, in-8, 20 pages); *Explication des neuf lettres données par l'archange saint Michel* (Explanation of the nine letters given by the archangel St. Michael) (manuscript, in-8, 34 pages); – *Explication du Tétragrammaton* (Explanation of the Tetragrammaton) (manuscript, 1886, 53 pages, small in-4°); – *L'image des sept transformations* (The image of the seven transformations) (manuscript, small in-4, 48 pages), etc...

These last three opuscules (manuscripts reputed to be among the most mysterious in the Carmel) would be truly worthy of the universal mockery. The filthy ignorance of the Baptist Doctor in matters of occultism is spread there in all its candour. We have not insisted on this ignorance, which is evident throughout the Pontiff's works, since our aim is not to demonstrate his ineptitude as a theosophist, but his impiety as a dogmatist and his ignominy as a sectarian: what is done, we think.

It seems that now we can cheer up, with the telling of one last anecdote, which refers to the year of grace 1886. These details come to us from a highly recommend-

MODERN AVATARS OF THE SORCERER

able source; it goes without saying, however, that an account passed from mouth to mouth cannot offer the guarantees of rigorous accuracy that are the hallmark of authentic documents.

That said, we dare to be adventurous.

Our great "Master of Wisdom" had been living for ten years in retreat, solitude and silence – and waiting too.

One might ask: what was he waiting for? Three things:

He was waiting for the angels, which were to bring him from Above the adamantine shield of invulnerability, the flaming sword of victory and the phallic sceptre of triumph...

Towards the beginning of March 1886, he declared outright that, having been invisibly armed with the invisible armour of Heaven, he was ready to conquer the world; he announced that the period of his *hidden life* was over and that the period of his *public life* was about to begin. "I am –he added–, John the Baptist, whom Elijah[83] prophesied: his mission is to cry out, and no ear shall be closed to his cry."

And he went to war.

A friend of progress and adaptations in all things, he immediately made concessions to the taste of the century; very different in this respect from another missionary from Heaven, who appeared last year on the world stage, under the name (perhaps too synthetic) of John and Peter, and who, after having been baptised with great pomp on the beach of Argelès-les-Bains by a kid and two little girls, solemnly rode on a great white horse devil, renewed from the Apocalypse, as he was baptised, and which answers to the zodiacal name of Sagittarius... – John the Baptist was more modern, having consulted the railway timetable, he simply took the *rapid* P.-L.-M. and disembarked in Paris without a care in the world.

What was he doing in Paris? – To preach to the people? To evangelise the passers-by on the boulevard? To be put in a cross on the wings of the *Moulin de la Galette?*... – Not at all. It is not that, for a prophet, this last perspective was not seductive; it would undoubtedly have been original to resemble both the Messiah and the Prince of the Apostles, and to suffer alternately, at the whim of the zephyrs, the passion of Our Lord and the martyrdom of Saint Peter!...

In any case, this ingenious destiny does not smile upon him.

His aim was above all – to visit a famous theosophist, who in fact enjoyed a certain fortune and whom he, the Baptist, believed to be disproportionately rich. Convincing X***! conquering him! attaching himself to him! what a triumph, and above all what a godsend for the sacred Carmel!

John the Baptist had from the outset been skilful enough (or happy enough) to seize Father Z***, an enthusiastic and generous nature, then a disciple of X*** and one of his best friends. The ecclesiastic in question, having fallen in love with the Carmelite convent, offered to act as intermediary and presenter. Could he have foreseen that the Pontiff wanted to enter his master's house, not to exchange lights, but in order to exploit, as far as possible, this gold mine?...

---

83 What embroilment!

Unfortunately, X***, informed (by Father Ch***, the brother of a victim of John the Baptist), informed, I said, of the moral value and the practices of the defrocked, refused to receive him. The latter did not hold himself to be beaten; he used the good will of Father Z*** to make a proper seat in the small hotel on rue V... – But no matter how many times the new catechumen in his daily visits multiplied his dithyrambs in favour of Elijah and John the Baptist, X*** had the prudence to stand firm.

So the Supreme Pontiff changed his tactics.

He wrote directly to Madame X***, imploring an audience, and swearing to God that he would cure this lady of the chronic ailment from which she had suffered for so long. Madame X*** gave in, in the vague hope of a possible relief: she made the Baptist answer that he was expected, set the day and time.

When X*** learned the result of these manoeuvres, he seemed very displeased, and declared that he would not tolerate that this lowly sorcerer be brought to the bedside of his sick wife, that he himself had not previously questioned the visitor himself, or even suspected him...

Around this time, X*** had daily contact with a brahmin pundit, an initiate from the southern pagodas of the peninsula, who was as expert on the hermetic path as he was on the *left path*: this brahmin, about whom X*** complained ever since, offered to look at John the Baptist, and soon brought him in; for the examination had not revealed him to be a rogue to be feared, at least in an enlightened environment.

Then an interesting scene took place in the flat of Madame X***.

The brahmin had made a point of exposing the latent sorcerer in the guise of the Doctor, on the assumption that he was (as some accused him of being) a formidable necromancer. – The Brahmin therefore became a Goetian, even a charlatan, to extort the secret from his interlocutor.

–*So, you are initiated?* he asked him out of the blue, in his full and resonant voice.

–Yes, no doubt –said the Pontiff, already taken aback.

–Your hand, then, Brother! It is perfect... Yes, alone I am bound; but between the two of us we will turn the world upside down.... Ah –said the brahmin, a philologist of consummate science–, what language do you speak? In terms of languages of mystery, we have Chinese, Sanskrit, Hebrew, Zend, Ethiopian...

–I don't know all the languages you're talking about here.

–But it is very necessary for an initiate. I would even say indispensable, to know at least one of the sacred languages of Esotericism... So be it! Do you speak Greek, at least? or German, or Russian? Oh, it's English, perhaps?

–I don't know English.

–But what language do you know, apart from French?

Baptist is confused, and he is at a loss for words: Latin.

Excellent! –he said, and immediately improvised a speech in the pure language of Sallustus and Caesar.

The other, who wanted to answer, stumbled at the first word.

–Come on –said the brahmin–, I see that you prefer to speak French. You can be a powerful wizard, after all, without shining with philological knowledge...

I've…, indeed, a little… forgotten.

–Well, well, let's not waste any precious time. Let's get to work today! Would you like us to perform some evocations…

–*Good Deus!* An evocation!…

–Your mother?

–No, Sir, no…, I dare not…, I do not know… these terrible operations…, my relig…

–Are you afraid, by any chance?

–Oh no, but…

But it's just like…

–And you, Madame X***, would you allow us to summon your mother?

–My mother? Well…

Baptist, when he received this unexpected answer, became pale, and although it was broad daylight, he moved behind a large armchair to secretly sketch out a sign of the cross.

Madame X*** and the Indian exchanged an indescribable look. Then the brahmin say with his loud voice, which became thunderous:

–Now then, Son of Shlomoh-ben-Ælohim, what are your familiar rites? Do you proceed with the *skull* or with the *serpent's skin?*

The poor man's knees, collapsed beneath him. He stammered.

–Oh, never… never… never… God! these forbidden sciences!… My methods are quite different: prayer, the supreme commandment to the Spirits of Light, by virtue…

–By virtue of what?

–By virtue… of Elijah…, the…

–Come, come, come, unite yourselves to me with the intention: Rise up! I am going to evoke, through incantations common to your religion as well as to mine. – The left hand in the air, the right hand shut tightly!…. All the fingers of the left hand closed in the same way, except for the thumb and the little finger… Are you there?

And the brahmin, with incredible verve and gravity, let go of the whims of his imagination, more or less in this manner:

"Mother of Mercy[84] whose baptism is of Ether and Central Fire, of heavenly and super-heavenly water! Open the zodiacal fountain to us, not normal ebb and flow, but retrograde flows, so that the Spirits, answering our call, come to us backwards in the descent, as they walked, their eyes towards You, when they climbed up the stairs of the Infinite in Your light!

Spirit, I adjure you; Soul, I beseech you; vital fluid, I command over you a sovereign union with the Son of Heaven, whose hand I hold and who unites himself to me in the evocative rite!

Angel with dead eyes, obey, white flower of the sepulchre, vain simulacrum of the one whom earthly life has left, and who at this hour climbs the paths of the mountain!… Angel of the eternal Maya, open your cooled sanctuary to receive once again the holy flame that will descend at my voice!

---

84 Need it be said that we do not answer for the terms of jargon uttered during this magical-comic exhibition?

Soul-Spirit, I call to you, I call to you, I adjure you! Come down at my command into the fluid prison of a new embryo... We are going to compel you, I the N*** and he the Baptist, united in will in Evil and in Good, *per fas et nefas*...

The Pontiff of Carmel could bear no more. He collapsed, all in one piece, still on his stomach rather than on his knees. When the brahmin looked at him, he saw him sprawled on the ground, covering himself with hasty signs of the cross, chewing with terror a whole rosary of paternosters...

–Fool! –murmured the oriental.

Perhaps Baptist had had the colic of dread. The fact is that he did not look for any pretext to hide from the hour, and took his leave with a misguided look on his face...

–Master –said the brahmin when the door was closed–, I know what I wanted to know, this funny man is harmless. He will never be able to do anything but harm weak minds and pusillanimous natures... He is a complete fool, and I can vouch for his ignorance in Goetia.[85] He has never taken seriously the *Path of the Left*, and if he ever tried it, he would die of fright, before he could pick a single one of the monstrous and fatal flowers which the intrepid of crime and madness reap there .

The brahmin turned to Madam X***:

–Madam, you can receive this silly sparrow without the slightest inconvenience: I answer for its harmlessness!

–But will you let me be treated by him?

–He only said that he intended to *operate* by prayer... Prayer, Madam, has never harmed anyone.

And with that, the brahmin took his leave.

I let myself be told that Baptist had turned his meeting at X***'s into a whole novel. I continue, according to third hand information, therefore with reservations.

He said that a brahmin ad come from the depths of India to see him, Baptist, and also a little –subsidiarily– to see X***. This brahmin had rushed at once to the knees of John the Baptist, saying: "Master, you are the one before whom all the Children of the Light bow down: command, we will obey!... Ah, if you wanted to be with us, the triumph would be assured by the Holy Carmel, and under your leadership we would turn the world upside down..."

At these words, John the Baptist *kindly raised the son of the suns of Asia* (sic), a Brahmin-Buddhist (*sic*) of the first order and a perfect initiate, and, forgetting his own rank, he gave him the *kiss of peace*. Thus the Prince of the Wise never deviates; for his charity smooths out unequal situations, levelling out spiritual castes...

---

85 This brahmin was too exclusive; we quote his opinion as it is, but we do not share it, not without reservation, at least.

It must be remembered that Baptist was presented to him as an initiate; he considers him insufficient as such. He is right. What he calls the *path of the left* is the path of a powerful follower who deviates towards evil, and becomes a *dougpa*. In the West we attribute another meaning to the word sorcerer.

We will agree with the brahmin, if it means that Baptist is unable to fight, on the astral plane, against a firm and enlightened will. But we know what evil deeds he may have done to superstitious and timid natures, and what makes him all the more dangerous is that he attacks the weak.

So Baptist saw Madame X***, prayed at her bedside, gave *commandments to the Spirits of Light* – all in vain... The cause of this failure lies in the faith of Madame X***, which is apparently not strong enough.

In addition, he gave Madame X*** a crystal medallion, mounted in silver, which (he said) contained relics and various holy things. In reality, this medallion contained a sacred host and other objects that it is better to keep secret; the apostate priest appeared there again.

Madame X*** could not refuse this medallion, which was indeed worth twenty-five francs, and was very upset about this.

For his part, the scholar X***, since Baptist had been received at his home, made the banal step of a short visit to this individual on the day of his departure. Translated in Baptist style: "He came to say goodbye to me, to thank me and to ask me for a word of order for the future. I gave him a guideline, I had to add a few tips, and before I left he received the kiss of peace. Then (which is not true) he took me to the Gare de Lyon."

What is true, however, is that the illustrious theosophist found the Doctor in a sordid room covered with patched clothes. It was still winter and the Pontiff hadn't made a fire... Not that he lacked money, since Mr. M*** had generously filled his travel bag. But it was fitting for John the Baptist to be, if not covered in cow dung, half naked and anointed with stinking fat, as in his first incarnation of the Precursor, at least to appear austere to excess. Who doesn't know, moreover, that in such a case a little dirt is not harmful?...

In short, the sight of the sickly-looking old man, plunged into such destitution, touched X*** deeply, already very embarrassed by the gift of the medallion. Before leaving, he asked for something to write on, slipped a hundred francs into an envelope, which he handed over to the Baptist's hands, with a penetrating air: "For your poor of the south," he said to him.

Later, Baptist, claiming to have shown X*** this medallion (an inestimable jewel, of an even more priceless price), claimed in the most natural tone that he had forgotten it in the rue de V... – Luckily, this art object had been religiously tightened in a drawer, and was immediately sent back to the Doctor, by registered parcel post. Baptist was frustrated; he could not make any noise from this adventure.

He compensated himself by insinuating that X*** was a *formidable magician*; the fact is that Vintras' heir left Paris in terror. He refused to explain about X***; only, in his minutes of expansion, he hinted that this terrible necromancer, confidant of the Powers of Darkness, was being served by the whole of Hell (*sic*).

Such suspicions must indeed have seemed abominable to a Chosen One, who is celestial every night at the kiss of the angels of Light, Sahael, Anandhaël and others, and is assaulted *a posteriori* by the lewd ghost of the circumcised Ezekiel.

This Israelite from beyond the grave proceeds in a curative, though unusual, manner – and it seems that one of his assaults alone is worth a purge and a bloodletting. Then he disposes, in favour of his partners, of the life-giving and beneficial fluids that make beings climb, step by step, the ascending ladder of life?

AND NUNC, LENONES, INTELLIGENT: ERUDIMINI, QUI JUDICATIS LUPANAR!

CHAPTER VII
Flowers from the Abyss
☦

The Chariot = the Septenary = Triumph
Consumption Plenitude = Wealth = Superfluousness
Flowers from the Abyss

A last word to those curious about Black Magic. Leaning with us over the abyss, from which they were able to grasp the escarpment and probe the dizzying night, perhaps they did not see without surprise blooming, on the edges and as far as the gully that leads to the abyss, some flowers of a wild and fatal beauty, of a heady and disturbing perfume...

Don't they know that Evil has its poetry? – From the mystery of abomination itself emerges a fantastic, attractive and disastrous ideal, where many have been seduced from time immemorial.

Let the curious beware! This is the great peril of eccentric excursions into worlds forbidden to profane whims. Whoever ventures without a guide on the trail of new emotions is already treading the path of his impending perdition, everything around him is conspiring for his ruin and the omen. On the door he is about to pass through, Dante could have engraved the threatening tercet of the *Inferno*:

Per me si va nella citta dolente;
Per me si va nell' eterno dolore:
Per me si va tra la perduta gente![1]...

Such, it is true, only ask Sorcery for the charm of art that is inherent to it[2] for those who are, much less is the danger. They stick to the rather superficial picturesque of the Grimoire; their teeth bite only the rind of the forbidden fruit.

---

1 By me one goes to the painful city;
   By me one goes to the eternal pain;
   By me one will mingle with the lost gent (the damned)!...
2 We still have in our ears a customary quip from one of our friends of letters, the subtle theorist of the "Symbolist School". Those who know the look and the accent of this poet

But others, daring as they are, savour the intimate poetry of Evil. The temptation for them was too strong; they did not know how to react. The spirit of mischief that seduced them now possesses them. From now on, they will sail in the fluid torrent of perversity, towards the abyss of unconsciousness that must one day engulf them. This suicide is the culmination of their destiny, willingly or unwillingly, all converge on it; some of them, by very circuitous routes. Such are the only way to abolish their individuality, due to the fever of an intractable egotism, to disappoint them in new peregrinations, in the conquest of an exclusive originality –sterile efforts, illusory conquest– they will succumb. Far from creating a fake "I", they will only have struggled to dissolve the real "I" within themselves.

The abyss of the Unconscious! This is the Maelstrom where the great Seducer imperceptibly attracts their poor vessels, fascinating the pilot's eyes with the phantasmagoria of fake mirages. A deaf murmur rises, which soon grows and rumbles; but the sailor, hardly distracted from his reverie, does not notice that the ship is moving in a circle, surrounded by a still distant whirlpool; that its course accelerates; that it leans to port, describing a spiral whose diameter narrows at a glance... However, the magic illusion has redoubled its captivating prestige... The abyss thunders a few cables away, but the pilot heard nothing. Already the gaping funnel has received the frail boat, which flies, carried like a feather to the pivot of the inner wall; but the pilot saw nothing, and here he disappears to the bottom of the vortex, his mind still in ecstasy and his eyes lost in the azure of his dream!

Initiates know why unconsciousness is the proper element of Satan-Pantheus, the central point where –fatally– the inflexible, logical Goetia brings back his direct or indirect followers, his sectarians of fact or intention. If we were asked to specify the symptoms by which this process of unconsciousness manifests itself in the followers of Goetia –conscious or unconscious– we would reply that it can be detected first of all by the abolition of logical faculties; by the proselytism of negative philosophies of free will and immortality; and finally, after death, by the retrogression towards the most minute forms of elementary nature.

Pure Satanism, avowed, deliberate and militant (if one may say so), is an exceptional evil. Figures as Gilles de Laval, David de Louviers, or the chanon Docre[3] are very rare, thank God! But cases of indirect witchcraft are not numerous.

---

emigrated from Hellas, who has the makings of a great French poet, will easily imagine the exotic and masterly tone of his exclamation when he approached us: *You are a magician, I am a sorcerer, and it is much more decorative...* And, in fact, Mr. Moréas is a bewitching artist. Let us open his *Cantilènes* (Cantilenas) to the pages of *Mélusine* and the Witch of Berkeley: we will agree that it would be difficult to grasp better the prestigious and decorative side of black magic, and to translate its impression in a more adequate and intense style.

Jean Moréas is a great sorcerer of letters – in the enviable and flattering sense of the term.

3 *Le Chanoine Docre* (The Canon Docre): a peculiar type of priest-sorcerer, in *Là-bas* (translated as *Down There* or *The Damned*), the last novel de M.J.-K. Huysmans. – *Là-bas* has recently galvanised the torpor of the materialist public, and we have every reason to be delighted that we have the opportunity to touch a word on it. This remarkable study, so conscientious about the monograph of the Sire of Raiz, appears riddled with inaccuracies and full of outrageous imputations towards contemporary occultists. – The answer is quite simple: if the pages in which the lord of Tiffauges relives his life are scrupulously documented, it is

Overly adventurous Mesmerians,[4] eccentric Spirits and Mediums, valetudinarians of a falsified ideal or devotees of a troubled mysticism, some of whom we dealt with in the previous chapter, go astray in pursuit of a marvellous without greatness, *the phenomenon at all costs*, – this is the rallying cry of the most fanatical. They will show you the supernatural, even if only in the kitchen, these bourgeois of the sorcery; or, as certified miracle-workers, you will see them on fairgrounds, performing authentic miracles.

Under this same heading of indirect sorcery, other examples, less unworthy of attention, can be catalogued; artists or thinkers, these are no less fatally lost, in search of their golden fleece; nostalgia torments them with some imaginary Olympus, of which they are the thundering Jupiter; or again the fever of an impracticable altruism; or the genius of a strange conception, sometimes monstrous and sublime, of philosophy, science or art. They are certainly the maniacs of genius, the patricians of modern witchcraft; they are entitled, in spite of their very aberration, to all our interest; we would almost say to all our sympathy. Without doubt, they are perverts. They are obsessed by the lyricism of evil; they only vibrate at these agreements of perdition, and even propagate them... For, besides the contagious fevers of intelligence, infernal proselytism is the rule among sorcerers of every caste and rank. – Our spirit rejects these powerful heresy of thought and feeling; where does it come from that our soul cannot hate them? – They are of the race of the *Ghibborim* of Moses and of the pagan demigods, Icarus of an ineffable firmament, they hovered very high before being precipitated; their dazzling fall illuminates the depths of evil – and this is the secret of our sympathy for them!

---

because M. Huysmans, curious about this evocative restitution, relied on it only on his own initiative as a bibliophile and palaeographer. What was he not always so jealous of finding out for himself?

His pages of modern investigation would equal those of retrospective scholarship, and the documentation of his book would be constantly maintained at the level of writing. There would be a masterpiece.

To hold Mr. Huysmans responsible for the factual errors –and, worse, for the gratuitous slander– of which he made himself the naive editor, his records would have to come from a third person, powerfully interested in lying. Now we know, from a very certain source, that the novelist wrote his work, with inconceivable lightness, on impostor documents that the awful drunkard executed in chapter VI of our work, under the pseudonym of Doctor Baptist, had made him hold. Mr. Huysmans was fooled by this venomous hypocrite, who had completely seized his confidence. This is so true that Mr. Huysmans confessed to one of his close friends that he had transcribed the notes of the defrocked man, without it even having occurred to him to check their accuracy. It would have been so easy!...

Moreover, the author of Là-bas charges the Rose+Croix with the most improbable accusations, without providing a shred of proof; we flatter ourselves, however, that we have not made any progress on Baptist, which we have not conclusively established. – The Pontiff of Carmel was fortunate enough to borrow a golden cup from which to pour out the gall and mire of his slanders; so much the better or so much the worse for him. As for Mr. Huysmans, if our sixth chapter should fall before his eyes, we have no doubt that he will not for a moment acknowledge his error, sorry in the soul to have made himself, in the best faith of the world, the propagator of a false concept and accomplice in a bad action...

4 Followers of Mesmer, the proposer of "animal magnetism", sometimes later referred to as mesmerism.

The seductive charm of the abyss is eternally exerted, and others will be attracted to it in turn... Don't bend over!...

An intoxicating aroma, emanating from below, undulates and unwinds its heavy volutes, slowly. It is a lascivious and languid exhalation, floating in the air; it infuses itself from one moment to the next... Here the contagion seems to have spread to the flowers of the ravine, whose chalice leans and wavers, weighed down with love. And like weary of themselves and sick with their own embalmed breath, all the corollas solicit the hand to pluck them.

And their intoxicating perfume makes you dizzy.

The abyss lights up from below. A misleading vision lights up in the dark depths of the unknown; it is, in blind glory, Satan himself, transfigured, disguised as an angel of light!

This sight dazzles – and makes you dizzy.

And that voice! It rises from the lowest depths of the abyss, melodious and treacherous like that of the sirens; a source of negation, an instigator of voluptuous despair...

Its song disturbs the ear and makes one dizzy.

This voice, which seems to exhale from the very essence of things, speaks to the distraught soul a dissolving language, very bitter and very sweet, which the soul hears, alas! without ever having learned it. It sounds like the confidential murmur of the atmosphere, as if living nature were revealing itself in its entirety in this voice, which identifies itself so deeply with your intimate verb, that it speaks within you all together and outside of you.

Inside, a curtain is torn: all the dark ideas are suddenly illuminated; all the hidden feelings, confessed to the tribunal of your Conscience, assert themselves as independent, accuse themselves of anarchy and reveal to your moral individuality the presence of another person, whom you did not suspect – and who lived in you. A mystery of uncertainty, languor and carelessness takes hold of free will with force, and the Ego panics at feeling angered, penetrated, violated by the Non-ego!

Soon the two opposites merge. You doubt everything and yourself. Anything is true, that seems possible to you; but nothing seems assured... This universal doubt, who formulates it? Is it your "I" that speaks, or the collective Self of the entities outside the "I"? You do not know.

What formidable spasm embraces you, irritates you and overwhelms you? What psychic pollution, inflicted on the universal nature, makes you commune with delight with the degradation of beings and things? – This multiple intoxication is latent in the atmosphere that bathes you, and you savour in spite of yourself the cup of false mysticism, where so many ecstasies mingle with so many setbacks!

False initiation..., cursed and false initiation, where the Initiator escapes and remains unknown! His word is incoherent, ambiguous and yet prodigiously suggestive, his word seems in turn to be that of a God, then of a demon. It is a teaching that mixes all the opposites, in order to remain equivocal. Truth is only formulated here to be prostituted at the coitus of Error. – Such is the very strange character of this lesson from the abyss; assertions and negations cross each other, embrace each other, marry each other? Is the voice ironic in asserting? Or does it deny only to refute its own negations? Does it blaspheme only to condemn its own blasphemy? – This is what the neophyte cannot discern, and his confusion increases.

We have heard this Voice, which is the Voice of *Satan-Pantheus*. What it teaches, what it suggests, no one will doubtless know, who will not have perceived its confidential, indefinite murmur... It would be futile to try to imprison this subtle essence in sentences; it vibrates, sonorous and fluid – elusive. We will only try to raise suspicion of its captivating accent, its enigmatic timbre.

We have heard this Voice... Perhaps, reader, you will hear it: God forbid you should ever listen to it!

The Kabbalah of Satan-Pantheus

* * *

–You have planted it in the heart of the Earth, your dazzling sword, Oh Kerub! In the heart of the unfaithful lover, who from the kisses of a god has kept in her womb only the seeds of lies and disappointment. You have planted it in the heart of the Earth, Oh Kerub! And the guard blossoms into a cross of light – like a flower.

Your manly sword is fertile, Oh Kerub, the wounds it has made; as soon as they heal, the wounds that have healed are matrices of light; and the breasts that you have pierced have become motherly; and the beings that you bless with your rigour give birth to light and life! But in vain hath thy sword passed through the womb of the harlot of nothingness: her womb hath not quivered, and is barren, neither shall her breasts be swollen with the milk of immortality... Wife of the old Kronos, she has kept only the saddest prerogatives of the virgin: two privileges of death – coldness and infertility.

Oh Earth, the kiss of your husband has not found you fruitful; your husband has cursed your sides, which are always frozen for him, and his vainly renewed ardour has not revived your marble; it only heats up in adultery, at the bite of the Adversary and under the embrace of the Evil One... Your constant infidelity conceives tirelessly and in turn gives birth to disappointing illusion. You have only given birth to ghosts, and the infernal larvae are the fruit of your criminal entrails.

But the Adversary is not; your wicked nights are a guilty dream, and your countless sons are deceiving appearances that disappoint your sterility.

* * *

And such are the blasphemies of your children:

–"ALEF! *The Absolute is not.* – BET! *Faith deceives us and Science deceives itself; and sterile is the eternal combat of these two differently lying forces.* GUIMEL! *Word of being, you are a nothingness like him; you are but the reflection of a shadow, or the shadow of a reflection.* – DALET! *The cubic stone is not secured at its base.* HE! *Matter alone is fertile, to serve the cult of Moloch: the Spirit does not give birth.* – WAV! *Love is an eternal struggle with no way out.* ZAYIN! *Only the Force is victorious in the present, as it has triumphed in the past, and as it will be glorified in the future...*"

Oh Earth, Oh Earth, listen: such are the blasphemies of your children!

CHET! *Balance is death by immobility; Movement is death by combat. Oh Life, you lie to yourself.* – TET! *The Ternary denies himself three times in the abhorred mystery.* – YOD! *The first cause is not Spirit.* – KF! *Force takes precedence over Right.* – LAMED! *Sacrifice is a sterile irony that insults itself.* – MEM! *Love does not give birth to Life, but to Death. Death thrones alone and imperishable over the manure of the ages.* – NUN! *Any Transformation is a decoy, any change is a decay: nothing grows but to offer more surface to destruction, more pasture to death. Progress resolves itself into an optical illusion; Universal Life is equivalent to an endless agony."*

Oh Earth, Oh Earth, listen: such are the blasphemies of your children!

–SAMECH! *The king of nature is Shatan, the one who asserts only to deny.* – AYIN! *Virtue, Art and Science build in the clouds their chimerical Babel, which the fire of the sky decapitates.* – PE! *The ideal exists only for those astrologers of sentiment, who spend their lives ogling the stars.* – TSADE! *In the struggle for existence, Perfidy is a tactic, Guile a necessity, Ambush a right, one must kill in order to live... or resolve to die, to make room for those who want to live by killing.* – QOF! *Gold is the only god whose altar men will never abolish. Be auspicious to us then, august divinity! In your light, star of glory, all virtue melts and dissolves, like wax or fire... Terrestrial and solar Jupiter, universal Don Juan, be favourable to our vows, for you can do everything about souls: omnibus luces, omnibus imperos; quis resistet tibi?* – RESH! *Matter is the eternal phoenix, which alone is reborn from its ashes. The soul, a succession of feelings and thoughts; Thought and Feeling, ephemeral sublimations of organised matter, die with it. At death, the brain ceases to secrete these volatile essences... Immortality? Chimera.* – SHIN! *Love? Stupidity or madness... Devotion? Role of dupe."*

Oh Earth, Oh Earth, listen to the blasphemy of your children! Here is the last one, which underlines and summarizes them:

–THAU! *The world is evil, and if God created it, it is God who wanted to be evil. If he has willed evil, he is a God in reverse: his name is not IOD-HEVE, but HEVE-JOD, that is to say Shatan!"*

* * *

Oh Earth, you have heard the blasphemies of your children. Thus exclaims the Sons of the Cursed, the reproach of your womb. The inductions of their human logic flash in sinister flashes, and thunder in imprecations against Heaven.

And Heaven cries out anathema to man's reason. The God from above repudiates the Goddess from below, the Goddess of Reason... On the cliff of his pride, man has built the citadel of rebellion. The fire of Heaven must reduce to dust this unholy temple, where an idol, rival of the Lord, is enthroned...

But have not you yourself, Oh earthly Bride, in your delirium glorified the fruit of an inexpiable adulterer, that spectre of thought, that breath of a day, the reasonable man? By contrasting the glory of the divine Logos with the incoherent vanity of the human word, have you not drunk the intoxication of a sacrilegious hope?

Oh Earth, have you not wanted to equal yourself in Heaven?

Hope is the only hope! Guilty thought... You thought: *I have sublimated the flower of my virtual energy; I have distilled the elixir of my own essence; I have raised up Man – this Living Reason – consubstantial with God!*

But here is that reasonable Man, deploying his Reason to confirm this chimera of identity, here is that Man has demonstrated that God is not, and that he himself has no essence, being a becoming... From now on, Heaven and Earth are level in the equality of nothingness!

Oh Earth, here then is your masterpiece – Man! And you, Man, the deplorable and dear illusion of a fallen consciousness and an abolished divinity; you, Man, here is your matrix of iniquity – the Earth! Listen to me, both of you.

You were mistaken, Oh Earth, in wanting to elaborate your essence towards an ideal celestial. Go back to your instinct: sleep and dream!

As for you, Man, who would have done better not to have been born under the illusion of conscious objectivity; since here you are, lie of the inferior Nature, pitiful counterfeit of the races of the Empyrean, go back to your instinct. – Whoever you are, at last, enter the unconscious sleep and dream!

Do you see this ethereal river, tumultuous and caressing, formidable and gentle, whose fluid gold sparkles as it carries the collective intoxication of engulfed existences through the worlds? Salute to the lascivious overflowing of impersonal Life; salute to the universal dissolving of artificial entities. Plunge into it. Try to drown yourself in it. It is deliverance! It is the happy life of the dream, or it is the dream of a life of happiness.

* * *

Who do you think I am? A voice from who knows where, who charms and consoles..., a messenger of hope, in any case!... If I am illusion, I still bring the failing Reality the comfort of a dream; if I am Reality, I erase the unhealthy nightmares of a satanic illusion.

Then come to me those who suffer and despair! I will lull them into a never-ending dream of light and fragrance... The dream! It is only illusory as an exception in earthly life. Suppose that the day before has become an exception, and the dream, a customary state, that is to say, a normal state... Thus it will be the Reality itself, the only true, the only lasting Reality; thus earthly life will appear only as an accidental and temporary nightmare.

To me, all the sorrowful, all the painful, all the calamitous... to me! For I bring the life of the Dream, or the Dream of this life!

* * *

The voice of Satan-Pantheus is undulating and multiple, like this physical Universe of which he is the soul. It speaks to each one his own familiar language; to the artist it speaks of art; to the mystic it speaks of occultism and to the man of action of intrigue. But, whatever it said –when it spoke– all the notions taken together leave the delirious soul in the grip of this single conviction, which gnaws at it like a cancer: everything is vain, nothing is certain... And from this chaos of uncertainty emerges one last imperative, peremptory concept: the urgency of individual moral abdication.

In the final analysis, what does this voice say? – Negations, the nothingness of the human verb, that is what it demonstrates; retrogression towards instinct, that is what it proposes; the apotheosis of the unconscious,[5] is what it celebrates. And as a means of attaining this false ideal, murderous to the soul, it suggests drowning in the bankless and bottomless river of universal physical life.

In this suicide, is the alpha and omega of Goetia (see chap. III. In order to resolve this, Satan-Panthaeus –who is also Satan-Proteus– makes an effort to disguise his invitation in the most unexpected and attractive forms. Goetia is not confined to the grossly picturesque work of the common sorcerer; we have defined it as the use of the occult forces of nature for evil, which is ready to creep like a subtle virus into all visible and invisible spheres, – wherever man's energy is deployed, this plague spreads its ravages.

And in fact, the arts, literature, philosophy and even theology were at all times more or less impregnated with the acrid ferment of pessimism that the great Seducer inoculated to the generations, as the surest way to make them listen to his voice, the instigator of moral suicide.

Flexible to all travesties, Satan-Pantheus does not allow himself to be transfigured into the glorious Christ – or even into Buddha. Haven't we seen him recently borrowing from India the charms of its exotic quietism and all the magic of its age-old traditions, to enchant novice eyes with insidious mirages, and to divert from the path those souls, more and more numerous by the day, who, repugnant to the materialistic quagmire and weary of the narrow horizons of academic eclecticism, tried to orient themselves on the barely encountered glimmer of an mystic ideal? A certain theosophy, distorting the most sublime concepts of esotericism, seemed to take on the task of making the will-o'-the-wisps of error shine with sparks of truth. This is how more than one so-called interpreter of the enigmatic Mahatmas spread useful teachings, while other brothers, depraving the notion of the Absolute to the point of instituting it as the basis of an atheistic synthesis, reduced the unfathomable Parabrahm to nothing. And, to make their morality worthy of their theodicy, they advocated, under the colour of altruism, the suicide of the true personality; it was their way of interpreting Nirvana (the state of the human sub-multiples reintegrated into the divine Unity); so much so that, on the way with their cohort of chosen ones towards this patibular ideal, they seemed as many butchers, marching with their herd on the way to the slaughterhouse!...

Some literature, like some philosophy, some mysticism, some art, therefore, belong to Goetia, of an immediate or mediate kind. It is because there is no place in which man's activity is carried on, which Satanism cannot invade and permeate, just as there is no place in which divine inspiration cannot ever endow and ennoble. The

---

5 According to the esoteric tradition, the earthly man, Individual *Consciousness*, is placed between two unconscious: the superior unconscious or Universal Spirit, and the inferior unconscious or Collective Instinct. According to whether he relates to one or the other, man receives: from above, Divine Inspiration, or from below, *Physical Intuition*. Each person is therefore free to assimilate one or other of these beverages, as far as he is able to do so, but he must not drown or dissolve his "I" in the universal Spirit any more than in the collective Instinct. – Moreover, the Universal Spirit is only called *Unconscious* (Superior) as opposed to Individual *Consciousness*, as it could be called *Non-me* (Superior), to distinguish it from the individual self. Does this mean that it is devoid in itself of consciousness or entity? To conclude in this way would be a play on words. – In this particular case, it is only the *lower unconscious*.

profound reason for this is in the essence of the human Word, a demiurgic agent and a mediator between the absolute and the relative, between spirit and matter, between God and Satan.

Whether good or bad – the magical Power resides here on earth entirely in the human Word. The human Word appears as an intermediary and convertible agent: the link from earth to heaven, the middle term of all extremes, the universal substratum of relationship.

In its relationship with the *Absolute Truth*, the human Word is formulated by an active virtue: Faith. – In its relationship with *contingent reality*, it manifests itself through a passive virtue: Science. – In its relationship with the *divine Word*, the human Word expresses itself through a power of identification from the relative to the absolute, from the finite to the infinite, from the sub-multiple to the unit: *Consciousness*, which is neutral, i.e. active with regard to Science, passive with regard to Faith.

The human Word, recognising itself by its own mirror, is Consciousness.[6] Its orientation towards Science or towards Faith thus opens up to the individual man a double sphere of action –positive and mystical– in which to unfold his potentialities; whatever the tendency of the individual, in either sphere, to rectitude or perversity, to Good or Evil.

These principles having been laid down, it will be better understood that Art also has its magic, dark or splendid, harmful or beneficial; since Art is only the adaptation of the human Word, modelled to the mould of each individual, and irradiating itself in emanations which are incorporated into adequate forms, symbolically expressive of this individual Word.

Every work of art seems, at first sight, to be the *embodiment of a thought*. – So be it; but is it true that this thought is immobilised, sterilised, extinguished by fixing itself? Is it true that the form in which it is imprisoned is its ultimate outcome? that in creating this bark, it has exhausted its virtual energy? – It would be wrong to think so. It is a law, in general physics, that force is transformed and never lost. A thought does not die, because it takes on a body. Like a soul, it only becomes incarnate to assert itself on a material level; it gets hold of a sensitive figure only to act on the senses; a plastic and objective form, only to acquire the right of citizenship in the plastic and objective world. This very form serves as a medium, a vehicle and an instrument, to deploy its energy in a new sphere. Every work of art is therefore burdened with a latent virtue of realisation, which will sooner or later require a series of real effects, in accordance with its innate principle; these effects produced will be the magical translation of the idea included in the work.

From this we can conclude, in summary: every work of art is a magical work, good or bad; the ideal that is its soul inclines its effective potential to the right or to

---

6 When in active mode, Consciousness can make use of its criterium, which is *Reason*; in passive mode, it cannot. And this is why Reason (the Criterion of Consciousness), is competent in the things of Science, incompetent in the things of Faith. For if, in relation to Faith, consciousness unfolds only in the passive mode, it cannot make use of its human criterium, which is Reason; it must, therefore, undergo the divine criterium (*sensorium coeleste*), which could be defined as the Logic of the Absolute.

the left; the virtue of latent realisation in it constitutes the magical agent of its determinism, for good or for evil. Finally, every artist is a wizard or sorcerer – more often, alas, a sorcerer than a wizard.

The magicians of pure art, and the Goetians of impure art! Theurgy or Necromancy of the pen, music and brush! What a beautiful book to write on this transcendental theme! But such a work would be above our strength in every respect.⁷ Required at least to sketch out in a few lines a synthetic scheme of art from this point of view, we would gladly borrow from the mythology of *Hellas* four quite distinct types, symbolic (it seems to us) of the four families of art that can be imagined to be primordial. These types –by their combinations–, these families –by their alliances–, would give a framework subdivided in a chessboard manner and suitable for methodical classification, like a genealogy tree.

The Art of Apollo, the *Chrysopoets* (almost all the great art; namely Orpheus, Virgil, St. John, Lamartine and Vigny; Raphael and Michelangelo; Bach, Mozart and Rossini. – *Astrological references*: ☉ and ♃; *Galen. corresp.*: the generous solar wines);

The Art of Hecate, *the Enchanters* (demonomists: Remigius and Bodin; dizzying mystics: such as Bœhme and Swedenborg; Poe, Hoffmann, Baudelaire and Rollinat; Rembrandt and Cahot, Salvator Rosa; Chopin, Berlioz: the Damnation of Faust. – *Astrological reference*: ☽ and ☋; *Galen corresp.*: opium and especially cocaine);

The Art of Eros, les Erotiques (Anacreon and Sapho, Catullus, Tibullus and Petronius, Claude Crébillon and the Marquis de Sade; Musset: poems; many XVIII century engravers; Prudhon: blue papers; Rops: etchings; Holmès; Massenet, in Esclarmonde.

The Art of Atropos, the Nihilists (Lucretius: De Rerum Nnatur; Voltaire: Candide; Jean-Jacques, Diderot; Goethe: Werther; Byron: Cain and Manfred; Stendhal: *Rouge et noir* (The Red and the Black); Musset: *Confessions d'un enfant du siècle* (Confessions of a child of the century); Richepin: *les Blasphèmes (The Blasphemies)*; Goya, Zurbaran. – Astrological reference: ♄ and ♂; *Galen. corresp.*: Datura, Conium, Hyosciamus).

It is enough; all the details we could add to this picture would not prevent it from remaining fundamentally incomplete and even inaccurate, since, in order to specify the class attributable to each artist, it would have been necessary to widen the tiny framework just described and open it up to the invasive scaffolding of the very complex subdivisions we have been talking about. How, moreover, can one locate in label boxes universal geniuses: Shakespeare, Leonardo, Beethoven? How can one square into the framework these prodigious natures of art, whose exuberant sap, overflowing in every direction, in defiance of the dividing classifications, would they make the whole framework disappear under bunches of multicoloured flowers? It would be madness to think about it... Are they an illusion, the types of art sketched above? – We don't think so. Allow us to make a comparison with the beautiful Theory of Temperaments by Mr. Polti and Mr. Gary, the analogy is very

---

7   Our friend Émile Michelet, author of a very remarkable essay on *l'Ésotérisme dans l'art* (Esotericism in Art), seems chosen to accomplish this task one day, worthy of a Platonic poet touched by modernism.

close, since we are dealing with temperaments of art. Well, isn't it quite exceptional, if not completely impossible, to find a subject that absolutely embodies one of the four primordial types (S, C, M or P),[8] to the exclusion of the other three? However, these four radical elements, which had to be selected and constructed from scratch –first by analytical dissociation and then by abstract synthesis– each have their own value and are in no way arbitrary; so much so that their classification, in order of predominance, makes it possible to provide the first examination with the physiognomonic formula of a subject. Perhaps formulas could be composed in the same way, based on the methodical combination of the four types of art: *Apollo, Hecate, Eros and Atropos*. We will not digress any further, having only wanted to point out a possible way forward.

We hope that at this time it will be discerned which works we have denounced as perfidious, under the emblem of the Flowers of the Abyss. It is neither the literary adaptation of occult theories to the framework of the poem, tale or novel, such as Cazotte's *le Diable amoureux* (The Devil in Love), Bulwer's *l'Étrange histoire* (Strange Story), or Lermina's captivating short stories, nor the fabulous legends of the East, or *Les Contes de ma mère l'Oye* (Tales of My Mother Goose). If such flowers were picked on the edge of the abyss, it must be agreed that they do not distil the poison; their subtle aroma has not made anyone dizzy from the black depths... No, it is not the marvellous in art that we will ever incriminate.

We have always had a weakness for the chatter of our ancestors; at the risk of lowering the esteem of the brave people, let us admit it straightforwardly, because that is how it is. Oh the delicious fantasies of the poet Perrault! But are these indeed fantasies?... The kingdom of fairies and geniuses must undoubtedly exist on some distant and dear planet, or else the migrating dreams of our childhood would have lied about it. We can't admit it; it's so sad, a dream that lies! The only reality should have the privilege of imposture. – Do you no longer want to believe in anything in this life, you disillusioned young man whose soul has been crumpled by the real world? At least don't deny the dreams of your childhood; let them be a refuge where the stream of the brutal century expires. It is sweet and comforting to relive them; it is healthy to breathe in their luminous mist... At the age of eighteen, we tried to make these beloved dreams take shape; they did so with a certain amount of bad grace, the incarnation was insufficient, so that they have retained a nebulous appearance and the appearance of ghosts. The contours imprecise, indefinitely vague. Since then, we have taken care to make people forget this stupid attempt, this work of mediocre quality, without colour and without accent. Well, without advising anyone to bite into the green fruit of our poetic inexperience, let us say that later on, as we reread these *Fantastic Rhymes*.[9] – Alas! They rhyme badly, the feeling that dominates in these verses, whose sincerity is their only merit, surprised and almost moved us; the vague, but very real awareness of a world beyond, emerges in all the stanzas.

Are the dear fairies really very far away?

---

8 The four temperament theory suggests that there are four fundamental personality types: sanguine, choleric, melancholic, and phlegmatic.
9 *Oiseaux de passage, Rimes fantastiques, Rimes d'ébène* (Birds of Passage, Fantastic Rhymes, Ebony Rhymes), by Stanislas de Guaita. Paris, Berger-Levrault, 1881, in-12.

–Grandmother, who narrates so well, tell us another story from the past! We are great children, and our ears, blasé to the high-pitched din of the modern city, will be able to open again, delicate and attentive, to the very soft murmur of miraculous springs; to tremble at the enchantment of music whose sounds no one has perceived except through the broken voice of the old women who tell, such as one perceives vague fluted melodies through the dull roll of a car on the stones. We will have tears for the unfortunate imaginary ones whose eyes remain dry at the distressing spectacle of real misery. Our dead heart can relive an artificial life, religiously half-opened to the love of an adorable Sleeping Beauty!

Make us smile and cry again –us and those whose melancholy has pale lips and dimmed eyes– make us cry and smile again, naive legend that comes to us from the dark past, on the rich, banal, flowery language, on the hereditary language of the unintelligent old women!... Nostalgia takes us to fantastic countries; love takes us to those who have only ever breathed inside the white curtains of the cradle of the sleeping child; only ever spoke, but in the breezes of an ideal springtime; to whom we have childish and superstitious regrets, regrets evocative of a country populated by dreams – and which our dreamy ignorance knows in depth...

Alas! Alas! We remain cold to the vibrant voices of virgins who would like to love, courtesans who seem to love, wives who love. But we find real tears and sincere kisses for the ghosts who appear in a moonbeam, in your broken voice, Oh Great Mother!

> **Note:** The first Septenary is closed; the other two will no longer be based on stories, facts and legends, but on theories of hermetic science and occult philosophy. – *The Key to Black Magic* will follow closely *The Temple of Satan*; the *Problem of Evil* will then close the series of the THE SERPENT OF GENESIS.

Index

A

Adramelech 170
Aggarath 171
Agrippa 78
  Occult Philosophy, the 15
  picture 50
Ahriman 39
Aiguillette 171
Albert
  great 15
  small (petite) 15
Albert Le Grand 171
Amulets 171
Androdamas 172
Android 172
Antichrist 46, 172
Apocalypse
  beast of 45, 174
Apple 172
Astral Light 11
Astral world 121
Astrolabe 172
Attractive plant 173
Avatars 173
Avestas 36

B

Bamboo, black 173
Baphomet 173
Basilisk 173
Bat 174
Beau-Ciel-Dieu 174
Beelzebub 40, 174
Bell 174
Belphegor 40, 175
Berbiguier 57
Bewitchment 100, 175
Bharat Cycle 72
Birds 175
Black Coq 175
Black Magic
  sacraments 95
Black magician 104
Black Mass 175
Blood 175
Bodin 124
Boguet 49
Bowl
  fateful 176
Britannicus 75
Broucolaque 74, 177

C

Cagliostro 152
Camaieu 177
Candles 177
Cantharides 177
Carcass 177
Cat 178
Catoblepas 178
Cazotte, trial of 162
Characters 178
Charm 179
Charms 98
  stupefying 107
  taciturnity 108
Child's skull 179
Cideville 212
Clavicle 179
Coca of Peru 179
Collin de Plancy
  Infernal Dictionary 17
Colours 181
Comets 181
Confarreatio 85
Cross 181

D

Decanter 182
Demon
  bearded 182
  of lightning 111
Demons 182
Devil
  almanac 171
  error, selfishness, ugliness 33
  lives in error 33
  pact 87
  sacraments of 201
  ubiquity 34
Divination
  instruments of 182
Divining Rod 183
Dove 183
Dragon
  red (Apocalipsis) 37
  red (book) 14
Drum, Magic 183

E

Egg
  white of 183
Eliphas Lévi
  bibliography 18
Elves 183
Enchanted Rod 183
Enchantment 100
Enchiridion 184
Ephialtes 184
Eugène Vintras (see Vintras) 212
Evil
  existence of 39
Evocation 184
Exorcism 107
Exteriorizations 219

F

Fabre d'Olivet
  bibliography 18
Fairies 82
Fakir burial 117
Farfadets 184
Faust
  picture, surrounded by demons 88
Fluidic Form. 187
Flying Pistol 187
Fumigations 187

G

Genius
  battle of 38
Ghouls 188
Gibborim 36
Gilles de Laval 135
Gnomes 188
Gnosis 76
Grandier, Urban (See Loudun)
  picture 50
Grimoires 188

INDEX

H

Hand of Glory 106
Hashish 189
Heva 43
High Hunt 89, 190
Hildegard, St. 37
Hippomanes 190
Hocque
  sorcery trial 97
Hoopoe 190

I

Idol 191
Illuminati 157, 191
Immortality
  elixir of 191
Incubus 115, 191
Infidelity 191

J

Jacobins 159

K

Kali 41, 191
Kardec, Allan 203
Knights Templar 142
  Manichaeism 144
  secret society 149

L

Laces 191
Lamps 191
Larvae 192
Laws against sorcery 128
Lemures 192
Leonard, Master 83, 192
Leviathan 43, 192
Lilith 43, 192
Lord of Retz 135
Loudun 51
  Laubardemont 52
  Ursulines 53

Louviers, possesions in the convent 140
Lycanthropy 74, 119

M

Magic
  cake 192
  circle 192
  mirror 192
  plants 193
  stiletto 204
  words 193
Magical Poisoning Charge 193
Magnet 194
Magnetism 194
Malefices 194
Mandigoës-Obi 101
Mandrake 194
Manes 37
Manichaeism 37, 77
Marks 195
Master Leonard 83
Medium 218
Melicertes 195
Mendes 40
  goat of 195
Mice
  white 209
Mochlath 196
Mole 196
Moloch 40, 73, 196
Monsters 196

N

Nagual 196
Nahash 36
Nahemah 197
Necromancy 74
Nehamah 43
Nenuphar 197
Nephilim 36
Numbers 197

O

Oak Mistletoe 197
Odyssey, evocation 113

P

Pact 198
Pegs 198
Perfumes 198
Phantom 198
Philtres 104, 199
Pierre de Lancre 49, 123
Pythoness of Endor 127
Pythons 199

Q

Question 199

R

Rama 4, 8
Red Dragon 199
Repercussion 220
Rhombus 200
Rings 200

S

Sabbath 81
  boiler 201
  goat 201
  High Hunt 89
  magic ointments 89
  queen of 84, 199
  transport 207
Sacrifice 201
Saint-Germain 153
Salamander 201
Sammael 43, 202
Satan 202
  avatars 42
  error, selfishness, ugliness 33
Satan-Pantheus 40
Satyres 202
Secrets 202
Serpent
  of Genesis 9
  symbol of 11
Shirt of Necessity 203
Signs 203
Simon the Magician 76
Snake Eggs 203
Sorcerer 67
Sortileges 203
Spells 96
  evil 100
  impotence 105
  taciturnity 108
Spike
  stroke of 214
Spiritism 203
Spirits 203
Stiletto, Magic 204
Strings of the Winds 204
Succubus 115, 204
Sword 204
Sylphs 204

T

Tables
  talking 207
  turntables 207
Taciturnity
  charm of 204
Talisman 205
Tarantula 205
Tarot 205
Tauroboly 206
Teeth 206
Templars (see Knights Templar) 142
Teraphim 207
Teutad 207
Thor 207
Thorel 212
Thugs 41
Toad 207
Tortures 131

U

Ulysses, evocation 114

INDEX

Undines 207
Upas 208
Urine 208
Usnea 208

V

Vampire 74
Vampires 208
Vampiric erraticity 116
Vintras 212, 231
Vitzliputzli 208
Volt 100, 208

Voodoo 102, 208
  god 102
  serpent 103

W

Wand 209
Water 209
Wax figure 100
Werewolf 119
Werewolves 209
Witchcraft 93
Witches 81
Wizard
  pond 82